THE COMMON CAMP

THE COMMON CAMP

Architecture of Power and Resistance in Israel–Palestine

IRIT KATZ

University of Minnesota Press
Minneapolis
London

The University of Minnesota Press gratefully acknowledges the financial assistance provided for the publication of this book by the Department of Art History at the University of Cambridge.

Illustrations in this book were funded in part by a grant from the SAH/Mellon Author Award of the Society of Architectural Historians.

Chapter 3 was published in a different form as "Camp Evolution and Israel's Creation: Between 'State of Emergency' and 'Emergence of State,'" *Political Geography* 55 (2016): 144–55. Portions of chapters 4 and 5 were published in a different form in "'The Common Camp': Temporary Settlements as a Spatio-Political Instrument in Israel–Palestine," *Journal of Architecture* 22, no. 1 (2017): 54–103, and in "Spreading and Concentrating: The Camp as the Space of the Frontier," *City* 19, no. 5 (2015): 722–35; both available online at http://www.tandfonline.com.

Copyright 2022 by the Regents of the University of Minnesota

All rights reserved. No part of this publication may be reproduced, stored in a retrieval system, or transmitted, in any form or by any means, electronic, mechanical, photocopying, recording, or otherwise, without the prior written permission of the publisher.

Published by the University of Minnesota Press
111 Third Avenue South, Suite 290
Minneapolis, MN 55401-2520
http://www.upress.umn.edu

ISBN 978-1-5179-0716-7 (hc)
ISBN 978-1-5179-0717-4 (pb)

Library of Congress record available at https://lccn.loc.gov/2021062272.

Printed in the United States of America on acid-free paper

The University of Minnesota is an equal-opportunity educator and employer.

31 30 29 28 27 26 25 24 23 22   10 9 8 7 6 5 4 3 2 1

We can no longer afford to take that which was good in the past and simply call it our heritage, to discard the bad and simply think of it as a dead load which by itself time will bury in oblivion. The subterranean stream of Western history has finally come to the surface and usurped the dignity of our tradition. This is the reality in which we live.

— Hannah Arendt, *The Origins of Totalitarianism*

Where there is power, there is resistance.

— Michel Foucault, *The History of Sexuality*

CONTENTS

Preface	ix
Glossary	xiii
Introduction: The Common Camp	1
1 THE CAMP RECONFIGURED Modernity's Versatile Architecture of Power	23
2 FACILITATING DOUBLE COLONIALISM British and Zionist Camps in Mandatory Palestine	57
3 GATHERING, ABSORBING, AND REORDERING THE DIASPORA Immigrant and Transit Camps of Israel's Early Statehood	87
4 FORCED PIONEERING Settling Israel's Frontiers	121
5 UNRECOGNIZED ORDER The Imposed Campness of the Negev/Naqab Bedouin	159
6 CAMPING, DECAMPING, ENCAMPING Palestinian Refugee Camps and Protest Camps and Israeli Settler Camps in the Occupied Territories	195
7 IN THE DESERT PENAL COLONY Holot Detention Camp for African Asylum Seekers	245
CONCLUSION, OR TOWARD AN EVER-EMERGING THEORY OF THE CAMP	271
Notes	291
Index	337

PREFACE

In the early years of the twenty-first century, the residents of the Bedouin unrecognized village Tarabin al-Sana were protesting against the plans of the neighboring Omer, my hometown, to expand over the lands on which they had lived for decades. It was clear that the violent clashes, which were followed by the eventual eviction of the village, could not be considered a single event. Rather, the events were part of Israel's ongoing approach to the tens of thousands of Bedouin living in the Negev unrecognized villages, suspending them there with no infrastructures or services and under a constant threat of expulsions and house demolitions, rendering them ever temporary and therefore ever displaceable.

As I grew up in the Negev and studied architecture in Jerusalem, it began to be apparent that spatial temporariness and violence are linked in both political aspects and spatial practices. Studying the destructive assaults inflicted by Israel on the Palestinian refugee camps in the second intifada and the invasiveness of the Israeli settler outposts that were erected not far from them made it evident that these environments were connected not only in political and territorial terms but also through architectural and material actions in which extreme force was intertwined with inherently temporary realities.

The research for this book evolved over two decades. During that time, new forms of similar spatial realities continued to be created by actors on all sides of the political spectrum, employing prefabricated or makeshift structures and swift construction. They have resonated not only with one another but also with the complex history of many other types of camps and temporary spaces created in the area in the past, such as Zionist settler camps and immigrant transit camps, some of which are long gone, while others have changed shape and function. While the differences between these spaces and their particular temporal and political realities were obvious, their commonness, it became clear, is deeply rooted in the spatial and political modus operandi that reshaped and still is shaping Palestine and Israel over the past century. The research has developed with the intention to understand this reality in Israel–Palestine and, through it, to investigate the spatiopolitical meaning of the camp.

This book was formed and facilitated thanks to the support of many. I owe my deep gratitude to those who contributed to it, either directly or indirectly, through stimulating conversations, correspondences, and debates, and to those who generously supported me along the way with their encouragement and guidance. I am deeply indebted to Wendy Pullan, who supervised my PhD, for her uncompromising intellectual sincerity. I am also thankful to Haim Yacobi, who first encouraged me to study the case of Tarabin and Omer back in architecture school, for his support and friendship. To Ariella Aïsha Azoulay and Adi Ophir, who first introduced me to Giorgio Agamben in my hermeneutical and cultural studies, I am grateful for providing the intellectual foundations for this work. I was fortunate to be their student. I am also obliged to Oren Yiftachel for urging me to quit my job as a practicing architect in London in favor of pursuing this research and for our continuous conversations.

I have had the privilege of working with great colleagues at the University of Cambridge, the London School of Economics, and the University of Sheffield, which created an invaluable intellectual community that significantly contributed to the development of my thinking. I am particularly grateful to Ash Amin, Suzanne Hall, Michele Lancione, and Max Sternberg for their intellectual support and friendship. I am also indebted to academics working on the spatial and political meanings of the camp, with whom I was privileged to discuss and test my ideas, including Claudio Minca and Diana Martin while coediting *Camps Revisited*, as well as Adam Ramadan, Romola Sanyal, Nando Sigona, Simon Turner, Fatina Abreek-Zubiedat, Camillo Boano, Silvia Pasquetti, Giovanni Picker, Roy Kozlovsky, and Aya Musmar. Special thanks to Diane Davis, James Sidaway, Duncan Bell, Ariel Handel, Matthew White, Mansour Nasasra, and Ronnie Ellenblum, who were all a great source of intellectual engagement and encouragement.

I thank my editor, Pieter Martin, the editorial team at the University of Minnesota Press, and the book's two reviewers for their constructive comments; all were invaluable in the transformation of this project into a book. In Israel–Palestine, I am grateful to all those in Yeruham, Rakhma, and other camps and related urban contexts investigated in this book, who gave their time and stories, and to all the NGO activists, state officials, planners, architects, archivists, and everyone who agreed to contribute their crucial perspectives to this project.

This work was generously supported by Kettle's Yard, University of Pennsylvania's Perry World House, Paul Mellon Centre, the Anglo–Israel Association, and Girton College's Graduate Scholarship Awards, with special thanks to Girton Fellows Frances Gandy and Peter Sparks for their help and support. The academic awards this project received along the way, including the SAH/Mellon Author award, the RIBA President's Award for Research, the Ben Halpern AIS award, and the SAHGB Morris Prize, were of great encouragement.

My family was the true force that made this book possible. I cannot thank them enough for always being interested and involved and for encouraging me in every possible way. This book is dedicated to my parents, Shoshana and Avraham Katz, with great appreciation, and in memory of my mother, who supported me in the difficult stages of this journey. Finally, my endless love to Alma and Ari, who fill my life with happiness: thank you for reminding me what the most important and urgent things are. And last, to Ze'ev, for our endless discussions since the very beginning of this project, which crossed with us cities and countries.

GLOSSARY

Aliyah: The immigration of Diaspora Jews to the Land of Israel

Ashkenazi Jews (plural, Ashkenazim): Jews who originate from Europe

Eretz Yisrael: The Land of Israel (biblical term)

frena **(plural,** *frenot***):** A Moroccan outdoor mud oven (similar to a Tabun/Taboon clay oven)

hamula: Extended family, which plays a vital role in Arab communities

kibbutz and moshav (plural, kibbutzim and moshavim): Israeli agricultural settlements based on cooperative communities

Likud: The major right-wing political party in Israel

ma'abara (plural, ma'abarot): Temporary transit camps for Jewish immigrants erected in Israel in the early 1950s during the mass-immigration period

mahanot olim: Jewish immigrant camps in Israel established in former British military camps at the beginning of the mass-immigration period

Mapai: A former left-wing political party in Israel (acronym for Hebrew Laborers Party of the Land of Israel) founded in the prestate period, later merged with the Israeli Labor Party

mawat: Dead land; a type of land tenure in the Ottoman Empire that was later adopted by Israel; similar to *terra nullius*, it is considered as empty land owned by no one, which therefore belongs to the state

Mizrahi Jews (plural, Mizrahim): Jews who originate from Muslim-majority countries (in the Middle East, North Africa, and so on)

Nahal: Acronym for *Noar Halutzi Lohem*, "pioneer combatant youth"

Nakba: (catastrophe); the destruction of Palestinian homeland and society and the permanent displacement of most of the Palestinians in 1948

Olim (singular, Ole): Jewish immigrants to the Land of Israel

p'zura: Term used by Israeli authorities to refer to unrecognized Negev Bedouin settlements (Hebrew for "scattering")

shig: The main Bedouin tent (or part of a tent) used for hospitality

xiv   Glossary

siyag/siyaj: The restricted zone under military rule created for the Negev Bedouin, to which many were transferred during and after the 1948 war (Hebrew and Arabic for "fence" or "enclosure")

sumud: An Arabic term for "steadfastness" or "steadfast perseverance," denoting a political strategy of remaining on the land to prevent its occupation by others

Yishuv: The Jews who lived in Palestine (Eretz Yisrael) before Israel's establishment (Hebrew for "settlement")

Abbreviations

HCJ: High Court of Justice

IDF: Israeli Defense Force

IDP: internally displaced person

JDC: American Jewish Joint Distribution Committee (Jewish humanitarian organization)

JNF: Jewish National Fund

PLO: Palestine Liberation Organization

RCUV: Regional Council for Unrecognized Bedouin Villages, a political advocacy group that represents the interests of the Bedouin in the unrecognized villages

UNRWA: UN Relief and Works Agency for Palestine Refugees in the Near East

INTRODUCTION
The Common Camp

Of the human settlements that have been formed over the centuries—villages, towns, cities—camps are considered a peculiar spatial entity. Whether they are erected as institutional spaces of detention or as makeshift spaces of refuge, camps are perceived as temporary environments that are created rapidly to respond to a specific situation and are expected to vanish as soon as that reality changes and things return to normal. Yet as some camps indeed appear and disappear swiftly and others exist for long periods of time, the multifaceted entity of the camp continues to emerge as a persistent space by which modern societies and political relations are managed and sometimes reworked. While most of us live in built environments that form the stable and predictable settings for our mundane activities, other people are torn from or disengage themselves from such a prosaic reality, living in situations that are transient and ephemeral. Camps are an inseparable part of the unstable realities created by forced displacement, colonial occupations, or acts of resistance and protest. They are often created ad hoc as spatial instruments, as means to an end to handle an urgent need or a change in a particular reality; they could also be created as pure means for political action or gesture; and they are also created as ends in themselves, as spatial voids that swallow and contain unresolved situations that stand at the core of modern politics. Once formed, camps are frequently suspended as spaces with no clear future, separated from their social and spatial surroundings, yet these spatial enclaves often do not remain still but, rather, dynamically stretch and transform as everyday needs and political demands are materialized and enacted through their spaces. While refugee, detention, and protest camps differ substantially in their functions, spatial forms, and modes of creation and organization, and while camps are often perceived as ambivalent sites of care and control, agency and oppression, temporariness and endurance, formality and informality, separation and connectivity, they are at the

1

same time recognized as various manifestations of the same ever-present spatial-political paradigm, one that is an important aspect of how we live today.

Over the past two decades, much has been written about the "return of the camp," mainly in relation to the post-9/11 "war on terror" and the global proliferation of camps that form part of the current migration age.[1] The camp as a space where civilian populations are contained en masse, however, had already appeared in the colonies as early as the nineteenth century and has not disappeared since. It was used extensively during the twentieth century, which will be remembered, as famously stated by Zygmunt Bauman, as the "Century of Camps."[2] In Israel–Palestine, camps were and still are commonly used to facilitate and resist the significant geopolitical changes of the twentieth century, most of them related to the Zionist and Israeli settlement and nation-building processes and to the Palestinian mass displacement they caused. Indeed, Israel–Palestine forms an extensive laboratory of camps, containing settler camps, immigrant camps, refugee camps, internally displaced person (IDP) camps, protest camps, and detention camps, which were created, sometimes changed, and often disappeared over the past century. As in other colonial, national, and postcolonial global settings of human movement and its restriction, where the camp was and still is extensively employed as a versatile instrument for transforming and controlling lands and populations, in Israel–Palestine camps form the modus operandi for responding to the drastic geopolitical changes the area has undergone and is still undergoing.

As prevalent as they are, however, camps seem to be everywhere and nowhere at the same time. Their disturbing images constantly appear in the news or rise from the archives as spaces that both constitute and represent urgent realities of crisis, emergency, expediency, and political turmoil, yet they remain distant and hidden from everyday environments and are rarely seen outside the reports of the media. Camps create flickering spatial entities that appear, transform, and disappear according to changing realities, and their patterns are therefore tricky to identify. As extraterritorial and extratemporal spaces existing on the outskirts and borderlands of cities and states, they are perceived as leftover temporary abject sites outside the perpetuity of ordinary environments and realities. They are also typically pushed to the edge of the architectural discourse, remaining in the periphery of discussions on modern built environments and on the architecture of modernity. Yet camps form intense sites of direct institutional power and of modes of resistance that are central to the way our modern built environments were and still are formed and to the way modern architecture was and still is being designed and created.

As a shadow that constantly follows modern life, camps are extensively employed by both authoritarian regimes and contemporary democracies as instruments of custody, containment, and abandonment. As such, camps are mainly analyzed as devices of power, created by, and mostly for, populations stripped of their basic rights, spaces that are managed outside society and ordinary state apparatuses in order to maintain, in Liisa Malkki's words, the "national order of things."[3] However, the camp is not only a space where powerless people are contained; while many camps are indeed inhabited by weakened populations excluded by stronger powers, others were and still are inhabited by and used by the strong as instruments to gain and extend control over desired territories. In addition, camps may also be transformed by their residents into platforms for their political struggles. If, as Walter Benjamin wrote, "there is no document of civilisation which is not at the same time a document of barbarism," then extreme spatial brutality would share the realm of architecture as a cultural product whose violence is often justified by political agendas in the guise of professional intentions.[4] For modern architecture, the camp would be one of the most visible manifestations of this spatial violence, whether as a space inflicting violence or as an instrument used to resist it.

The word "camp" is etymologically derived from Latin *campus*, related to an empty space, a plain, or a field. Camps are indeed created on unoccupied areas, often with the open field remaining between their temporary structures, ready to return to its previous unpopulated condition. As such, at least in their initial creation, camps are not inherently related to the area where they appear; they are *in* a particular space but not *of* the space they occupy. "To camp" is also a verb, and camps could also be seen as an action, a space that is also a practice formed and performed as a temporary event in which certain people (or materials or powers) camp and move on, maintaining fluid positions while sometimes permanently changing the realities around them. Importantly, the word "camp" is also about a group of people collectively defined around a particular idea. Camps are therefore also about social, political, and other imposed or self-defined identities and the struggle over and against them. As such, camps seem to combine a field (space), an action (event), and possibly also a particular group (identity) by or around which they are formed. In Hebrew, the word "camp," *mahane* (מַחֲנֶה), means both a place of temporary and often collective inhabitation, where tents or ephemeral structures are erected, and also a group of people who make up one side of a debate or argument. It is derived from the stem verb *hana* (חָנָה), meaning to temporarily park in one place. In Arabic the most prevalent word for "camp" is *mukhayyam* (مُخَيَّم), a name for a place that is installed for a specific purpose, often for an unclear duration. It is derived from the stem verb *khayam* (خَيَّم), meaning "he/she installed a tent," a verb with the meaning of often-collective inhabitation.[5]

Rather than being regarded as mere spaces, camps are seen here as purposeful and collectively populated spaces that are also identified and defined through the element of time as spatial events or actions. They are created and endure between the empty, the occupied, and the no-longer-occupied; between arriving, claiming, moving on, or remaining for an unforeseen period; between the ephemeral, the suspended, and the potentially permanent. This spatial flexibility, however, which could be seen as potent (as much as unpredictable) in specific circumstances, also brings with it stretched situations of prolonged suspension, with their diverse affects ranging from uncertainty and fear to hope and agentic forms of waiting.

"The common camp" is a term that pulls the camp out of its marginal position, establishing it as a common space at the center of the way modern politics is shaped and organized. The camp is common because it is prevalent; it is common in the sense of being widespread despite efforts to make it invisible. In Israel–Palestine's ongoing state of exception, the camp is indeed so common that it has almost become an ordinary, typical space. The camp is also common in the sense of being a joint phenomenon that influences many, a sort of a spatial common denominator that links varied ethnic groups, historic periods, and political actions. While the meaning of the word "camp" itself indicates separation, the fact that it is used by or for so many groups of people makes it in some sense a common ground of segregation and exclusion—either willingly generated from within or imposed from the outside. This term could be looked at as the other side of the Hobbesian Commonwealth:[6] while Hobbes's term means a political organization of people under one sovereign, "the common camp" implies a variety of social, spatial, and political separations and different kinds of exclusion enacted by or on different people by the same multifaceted tool, where some people might create the subversive space of what Stefano Harney and Fred Moten call "the undercommons."[7] Camps, however, not only separate but also sometimes create new common spaces within themselves, new commons where unique alliances and political subjectivities evolve, often through the intrinsic and dynamic creation of the camp's space itself. The various types of camps created over the years in Israel–Palestine allow us to reinterpret and conceptualize the spatial vocabulary of the camp and its political meaning while also illuminating new aspects of the constantly evolving global reality of camp spaces.

The Spatiopolitical Mechanism of the Camp

Camps have multifaceted spatial features that appear in highly rationalized institutional spaces and in self-made, makeshift environments, both often created to provide the bare minimum for their residents. Institutional camps created for civilians are incarnations of a distinct disciplinary facility: the military camp, originally designed to manage a specific population—soldiers—in a strict, controlled manner. The basic blueprint of the military camp and military technologies of containment were appropriated in the nineteenth century in the colonies and later in Europe and worldwide for the mass control and care of people in a variety of famine camps, plague camps, concentration camps, and refugee camps.[8] "Apparently nobody wants to know that contemporary history has created a new kind of human being—the kind that are put in concentration camps by their foes and in internment camps by their friends," reflected Hannah Arendt in her 1943 essay "We Refugees" on the tight connection between concentration camps and camps where refugees were contained out of sight and out of mind.[9] The camp, reflected Arendt later, "was the only 'country' the world had to offer the stateless" and "the only practical substitute for a nonexistent homeland."[10]

Concentration camps and refugee camps use the same techniques, addressing the minimal aspects of the biological lives of those contained in the camp, providing basic needs such as food, shelter, hygiene, and security. Such techniques could prevent or create a humanitarian disaster not only within but also *by* the camp, according to the camp's objectives and according to how this isolated and isolating space is managed. Other camps, ones that are not institutional facilities, were and still are created or altered by their inhabitants as ad hoc makeshift spaces, which sometimes urbanize. While the city and the camp are often seen as spatial entities that stand on the two sides of a "strict analytical dichotomy," the relationship between camps and cities is often composite and entangled.[11] The camp's military–civilian link and its complex connection to the city, both appearing in many forms in the camps created in Israel–Palestine, have existed since antiquity. Roman military camps were established on the principles of Roman towns; the military camp was created as "an improvised city," in the words of the Roman historian Flavius Josephus (c. 37–95); some of those military spaces later transformed into civilian settlements, including some cities we know today, such as Vienna and Manchester.[12] Yet, importantly, the camp is not only a space but also a social and political structure defining a particular group. "Camp thinking" is the term Paul Gilroy uses to describe the fixed racial, national, and cultural categories, based on sameness, that separates humans into biological and cultural hierarchies, often leading to the separation and containment of people in actual camp spaces.[13]

"Today it is not the city but rather the camp that is the fundamental biopolitical paradigm of the West," argued the Italian philosopher Giorgio Agamben, whose influential theory brought the idea of "the camp" to the front lines of academic research.[14] Agamben's theory of sovereign power and the state / space of exception, presented in a number of books, particularly *Homo Sacer: Sovereign Power and Bare Life*,[15] places the camp at the center of modern (bio)politics, together with the figure produced in the camp: *homo sacer*, an exposed person, or "bare life," whose rights and social, political, and human existence are denied. Following, though not always explicitly, the observations of Hannah Arendt, Michel Foucault, Carl Schmitt, and Walter Benjamin about modern society, sovereignty, and politics, Agamben sees the hidden matrix of the modern political order in the incorporation of bare life into the political realm by its exclusion in the camp. For Agamben, the Nazi camps were not a historical anomaly but, rather, an example of the thanatopolitical space of the camp as the *nomos* of the modern, where the classical Aristotelian separation between life and politics collapses and where power directly confronts stripped life in its most dehumanized form. The camp for Agamben is the fundamental (although not the only) space of exception; its particular juridico-political structure creates a place where, in Arendt's words, "everything is possible."[16] Camps, contends Agamben, emerge as particular spaces where law and fact become indistinguishable whenever the central nexus of the modern nation–state—land (territory), inscribed life (nation), and order (state)—enters into an ongoing crisis.

Since its publication, Agamben's theory has become an almost-mandatory rite of passage for scholars discussing the camp, with scholarship shifting between universally and concretely embracing the theory to utterly rejecting, even condemning, it.[17] Examining camps as actual spaces, scholars have highlighted particular geopolitical situations that contradict Agamben's theory, such as the fact that many camps were and still are being created outside the nation–state–territory triad, particularly in colonial and offshore contexts.[18] The investigation of the camp should not be limited to the formation and function of the modern nation-state, with Arendt herself famously exposing the colonial roots of the Nazi concentration camps.[19] The fortified territories and "shifting borders" that structure human movement and its spaces in the Leviathan we call the globalized world, by combining "border barriers, corridors, and transit camps," show that camps are now part of the global order both within and beyond the nation-state.[20] Even more importantly, Agamben's theory has been rejected for failing to consider the complex and dynamic power relations within the camp, reducing people in the camp to helpless biological beings while ignoring the resourceful ways in which their political agency and subjectivity are enacted and rearticulated in camps around the world.[21] Yet Agamben primarily sees the camp as a *paradigm* of the contradictions of modern biopolitics,[22] and abandoning the Agambenian theory completely might risk overlooking his insights into the core meaning of the camp to modern societies and political thought.

That camps are not only the spaces of *homines sacri* (that is, bare lives stripped of appropriate legal and political protection) is obvious when we consider the multifaceted camp forms and functions in the ever-growing inventory of camp spaces around us—refugee camps, holiday camps, mining camps, protest camps, detention camps—with their indeterminate and occasionally interchangeable functions.[23] Yet what links these different forms—the fact that they facilitate particular spatial practices, such as speedy creation and potentially rapid further change, either to liquidation or to further versatility—is also what makes the camp such a highly responsive political mechanism. Its rapidly created, rapidly changed, flexible spaces, with their often-tangled top-down and bottom-up formations, can be created as instruments for the immediate control of people (and lands), but they can also be seized by inhabitants as emancipatory instruments of political agency. The political understanding of the camp, therefore, must examine it beyond a solely theoretical paradigm and embark on a genealogical account that investigates the camp from its colonial past to nation-states and locates it in the global (post)colonial present.

Architectural, material, and spatial analysis becomes crucial in such an investigation. Camps can be, at the same time, spaces of power and resistance, and this book traces how the changing political roles of these spaces are being worked out through their materiality and built worlds, but also through their metaphorical existence as the empty core of modern politics. In examining particular spatial practices and material worlds and the geopolitics that creates the camp's various and often changing taxonomies, we can decipher the meaning of the multiple spatial practices that create and transform the camp in relation to the various and occasionally changing politics that it shapes. It is important to note that architecture here is perceived not as a mere representation, symbol, or illustration of preexisting politics but, rather, as a central realm through which politics and social and cultural meanings are enacted, mediated, and reshaped through specific embodied and often performative spatial practices. This is happening in the most basic spatial registers through acts of construction and destruction, through design and its overt or hidden logistics and logics, through particular modes of use, and through symbolic value, whether in everyday spatial contexts or in history and theory. The work of architects who designed and employed camps and camp-related spaces in Israel–Palestine is discussed in this book, reframing the means and the ends of architectural projects and expertise.

While the camp is a multifaceted, versatile spatial entity, most of the attempts to understand and conceptualize it as a political space, in both theoretical and empirical investigations, focus on one type of camp, whether the concentration camp, the detention camp, or, most commonly, the refugee camp. These camps are investigated in both historical and contemporary contexts, and while they are different from one another, they share an inherent similarity: they are spaces created by stronger powers to contain specific people (insurgent colonized populations, irregular migrants, refugees). Yet camps are not created only as spaces where the strong dominate the weak, who then may or may not adjust them to meet their everyday needs and their political ambitions. From their ancient creation in the Roman world to their modern colonial uses, camps were also formed by and for military and civilian forces as spaces that enhanced their power—for example, by moving through or expanding into new territories. Considering these and other camps by and within which the political (broadly conceived as the domain of power) is enacted and reworked will enable us to further decipher the particular logic the camp represents and constitutes.

Trying to avoid an essentialist approach that ascribes necessary and common characteristics to all camps, and at the same time aiming to better understand the camp and its workings, this book combines a genealogical and theoretical approach to interpret and conceptualize the camp in general and in Israel–Palestine in particular. Theoretically, the book situates the camp in relation to modernity, including its most prevalent political constellations: primarily colonialism and the nation-state, including their entanglements in settler societies, as well as more recent globalized political forms. As such, the camp is explored in relation to core concepts in which modern politics is grounded—namely sovereignty, including juridical and governmental orders; territory, with its particular spatial apparatuses; and people, reflecting on the national, ethnoracial, cultural, social, and ideological frameworks according to which they are divided and categorized. In addition, the rapidly changing modern material world is carefully considered as the very stuff camps are made of. These aspects enable us to locate the camp as a governmental and material force and as a spatial and human constellation that is distinct in its settings and will form a foundation to conceptualize the camp not only as a paradigm but also as a concrete space that generates specific forms of power.

Political thinking assumes a multiplicity of forms, and the camp's complex politics is examined in this book through the writings of political thinkers, including those already mentioned here, who reflect on the camp and other modern spaces as instruments and realms of power and resistance. These examinations include particular notions and theoretical accounts, such as Zygmunt Bauman's understanding of modernity as a quest for order and Gilles Deleuze and Félix Guattari's conceptualization of processes of becoming minor as a way camp spaces are deterritorialized and politicized by their dwellers.[24] These investigations are based on and generated by actual camp spaces and architectures and by an examination of those who created, managed, and inhabited them, all functioning as the book's primary sources. Whether those sources are analyzed through spatial ethnography or archival research, they are all imbued with ontological and epistemological value that infuse their theorization.

Importantly, in addition to these theoretical and empirical foundations, this book is based on a genealogical approach, enabling us to move beyond the word–concept relations and bring in things, practices, and the workings of power to gain a better understanding of what the evolving meaning of the camp is, particularly in the context of Israel–Palestine. Genealogy, perceived as the historical examination of the conditions of possibility of things being as they are, enables us to reinterrogate narratives while making legible the material, cultural, and political kinships that subtend them. This is about telling the story both backward and forward, tracing how the contemporary experiences and practices of the camp have emerged from different sources in an extended process in which their earlier modes were reinterpreted by later ones, while continuing to create multiple different outputs, some of which have been formed as this book evolved. According to Nietzsche's reflection on genealogy, each examined phenomenon is "continually interpreted anew, requisitioned anew, transformed and redirected to a new purpose," making the reinterpretation a conflictual process with contingent and variable outcome. "The form is fluid," Nietzsche contends; "the 'meaning' [Sinn] even more so."[25] As Foucault constantly emphasizes, genealogy "opposes itself to the search for 'origins.'" Nor is it about imposing "a predetermined form to all its vicissitudes."[26] Instead, genealogy is about acknowledging the dispersion of passing events, identifying the minute deviations, the accidents, or, conversely, the complete reversal and faulty calculations that gave birth to the things that continue to exist around us, including their ever-changing attributes and shifting and eroding meanings. Camps are spaces that often shift rapidly in function, form, and meaning in relation to historical, geopolitical, and cultural contexts, and so their genealogical explorations enable us to situate particular environments, experiences, and practices as part of the camp as a particular group not because all its members share exclusive generic characteristics, but because they stand in a particular historical relationship of reinterpretation to one another.

The Common Camp, therefore, is about how particular spaces, practices, experiences, concepts, and political implications of the camp are connected to one another through complex and overlapping processes of drift in meaning created by the shifting workings of the powers forming and interpreting them. In the settings of Israel–Palestine, the common camp is traced as the territory's hidden gene of a spatial practice that changes, mutates, disappears, and reappears in relation to the shifting geopolitics in the area. This act of interpretation is therefore admittedly political. It uncovers latent relations intertwined with the workings of power, even if these are linked to actors, contexts, and periods that are often examined as detached and unrelated. Unavoidably, the space and concept of "the camp" here is open to interpretation and receives new meanings in relation to its multifaceted roles, settings, and changes.

The Common Camp in Israel–Palestine

Camps and temporary settlements are prevalent in Israel–Palestine. Erected ad hoc for various reasons, in diverse shapes and forms, by and for different populations and actors, some camps create rigidly organized, totally ordered spaces, and others are makeshift spaces with no apparent organizing principles. However, the continuous appearance of these camps over the last century in this territory requires further explanation of a situation of which temporariness is an enduring feature. The Palestinian refugee camps erected following the 1948 Arab–Israeli war, which still exist today, are probably the best known, yet many other camp formations can be identified within this territory.

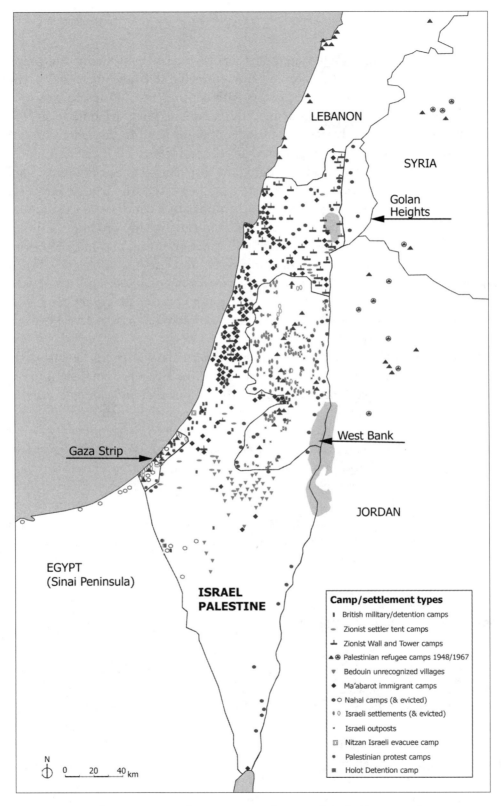

Map 1. Camps and temporary settlements created in Israel–Palestine over the past century.

The unique camp-cum-laboratory of Israel–Palestine—with its settler and detention camps of the early Zionist and British colonial periods; immigrant transit camps, refugee camps, and IDP camps of the Israeli nation-building internal colonization period and Palestinian mass-displacement period; and later colonial, decolonial, and postcolonial settler, protest, and migrant detention camps—allows us to study the meaning of this architectural instrument in its various manifestations, uses, and articulations. This book by no means makes a comparison between the camps of the destitute and those of the privileged, between the spaces of the dispossessed and those of the people who are still actively expelling them. Rather, this study traces the camp as it changes in relation to the shifting powers in the area, exposing the camp as a sophisticated instrument of power and of occasional resistance to it, while bringing the camp's centrality to the attention of the architectural discourse and of those who look at the relations between space and power in Israel–Palestine and beyond. Importantly, the many types of camps that have appeared in the territory, and in places related to it, over the last century form a distinctive paradigmatic pattern, and the study of camps in Israel–Palestine reveals a crucial aspect of the way the territory was and still is managed, organized, negotiated, and reshaped.

Camps have been an inseparable part of the spatial and later territorial changes in the area since the beginning of the twentieth century, when Zionist settlers erected tent camps in remote locations. Under British rule (1917–48), these evolved into prefabricated fortified camps as part of the ambition to expand the territory of a possible future state, and detention camps were later constructed by British authorities to prevent illegal Jewish immigrants/refugees from entering the country. Following the 1948 Arab–Israeli war, Palestinian refugee camps were founded in neighboring Arab countries and in the West Bank and the Gaza Strip, and makeshift camps were also created within Israel's 1948 boundaries by internally displaced Palestinian populations. At the same time, other camps were created by the new Israeli state in order to absorb and later spread the waves of Jewish immigrants entering the country, and military–civilian camps of the Israeli army were also created to fortify the state's new frontier areas. As the geopolitical map changed, new camps appeared: after the Israeli occupations of the 1967 war; during the Palestinian uprising of the 1980s (the first intifada); during the new wave of Jewish mass immigration in the 1990s; after the 2005 Israeli evacuation of the Gaza Strip; following the arrival in Israel, from the mid-2010s, of African asylum seekers to Israel; and during the ongoing civilian occupation and protest in the Palestinian-occupied territories. Thus, over the past century, dozens of settler camps, transit camps, detention camps, and protest camps were erected in Israel–Palestine by and for different populations, actors, and purposes.

This brief list of examples, part of which will be further examined here and throughout the book, demonstrates that while these spaces differ significantly in their political objectives and spatial forms, reliance on camps seems to be a central pattern in the way space and populations are managed in the region. What is common to these camps? What do their differences mean? And finally, why are they so prevalent in Israel–Palestine? This book attempts to answer these questions while advancing our understanding of the camp itself as a versatile spatiopolitical instrument.

Israel is an important example of the settler colonial and national creation and territorial redefinition of states in the nineteenth and twentieth centuries, using different techniques to manage and reorganize populations in space. The vast mosaic of camps in Israel–Palestine is grounded in this particular history and in the character of the radical geopolitical changes this territory has undergone over the last century. These changes were not a consequence of arbitrary or uncontrollable events; rather, they were part of a political idea that turned into a national movement, then into a grand plan, and then eventually into a national project—the Zionist project, whose goal was to make historic Palestine, or the Jewish geotheological Eretz Yisrael (the land of Israel), the national home of the Jewish people.

When the Zionist project began to develop in the late nineteenth century, it was accompanied by the famous motto "A land without a people, for a people without a land," which depicted Palestine as an unsettled land waiting to be redeemed. But Palestine was, of course, already inhabited, primarily by Arab populations, and its territorial conquest required the recruitment of particular means.[27] Camps were readily adopted by Zionist settlers and later by Israeli national powers as one of the primary mechanisms both to change Palestine's territorial and demographic reality and to deal with the consequences of these radical alterations.

Like other encompassing state projects of social engineering and territorial ordering, the Zionist project also included a utopian vision and a high-modernist ideology.[28] In the case of Zionism, this was supplemented by a modern messianic spirit appropriated to achieve national goals; its radical religious version generated further geopolitical alterations after the 1967 war, almost two decades after Israel's establishment. Outpost camps and other forms of temporary spaces are central to these changes, which continue today in the effort to gain control over the West Bank, part of what the current messianic settlers perceive as the entire Eretz Yisrael. This time Palestine's geopolitical alterations are pursued not by the relatively fragile political powers of an ethnic minority struggling for survival, as in the beginning of the twentieth century, but by settler forces backed up by the strong military and governmental powers of the Israeli state.

It is crucial to understand Israel–Palestine in relation to settler societies as a form of colonialism, which in the Zionist context has been described as colonization for the survival of the Jewish ethnicity.[29] Zionism combined colonial and ethnonational elements from its earliest stages, encouraging Jews to settle in the remembered Land of Israel as a form of collective survival in the face of the threats of anti-Semitism and persecution that increased in nineteenth-century Europe. The gradually developing goals and actions of the Zionist movement were colonial and later national and territorial par excellence: to purchase and settle land, attract settlers, develop agriculture, and launch an international campaign for Jewish political sovereignty. As Oren Yiftachel argues, the Zionist settlers' territoriality became a continuing attempt to Judaize the land "in the name of national self-determination in a Jewish homeland."[30]

Israel–Palestine's genealogy of camps emerges from the initial approach and actions of the Zionist settler society and its national modernist tools and ideology. Camps were used from the earliest stages of Zionist expansion to "the frontier," the "taming" and settling of which was a central icon in Zionist discourse. The camp was initially adopted during the first, second, and, especially, third *Aliyah* immigration waves, when temporary tent camps were used by idealist Zionist settlers, defined as pioneers (*halutzim* in Hebrew), who settled in remote areas as part of the effort to "build the country," cultivate the land, and thus spread across the territory.[31] The best-known type of prestate settler camps were the prefabricated, fortified "wall and tower" outpost camps, of which over fifty were erected in what were considered frontier territories during the years of the Arab uprising (1936–39). All of these Zionist settler camps were fundamental to the creation of a continuous Jewish territory later acknowledged in the UN partition plan for Palestine. Like other camps for civilians, settler camps are also deeply rooted in colonial history, as can be seen in Australia, the Americas, and South Africa as well. Thus, the specific Zionist example can be placed in the wider context of colonial settler societies. It is worth mentioning that while this form of settlement was supported by the British authorities at the beginning of the British Mandate, their attitude changed drastically during the Arab uprising, when strict limitations on Jewish immigration to Palestine were enforced by containing illegal Jewish immigrants/refugees in detention camps in Palestine and beyond. These camps were yet another type of camp that appeared in the area during the period, similar to many other examples of internment camps in what Aidan Forth calls "Britain's empire of camps," as well as in other colonial areas examined in this book.[32]

However, it is only by looking at the period after the establishment of Israel in 1948 that we can see how the camp was widely adopted as a multifaceted mechanism to manage and reorganize the Jewish and Arab populations within and outside the territory. While the prestate settler camps had a mainly territorial meaning, the intensified role of the camp during the first years of statehood was more complex, as it was used for complementary spatial and political purposes. The camp was a territorial mechanism that allowed one population to spread while concentrating and suspending another, and it was also a mechanism that enabled

14   Introduction

the implementation of a modernist ideology of creating a planned new order while facilitating an ethnic if not racial division of Israel's Jewish population.

Camps, created and managed by the Jewish Agency and the state, were used to absorb and then spread mass Jewish immigration, which in Israel's first three years doubled the size of the Jewish population to 1.2 million. This immigration came from two main sources: first, European Jews who had survived the war, including the Nazi concentration and death camps of the Holocaust, many as displaced refugees who had lost their homes and families and were suspended in displaced persons or transit camps, waiting for the gates of the new country to open after the closure imposed by the British authorities; and second, Jews from Arab countries who wished to come to Israel because of religious aspirations, who feared violence due to the Arab–Israeli war and a number of violent attacks on their communities, or who were persuaded by Zionist propaganda that enticed them to leave their homes and settle in the new state.

Camps were created abroad by Jewish institutions such as the American Jewish Joint Distribution Committee (JDC, or the Joint) in order to gather together Jewish immigrants before transferring them to their new state. The first immigrant camps in Israel were established in the abandoned British military camps, followed by a multiplicity of smaller-scale immigrant transit camps—the *ma'abarot*—which were constructed across the country, including in frontier areas. This immigrant transit camp project and the modern frontier development towns that followed have generated an internal Jewish ethnic division in Israel based on territorial ordering: while the founding group of European Jews (Ashkenazim) tightened its hold on the upper social spheres in Israel's central cities and in the early kibbutz and moshav settlements, the "eastern/oriental Jews" (Mizrahim), who came later from Muslim countries, were marginalized, relegated to the state's periphery in the ma'abara camps and, later, development towns.

The distorted mirror images of these camps are the Palestinian refugee camps created by the UN Relief and Works Agency for Palestinian Refugees in the Near East (UNRWA) in neighboring Arab countries for those who fled or were forced out of their homes during the 1948 war and were not allowed to return to what had become part of the new Israeli state. These camps appeared in the same years as the Israeli immigrant and transit camps and supported a population of about the same size. However, while the Jewish migrant transit camps were liquidated after a few years and many of their dwellers were moved into the government-planned development towns, the Palestinian camps still exist today, gaining a particular political meaning of the refugees' resistance to their situation of continuous displacement and demand for the Palestinian right of return (ḥaqq al-ʿawda in Arabic or *zekhut ha'shivah* in Hebrew). Camps were also used by the Israeli army to detain thousands of Palestinian civilians during the 1948 war, and makeshift camps and settlements were created within post-1948-war Israel by the internally displaced Palestinian populations, including the Bedouin. Over the years, some of these have become unrecognized settlements where Palestinian populations have been suspended for decades with no basic infrastructure or state services. Many Negev Bedouin live in these conditions to this day.

The appearance of camps in Israel–Palestine is closely connected to the discrepancy between Israel's territorial and ethnic boundaries, as well as to its emergence as a modern state for the Jewish people on a territory that was mainly inhabited by Arab populations. Many of these camps form part of the indefatigable efforts of the Zionist movement, followed by the Israeli state, to establish Jewish domination over the territory while destabilizing the Arab presence and reducing it to a minimum. The scope of this phenomenon and its particular manifestations show that these camps are not only related to the actions of early statehood, which included the "purification" of the Israeli population by the containment of marginalized "undesired" minorities. Rather, these camps are part of Israel's drastic yet persistent geopolitical reformations and to their related continuous *state of emergency*, which is tightly bound to what seems to be an everlasting yet well-calculated *emergence of state*.

Indeed, detention, settler, and immigrant camps have continued to appear in Israel–Palestine following the additional territorial and demographic changes in the area. The *Nahal* (the Hebrew acronym for *Noar Halutzi Lohem*, "pioneer combatant youth") military–civilian agriculture camps that fortified Israel's frontier areas after the state was established were also erected by Israel after the 1967 war in the newly conquered territories in the Sinai Peninsula, the Golan Heights, the Gaza Strip, and the West Bank, and Jewish settler outpost camps were also continuously erected in the Palestinian occupied territories. During the 1980s, an internment camp was opened to confine the Palestinian population participating in the first uprising against Israel (the first intifada). During the 1990s, a second generation of immigrant camps appeared in peripheral areas to accommodate a new wave of mass immigration arriving from the former USSR and Ethiopia, while a new series of settler outpost camps were created following the Oslo Accords. In 2005, a camp was constructed to temporarily house the Israeli settlers evicted from the Gaza Strip. More recently, in 2013, a detention camp for African asylum seekers was opened in the Negev desert, while Palestinian protest camps were erected over the last decade in the West Bank and along the fortified border fence erected by Israel as part of its blockade of the Gaza Strip.

The ethnically oriented spatial policies in Israel–Palestine, including the different camps, have been examined by numerous scholars, and their work is taken up in this book; however, most analyses have focused on specific spaces, populations, and periods and have not addressed the encompassing and ever-changing apparatus of the camp itself. Other scholars, in work that is also fundamental

16   Introduction

for this study, have identified Israel's ethnocratic and racialized spatial and geo-political patterns as an ongoing national regime, controlled by a dominant ethnic group, that spans spaces and periods, yet the wider role of the camp as a versatile spatiopolitical tool in the territory has not yet been examined. In addition to the scholarship on the camp discussed earlier, this book is deeply rooted in the work of historians, architectural historians and theorists, geographers, sociologists, an-thropologists, and political philosophers who examine the ways space and popula-tions were and still are managed in Israel–Palestine in general and in relation to the camp in particular. The advantage of examining different sorts of camps is that it allows us to expose systematic spatiopolitical patterns, and drastic diversions from them, in spaces that are mostly analyzed as completely different phenomena.

The camps in Israel–Palestine differ substantially. They were created in many forms, from modern prefabricated temporary units, to makeshift camps, to enduring and appropriated camp spaces; they were made by and for different populations and actors; they existed for different lengths of time, a few years or generations; and they served different purposes, primarily to spread the Jewish population over the territory, to concentrate and suspend the Arab populations within or outside the territory, or to resist these imposed state and civil actions of occupation, expulsion, concentration, suspension, and expropriation. These dif-ferences are much more complicated and less binary than what is presented here, but illustrating these basic patterns is required for an initial understanding of this complex reality, which is unfolded in this book.

Capturing Architectural Ghosts

Complex and dynamic systems and mechanisms are not easy to decode. In some cases, a new language and new concepts are needed to capture a transforming and multifaceted apparatus and to understand it as a specific yet evolving instrument, in all its intricate modes of operation. The arguments and conceptualizations of the book aim to open a wider understanding, both theoretical and genealogical, of the camp as a dynamic device. Through an examination of camps in Israel–Palestine in relation to other situations and contexts, the book offers an account of the camp's appearance and change, from the beginning of colonialism, through national and state-building projects, to its current global proliferation. The theo-retical foundations for examining these camps are explored deeply in chapter 1, but the meaning of the differences between these camps is further analyzed in the following chapters. This investigation allows us to understand the complexity of the camp itself as an ever-changing mechanism and thus to go beyond its gen-eral conceptualization, and it also allows us to examine the various ways camps were and still are used as a determining factor in the continuing rearrangement of Israel–Palestine and other modern societies and territories.

The book explores the camp through three complementary modes of investigation: theoretical, historical–genealogical, and spatial–material. Together, these investigations enable us to reflect on the camp's meanings in Israel–Palestine's changing geopolitics. First, in order to understand the situation of the camp, it is necessary to establish a theoretical understanding that allows different spatial types to be read as a group of related spatiopolitical phenomena. Agamben's theory is the basis for this initial approach, yet a critical examination of his theory as it relates to the multifaceted camp types in Israel–Palestine and beyond and in light of the emerging critical scholarship on the theory allows us to form a wider theoretical foundation. This foundation defines the camp first and foremost as a spatiopolitical apparatus that, together with its substantial sociopolitical attributes, creates an instrument that may drastically affect populations, territories, and political negotiations. Second, to understand the prevalent role of the camp in Israel–Palestine, we must also understand the history of the region, including the history of the different political attitudes, policies, and modes of governance established in relation to historical events (such as mass immigration, or the Arab–Israeli conflict). These historical studies are intertwined through the book as a necessary background for understanding the centrality of the camp as an instrument widely used to deal with specific situations in the territory.[33] Third, an empirical study of very different examples of camps that also have commonalities (such as in the ways they are inhabited and evolve spatially and politically) allows us to discuss the specific spatial, social, and political aspects of the camp as a real, physical space.

The book operates between various levels of analysis. This is not only because it reflects on camps created in very different periods, from those of the British Mandate, to the camps of the state-building period, with its displacements and emplacements, to contemporary camp environments. It is also because the book analyzes multiple types of camps, aiming to illustrate a comprehensible genealogy showing how they were differently used in Israel–Palestine and changed throughout the years. In some cases, broad types and alignments of camps, such as the Zionist settler camps and the Palestinian refugee camps, are examined. In other cases, the book zooms in to examine a specific camp, such as the Tel-Yeruham immigrant transit camp, the Rakhma Bedouin camp, or the Holot detention camp for African asylum seekers, enabling us to discuss them as particular places with specific people, spaces, and (his)stories, but always in relation to the larger apparatuses that created them.

The inherent differences between the camps created in different periods also means that various methodologies were used to examine them, involving hermeneutical historical and archival research as well as qualitative ethnographic research strategies, such as observational research, mapping, and interviews.[34] Because one of the most significant attributes of the camp is its temporariness, researching these spaces often involved chasing architectural ghosts, as many camps no longer exist as real physical places but only as archived documents, archeological remnants, or oral histories. Ghosts, as Derrida tells us, are entities that, despite not being present or presently living, still have power to influence the lives of those who are, as an ongoing intergenerational trauma.[35] While some of the camps in Israel–Palestine are still very much living entities, the specters of others that have been erased and are long gone still have a grip on the area's spaces, people, and troubled politics.

As clear evidence of Frantz Fanon's argument that the "settler makes history and is conscious of making it,"[36] many of the camp spaces related to the modernist Zionist movement and the Israeli state creation process were frantically documented and meticulously archived as a testimony to the essential scaffolding of progress and national creation, and as a pure expression of power. Certain Palestinian spaces of refuge were also closely documented by international powers in what could be seen as part of the link between humanitarian practices and colonial legacies of control over the documented image. At the same time, other temporary spaces were thoroughly wiped away, with the intention of leaving no trace, and are missing from the archives, which are never innocent but impose, in Achille Mbembe's words, the "identification and interpretation" of the powerful.[37] These missing spaces and the documents related to them, many of which are still classified by the state or are still actively concealed,[38] remain hidden and muted and are recovered here through the oral histories of those who experienced them. On the other hand, because other camps studied here still exist today as part of an unstable political reality, this study also examines them as lived spaces, while following the spatial and political changes they underwent over time.

It is important to mention how sensitive the subject of "the camp" is in the region. For the Jewish population, the word "camp" immediately calls up haunting images of the Nazi concentration and death camps of the Holocaust (the Shoah), the horrific genocide of European Jewry during World War II, with the mass murder of six million Jews, men, women, and children. Differently, for Palestinians, the word relates to the ongoing situation of the refugee camps created after the 1948 *Nakba* (the Palestinian Catastrophe) and the 1967 war, to host the two waves of Palestinian refugees and still in existence. These spaces are inherently linked to very different, dreadful realities and traumatic memories, which are also used politically by both sides. We need to acknowledge that these reminders are always in the background, and they occasionally appear in the book as difficult associations for their survivors and victims. There is no attempt here to obscure or compare their singularities. This book, indeed, deals with contested concepts and materials, sensitive for all sides involved, a fact that influenced its writing and production

Introduction   **19**

until the very last phases. It was not easy, for example, to obtain permission to use photos from archives that work for and represent opposite ideologies and political interests, such as the archives of the Jewish National Fund (JNF) and UNRWA, where I had to explain the essence of this work. Instead of the pure oppositional potential of these photos, I allow them to speak to one another, as Ariella Aïsha Azoulay suggests in her account on photography's civil contract, as part of "an attempt to rethink the political space of governed populations," including the domination of the powers controlling their images.[39] Part of what this book attempts is to dismantle the stereotypes of these difficult environments and expose their workings and experiences, going beyond the politics that appropriates their histories. The identification of the camp as an instrument generating similar experiences, such as imposed separation, suspension, and discrimination, that many groups in this territory have in common might have a political meaning in itself. By recasting Israel–Palestine's political scripts and histories through bringing into a dialogue interlinked and common realities of oppression that are often examined separately, *The Common Camp* might form a point of departure for new understandings between different groups who were governed by the same violent mechanism, or at least challenge and displace the strict partition between them.

The book traces and analyzes the camp's appearances and variations from early modernity to the present, examining its manifestations and dynamics in Israel–Palestine and beyond. The camp is first theoretically discussed as a spatiopolitical mechanism of modernity. Then, each chapter explores specific camp types in relation to a particular geopolitical situation and related historical period and theoretical aspects. These camps are connected in a genealogical account, illustrating how the camp has transformed over the past century.

Chapter 1 offers a theoretical framework for investigating the camp as a versatile mechanism of modern politics. Through the writings of political thinkers such as Arendt, Foucault, Agamben, Mbembe, and others, the chapter investigates the camp in relation to core political and spatial concepts, including sovereignty, territoriality, population, and materiality. The chapter also examines the inherent connection between the camp and colonialism, and colonial settler societies in particular, and its adaptation to serve the needs of national and global political orders and their changing geopolitical frontiers.

The next six chapters discuss the camp in specific contexts and periods in Israel–Palestine and beyond, while unpacking its changing architectural and political meaning. Focusing on the period of the British rule over Palestine (1917–48), chapter 2 discusses the multifaceted roles of the camp in relation to the intertwined British and Zionist colonial powers. The chapter centers on three different types of camps: the British military camps that evolved after the occupation of the territory during World War I; the Zionist settler tent camps that later evolved to the wall and tower fortified camps, creating the initial Jewish agricultural frontier territorial settlements; and the British detention camps where Jews and Arabs who resisted the British rule, as well as Jewish immigrants/refugees who entered the country illegally, were detained. In this chapter, I begin to develop the themes that are discussed throughout the book, primarily the existence of the camp on a military–civilian continuum, the creation of camps as frontier spaces, and the camp's roles of not only spatial exclusion, expulsion, and expropriation but also of territorial expansion.

The next three chapters examine the central role of the camp in Israel's state-building projects as an instrument that, on the one hand, facilitated the absorption of Jewish immigrants and their dispersal over the territory and, on the other hand, was used to concentrate and suspend the internally displaced Arab populations remaining in Israel after the 1948 war. Chapter 3 examines the camp as an ordering mechanism by exploring the camps created during the Israeli mass-immigration period (1948–51). These include the immigrant camps established abroad (in places such as Algiers, Aden, Marseille, and Brindisi) to gather Jewish immigrants before bringing them to Israel, the closed immigrant camps created in Israel in deserted British military camps to absorb and contain Jewish migrants, and the ma'abarot, the immigrant transit camps used to absorb Jewish immigrants and later to spread them across the territory. Based on Zygmunt Bauman's and James Scott's theories of modernism and order, the chapter analyzes how the camp helped facilitate Israel's profound geopolitical and spatial changes, allowing it to be established as a state formed by two allegedly contradictory but in fact complementary conditions: it was the product, on the one hand, of a chaotic state of emergency created by mass immigration and, on the other hand, of an ambitious and comprehensive modernist project. Arieh Sharon, the architect who was head of the governmental Planning Department in Israel's early years, is one of the main figures discussed in this chapter. He was the leading architect of Israel's National Plan, the state's first encompassing master plan, and camps were one of the means for its implementation.

Chapter 4 analyzes the camp as an instrument of population management and territorial control by looking closely at the central role of the frontier ma'abara transit camps used by Israel to disperse the new Jewish immigrants across the country. The chapter focuses on the story of Yeruham, established in 1951 as an isolated ma'abara camp in the Negev desert, which eventually became a permanent town. The chapter follows Yeruham's early years closely, analyzing it as a frontier camp whose function was based on its isolated location and spatial temporariness, a centralized mode of governance, and a strong ideology of modern development and planning that allowed immigrants to be used as pawns in the creation of Israel's new social and territorial order. The ma'abara camps are also analyzed here as the initial tool causing the spatial segregation of Jewish society in Israel along ethnoracial lines. The spatial and architectural connection between the camp and the modern tenement blocks of Israeli development towns is also examined in this chapter, as are the minor acts of resilience and resistance engaged in by immigrants coping with the reality of the camp that was imposed on them.

The complementary side of chapters 3 and 4 is presented in chapters 5 and 6, focusing on camps created as spatial instruments for containing and suspending internally displaced indigenous Palestinian populations in Israel and Palestinian refugees, as part of the state-building process and in later years. Chapter 5 analyzes the encampments and makeshift settlements created by internally displaced Palestinian populations that later developed into unrecognized villages, telling the story of Rakhma, a makeshift unrecognized Bedouin settlement neighboring Yeruham, which was created in the late 1950s when the population was displaced to the area by the Israeli army. The imposed campness of the makeshift village is discussed as an instrument that allowed and still allows Israel to suspend indigenous populations as temporary inhabitants as a tactic to further concentrate and urbanize them according to the interests of the state. The chapter examines the architectural meaning of the "chaotic" environments of the unrecognized settlements that are managed by Israel as de facto makeshift camps, interpreting their deep sociospatial order, often invisible to Israeli authorities, against the "total order" of institutionalized camps. Rakhma's actions to resist its imposed situation through spatial initiatives are analyzed as a tool of cultural negotiation and political struggle for their denied resources and rights.

Chapter 6 focuses on the very different camps that formed and changed in the territories occupied by Israel following the 1967 Six-Day War. Through an analysis of the Palestinian refugee camps and the Palestinian protest camps in the Palestinian occupied territories, it examines how the camp, on the one hand, was used as a tool of resistance, protest, and struggle against the Israeli occupation, while it also, on the other hand, became the target of Israeli efforts to reduce and rearrange the population of Palestinian refugees in those territories. Through an analysis of Israeli settler camps created by different groups in the Sinai Peninsula, the Golan Heights, and the Palestinian occupied territories of the Gaza Strip and the West Bank, the chapter also examines how the settler camp has facilitated Israel's continuous colonial occupation. The chapter looks at how the space of the refugee camp enables its residents to articulate and enact a new political reality, while shaping interactions through its built environment as a form of architectural resistance. It also shows how the Israeli settler camps and the infrastructures that connect them are together used as a territorial instrument that further encamps the Palestinians in separated, shrinking, and controlled territorial enclaves.

The Holot detention camp for African asylum seekers, opened in 2013 in the Negev desert as a space of containment and banishment, is the focus of chapter 7. The chapter shows how this camp, originally conceived as a border camp intended

22 Introduction

to control the movement of newcomers to Israel, was mainly operated to remove this vulnerable population from Israeli cities and to pressure them to "willingly" leave the country. The camp, where Israel detained asylum seekers for various periods of time, is discussed in the broader context of the contemporary global penal colony, an ever-changing infrastructure of camps where unwanted populations are suspended and managed.

The conclusion discusses the book's main understandings of the camp as a result of its genealogical analysis: its function as a versatile multifaceted instrument based on spatial temporariness and the management of specific populations outside the normal state order and through particular modern technologies and materialities; its complementary use for concentration, containment, expulsion, and expropriation as well as for mobility and territorial expansion; the complex meaning behind its various "ordered" and "chaotic" spaces; its function as a political instrument of control, exclusion, protest, and resistance; its relation to the city; and its transformations as Israel–Palestine's hidden spatial gene, a gene that drastically influenced the territory's political and spatial formation. The conclusion also highlights how the extremes of the camp allow fundamental spatial and architectural perceptions to be challenged and reconceptualized. The camp's role, the conclusion shows, is that of a modern instrument that has been and still is— from the early days of colonialism, through state-building processes, and in the present global political order—used to reorganize, control, and negotiate territories and populations. It suggests that the instrument of the camp will continue to transform and emerge according to political changes as a space that materializes through the everlasting struggles between the power *over* human life and the power *of* human life to resist a certain reality and struggle to change it.

The Common Camp aims to reveal the camp not only as a space but also as a spatial practice that produces a politics proper to itself, a politics that is not only constituting the camp but is also constituted by the camp and because of its existence. Its prevalence in Israel–Palestine tells the story not only of the camp but also of this unstable territory, its violence and politics, which has affected the lives of many. Though this book analyzes multiple and various camp spaces, its intention is not to present a typology of camps created in Israel–Palestine over the last century (nor does it claim to be an exhaustive collection of types), nor to be an inventory of camps through which the history of the region can be understood. Rather, the book aims to develop an understanding of the camp as a certain logic, which it at once forms and represents. A more generalizable understanding of the common camp would reveal a logic of a spatial and material culture that is constitutive to the political history of Israel–Palestine and beyond to the current evolving global reality of encampment.

1

THE CAMP RECONFIGURED
Modernity's Versatile Architecture of Power

Modernity was born under the stars of acceleration and land conquest, and these stars form a constellation which contains all the information about its character, conduct, and fate. . . . Spatial expansion was the name of the game and space was at stake; space was the value, time was the tool.
　　　—Zygmunt Bauman, *Liquid Modernity*

For surely it is one of the unhappiest characteristics of the age to have pro-duced more refugees, migrants, displaced persons, and exiles than ever before in history, most of them as accompaniment to and, ironically enough, as afterthoughts of great post-colonial and imperial conflicts. As the struggle for independence produced new states and new boundaries, it also produced home-less wanderers, nomads, vagrants, unassimilated to the emerging structures of institutional power, rejected by the established order for their intransigence and obdurate rebelliousness.
　　　—Edward Said, *Culture and Imperialism*

The camp is considered a paradigmatic yet concealed space of modern politics. Whether we discuss the colonial "empire of camps," the camps emerging out of the "political system of the modern nation-state," the complex relationships between "the city and the camp," or the current expanding "global archipelago of encamp-ments,"[1] the camp is often invisible yet central to the colonial, national, urban, and global enmeshed politics of modernity, which are all grounded in space. The significance of the camp as the hidden matrix, the *arcanum imperii*, of modern politics, with its unaccountable actions, is set in the way particular people, ma-terials, and territories are administered, negotiated, and manipulated within and in between political frameworks, primarily that of the modern state. As we live today in a world of states, in which almost every part of the globe is the territory of some state (while not all people are *members* of a state), contemporary camps are mostly discussed as threshold spaces of the encompassing national framework that orders, regulates, and controls people in space.[2] Refugees, irregular migrants, and "war on terror" suspects are now the main actors contained in camp spaces, as they are seen as challenging, disrupting, or threatening stabilized state orders. If we add those deemed undesirable and held to be members of "dangerous groups" in the past—such as Jews, Roma, and homosexuals in the Nazi concentration and extermination camps, or Boers, Nama, and Mau Mau peoples in the colonial camps—the list of those who were contained in camps is much longer.

Modern politics, however, involves not only people, space, and political structures but also the constantly unfolding modern technologies and the particular materials and apparatuses that people use and through which they are governed. As these material elements and their logistical and spatial apparatuses are invented and developed, they become inherent parts of the evolution of modern governmental structures and political practices, including the way particular human environments, such as the camp, are created, managed, and transformed. Indeed, the camp is not only a governmental tool; it also has distinct material characteristics that not only enable it to act on people, lands, and other matters, but also allow it to be used as a space for people to act through its often-flexible material and spatial constellations. As a space that can be swiftly erected, altered, and demolished, the camp is not only influenced by politics, but can also itself constitute a new form of politics emerging from its particular attributes that create rapidly evolving political realities and practices. As such, it is not only a space that is used by power, but also a space through which people are speaking back to power.

What, then, is the relation between the camp and modern politics, including its broader situations and aspects? What distinguishes the camp, in its multifaceted varieties, from other spaces and political constellations? This chapter offers a theoretical framework for the camp as a versatile spatiopolitical instrument while examining it in relation to the fundamental attributes of modernity, including modernity's political and material structures and technologies.

The Modern Reordering of Things

Modernity, as a historical period and a cultural and social category, encompasses many things, and its various attributes, from the secularization of society to its rapid industrialization, have substantially reshaped politics and the way societies are governed. Among the many different markers of modernity, Zygmunt Bauman has identified two attributes as crucial. The first is the changing relationship between space and time: modernity emerged from the technological innovations leading to the acceleration of speed in moving through space, with velocity expediting spatial expansion, land conquest, and colonization while imposing immobility on the colonized.[3] The second attribute of modernity is the quest for order, which includes an ambition to struggle against chaos and ambivalence and to give the world a defined structure.[4] The camp, as a spatial mechanism of speed, containment, and ordering, is closely related to these attributes.

Migration, refuge, and the mobility of peoples are as old as human existence, yet in modern times, with new technologies of mobility, the scale and speed of moving people and things from one place to another has risen drastically, and at the same time, new social and political forms of ordering have also been created in the attempt to organize society and control people in space. Both colonialism and the rise of the state as the most prevalent modern form of governance are tightly connected to modernity's sociocultural ordering mechanisms and technological transformations. These transformations influenced not only political forms but also their ever-evolving governmental and related spatial apparatuses, including the camp, which, in turn, created new political and human relations.

Over the last century the camp has gradually become entangled with the framework of the state, creating a designated space for those who are not yet admitted to, or who "had been ejected from," in Arendt's words, "the old trinity of state–people–territory" that created the modern state.[5] The tight nexus between the three basic entities of people, state, and territory can already be identified in Max Weber's traditional definition of the state as "a human community" (population or nation) with a "monopoly of the legitimate use of force" (state or governance) acting "within a given territory."[6] With the frantic reordering of the world into nation-states over the last century in the attempt to achieve a humanity that is accurately organized within the global territorial political map, the camp seems to be a space formed when those entities do not overlap.

As an instrument to reorder the world around state and colonial political contexts, including postcolonial and neocolonial situations, the camp continuously appears as a device to prevent or suspend the movement of people to and within particular territories. Yet with the ability to swiftly create and transform both its function and its form, the camp is a space that not only facilitates immobility but also supports rapid mobility and self-initiated movement through specific political and material components.

In this chapter I examine the prominent social, political, and material aspects from which the camp emerges as a multifaceted modern spatiopolitical instrument. These aspects serve as the baseline for the discussion throughout the book and relate to key elements in which the camp is distinguished from other spaces, primarily those of the modern state and colonial apparatuses. They relate to modernity's stabilizing formations and their associated order, primarily the state–people–territory triad of the modern state and its legal, governmental, social, and spatial apparatuses. They also relate to the heterogeneous actors and elements of modern technologies, materiality, and sociopolitical assemblages and their associated bottom-up provisional yet inventive practices and politics. As such, the common camp holds in tension aspects of agency and structure, revealing, through its multifaceted appearances and evolution in Israel–Palestine, how these are constantly negotiated.

The ever-changing practices and attributes of the common camp discussed throughout this book are examined through a variety of camps created in one location yet across sovereigns, populations, and territorial constellations. In this chapter, these three aspects—state/sovereignty, people/nation, and territory/space—also form the core structure through which the camp is discussed. These aspects, which are examined in relation to other camp components, such as modern forms of (im)mobility, materiality, and violence, enable us to distinguish the camp from other spaces of modernity and to establish the kinds of politics it enables.

Sovereignty, Modern Politics, and the Camp

Over the past two decades, the camp has been primarily theorized through the influential work of political philosopher Giorgio Agamben on the camp as the paradigmatic space of modern biopolitics. Agamben addresses both the idea of "the camp" and specific camps as particular material spaces. Building on the ideas of Arendt, Benjamin, Foucault, Schmitt, and others, Agamben holds that the camp forms a "space of exception" that is included within a state's territory through its exclusion from the state's normal juridical order, and is "produced at a point at which the political system of the modern nation-state, which was founded on the functional nexus between a determinate localisation (land) and a determinate order (the State) mediated by automatic rules for the inscription of life (birth or the nation), enters into a lasting crisis."[7] The state here functions as a juridical and governmental entity that might exceed its "legitimate use of force," to use Weber's words, through the extensive use of violence in the camp. In order to understand the camp's exceptionality within the state order and in other related contexts of modern sovereignty, we must examine the principles (and paradoxes) of modern sovereignty that encompass both the exception and the norm.

Sovereignty and the Right to Decide

The concept of the modern state developed alongside the idea of sovereignty. The word "sovereignty" derives from the French term *souverain,* "supreme ruler," and sovereignty is characterized in two complementary ways that reflect the dual political arenas in which it exists. First, sovereignty is the primacy of the domestic authority within the state's boundaries, which includes the right to make laws and to make final juridical decisions. Second, sovereignty implies the independence of individual states and their power to secure their independence from other states.[8] But what constitutes a sovereign? And how does the camp relate to the way modern sovereignty functions?

It was probably Thomas Hobbes in his seventeenth-century book *Leviathan* who began to think theoretically on the idea of the modern state, where the equality of people and the absence of a clear natural hierarchy of power relations are the primary reasons for the need for a sovereign.[9] In what Hobbes calls a "State of Nature," "where every man is enemy to every man," resulting in people living in "continual fear, and danger of violent death," it is impossible to maintain an active social life of creativity and comfort.[10] With the use of reason, therefore, people establish a "multitude . . . united in one person . . . called a Commonwealth . . . that great Leviathan . . . that Mortal God, to which we owe . . . our peace and defence."[11] The sovereign, for Hobbes, is the one to whom (or to whose representatives) the community transfers the right to use violence; the sovereign exists outside the community and ensures its peaceful existence. In Hobbes's political machine of the state, although the subjects are protected from each other's violence, the sovereign itself remains in the violent State of Nature in relation to other sovereignties, in a situation that also constitutes the sovereign's exclusive power, keeping war away from its community and outside its borders. The exclusive and violent character of sovereign power was already recognized by the sixteenth-century political philosopher Jean Bodin, who identifies the abilities that mark sovereign power as "properties not shared by [its] subjects."[12] What is implicit in Bodin's text is that sovereignty is an *effect* of the sovereign's actions, such as enforcing law and declaring war, and that these actions should be performed frequently to maintain the sovereign as the central referent.

For both Hobbes and Bodin, the sovereign is placed—like a god—outside the juridical order, constituting itself by the right to decide (on laws, on wars) and through violent performances of this right whenever this order is violated (by criminals, traitors, or anyone else who threatens its power). These rights are embodied in what Foucault identifies as one of the sovereign's basic attributes in the classic theory of sovereignty: the right of life and death. In premodern sovereignties, Foucault argues, the right of life and death was exercised only when the sovereign could kill—"the right to take life or let live."[13] The concrete manifestation of this power is seen in the great public ritualizations of death—spectacular ceremonies of torture, execution, and other punishments performed publicly in central squares, ceremonies in which the whole of society participated.

Both Hobbes's and Bodin's political theories are products of northern and western Europe in the sixteenth and seventeenth centuries, when kings possessed both secular and divine authority, embodied in the person of the monarch. The sovereign's right "to take life or let live" was an acceptable performance of power, as he was not an equal member of the community but was in a position closer to God. The increasing independence of humanity from the divine, however, together with other economic, technological, and social changes of modernity and modernization, signaled the decline of absolutist and authoritarian states and the need to eventually develop other instruments, including the camp, through which sovereignty is asserted.

The emergence and evolution of popular sovereignty in the eighteenth century expressed the increasing power of groups of wealthy and educated people who demanded a measure of sovereignty as individuals. As French philosopher Claude Lefort argues, the revolutionary feature of democracy is that it changed the locus of power into an *empty place*, preventing its appropriation by permanent political figures. Only the mechanisms by which it was exercised could be recognized; it remained the symbolic agency by virtue of which society framed itself as a unified political entity.[14]

The French Revolution played a prominent role in codifying the new idea of the sovereign "people" in the transition to the emergent system of the nation-state. The crucial indications of sovereign power—indivisibility, self-reference, and transcendence—were now embedded in the citizens, and violence was now the weapon of reason for the preservation of their basic right of freedom against external threats and internal enemies.[15] New radical principles for organizing a democratic society that emerged at the time are still central to modern political thought, such as Jean-Jacques Rousseau's idea that all human beings are free and equal. In *The Social Contract*, Rousseau suggests the optimal conditions under which sovereign power could maintain the basic human rights of freedom and equality and express the will of its subjects, containing simultaneously the loss and the protection of freedom.[16] The "individual will" joins all the other wills, forming the "general will," reflecting the reason of all individual wills that are part of the contract. Sovereign power here is legitimate only if it represents the "general will," and although people lose their "natural freedom" under it, they gain civic freedom, legal equality, and moral freedom, which enforce obedience to the laws that people set for themselves. Unlike the Hobbesian sovereign, who is separate from its subjects, Rousseau's ideal sovereign functions like an organic whole: "This multitude is so united in one body, it is impossible to offend against one of the members without attacking the body."[17] However, while the question of *decision* is resolved in Hobbes's theory, as the sovereign is a separate entity, *The Social Contract*'s contradictory principles make it more problematic: the *concrete decision* of the "general will," which expresses the majority of all individual wills, might contradict the *ideal* "general will"—the common denominator of all individual wills.[18]

While the concrete decision is identified as the potential problem in Rousseau's social contract, for the twentieth-century conservative political thinker Carl Schmitt decisionism is the defining doctrine of sovereignty and its expression.

"Sovereign is he who decides on the [state of] exception," and this is how the sovereign asserts its power.[19] Only the sovereign has the right to decide whether "the constitution needs to be suspended" in a case of an extreme emergency. Schmitt, observing the weaknesses of liberal constitutionalism and cosmopolitanism (while being actively involved with Nazism), sees sovereignty as a "borderline concept," determined by the borderline case of such a decision (of what should be declared a state of exception and what should be done about it).[20] Emergency, in English, is "defined by a state of *emerging*," that is, a volatile condition in which forms are no longer stable, when potentially dangerous or revolutionary new forms of political life might arise. In German, the *Ausnahmezustand*, which is literally "state of exception," reflects the notion that the exception to the law defines the very essence of it.[21] The sovereign, in the state of emergency, stands outside the juridical order in which he is included through its necessary suspension.

Building on Schmitt's understanding that although the sovereign "stands outside the normally valid legal system, he nevertheless belongs to it," Agamben identifies this paradox of sovereignty as its logic, arguing that "the sovereign is, at the same time, outside and inside the juridical order."[22] As, according to Agamben, the issue of the sovereign exception is "the very condition of possibility of juridical rule, and, along with it, the very meaning of state authority," the state of exception when the law is suspended is what defines the rule of law and what makes the validation of the juridical order possible. The exception is taken outside *(ex-capere)*, and the outside is included "by letting the juridical order withdraw from the exception and abandon it." It is here where the camp, according to Agamben, emerges as the physical appearance of the state of exception, and as a space that is both inside and outside sovereignty: the camp is *"the space that is opened when the state of exception begins to become the rule,"* and in the camp the essentially temporary state of exception "is now given a permanent spatial arrangement."[23]

As a space created ad hoc, not part of prior long-term planning and legal order, the camp is not the outcome of the state's democratically agreed mode of governance but, rather, *"a hybrid of law and fact in which the two terms become indistinguishable."* While under the normal legal order the subject is protected from the violence of the sovereign, in the camp "power confronts nothing but pure life, without any mediation." For Agamben, the Hobbesian "state of nature" is not a prejuridical or extrajuridical condition with no relation to the internal legal order; rather, "the state of nature is, in truth, a state of exception,"[24] where outside and inside enter into a zone of indistinction that stands at the core of the juridical order of the modern state.[25] The prison, where individuals are interned because they have committed a crime and are therefore subject to the state's penal system, sits firmly within its juridical order. By contrast, those in the camp are not interned as individuals because of what they did, but en masse because of what they are (Jews and Roma in the Nazi camps, refugees and irregular migrants in today's refugee and detention camps)—that is, undesirable people who are perceived as a threat or are determined by the sovereign to be "life that does not deserve to live," at least not as part of the "normal" state order.[26] The camp has become the place were citizens, noncitizens, and no-longer citizens, men, women, and children, could be detained, abused, and, in the Nazi death camps and other camps, also systematically murdered, and where no one is entirely protected from anyone else or from the violence of the sovereign. As Walter Benjamin observed, "The tradition of the oppressed teaches us that the 'state of emergency' in which we live is not the exception but the rule,"[27] which led Agamben to recognize that in the Western modern state of the twentieth century the state of exception began not only to coincide with the normal order but, increasingly gripping the logic of the norm, to "appear as the dominant paradigm of government in contemporary politics."[28]

In Israel–Palestine, emergency regulations are indeed central to the juridical system. An official state of emergency was adopted by Israel as part of the first legislation following its declaration of independence in May 1948, effectively incorporating the 1945 emergency British Mandatory regulations in Israeli law in the form of a national state of emergency that has been extended every year since. This state of emergency has served as the juridical background to some of the camp spaces examined in this book, which have morphed according to Israel–Palestine's ever-emerging exceptional realities and ongoing "genealogy of emergency."[29]

The State as a Mode of Governance

It is not only the juridical state of exception in the camp that makes it such a central space of modern state sovereignty as its internal "constituting outside," but also the way the camp is located within the state's mode of governance. As Foucault shows, the modern state was created following a political transformation during the seventeenth century, with the breakthrough of "governmental reason"—*raison d'Etat*—which "delineated the state as both its principle and its objective"; the state became "the regulatory idea of that form of thought, that form of reflection, that form of calculation, and that form of intervention . . . as a rational form of the art of government."[30] With this, the machine of the state continuously reproduces itself through its mode of governance, its practices, and its logic.

Since the emergence of governmental reason, the naturalized entity of the state increasingly appears almost everywhere: in formal juridical, bureaucratic, and political discourse as well as in many other spheres, such as spatial and economic formations, and it is the sovereign that brings together this multiplicity of powers and potentials under one political unity of power. The state is not only an abstract appearance; rather, it is connected to the way specific entities such as population, space, and goods are closely managed and controlled by multiplying governmental apparatuses, and in ways that since the eighteenth century have become increasingly bureaucratic, distant, and less personal. Importantly, as Foucault reflects, freedom was inserted within this governmentality "not only as the right of individuals . . . but as an element that has become indispensable to governmentality itself"; from this point forward, "a condition of governing well is that freedom, or certain forms of freedom, are really respected." Freedom, therefore, including freedom of movement, among other freedoms, is central to this democratic governmentality; "the idea of government as government of population" makes Rousseau's problem of the foundation of both sovereignty and freedom even more acute.[31]

As an enclave where people are managed temporarily, the camp is not only a space but also a specific mode of governance that works simultaneously within and outside the unified juridical *and* governmental orders of the state, including its territorial ones. This is where various forms of freedom are limited, but it might also be the place and the means through which the limitations of freedom are challenged, such as in some refugee camps and protest camps. When this separated and separating form of governance is coupled with the way the impersonal bureaucracy and logistics deal with the masses, the camp might become a lethal machine owing either to active violence or to mere neglect and abandonment of the contained population. Because the camp is a space of exception existing both within and outside the unified order of the state, the particular power relations and modes of governance in the camp are often recognized as "contested," "hybrid," "ambiguous," "contentious," or "patched" sovereignty and governance that control or activate the camp rather than representing its residents, unlike other spaces of the modern state.[32] As a space that could be rapidly created to answer an urgent and unexpected state of emergency, a camp could be seen as part of what Alex Jeffrey calls "the improvised state," which conducts "structured improvisations" through multifaceted practices of performed resourcefulness, which often do not coincide with its own governmental and legal order, as could be seen in many of the camps created by Israel and examined in this book.[33]

The camp, as a way of governing people by containing them en masse, is seen as emerging from military technologies of containment developed in the late eighteenth century for holding prisoners of war (POWs), such as the POW camps that were built across Britain before and during the Napoleonic Wars and those of the American Civil War. They are also related to Victorian England's relief practices, where institutions such as the workhouse were created to support (and control and exploit) the poor.[34] Yet it was in the colonies where the governmental technology of the camp evolved to control civilian populations in disaster situations, with imperialism giving rise to interconnected series of crises, including famine and war, for which the offered solution was mass encampment.[35]

The Colonial Laboratory of Modern Governance

The origin of the camp as a modern spatial instrument for managing civilian populations is inherently connected to colonial history. As Thomas Blom Hansen and Finn Stepputat argue, the colonial sovereignty remained a naked version of sovereign power, the raw racist and violent "truth" of the modern nation-state.[36] Camps were a significant part of the colonial laboratory of modernity, and in *The Origins of Totalitarianism* Hannah Arendt was famously one of the first to recognize how new racial forms of power mechanisms were tested within the colonial matrix. Arendt identifies the link between the colonial concentration camps for "undesirable elements," which emerged in South Africa and India at the beginning of the twentieth century and "were used for 'suspects' whose offenses could not be proved and who could not be sentenced by ordinary process of law," and the concentration camps of the Third Reich, which were central to the development of totalitarianism and its associated genocide.[37]

The extensive use of camps to intern and concentrate civilian populations is now widely acknowledged as part of the continuities between not only colonial and totalitarian but also democratic and liberal regimes. As a spatial technology of power born and experimented with during the colonial wars, the colonial concentration camps—such as those in which the English contained the Boers in the late nineteenth century or the *campos de concentraciones* created in Cuba by the Spanish in 1896—are often mentioned as the first historical examples of camps for civilians.[38] The colonial concentration camps are strongly connected not only to the aforementioned POW camps and the Victorian relief institutions for the "dangerous classes" of the poor, but also to other colonial camp formations, such as the famine camps, plague camps, evacuation camps, and camps or networks of enclosed settlements for "criminal tribes" in British India and elsewhere.[39] These colonial concentration camps, which consolidated the connection between concentration, forced labor, and extermination before migrating to the West,[40] are also linked to the colonial mining camps where the massive appropriation of laboring bodies was facilitated from the early days of colonialism.[41] These camps are what sociologist Erving Goffman described as the "total institution," which imposes a "total life" cut off from the wider society, a formally administered life from which it is difficult to escape.[42]

The colonial concentration camps for civilians evolved as a military tactic responding to new forms of conflict. In South Africa, as irregular Boer guerrilla groups, aided by local civilians, attacked British forces, scorched-earth warfare was initiated, displacing the Boers from their farms and concentrating these scattered and often famished civilians in a system of concentration camps as spaces of (inadequate) care and control.[43] In 1901, a network of some forty such camps, composed of tents laid out in grids and resembling military camps, became the spatial apparatuses where more than twenty-eight thousand Boers, mostly women, children, and elderly men, died of starvation and diseases. Lack of food, blankets, fuel, clothes, sanitation, and other core necessities proved fatal in these overcrowded and severely neglected spaces. A parallel system of makeshift concentration camps for displaced black African families was created on vacant land near the British guarded railway system and around the Boer camps. Those who were "dumped" in these areas were required to construct their own temporary shelters, of tin and wood frameworks covered with sailcloth or sacks, while being regarded as a reservoir of labor.[44]

The substantial death rates in the colonial camps, such as those containing the Boers or those created by the Spanish colonialists in Cuba (where half a million were contained and at least one hundred thousand died from disease and starvation) revealed the camp as an efficient instrument for the mass killing of entire populations. Shortly after the German government criticized the cruelty of the British in the South African camps, it created its own camps for the Herero and Nama in German South West Africa (Deutsche Südwestafrika; now Namibia) with a gruesome shift in the evolution of the camp: extermination became its primary purpose, leading to what is now recognized as the first genocide of the twenty-first century. This new spatial weapon developed in the colonies was later imported to the West, creating the racialized architecture of the Japanese American concentration camps during World War II and serving the genocidal Nazi regime in Europe, first to concentrate and contain and also, later, to systematically exterminate millions of those deemed undesired populations, such as Roma and, primarily, Jews.[45] Colonial internment camps have continued to be created in multiple settings during the twentieth century, before and after World War II: the Italian concentration camps for Bedouin in Libya in the 1930s, the British camps for the Mau Mau in Kenya in the 1950s, and the French *camps de regroupement* for the forcibly relocated people in Algeria during the revolution of the 1950s and 1960s.[46]

Whether the abandonment of particular and often native populations in the camp to diseases and starvation was a form of deliberate population control or a result of mere indifference to their deaths, racism was at the core of the concentration camp from its initial creation. In the colonies and later in the West, the modern state used these camps to segregate racialized populations out of the political community and organize them as (undesired) biological beings.

Settler Colonialism and the Camp

There are many forms of colonialism, as Ann Stoler argues,[47] and these forms also create multiple kinds of camps for different populations and settings. In Israel–Palestine, the camp appears, in its various uses, as part of the area's intertwined colonial and national processes, which are primarily linked to the ongoing Zionist and then Israeli settler colonial project. Colonialism's common form included the appropriation of land, resources, and labor by a relatively small group of European administrators, merchants, missionaries, and soldiers. By contrast, colonial settler societies were formed by a substantial number of Europeans arriving for permanent settlement, with some settlement models involving direct control of land and economy based on "white labor."[48] Together with the forced removal or destruction of the indigenous population and its spaces, which could often be identified as ethnic cleansing in a different scope and extent,[49] this enabled white European settlers to regain a racially based sense of ethnic and cultural homogeneity that was also identified with nationality as a European concept. Such colonies are claimed to be the most appropriate model for the Zionist–Israeli case,[50] and they have used various coercive, ideological, legal, and administrative mechanisms to exclude and exploit both indigenous and alien populations, often on an ethnic or racial basis.[51] As Israeli sociologist Baruch Kimmerling argued, "The Israeli state, like many other immigrant-settler societies, was born in sin, on the ruins of another culture, one which suffered politicide and a partial ethnic cleansing," even if Israel did not completely annihilate the native culture as many other settler societies did.[52] These practices, based on different modes of self-initiated and imposed mobilities, divided such settler societies into three main ethnoclasses: a founding (European) group, a group of later (often non-European) immigrants, and a dispossessed indigenous group; a fourth stratum, of legal or illegalized foreign workers, has recently emerged in many settler societies.[53]

These various ethnoclasses and racial divisions of colonial settler societies, which have also emerged in Israel–Palestine, are also reflected in the different camp types created over the years to facilitate both territorial expansion and related expulsions and expropriations: the first Zionist settler tent camps and wall and tower camps were created by the Zionist founding group; the Israeli immigrant camps and ma'abara transit camps were created for the later Jewish immigrants; the Bedouin and Palestinian camps were created for and by the dispossessed and displaced indigenous groups; and a detention camp was created for African asylum seekers, who are classified by Israel as illegal migrants. These camps were not only created as biopolitical mechanisms of the "national body" acting on the "people" (or the population as a whole) as something that should "continually be redefined and purified through exclusion";[54] they were also created to build, educate, and expand this national body and its territory, with these various forms corresponding to modernity's ordering efforts, displacing and emplacing different populations according to a national and often ethnocratic and racial logic. But in what ways are these ethnic and racial divisions connected to the biopolitical logic of colonial apparatuses and the nation-state? And in what ways does the camp become an instrument to assert this logic within particular modern political formations?

Populations, Nations, and Racial Formations: Biopolitics, Necropolitics, and the Camp

One of the most important historical phenomena related to the modern state is the appearance and continued expansion, splitting, and multiplication of more and more state apparatuses that are primarily concerned with managing people's lives rather than with only subjecting them to the law.[55] The inherent link between these apparatuses and the instrument of the camp is related to the close management of the life of the state's population as a society, a process connected to modernity and to the perception of the state's population as a nation that is taken care of by its state.

In *The Human Condition*, Arendt analyzes the fact that, with the rise of modern society, biological life as such gradually came to occupy the center of the political scene of modernity, transforming the political realm by giving natural life primacy over political action. Instead of focusing on political life as a sphere of plurality, worldliness, and freedom, where people are the subject and their human essence is being realized, society turned its interest toward the continuation of the life process itself, with the only aim being the survival of the "animal species man."[56] Foucault's writing on this process, which started at the threshold of the modern era, by which natural life began to be included in the mechanisms of state power and politics became *biopolitics*, is crucial in understanding the relations between population, governance, space, and the camp.[57] Unlike disciplinary power, which is addressed to the single body, biopolitics and biopower deal with the population's multiple bodies, administering "the population as a political problem, as a problem that is at once scientific and political, as a biological problem and as power's problem."[58] Biopolitics intervenes at the population's general level through state mechanisms that include statistical estimates, forecasts, and other overall measures. Mortality rate, birth rate, and life expectancy are all balanced to regulate society's biological processes for maintaining "man-as-species," and society's docile bodies become the main object of government.

The greatest transformation political rights underwent in the nineteenth century, Foucault argues, was the penetration of the old sovereign right "to take life or to let live" by the new power of "making live and letting die."[59] As the spectacular public ritualization of death began to disappear, the purpose of modern state mechanisms that regulate the population began focusing on improving life.[60] This is what connects "the power of regularization,"[61] the biopolitical mechanisms the state uses to deal with populations rather than with individuals, to the power over human life. The power of the state's disciplinary or regulatory technologies "takes life as both its object and its objective," and its "basic function is to improve life"; how, then, asks Foucault, can biopower "expose not only its enemies but its own citizens to the risk of death"? "How can a power such as this kill?" The answer is that this is where racism intervenes. Racism, argues Foucault, is a way of introducing a distinction into the domain of life under the control of the state between "what must live and what must die."[62] Racism fragments the biological human life controlled by state power, allowing it to separate out and kill racialized groups within the population, as did the Nazi regime Foucault refers to, with its "final solution" of systematically concentrating and then annihilating all Jews. It establishes a biologic caesura within the population, subdividing "the species it controls, into the subspecies known, precisely, as races," and creates within the state itself a biological relationship in which "the more [the] inferior species die out," the more the other "species" proliferate. It allows us to understand biopower as a form of power that enables the state, in Foucault's words, "both to protect life and to authorise a holocaust."[63] It also allows states in other contexts, such as colonial, settler colonial, and postcolonial societies, to abandon certain racialized groups, such as indigenous or certain migrant populations, and let them diminish.

Biopolitics, as the power of the modern state over life, and racism together create a new threshold between life and death in which society acts against itself, and the camp functions as one of its central mechanisms. The population that is legally protected by the normal juridical order from direct violence by the state is also biologically protected by the state's regulatory technologies. These protections recede in certain types of contexts, such as the camp, where the detainees/residents are abandoned, either by direct state violence or by the state's failure or refusal to provide them with the systems and infrastructures necessary to support life. The mechanisms that tighten the bond between the population and the state, such as infrastructures or social services, are the same ones that "make live," if they are supplied to the "normal" citizen, or "let die," if they are denied in the camp. But who are the populations who are excluded, who are detained in the camp? And how does their exclusion relate to the political foundation of the modern state, including the colonial settler state?

Unpacking "The Nation"

The habit of interchanging "nation" and "state" as abbreviations for the "nation-state," writes the political scientist Walker Connor, overlooks the fact that this hyphenated term marks the vital difference between the two.[64] "United Nations," "international law," and "national income" are all misnomers obscuring the difference between state and nation, a terminological confusion that is a syndrome reflecting the blurriness of the meaning of "nation." While its Latin origin *natio*, literally meaning "birth," conveys the idea of common blood ties, its later use may merely describe the population of a country, regardless of its ethnonational composition. But while the world is often conceived as being largely composed of nation-states, in fact less than 10 percent of states can be justifiably described so, and nation-states are usually multinational states. The fact that states (Germany or Spain) are often named after nations (Germans or Spaniards) creates integration between the state, as sovereignty and multiple governmental apparatuses, on the one hand, and its subjects, who are imagined as *the nation* or *the people*, on the other. The name of the state is a means to proclaim its unity: a reassurance of the wholeness of the subjected population group to which the state belongs and a guarantee of their safety and well-being. However, who the nation is, what its boundaries are, who belongs, who remains outside, and how people either join from the outside or are excluded from within are all decided by the sovereign in the name of the state, which acts in the name of the nation. And this is exactly what the term "nation" blurs, making the state appear to be a natural framework of partnership and belonging. In popular sovereignty, as declared in the French Declaration of the Rights of Man and of the Citizen, "the source of all sovereignty resides essentially in the nation,"[65] meaning that the question of who is a part of "the nation" had, and still has, substantial political importance.

"Nation, nationality, nationalism—all have proved notoriously difficult to define," states Benedict Anderson, who proposes a definition of the nation as an imagined political community.[66] While the various definitions of "nation" differ tremendously on what these imagined communities have in common, they all agree that certain characteristics construct a nation's identity and distinguish it from other nations. As the nation-state evolved during the nineteenth century, the abstract "human community" began to be actively transformed into a nation. Rituals and symbols, including customs, holidays, flags, national anthems, a common history, and the honoring of any heroism or sacrifice of life in war, created common signifiers for national identity in the symbolic level, while legal and regulatory state mechanisms, including benefits such as education and health care, were the social and biopolitical technologies that formed "the nation" on the more practical level. The ethnic–linguistic definition of nations was invented, according to Eric Hobsbawm, in the second half of the nineteenth century, and Hobsbawm uses Zionism as the most extreme example of a national ideology forming a language, a culture, and a territory in order to pursue its program.[67]

With the decline of real communities like the village, the extended family, and the parish, the nation-state took over, instituting citizenship as a legal form of belonging, using the associated emotions on a scale that could be adopted by modern society only on technical and metaphorical levels. The imagined community of "the nation" filled the void left by disappearing communities and was recruited by the political needs of the state. Governments reached down to each citizen through agents who were part of citizens' everyday lives, such as policemen and teachers (and later television hosts), and these agents encouraged citizens' patriotic commitment to the state and "the nation" as a new civic religion. Paul Gilroy talks of "camps" as the national and governmental formations where nation and race are closely articulated, creating martial phenomena involving flags and mass spectacles in which "the national camp's principles of belonging and solidarity become attractive."[68]

But while state nationalism (whether real, intensified, or imagined) created a feeling of collective belonging for some, it alienated those who could not and did not belong, did not wish to belong, and sometimes resisted the official nationality, language, and ideology. The increasing national homogeneity that included many also excluded others for their ethnic, cultural, ideological, or other differences. The internal disintegration of the nation-state began, according to Arendt, after the peace treaties following World War I and the ever-growing refugee movement of minorities and stateless persons, people who were forced to live under "the law of exception of the Minority Treaties" or "under the conditions of absolute lawlessness."[69] What troubles Arendt in the nation-state is that the imagined ethnocultural homogeneity of the nation as an entity came to be attached to the state's juridicopolitical institutions; denationalization became a powerful weapon of totalitarian politics, and other European nation-states did not guarantee human rights to those stateless people who lost their nationally guarantied human rights. Citizenship and its rights came to be solely the domain of the nation-state, while the state's legal institution of citizenship became the internal divider between those who can enjoy various degrees of rights, such as the right to freedom, security, mobility, work, welfare, education, and health care (citizens), and those who cannot (noncitizens). The connection between national citizenship and human rights becomes particularly problematic in relation to the stateless and minorities, who find themselves exposed without such citizenship and without what Arendt calls the fundamental "right to have rights."[70]

Thus, instead of being a universal institution with legally protected equal rights for all within its geographic boundaries, the state became an institution that was racially and ethnically oriented to particular people and excluded others, bringing forward a nationalist ideology whose program was, as argues Hobsbawm, "to resist, expel, defeat, conquer, subject or eliminate 'the foreigner.'"[71] Following Arendt, Judith Butler argues that "the nation-state as a political formation requires periodic expulsion and dispossession of its national minorities in order to gain a legitimating ground for itself"; such expulsion can take the form of containment, when the expelled minorities are contained within the territory as inclusive exclusion where constitutional protection is suspended, such as in the camp.[72] Indeed, it was the camp, as both Arendt and later Agamben indicated, that became the space of "the wretched, the oppressed and the defeated" whom the state and the nation refuse to include.[73]

Between Bare Life, Everyday Life, and Life That Resists

Drawing on Schmitt's idea of the exception and Foucault's and Arendt's ideas about society, biopolitics, and the camp, Agamben makes the idea of *homo sacer* (or "bare life," with "bare" corresponding to the Greek *haplôs*, pure Being), a person denied all rights and banned from society, an essential concept in modern politics. The realm of bare life, the dispossessed life naked of its humanity and "stripped of every political status," a life that may be killed yet not sacrificed, coincides with the political realm of state power in the state of exception: "At once excluding bare life from and capturing it within the political order, the state of exception actually constituted, in its very separateness, the hidden foundation on which the entire political system rested."[74] In contrast to theories of political communities that regard their essence as a common belonging in a shared national, religious, or moral identity, Agamben argues that the *ban* is the original juridicopolitical relation in which the state actively excludes a specific life while capturing it in the political order through its exclusion, and in so doing constitutes its sovereignty. As "Western politics is a bio-politics from the very beginning," political life is redundant, and it is only for the sovereign to decide who is entitled to full human qualified life *(bios)*, and who will be condemned to the dehumanizing bare life of nothing more than exposed existence common to all living beings *(zoë)*, in a space where "exclusion and inclusion, outside and inside, *bios* and *zoë*, right and fact, enter into a zone of irreducible indistinction."[75]

The camp, Agamben argues, is the paradigm of contemporary politics' zone of indistinction, a space that makes a biopolitical machine where the most absolute *conditio inhumana* is realized and bare life is produced. In the realm of the nation-state, the camp is where the sovereign excludes populations within its territory in order to constantly reform and endlessly purify the national body by stripping people of their humanity and political power (and in the case of the Nazi death camps, by industrially killing them). Butler notes that the camp is not merely a state of exception but also a state of desubjectivation, a space where, under a state of emergency, "certain subjects undergo a suspension of their ontological status as subjects."[76]

It is important to remember that these processes started not in the twentieth-century European nation-states but in the continent's testing grounds in the colonies. Colonial camps, where human bodies of entire populations were contained en masse only to be neglected and destroyed through structural racialized violence, clearly reflect Achille Mbembe's post-Foucauldian notion of necropolitics: a political violence through which a particular population group is administered under the threat of death—a threat often carried out. With the sovereign right to kill freed from restrictions in the colonies, and with colonial warfare not being considered a legally codified activity, colonial occupation also meant colonial

40   The Camp Reconfigured

terror. This, as Mbembe argues, relegated the colonized natives to "a third zone between subjecthood and objecthood,"[77] where their lives were constantly subjugated to the power of death, creating "death-worlds" where the status of "living dead" was conferred through the conditions of life. This is a zone where, following Agamben's understanding of the camp, fact and law, outside and inside, norm and exception, *oikos* (the household, as the sphere of life) and *polis* (the city-state, as the sphere of the political) become indistinguishable and are therefore exposed to the violence of sovereign power. The notion of "nativity" has quite a different meaning in the European and colonial contexts. "Nativity" is inherent to European nationality, which questions that of particular groups such as ethnic minorities who are considered "the Other." In colonial contexts, "the natives" who lived in an area before its colonization are often seen by the colonizers as a racialized group that should be subordinated, with the colonizers, in the case of settler societies, turning themselves into the new "natives" of the place.[78] What connects colonial environments, including the colonial concentration camps, and the camps of the nation-state—beyond their similar structure and mode of governance through containment, exclusion, and abandonment—is that in these camps a *specific population* is excluded, on the basis of ethnic, racialized, or other particular definitions of what its people are. This is reflected in the context of Israel–Palestine and in many of the camps and camp-like spaces discussed in this book.

Camps, however, were and still are being created not only to contain, control, and abandon specific populations, but sometimes also for the opposite reason—that is, to facilitate the life, protection, and movement and expansion of particular populations in what are considered hostile environments. The camps in Israel–Palestine examined in this book were indeed all formed by or for specific populations, often based on their ethnic or racialized origin, such as the camps containing Mizrahi Jewish immigrants or Palestinian refugees. The specific populations of many of these camps were indeed excluded and abandoned in various ways, and violently "let [to] die" by the sovereign power. However, unlike the camp as seen by Agamben and many others, some of these camps were not only spaces of exclusion from the national body but were also appropriated for the territorial and national expansion, formation, and grounding of that body. Some of these camps, created by colonial and national powers, allowed a new geopolitical order to be established almost from scratch, facilitating the assembling, transportation, and absorption of Jews from different parts of the globe in a specific territory and their dispersal throughout its frontiers as a new nation, while displacing and expropriating native populations. In addition, in Israel–Palestine and in other contexts, camps were and still are also created and reshaped in order to protest, resist, and act against these and other violent national and colonial powers and their actions. As some of the populations in these camps were or became active in reappropriating the camp's spaces to answer their cultural, social, and political needs and demands, transforming them into new fields of possibility for social, cultural, and substantial political action, the camps' residents could not be generally considered dehumanized *homines sacri*; rather, they could also be seen as people possessing agency and subversive power.

Indeed, critical scholarly work on refugee, detention, and concentration camps created by sovereign powers have analyzed actual camp spaces, based on Agamben's writings, as sites that transform people into mere exposed bodies.[79] Yet a growing literature attempting to implement Agamben's theory on camp spaces that materialize the political struggles of their inhabitants has argued that it does not provide a fully appropriate analytical tool for understanding the social, political, and related architectural complexities of real camp spaces. Camps, these scholars propose, should also be analyzed as social and political spaces of human agency, resistance, and contestation that may also allow for the emergence of new political subjectivities. Some of these works examine camps that were constructed or appropriated by their inhabitants (whether migrants, refugees, or protesters) as a social and political *lived* space in which people negotiate, fight, resist, and practice citizenship through their own resourcefulness and spatial actions of everyday life in the camp.[80] Such accounts remind us that even in the horrible Nazi death camps there was always the possibility that human actions might constitute a social and political sphere within and through the camp by which the detainees might resist their dehumanization even in the darkest moments.[81]

These studies show that camps can become spaces of agency and struggle where people recover their political power through active forms of resistance, where rights, obligations, entitlements, and objectifications are bent, formed, adjusted, reshaped, and activated through everyday interactions and direct political actions. When these political acts are discussed beyond the camps in which they are enacted, sometimes globally, "bare life" is repudiated, as Patricia Owens argues, and, as Michel Agier suggests, "life that resists" is embraced.[82] It is important to remember, however, that while Agamben mentions particular examples of camps and other dehumanizing spaces, his argument is ultimately about the camp as *paradigm,* that is, about the topology of modern biopolitical sovereignty and the law to which the camp is paradigmatic as a space of exception, rather than an encompassing claim about actual camp spaces.[83] While his theory exposed the camp as a central space of modern biopolitics, the investigation of actual camps and their complex genealogy reveal them to be embodied spaces that function as both instruments and arenas where the political is not only eliminated but also asserted, claimed, and reconfigured.

In Israel–Palestine and elsewhere, camps were not only created by strong groups to control undesired and weak populations; they were also initiated by groups who acted to change their world through the camp by using it for settlement and protest. These latter camps were created by those who defined themselves through their shared political aspirations, for which the camp was an effective means. Here, the intricate political and human dimensions of the camp begin to be revealed beyond their paradigmatic biopolitical and necropolitical understanding, with the population groups and politics of those encamped differing not only by external and imposed roles and divisions but also by their resourcefulness and ability to act and regain human agency, and sometimes political control, through and within these spaces.

The camp, as we have seen so far, incorporates a specific mode of juridical and governmental order, and it is also a space that "deals with" specific populations for the "purification" or "creation" of certain colonial and national realities. However, as the camp is profoundly a spatial mechanism, its understanding also requires spatial investigations. How does the camp, in its various forms, differ from other spaces? This exploration is inherently related to the understanding of *territorial* and *material* apparatuses as a system of spatial practices that are inseparable from the modern state and colonial and globalized mechanisms of which the camp is a part.

The Territorial, Spatial, and Material Instrument of the Camp

Camps are multifaceted instruments with very different spatial conditions. While some are created as rationalized, ordered spaces, often with standardized, repetitive, prefabricated shelters designed to provide for minimal needs, other camps are formed of self-built shelters as precarious makeshift environments. These distinctions between camp spaces are anything but clear-cut, static, or linear; while institutional camps might go through processes of reappropriation, informalization, and change, makeshift camps might institutionalize, morphing into very different, ever-changing, and often unexpected spatial landscapes.[84] Importantly, the camp's spatial and material characteristics are also inherently linked to the way modern spatial and territorial constellations of states and related colonial situations are being formed, managed, and resisted.

Territory and Territoriality

The seventeenth-century philosophical–mathematical Cartesian understanding of the world in terms of numbers and points, together with the redrawing of the map of political power in Europe and the colonization of the New World, developed into the cartographic ability and the political demand to divide the globe into defined territories. Yet although today the idea of a space that is not part of any state is rare and sounds almost fantastic, the situation in which the whole earth is divided into states is relatively new. The division was only completed during the second half of the twentieth century with the collapse of the colonial order and the establishment of nation-states in Africa and Asia; since 1945, the total number of states has more than tripled.[85]

Territory is traditionally seen as a bounded space under the control of a group of people, usually a state, with the understanding that a state cannot exist without a territory and the authority of the state is essentially territorial. Yet territory, as Stuart Elden argues, has existed since antiquity, and we need to understand it in its specificity as historically and geographically dependent social and spatial organizations, each with its particular techniques and laws.[86] While in modern geopolitics territory is conceived of as an integral part of the modern state–nation–territory triad, states and territories preceded modern articulations of the nation, and it was only later that some nations aspired to statehood and territories they could control as their own.

The traditional notion that the 1648 Peace of Westphalia was a landmark historical point for the creation of the sovereign territorial state has now been dismissed as a myth.[87] But other political changes in the seventeenth century, such as the shift from dynastic to parliamentary sovereignty in England, did begin to create what we know now as the modern state.[88] Beginning in the eighteenth century, territory became increasingly associated with the nation that occupied it, and nationalist sentiment was propelled by changes in territorial security needs.[89] Territoriality turned into both the motive and the tool to build national identity as part of a defense against external threats, and it was necessary to establish a sense of national territorialization by regulating relations between state, people, and land. The dual definition of territory—from the outside by internationally defined border agreements and from the inside by legal and administrative systems—was also a dual action of power and politics. It required the ability to rationalize the definition of states as separate territorial units and to create an internal spatial and political construction that rationalized relations between the state and its subjects. "In the chaos of relations among individuals, groups, class fractions and classes," writes Henri Lefebvre, "the State tends to impose a rationality, its own, which has space as its privileged instrument."[90] Indeed, the state uses various spatial mechanisms, such as maps, infrastructures, and planning regulations, to naturalize and stabilize relations between people, identity, and territory. The instrument of the camp often functions as part of these stabilizing mechanisms, but it can also have the opposite effect; it can be used to temporarily contain territorial and other geopolitical changes, and it can also be used to initiate or facilitate such changes.

Unlike "territory," "territoriality" makes up part of the particular strategies and processes directed at a territory, and it is also a form of active spatial behavior to influence or control resources and people by controlling and shaping an area. Territory can be used to contain or restrain, it requires constant territorial and other effort for its establishment and maintenance,[91] and as an effect of networked social–political–technical practices, it is always in a continuous process of becoming.[92] Foucault suggests that "*territory* is no doubt a geographical notion, but it's first of all a juridicopolitical one; the area controlled by a certain kind of power."[93] Indeed, like ever-changing political realities, territory, as Elden argues, "is in itself a process, made and remade, shaped and shaping, active and reactive," and the camp could be described as part of such territorial processes.[94] In Israel–Palestine, territorial actions are indeed a constant work in progress, and the camp makes up part of the constant processes of territorialization, deterritorialization, and hyper-territorialization happening there simultaneously, often in relation to colonial and decolonial processes.

Yet it is important to remember that, as legal scholar Kal Raustiala shows, nation-state sovereignty, with its offshore detention camps and similar facilities, "has become progressively 'unbundled' from territoriality."[95] In practice, then, the nation-state–territory triad is a much less stable and comprehensive reality, as it happens in Israel–Palestine and other contested territorial constellations in which the state is not only including the outside by its exclusion, as per Agamben's tight formula, but is also outsourcing the outside and expanding it in a variety of dubious juridicopolitical arrangements. Camps are also not necessarily bound within the nation–state–territory model, and while they are inherently connected to the state, they must also be understood within broader geopolitical contexts.

State Space and the Camp

As the state is a spatial as much as a territorial entity, and territory is only one type of spatiality, it is important not only to comprehend the difference between the two but also to understand the central role of space in asserting and negotiating power. While territory is a claimed space, space—beyond the reduced homogenous Cartesian space—is where objects, people, and events have relative position and direction. In her seminal *For Space*, Doreen Massey famously discusses space as the product of interrelations between different identities/entities constituted through interactions in various scales, and as a sphere where multiplicity and plurality exist in a form of coexisting heterogeneity that is always under construction.[96] Space, then, like territory, is an ongoing process that is never finished or closed. And while territory is only one aspect of space, when discussing the state, they are very closely related.

Space can be appropriated for state actions which are often territorial and inherently violent. In *The Production of Space*, Lefebvre discusses the link between space and state control, arguing that "sovereignty implies 'space,' and what is more it implies space against which violence, whether latent or overt, is directed—a space established and constituted by violence."[97] Force and violence in this context is not only used to protect state territory from the outside but also to spatially organize and protect it against internal threats that undermine its ability to reproduce social relations. As Neil Brenner and Stuart Elden put it, Lefebvre sees "state space *as* territory"; for him, "territory is the political *form* of space produced by and associated with the modern state," and this territorial space requires attentive theorization based on its excavation and historicization.[98] In rapidly changing environments such as the camp, where most of the physical remnants are already gone, spaces could be traced back from the territories they created, as is sometimes done here in the case of Israel–Palestine.

The Gramscian concept of cultural hegemony, in which the ruling social class manipulates a society's values and norms to establish a worldview that justifies its dominance, is used by Lefebvre as a starting point for his theory of the production of social space. The active role of space is demonstrated in the preservation of the existing mode of hegemonic power, which uses space to establish a system that facilitates its endurance with the assistance of professional knowledge and technical expertise. Architecture and planning have developed as professional disciplines that allow the state to plan and supervise the form and function of the built environment, and in so doing the state manages the personal and social behavior of the individuals and populations inhabiting it. While in the past architects were involved only in complicated projects, such as cathedrals and palaces (for the immortal and mortal gods), and the design and construction of regular houses was undertaken by builders or the inhabitants themselves, in the modern built environment architecture has become synonymous with almost any built form. According to Foucault, these forms combine the disciplinary techniques and regulatory mechanisms that state institutions use complementarily, as exemplified in the rationally planned layout of model towns. What is common to both disciplinary and regulatory technologies, argues Foucault, is the *norm* that can be applied "to both a body one wishes to discipline and a population one wishes to regularise."[99] The state, through its governance, policies, regulations, laws, and mechanisms, imposes a conceptual spatial grid by dividing, parceling, bounding, registering, and designing space, and by doing so it also imposes a grid on its populations, approaching them as clusters of individuals who should be identified and located.[100]

Whereas the norm is the hegemonic form of the population to be managed by the state, the camp is a space created and regulated both within and outside the norm. This means that its spatiality is not a result of the (often) agreed relation between state and population mediated by architects and planners; rather, it is a space often created with no legal, disciplinary, or regulatory mediation. Camps are exclusionary spaces; either they are imposed by the state or other major political or humanitarian forces, creating rigid rationalized environments whose human aspect is often neglected, or they are formed as makeshift spaces outside the grid and without the state's formal consent, bound to occasional violent state interference such as evictions and demolitions and to precarious living conditions. This may explain the camp's very different spatial manifestations, formed as a result of violent intervention intertwined with violent abandonment. As political philosopher Adi Ophir states, the camp "is the perfect combination of the sovereign authority to distance and abandon and of the sovereign authority to intervene and manage."[101]

The camp is closely linked to the exceptional aspects of state space, territory, and territoriality, and it could be employed by states and other powers as an instrument to control certain, including colonized, populations and territories. In areas of colonial occupations, the camp could be seen as part of what Frantz Fanon described as the particular spatialization of the colonized, "a world divided into compartments, a motionless, Mechanistic world."[102] These compartmentalized "imperial formations" are characterized by Stoler as "macropolities whose technologies of rule thrive on the production of exceptions and their uneven and changing proliferation" and whose critical features include territorial ambiguity, redefined legal categories of quasi membership and belonging, the shifting "geographic and demographic zones of *partially* suspended rights," and the "legal and political fuzziness of dependencies, trusteeships, protectorates, and unincorporated territories."[103] Within state territories, the camp is often created as an "extra-territorial space,"[104] to contain, manage, and suspend—but also to disperse and support—specific populations in order to form or "purify" the national body and territory. Yet the embodied space of the camp, as examined earlier and as discussed in this book, is also a space that, under certain conditions, could itself be used to subvert the realities and powers that initially created it, becoming an instrument for its own deterritorialization that might enable alternative forms of politics and social order to be enacted.[105]

The notion of *nomos*, based on Schmitt's definition of the "*nomos* of the earth," is used by Agamben to describe the sovereign "ordering of space" and is important for the understanding of the camp as a space related to modern politics.[106] *Nomos*, according to Schmitt, is a structuring combination of localization *(Ortung)* and order *(Ordnung)*.[107] *Nomos* comes from the Greek *nemein*, meaning "to divide" and "to pasture."[108] Thus it is "the immediate form in which the political and social order of a people becomes spatially visible."[109] The Schmittian "*nomos* of the earth" is the spatial, political, and juridical system that is mutually binding in the conduct of international affairs, a system that from the early colonial age until World War I was embodied in European "international law."[110] It was specifically based on the spatially grounded distinction between European state territory, recognizing the unity of the European spatial order and the equality of its members, and non-European space, seen as free for occupation. Notions of "humanity" and "civilization" strictly meant *European* civilization; any non-European space was considered to be either uncivilized, partly civilized, or even empty, an "empty field" on which camps are created.[111]

According to Schmitt, "Everything that occurred 'beyond the [European] line' remained outside the legal, moral and political values recognised on this side of the line"; in the "immeasurable space of free land—the New World," European law was not in force.[112] Thus, this "*nomos* of the earth" contained both the European spatial order and the colonial world as a state of exception. Colonies were considered, as Mbembe argues, to be "the zone where the violence of the [colonial] state of exception is deemed to operate in the service of 'civilization.'"[113] With the collapse of the old "*nomos* of the earth," when the "outside" of colonies as uncivilized empty land—or *terra nullius,* "nobody's land"—begins to vanish, the colonial space of exception begins to appear within the European nation-state as the space of the concentration camp,[114] which is then exported again to the rest of the world in the form of the refugee camp and the detention camp. For Agamben, the camp is the disjunction of birth (life) and the political order of the nation-state (which excludes particular life), a place of *"dislocating localization"* where an order without localization (the state of exception) is given a localization without order (the camp itself). In this national and global era, in which the states "outside" could be formed mostly within the territories of the states into which the earth is almost hermetically divided, it is the camp, for Agamben, that "is the new biopolitical *nomos* of the planet."[115]

The Camp and the Frontier

The colonial situation and its legacies did not disappear with the globe's division into states, and it could still be located, as seen in Israel–Palestine and in other settler colonial and postcolonial contexts, in what could be described as the globe's constantly reshaping internal frontiers. According to Howard Lamar and Leonard Thompson, the frontier, in its colonial context, is not "a boundary or line, but . . . a territory or zone of interpenetration between two previously distinct societies," one usually indigenous to the region. The frontier "opens" when the new society arrives and "closes" when "a single political authority has established hegemony over the zone." The essential elements involved in any frontier situation are "territory; two or more initially distinct peoples; and the process" by which the relations between them "begin, develop, and eventually crystallise."[116] In contrast to stabilized hegemonic space and territory, the frontier is a zone of a political conflict of acts and counter-acts that create continuous movement, a space integrated with action.

In frontier regions of settler states such as Israel, argue Yiftachel and Meir, the collective employs forceful ethnic control practices characterized by the "exclusion of the groups that fall outside the ethnic definition of the nascent nation (such as indigenous people), and by the forceful inclusion and assimilation of others (such as subsequent migrants)."[117] In these and other frontier spaces, camps are used as spatial mechanisms to transform the geopolitical reality according to the interests of the founding settler group. The frontier is a central icon in Zionist discourse, and its "taming" or settlement was glorified as essential to the nation-building process.[118] Most of the camps discussed in this book were used in frontier zones to shape populations and territories, while often marking what geographer Stephen Graham has defined as "the crossover between the military and the civilian applications."[119]

As the geographical zone of the frontier shifts and changes following political changes, so does the camp's geographical area. In Israel–Palestine, camps created by the Zionist movement during the 1940s in order to expand the territory of the possible future state have become settlements in Israel's geographical center since the state was established. In areas that are still considered frontiers, such as the Negev, camps and camp-like spaces still exist (such as the unrecognized Bedouin settlements) and are being added (like the Holot camp for African asylum seekers). The Palestinian occupied territories, which are still at the center of political conflict, are also a frontier area where Palestinian refugee and protest camps and Israeli Jewish outpost camps are still constantly created and reformed.

Camps such as the Zionist settler camps in Mandatory Palestine, the Palestinian refugee camps, and the Israeli outpost settler camps and Palestinian protest camps in the occupied Palestinian areas, do not sit comfortably within Agamben's theory, nor within any state's container; rather, they are spaces created where the boundaries of the state are contested or extremely vague. The frontier is not only a territory, but a "territory combined with action,"[120] a territory where struggles and negotiations over the land or over certain rights, such as the right to enter particular states and ask for protection, have not yet been settled. The camp, which combines space and action, is an instrument inherently related to the frontier and the struggles within and over it, such as the constant struggles in Israel–Palestine, where ongoing temporariness is an inherent part of prolonged suspension and waiting, and frantic spatial mobilities and processes of construction and destruction. As Georgine Clarsen notes, "Settler colonial societies are, after all, stridently mobile formations."[121]

Temporality, Power, and the Camp

The modern state space is usually perceived to be a permanent spatial entity. As the outcome of a long process of planning, design, and construction; as the product of a great investment of time, money, and effort by builders, professionals, and experts; and as a spatial form that usually exists for a long period of time, the state space with its architecture and infrastructures is created as stable and long-lasting.

Yet the relation between architecture and time is not a given; it is also part of the reproduction of social relations and of the architectural discipline itself, with its conservation projects, educational systems, and history books. Although most architectural projects built today are planned to exist for only a limited period, the state, the market, and architects themselves promote architecture as a permanent creation. The conception of permanency affirms the stability of the state's control over its space and territory, dominant culture, and society; justifies the price of real estate; and gives the profession the glory of being part of the eternal. Camps, in contrast, are perceived as temporary spaces created to exist for short periods of time. Their status is similar to that of other built environments dismissed as provisional, transitory, and not "proper architecture": spaces created by marginalized people who survive outside the axis of global capitalism and national identities.

However, in many cases the actual situation is rather different. While territory and space should be regarded as an ongoing process, and architecture and infrastructures indeed often change over time, with buildings being demolished and reconstructed after a few decades, camps sometimes endure for decades or even generations, and sometimes they are transformed into permanent settlements. Although many camps are indeed temporary spaces that vanish after a short period of time, others are suspended in an ongoing temporary status or exist as permanent facilities used to hold people temporarily. Thus, the comprehension of architecture and hegemonic built environments as permanent and camps as temporary is not (only) based on their actual physical endurance; rather, it is primarily driven by other considerations that render one environment stable and the other transitory. These categories are fundamentally linked to modern state mechanisms, which establish and maintain a mode of stability and predictability related to territory, governance, and population and at the same time use temporariness to maintain a mode of uncertainty and precariousness in which everything and everyone that does not suit the state's political objectives is suspended and excluded.

The camp has become a "permanent spatial arrangement," in Agamben's words, not only because many camps endure for years or are created as permanent spaces for the prolonged detention of people.[122] The camp is also permanent because it became the versatile space bridging the gap between law and a sudden crisis or political need. It became a space that stretches between a stabilized legal, spatial, governmental "normal" order and the unmediated practices beyond it (whether well-organized or unruly), creating a space for political maneuvers that is also a space of exception. As temporary embodied and often flexible spaces, camps could form emancipatory environments where residents/fabricants can recover their agency by producing spaces through which they negotiate their everyday and political existence and lay political claims, enabling new mobilizations and insurgent identities to appear. They could also form stripped spaces where people are arbitrarily exposed to violence outside the constraints of the law, because "when everything is temporary," as Ophir notes, "almost anything—any crime, any form of violence—is acceptable, because the temporariness seemingly grants it a license, the license of the state of emergency."[123]

As the poet Yousif Qasmiyeh aptly writes, "The camp is a time more than it is a place."[124] Camps are indeed created not only as specific spaces but also as distinct temporal constructs. They form not only multifaceted landscapes but also complex timescapes with unpredicted layers of spatial and human temporalities that penetrate and reshape one another: the precamp *past*, when the camp did not exist and could not be imagined and other lost realities existed instead; the *present*, stretched to the unknown as an enduring existence of waiting that, though in motion and sometimes agentic, is nevertheless suspended and in which the ability to anticipate, plan, and act according to certain assumptions is compromised by obscured horizons of possibility; and the often unforeseeable *future*, when the camp will eventually cease to exist, at least as a camp, and something else will emerge instead, whether welcome or not.

Camps have their own unique temporalities and speed: they are rapidly created as spaces that come into being all of a sudden; they may endure as temporary environments for different periods—days, weeks, years, generations; they can be highly ephemeral spaces flickering between existence, nonexistence, and reappearance in different versions, locations, or constellation; and they may be permanent spaces where people are held temporarily. While cities are often experienced as incremental spaces formed and developed over time, and while their origins occasionally emerge through the layers that have accreted over time, the camp is often experienced as a spatial tabula rasa where shelters abruptly appear all at once, a time machine whose clock begins to tick when it is erected and occupied and stops when it reaches its predicted eventual destruction and erasure, as if it had never been there. These camps create enclaves that are not only spatially but also temporally restrictive for an unpredicted period of time, spaces of suspension and stuckness where time is divided and stretched differently, outside the everyday social–temporal divisions. Existing between temporariness and permanence, it is a space where people are suspended *in time* while being subjected *to time*: they grow up and grow old while waiting between the "not anymore" and the "not yet" for a certain political, physical, or other situation to change so the camp itself will be redundant. Yet temporality has a dynamic nature even in situations of chronic suspension and lingering waiting, a nature that should not be conceptualized as active or passive realities but as variegated affective situations consisting of many different planes, including the one of potential, anticipation, desire, and also possibly dread of the promised "event-to-come."[125] Yet while the camp is often the space of the displaced, it could not be regarded as that of the dis-timed, as even within the uncertainty of displacement, as Catherine Brun shows, people find ways to make uncertainty meaningful in what she describes as "agency-in-waiting"—that is, the capacity to act in the time of the everyday, generating new possibilities in the time of the present while coping with the uncontrollable and unpredictable future.[126]

The embedded temporariness of the camp, however, is inherent in its exceptionality as a modern state space and could be related to such physical attributes as the provisional materiality of its structures, its lack of adequate infrastructures, its legal status as a temporary space, or the status of its inhabitants as temporary within it. Temporariness here becomes a political mechanism of the state to exclude populations, a mechanism that not only abandons people legally and physically but also negates a substantial existential aspect of their lives, their control over time. The compulsory suspension and obscurity of time in the camp, disconnecting those suspended in it from the flows and divisions of normal social temporality and its inherent connection to the time-bounded human life, makes the suspension in the camp an inhumane act in itself, an act that undermines the individual and society's sense of being.[127] "People become aware of the centrality of time to their experience when confronted with an event that stops the flow of time," reflects sociologist Amal Jamal in his analysis of the suspended Palestinian temporality, seeing the condition of suspending time as inherently colonial.[128] The camp could be seen as one of the salient mechanisms for this suspension, but it is also sometimes revealed as an arena to resist it.

Arendt reflects on the importance of existence in time due to the distinctiveness of each human being in a unique and time-bounded life story. In *The Human Condition* Arendt distinguishes among three interconnected modes of human existence in time: The first is the *cyclic temporality* of human biological life, with its repetitive and ephemeral activities sustaining life's bare necessities. A second is the more *enduring, permanent, accumulative, and potentially immortal* "man-made world of things," which she sees as essential for anchoring human life (which would otherwise be intolerably unstable).[129] And the third is made up of the *events* or *temporal happenings* in this human world, where the political sphere appears as contingent and transitory situations when people are acting together *at the same time* to change their world. The interconnected durable worldliness and unexpected emergence of new political powers could be linked to Henri Bergson's temporal notion of duration, describing the dynamic human conscious existence that passes and endures from state to state, while its pure heterogeneity also entails an ever-inventive and unpredictable emergence.[130] Bergson, as Elizabeth Grosz reflects in *Time Travels*, "is above all a thinker of dynamic movement, action, change."[131] Similarly, Arendt's political time, unlike the cyclical biological time and the stabilized and linear worldly time, has the inherent possibility to be reborn, restored, and redeemed as an orchestrated event that diverges from our predictable reality, a moment created not as a site of fixity or stasis but as a potential and possibility. Politics, here, has an extratemporal standpoint. As a political community could be born only when it deviates from cyclical, linear, and stabilized time, it exerts its rejuvenating potential by the power unleashed by human encounters of those acting together to create their desired common world.[132]

This idea of the political and its particular temporality is quite different from Agamben's understanding of Western (bio)politics through the (permanent) exception, and it enables a quite different interpretation of the camp as a spatial and political instrument with a specific temporality. As embodied spaces created ad hoc to bring people together or to coercively concentrate them, to either exert or extract power, camps could be seen as events in time that are inherently political, yet in different ways. As a potentially highly responsive spatial configuration, the camp creates a versatile instrument for improvisation, whether by powerful actors such as the state or by the powerless whom the state excludes. The camp could be created as a depoliticizing space of coercion and conditional care, yet other contingent camp spaces, such as protest camps, create embodied spatial actions that articulate a political claim.[133] Yet as exceptional instruments of power that coerce people en masse, camps that were created by the powerful to restrict the powerless could also unfold as ongoing political events when politics is seized by those encamped through an array of (spatial and other) actions through which they together object to and change their enforced realities. Such camps are continuously emerging as an embodied temporal–spatial happening, making the camp not only the materialization of certain politics but also the instrument for the articulation of alternative politics.

Camp's Materiality

Analyses of the camp usually focus on its social and political role as a space of exception and its historical transformations as a space created for the violent sociopolitical ordering and control of modern societies. Yet because the camp is a physical space with different degrees of temporariness, one that is often detached from everyday environments and has particular modes of creation, existence, and liquidation, its materiality is key for grasping its function and evolution as a modern spatiopolitical instrument. Among modernity's important aspects, as discussed earlier, are not only the quest for order to which the camp is linked, but also the new technologies that became significant forces in the rapid movement of people and objects and in the conquest, occupation, and creation of spaces, and that are highly significant to the way the camp has been and still is being produced and evolving.

Materials and material culture are constitutive to political realities and histories, and the camp should be discussed in relation to the ways these "matters" influence its formation and transformation. This could be framed within the ideas of "new materialism," which includes diverse approaches from assemblage thinking to actor–network theory (ANT), examining the effect of material realities and objects on social and political formations, understanding their constantly changing networks and relationships beyond discursive and ideological interpretation. By focusing on the affective and generative powers materials have, on their formative capacities, and on their processual nature involving both human and nonhuman factors, the definitive influence of materials emerges as an active force on social and political realities. Materials here, even those considered banal and insignificant, are not only produced and morphed by social, political, and human worlds; materials also condition, coproduce, and enable them, sometimes unintentionally and indirectly. As Latour suggests, the investigation of these materials, which are an active part of society, should be concerned with not only *who* but also *what* is to be considered.[134] The concept of "assemblage," though an inaccurate translation of Deleuze and Guattari's notion of *agencement*, is often used to capture the ongoing process in which multiple, heterogeneous, and contested human and nonhuman elements come together, bringing objects and subjects into mutually constitutive relations while forming and influencing, among other things, political techniques, technologies, and spaces such as the camp.

The constantly evolving material ontologies of modernity are indeed fundamental to the evolution of the camp as a political instrument, and the varieties of its political roles and spaces were greatly affected by the ever-shifting modern material world. Technologies used for both the facilitation and restriction of human and material mobilities were central to the emergence of the camp as an instrument that forms an isolated and isolating environment of control yet must also be well connected if it is to be rapidly created, rapidly populated, and able to contain and sustain its population away from society. These technologies and the particular material and spatial realities produced from them—from mobile prefabricated shelters and other materials and objects enabling the creation of ad hoc spaces, including the infrastructures and vehicles needed for their logistical transportation, to the barbed wire that controls movement—were and still are fundamental to the camp's continuing emergence as a facility of control and (often compromised) care but also as a space of colonial expansion and an emancipatory space of resistance.[135]

The colonial concentration camp, as Benjamin Meiches shows, emerged from the entanglement of the modern invention of barbed wire, the rise of motorized transport, and the changing colonial warfare involving guerrilla fighters, changes that generated both the need and the means to spatially concentrate, control, and sustain (or abandon) people.[136] Such technologies and materials, which combined new levels of intensities and speed, enabled the formation of the camp as a powerful modern spatial instrument that could radically change the relationship among people, land, and other resources. Indeed, vehicles and infrastructures—trucks and roads, ships and ports—repeatedly appear in this book as an inseparable part of the material apparatus that creates and sustains the camp not only as a detached enclave but also as a connected (yet often tightly controlled) material and human junction. In this sense, the camp is not only the product of new forms of colonial warfare and racial social ordering; it is also the offshoot of new modern systems and materials of mobility and logistics and their experimental use. It is a space of "high mobility and elasticity," which makes it an adaptable instrument that can be rapidly redesigned for new roles and situations.[137]

Indeed, the evolving instrument of the camp was and still is generated by its own transforming assemblages, such as its lethal potential, discovered in the colonial concentration camp and evolved to the aforementioned abominable genocidal instruments of the colonial and later Nazi extermination camp. At the same time, the particular material and sociopolitical environment of the camp might also enable those contained in it, in certain conditions, to alter and reappropriate their spaces, often beyond the reach of professional architects and planners.[138] That alteration and reappropriation can, as Nasser Abourahme reveals in his analysis of cement in Palestinian refugee camps, go so far as to spill over the boundaries of quotidian life to become an action of political subversion.[139] These material analyses enable us to understand the camp's political dimensions as correlated not only with spatial and social forms but also with fluid material constellations that could be transformed as an outcome of their own unexpected human and nonhuman entanglements and affects. Camps, therefore, both represent a certain logic and may also constitute one in their creation and existence as versatile and unpredictable forms that could be formed by and translated to certain materialities, temporalities, forms of governance, subjectivities, and actions, including subversive political ones.

A Spatial and Political Instrument within and beyond the State

Discussing the camp as it relates to modernity's ordering ambitions and technological transformations and to the modern state–people–territory triad enables us to examine it with respect to the central elements of modern politics. Indeed, the camp's central attributes emerging from this discussion put it in an exceptional relationship with the state, including its colonial apparatuses. While camps are created in different forms and for different functions for and by a variety of actors, they make spaces to which temporariness is central, with a spatiality and materiality that form them as spaces that in many ways are disconnected from their immediate environments while also being connected to particular forms of material and human (im)mobility, infrastructure, and speed. They are formed and function in a particular form of governance, and they are created for or by distinct populations. As such, camps are often tactically used to reform or contain a specific situation until it becomes part of the (sometimes new) desired order. But camps may also be more flexible and adaptable to change, including changes made by their residents counter to the purposes of their original creation.

In the genealogy of camps in Israel–Palestine examined in this book, the camp functions not only as a tool to include the exception within a stabilized nation-state territory, but also as an instrument constantly involved in the ongoing territorial changes and (re)creations of Israel–Palestine and in the formation of the spaces and political subjectivities of both the colonizers and the colonized. In the following chapters, camps in Israel–Palestine are discussed in relation to the different sovereignties, populations, and territorial constellations that emerged and changed in the area over the last century, further revealing the camp's conditions and workings. While the camp will appear in many manifestations and contradictions—existing between ordering initiatives and disruptive actions, between modern technologies of speed and logistics and precarious makeshift practices, between concentration and expansion, between temporariness and endurance—it also emerges as a complex spatiopolitical instrument that had and has a central influence on the geopolitical realities in Israel–Palestine from the past until the present.

2

FACILITATING DOUBLE COLONIALISM
British and Zionist Camps in Mandatory Palestine

Above all, camps reflected imperial Britain's habitual anxieties about "order." . . . The colonial world presented Europeans with the spectre of unordered space: of teeming and potentially dangerous masses; of disorienting and unfamiliar environments; and above all, of dirt, degeneration, and disease.

>—Aidan Forth, *Barbed-Wire Imperialism,* 2017

This is the camp in which our forefathers dwelt—the two men with the sticks are the night guards and now, in the morning, they are waking the forefathers to work, beating with sticks on the tents and shouting, "Wake up! Wake up! To work on the road!"

>—M. Shweiger, "And It Happened at the End of Days," 1924

The British rule over Palestine, a period of ongoing geopolitical transformations over about thirty years, could be considered a pertinent point of departure for a spatial genealogy of camps in Israel–Palestine for two main reasons. The first reason is territorial: Palestine was defined as a distinct modern territory, as it is recognized today, only after it was conquered by the British during World War I, after the Ottoman Empire had ruled the area for almost four centuries. Until then, Palestine had formed no independent geopolitical unit, and its names, borders, and populations changed over time. The second reason is spatial: camps, as modern political instruments for the management of lands and populations, appeared in the area as a significant political tool during this period, while continuing to evolve in response to the geopolitical transformations that followed.

These camps were formed in Palestine following the arrival of two different yet connected powers. The first was the Jewish Zionist settlers who arrived in the early 1880s but remained a marginal element in the region until World War I.[1]

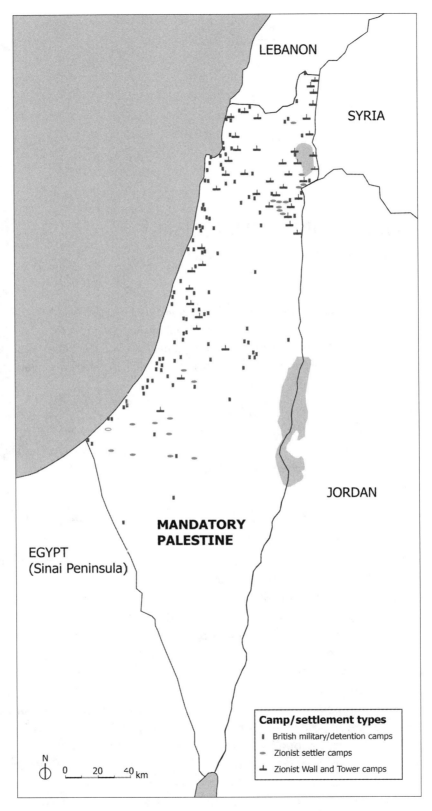

Map 2. British military and detention camps and Zionist settler camps created in Mandatory Palestine, 1920–1948.

Zionist settlers were already using tent camps to create new agricultural Jewish settlements in the early 1900s, yet these settler camps multiplied and changed during the British rule, being erected later in those years as fortified agricultural settler camps. The second power was the British forces, who created two more types of camp in the area, similar to the camps used in other colonies. Military camps were created immediately following the British conquest and developed significantly during World War II. These camps, accompanied by work camps accommodating local Jewish and Arab builders, were later used by Israel for both military and civilian purposes. In addition, detention camps were also created to control civilians, both Jews and Arabs, who resisted the British rule and to prevent illegal Jewish immigrants or refugees from entering Palestine. These different types of camps were formed and transformed by and for both civilian and military powers, sometimes through ad hoc material inventions answering particular needs. While this book focuses on camps for civilians, British military camps are relevant because many of them later changed their status and function, shifting from military to civilian use. Indeed, the camps discussed in this chapter exist on a military–civilian continuum, revealing their transformation around the lines stitching together the patchwork formed by colonial military and governmental frameworks and settlement actions in a continuously changing situation of a contested political, demographic, and territorial reality.

The creation of these various camp types in such a short time indicates the exceptional political situation in Palestine in this period; it was a territory that went through negotiations and struggles between Jews and Arabs under British rule, and it was also subject to contradictory political promises and agreements. The confidential Hussein–McMahon Correspondence (1915–16) promised during World War I that Great Britain would be "prepared to recognise and support the independence of the Arab" over their territories in return for an Arab–British revolt against the Turks.[2] By contrast, the Balfour Declaration of November 1917 stated, "His Majesty's Government view with favour the establishment in Palestine of a national home for the Jewish people."[3] Meanwhile, the secret Sykes–Picot Agreement of May 1916 between France and the United Kingdom shows that during the war the two countries had already planned to divide between them the occupied parts of these lands, which were ostensibly promised to various peoples and national movements, with priority given to retaining the colonial European balance of power rather than to serving the interests of local actors. The British interests in the territory, then, were primarily strategic, and colonial history is the broader framework in which the European policies toward Palestine should be considered.[4]

The emergence of Great Britain as the hegemonic power in Palestine started with its conquest of the land during World War I. In 1917 the Anglo–Egyptian Expeditionary Force under General Edmund Allenby conquered Sinai and the Negev desert, southern Palestine up to Gaza, and later Jaffa and Jerusalem.[5] The mandate system, established at the international 1920 San Remo Conference of the post–World War I Allied Supreme War Council, divided the Middle East between Britain and France. Syria and Lebanon were to be administered by France; Iraq, Transjordan, and Palestine were to be administered by Britain; and Egypt became a British protectorate.

It was indeed colonial rule in a new appearance, and it was conceived as such locally.[6] As declared in Article 22 of the Covenant of the League of Nations (June 1919), the "colonies and territories, which as a consequence of the late war had ceased to be under the sovereignty of the states which formerly governed them, and which are inhabited by peoples not yet able to stand by themselves under the strenuous conditions of the modern world," were handed, under the new regime of international law, as a "sacred trust of civilization" to the guardianship of experienced, and of course Western, "advanced nations."[7] Modernity's "strenuous conditions," then, were the justification for maintaining European powers in the area, bringing with them the modern mechanism of the camp to control locals who resisted their presence.

While most of the Arab territories of the former Ottoman Empire (such as Syria, Lebanon, and Iraq) qualified for the class A mandate, which enabled them to seek independence under the guidance of a European power, Palestine was an exception. According to the British understanding, because of the "Jewish question," the territory was subject to special regulations and was given a different status. Whitehall gave increasing (yet certainly not unanimous) support for the Zionist movement, viewing it as a motor for colonial development in Palestine and "a useful tool for Britain's colonial expansion into the Eastern Mediterranean."[8] The military authorities in Palestine, at the end of March 1919, gave a population estimate of 648,000 people: 551,000 Muslims, 62,500 Christians, 65,300 Jews, and 5,050 "Others" (such as Druze and Armenians).[9] These numbers, and their geographic spread, were to change significantly during and following the Mandate period, with camps playing a central role in these demographic and later territorial changes.

The British Military Camps

The tight link between military camps and camps for civilians and related civilian spaces and infrastructures, which appears throughout this book, could already be identified in the camps created by the British military forces in Palestine. While many of these camps have since become the core of Israel's military alignment, others were later employed for civilian purposes in Israel–Palestine: from camps used to absorb Jewish immigrants in the early years of Israeli statehood and camps used as emergency shelters for Palestinian refugees, to camps that became part of civilian infrastructures and are still identifiable in the Israeli built environment. The facts that the British military camps created the foundations for the alignment of camps and infrastructures for civilians in Israel–Palestine and that some of them eventually developed into everyday urban fabrics show the significance of the ever-shifting military–civilian relations.

The first British camps to appear in Palestine were temporary military tent camps erected during the progress of the conquering army, and more permanent camps started to appear from 1918 onward. The first priorities of the Entente Powers were to establish firm control over the occupied area to stand against local resistance and international competition, and to deal with relief and rehabilitation of the local population, who had suffered greatly during the war.[10] These first camps expanded and multiplied to serve both local and international political and military needs, such as in response to the 1921 Jaffa riots, the 1936–39 Arab uprising, the Jewish violent resistance, and World War II.

Sarafand, known today as Tz'rifin, is an example of a military camp that expanded during this period. Created in 1918 as a minor tent camp near the Arab village of Sarafand El-Amar, about five kilometers northwest of Ramla, it was developed by the British army during the Mandate period and became the largest military training base in the Middle East (Figure 2.1). In 1936, a detention camp for Arab political prisoners was added, and from 1939 the camp was used to detain Jewish political prisoners and illegal Jewish immigrants. As with most other British military camps in Palestine, its major construction occurred during World War II. The objective of the UK's military deployment in Palestine during the war was to secure UK assets in the Near East and to function as the rear front for the Allied forces fighting in Iraq, Syria, and North Africa. For this purpose, the army built a massive alignment of training camps and the Royal Air Force (RAF) built airports.[11] The camps were built mostly by local Arab and Jewish workers who lived in temporary "work camps" erected next to the army campsites. Around fifty thousand Arab and Jewish construction workers labored together for the British army during the war, which some saw as part of a joint war effort.[12]

The camps were deployed on the basis of geographical features and the locations of the main roads and railroads on which soldiers, weapons, and equipment were transported, showing the strong spatial and material connection between camps and the infrastructures that maintain them.[13] The large main camps and the important airports were constructed along the coastal plain, with many camps concentrated near the main port in Haifa; the second largest concentration was near Jaffa and Tel Aviv and near the central airport in Lydda (now Lod); and others were constructed adjacent to large concentrations of civilian population because of the need for services and supplies for the military units situated within them. In

Figure 2.1. The British military camp at Sarafand, 1940. Photograph by Zoltan Kluger, National Photo Collection of Israel, Government Press Office.

all but a few cases, the camps were erected on private lands owned by the Arab and Jewish population, lands either leased or confiscated by the British army.[14]

Prefabricated Structure: The Mass-Produced Military and Colonial Building Block

The British military camps were rapidly erected following a standard plan of the site depicting the outline and description of the numbered huts. Tents were used for most of the soldiers' accommodations, and facilities like offices, dining rooms, and watchtowers were usually placed in temporary preplanned structures.[15] These huts were made from standard light materials, such as plaster on canvas, fixed to timber framing with a corrugated-iron roof, concrete floor, and prefabricated doors and windows.[16] One of the best-known hut designs is the Nissen hut, a prefabricated steel structure made from a half-cylindrical skin of corrugated steel, designed during World War I by Peter Norman Nissen, a lieutenant colonel of the Royal Engineers of the British army. Steel ribs were used for structure and curved corrugated panels enclosed the hut. Produced in two models, more than one hun-

Facilitating Double Colonialism 63

Figure 2.2. Nissen huts in a former British military camp in central Israel that became a transit camp for new Jewish immigrants, 1948. Photograph by Hans Pinn, National Photo Collection of Israel, Government Press Office.

dred thousand Nissen huts were deployed to support British troops in war zones, including Palestine, where these huts were erected from 1922 on and were also adopted later for civilian use (Figure 2.2).[17] The British Nissen hut, followed by the better-insulated American Quonset hut, were key structures in the evolution of prefabricated, portable, demountable structures, and they are often cited as the first completely mass-produced building.[18] The arched shape gave the building a structural advantage in strength, and the structure was easy to carry and assemble, with each component being light enough to be handled by two people. The huts were supplied in kit form, and the entire hut, measuring 8.2 by 4.9 meters, could be assembled by four people in four hours using only a wrench.[19] These huts, with their particular curved form, were designed as a placeless and detached spatial product and appeared in different places around Palestine, landing there as foreign

64   Facilitating Double Colonialism

and peculiar architectural spaceships. Although they were constructed as temporary structures, they existed for decades after the British forces left as identifiable alien marks on the landscape.

While the Nissen hut was at the time a new invention that served British military and later colonial forces in Palestine and other areas around the world, prefabricated transportable huts were a core spatial invention that was already serving colonial powers decades earlier. The British use of prefabricated structures for colonial purposes dates back to the late eighteenth century and is historically connected not only to military objectives but also to civilian ones, with the Manning Portable Colonial Cottage for Emigrants marking the establishment of industrialized prefabrication as a technical means to facilitate colonial settlement in the first half of the nineteenth century.[20]

Prefabricated portable huts in different designs, materials, and sizes became the building blocks of camps in Palestine, serving colonial and other political, territorial, and demographic purposes. As a modern mass-produced invention that could be easily transported and erected, the prefabricated structures and shelters have become a widely used architectural mechanism to deal with population mobility and the displacement it often generates. Modern materials and technologies, with their assemblages of infrastructures, prefabricated structures, and motorized transportation that enabled the logistics of rapid operational movement of goods and people, were of paramount importance to the creation of camps. These specific material elements were key to the formation of these camps as part of larger logistical and military apparatuses in which the ability to quickly create spaces translated to territorial and colonial abilities. These assemblages, however, have continued to evolve in response not only to technological advancement but also to the changing realities and material resources that required improvisation and ad hoc adaptation.

Ad Hoc Architectural Inventions

Local inventions and ad hoc solutions were needed in order to create camps while dealing with the fast-changing realities in the region. Owing to the local lack of standard materials in Palestine during World War II and the logistical difficulties of transporting them from elsewhere, there was a severe deficit of building materials in the area, as evidenced in the chief engineer's monthly report from September 1940:

> Until the end of October at the earliest, building materials are going to
> be extremely scarce in Palestine. . . . Cement, Brick, Timber and probably
> Lime are the main items of which there is an acute shortage. . . . Owing to

the shortage it will be necessary to carry out as much work as possible in local material. i.e. mud brick, mud floors, mix-in-place paths, etc.[21]

In order to address the deficiency, an extensive and quite creative search for appropriate local building materials and building methods was conducted:

> Explored the question of using clay as a building material. Approached the Chief Architect of P.W.D. and Father Eugene of Franciscan Order of Monks to search through libraries on how ancient Arabs used clay. Sent Khoury into towns of Bethlehem, Beit Jala & Ramallah to find out how clay houses are built. In the meantime I remembered that in an old book on Palestine written by Charles Warren R.E. and published in 1860, stated that in his day Arabs used a mixture of olive oil and clay for building purposes. . . . Asked Manager of Shemen Oil Factory whether the use of olive oil and mud could be effective for building purposes. . . . P.W.D. architect suggested cow dung and mud but this was out of the question as there is not sufficient cattle in Palestine to produce anything like the quantity of dung which would be required.[22]

Beyond the exotic nature of this investigation of building methods and materials—in which there is a peculiar intersection of elements such as mud, oil, and cow dung and a variety of places and people, including an oil factory manager, a priest, and an architect—it is clear that in order to quickly build the required camps during the unstable time of war, original and imaginative inquiries and inventions were needed. As part of the search, varied options were examined, and experiments were conducted by local professionals, such as "Gut Gourevitz, Engineers, of Tel Aviv" making "15 experiments with clay, chopped straw, kerosene and colas."[23] Indeed, the arched-wall Gut hut is an example of such building investigation. Designed in 1940 by British and local engineers, it combined traditional pressed-clay blocks with modern hut design and prefabricated parts such as dormer windows and precast concrete foundations. With this assemblage of modern and traditional materials and building methods, a new local type of hut was created, replicating the Nissen hut's curved shape yet differing substantially in design and materiality (Figures 2.3 and 2.4).

At the end of the war neither the British army's presence in Palestine nor its infrastructure was reduced, with the Mandatory government declaring a state of emergency following the increasing anti-British Jewish resistance.[24] During the summer of 1947, when the British forces started to leave, the army in Palestine included close to one hundred thousand soldiers—one-tenth of the entire armed forces of the British Empire—occupying around one thousand facilities such as

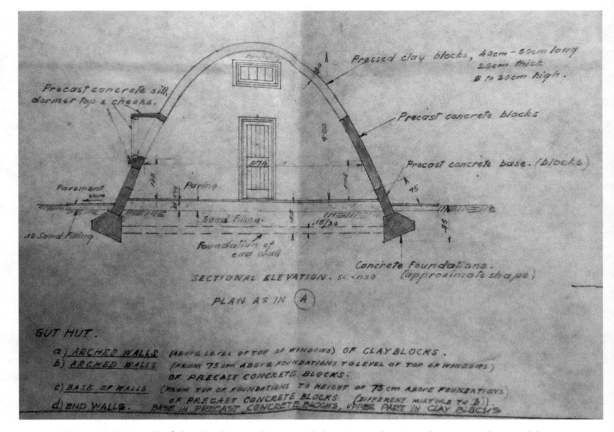

Figure 2.3. Detail of the Gut hut architectural drawings, showing the material assemblage of precast concrete blocks and foundations, pressed-clay blocks, and prefabricated details such as windows and doors. Ref. WO169/152, British National Archives.

camps, airports, depots, and offices in various sizes and of various construction methods.[25]

While the deployment of the British military camps in Palestine would later provide the built foundation for the Israeli army, around thirty British camps were used by the Jewish Agency to absorb the massive wave of Jewish immigrants who entered the country between 1948 and the early 1950s, and camps in the Gaza Strip were used to shelter Palestinian refugees.[26] The camps were therefore reappropriated to related forms of population management—of immigrants coming to the new state and of refugees displaced from its territory—according to the location of the camps and their material and spatial suitability for mass provision and control. This spatiopolitical evolution has continued, with some of the structures and infrastructure of these camps still in existence. In the city of Rosh HaAyin, for example, it is still possible to trace the remains of the British Ras el Ain RAF supply camp that became a camp for Jews from Yemen and later evolved into

Facilitating Double Colonialism   67

Figure 2.4. British military huts of stone and concrete with corrugated-steel roofs in Mahane Israel, a former British military camp converted into an immigrant camp, near Lod, 1950. Photograph by Zoltan Kluger, National Photo Collection of Israel, Government Press Office.

a city (Figures 2.5 and 2.6).[27] Thus, although the British military camps were conceived as temporary spaces, created, enlarged, and multiplied in response to the army's emergency requirements, many of them became the initial structures and infrastructures of later civil environments.

The Zionist Settler Camps

The Zionist settler camps underwent an evolution opposite to that of the British military camps. While some British military camps were later adopted for civilian use, civilian Zionist settler camps went through a significant process of militarization during the Mandate period, developing a mode of operation that later became prevalent in Israeli society and governance, in which the military–civilian distinction is blurred where frontier settlements are concerned.

Grounded in European models based on national narratives and myths and in colonial ideas and practices, the notion that the Jews would "reunite" as a nation

Figure 2.5. Rosh HaAyin immigrant camp in former British Ras el Ain RAF supply camp, 1950. Photograph by David Eldan, National Photo Collection of Israel, Government Press Office.

in the biblical Eretz Yisrael, the Land of the Forefathers *(nahalat avot)* that the (Zionist) Jews must redeem *(ge'ulat ha'aretz)*, was based on the action of colonial settling *(hityashvut)*. Employing devices like the term *Yishuv*, meaning "settlement," to refer to the community of settlers, Zionist journals with titles like *The Colonist (Der Kolonist)*, and institutions such as the Jewish Colonization Association (JCA, or ICA in Yiddish, established in 1891), the Jewish Colonial Trust (JCT, established in 1899), and the Palestine Jewish Colonization Association (known by its Yiddish acronym PICA, established in 1924),[28] settler colonialism was at the heart of Zionism as both a practice and a narrative, and camps, temporary settlements, and ephemeral structures were used by settlers from the early days of Zionist frontier settlement. Indeed, as Maxine Rodinson and Edward Said argue, Israel should be interpreted as a colonial settler state, as part of "the culmination of a process that fits perfectly into the great European–American movement of expansion in the nineteenth and twentieth centuries."[29] The Zionist project, however, was different from other colonial projects in the fact that its national goals were prior to economic and even, at its beginning, to territorial settlement.[30]

Facilitating Double Colonialism 69

Figure 2.6. A hangar made of bricks with a corrugated-steel roof at the British Ras el Ain RAF supply camp, in today's Israeli city of Rosh HaAyin, 2013. Photograph by the author.

The first Zionist communal rural settlements were composed of small agricultural groups of young "pioneers" (*halutzim*—derived from the biblical *halutz,* the one who went ahead of his people and in their service) who tended to work and erect tent camps in remote, desolate, and, often, temporary locations. The ethos that combined agricultural cultivation with securing control over the land has adopted a territorial jargon for land and occupation, with the slogans "conquest of labor" *(kibbush ha'avoda)* and "conquest of the wasteland" *(kibbush ha'shmama).* The anti-Semitic European figures of the "wandering Jews," merchants and moneylenders who rely on the labor of others, are turned into laborers and fighters invested in conquering the frontier as an act of individual and national fulfilment *(hagshama),* redeeming Eretz Yisrael and "returning" it to its "rightful" owners through its cultivation.[31] Tents were the first dwellings in many of the first communal kibbutz settlements established during the British rule, when they were often created in temporary locations before becoming permanent.

Ein Harod kibbutz was one of the first of the settlements founded as tent camps. It was created in 1921 by Jewish settlers who were members of the Labor Battalion (Gdud HaAvoda), a Zionist socialist group created with a mission of Jewish labor, settlement, and defense. The group, which was one of a number of Zionist national settler movements promoting socialist values and frontier rural

70   Facilitating Double Colonialism

settlements that together created the Labor Settlement movement *(HaHityashvut HaOvedet)*, was immersed in the ideology of Yosef Trumpeldor, a Zionist activist who became a national hero after he was killed in 1920 while defending the settlement of Tel Hai. A quotation attributed to Trumpeldor—"Wherever the Jewish plough cultivates its last furrow, that is where the border will run"—expresses well the relation between Zionist agricultural settlements and territoriality.[32] His ideology defined the strong Zionist ethos of the "redemption of the land";[33] it also expressed the discipline of those dedicated to the task:

> We must raise up a generation that has no interests and no habits. Iron bars pure and simple. Supple—but iron. Metal from which all that is required for the national machine can be forged. A wheel is lacking?—I am a wheel. A nail, screw, a flywheel?—Take me! Must the soil be dug?—I am a digger. Is there a need to shoot, to be a soldier?—I am a soldier. . . . I have no face, no psychology, no emotions, I don't even have a name: I—the pure concept of service, prepared for anything, I am not tied to anything; I know only one imperative: to build![34]

Ein Harod's settlers were an inherent part of Zionism's modernist national machine. They created their first camp by pitching their tents near the Harod Spring in the Jezreel Valley in order to cultivate land purchased by the Zionist Palestine Land Development Company, and in 1930 the collective relocated to an adjacent place to form a permanent kibbutz settlement (Figure 2.7). Many other kibbutzim were similarly initially established as temporary tent camps that later became permeant settlements. In Beit Hashita kibbutz, two timber huts and a few tents served the settlers for the first ten years: "My own wedding present to my bride was a new tent, with windows opening to the sky, which I sewed by myself and erected at somewhat of a distance from the common camp" wrote one of the settlers; he continued, "This is where we lived for ten good years, where our two children were born."[35] These forms of settler camps also seemed to meet the basic principles of frugality, equality, and rejection of private property adopted by the kibbutz movement, a mixture of Marxist revolutionary enthusiasm and Tolstoyan ideas about being close to nature.[36]

In *Land and Desire in Early Zionism*, Israeli historian Boaz Neumann shows the intense relations that blurred the boundaries between the land and the pioneer "who moistens the soil and senses himself as part of it"; "through labor, the halutzim [pioneers] 'unite' and 'merge' with the land, are 'assimilated' and 'soaked up' by it." This action also created boundaries, because when "the pioneer[s] moisten[ed] the land, thus making it 'Jewish,'" they were also "constituting a boundary between Jewish land and Arab land."[37] The settlers' tent camps made it possible to both develop this intense, unmediated, embodied, almost-existential

Figure 2.7. Ein Harod settler tent camp, Jezreel Valley, 1921. Photograph by Avraham Soskin, Ein Harod Archive.

connection between the pioneers and the soil and to broaden the boundary of the "Jewish land" at the expense of the "Arab land." As many of the first pioneer groups moved their camps frequently, to wherever they could find work or agricultural lands to cultivate, the mobility and physical temporariness of the tent camps, the fact that they could be easily moved to different locations, meant that a given temporary camp could potentially occupy other spaces almost simultaneously and that the pioneers were potentially everywhere—cultivating lands and "making them Jewish" in many areas at the same time. As the agricultural and building activities of the pioneers changed the land itself, and because their temporary camps meant they could easily move in space, this spatial mobility let them leave as many marks as possible, until the land was fully occupied and "owned" through its cultivation.

The spatial and material temporariness of these camps meant they were in a constant process of evolution and change. Timber huts were gradually constructed in the kibbutzim that settled in a specific place, although these were mainly public structures, particularly the kibbutz's children's house, which signified planning for a long-term future in the new homeland. As the mother of the first child in Tel Yosef kibbutz recalls:

> It was a great event for the entire camp—the first child. . . . All that time I was troubled with the question: where shall we house the baby? In the tent? What about the days' heat and nights' wind? But behold! The comrades built us a palace. A square shack made of straw mats with a tin roof, a true palace.[38]

The permanent kibbutz settlement developed in close relation with the camp not only as its initial temporary space but also as a communal way of living. In the first days of many of the permanent kibbutzim, their members lived in one structure, all together or divided according to gender, with no minimum level of privacy. Even in later stages of development the small private dwellings of kibbutz members were called not homes or houses, but rooms (*hadarim*; singular *heder*), while members ate their meals in a common dining room and their children slept in the common children's houses. These communal kibbutz settlements resembled military life in a camp, where its pioneer-cum-soldiers were relying on one another for everyday tasks and survival in hostile frontier environments. As Yigal Allon, an Israeli general and politician and one of the founders of Ginosar kibbutz, would later write, there is a "great resemblance between a kibbutz and a military unit," both being built on discipline, volunteerism, and dedication to the group.[39] Both, it seems, were also based on the formation of the camp.

Fortifying the Settler Camps

The form of the settler camp, many of which became new kibbutz frontier settlements, did indeed evolve and enhance its military character during the prestate, early state, and later periods, while also becoming increasingly territorial. One of the most famous of these camp-settlement models is the wall and tower (*homa u'migdal*) method of erecting fortified settler outpost camps, adopted during the Arab uprising of 1936–39. This method allowed the construction of prefabricated, secured agricultural kibbutz outpost camp settlements in one day by using military tactics in their design, transportation, and construction, a model that significantly changed the Zionist territorial map in Mandatory Palestine.

The first wall and tower camp was constructed in 1936 by the members of Kibbutz Tel Amal in order to seize control of land that had been purchased by the Jewish National Fund (JNF) (Figure 2.8). Adjacent to the Asi River in Bet-She'an Valley, the land could not be settled owing to the violent acts of the neighboring Bedouin encampment as a part of the Arab uprising.[40] The building method, based on the hasty construction of a prefabricated fortified outpost camp, developed fol-

Figure 2.8. Tel Amal wall and tower camp near the Asi River, Bet-She'an Valley, 1937. Unknown photographer, Central Zionist Archives, NPS\200979.

lowing discussions between the kibbutz members and the JNF. Because of security needs, the prefabricated outpost camp had to be transported and constructed in six to eight hours so that its inhabitants would be able to defend themselves immediately, day and night. The camp's walls were prefabricated wooden molds filled with gravel, which enclosed a square area of 35 meters by 35 meters. There were two bastions for gun emplacements in its corners, and the whole was surrounded by two fences of barbed wire that protected the "conquering troop" from intruders, snipers, and hand grenades. It was then completed with four shacks to accommodate forty people and a prefabricated watchtower with a searchlight to overlook the surrounding area.[41]

Preparations for the construction took place in the nearby Beit-Alfa kibbutz, and the camp components were ready a few months before the settling action was approved by the Jewish Agency in Jerusalem, which was quite reluctant about this new invention. On 10 December 1936, five trucks transported the prefabricated parts for the camp, which was erected within six hours with the help of members from the surrounding kibbutz settlements.[42] Shlomo Gur, the kibbutz member who planned and organized the first Tel Amal settlement, continued to develop the method with the support of Yohanan Ratner, the chief architect and strategic planner of the Ha'gana (the prestate army).[43] After the success of this

Figure 2.9. Zionist volunteers on trucks carry building materials to establish the new wall and tower outpost of Kibbutz Ein Gev at the Sea of Galilee, 1937. Photograph by Zoltan Kluger, National Photo Collection of Israel, Government Press Office.

prototype, this initiative was enthusiastically adopted by the Zionist institutions during the Arab uprising.[44]

The construction of a wall and tower settlement was planned like a military action. The area for the new settlement was agreed upon in advance, and a few days before D-Day, the specific site was chosen. The settlers, together with the supporting organizations, arranged the construction of the prefabricated components of the camp, their transportation to the site by trucks, and additional help to assemble them (Figures 2.9 and 2.10). At first, the construction of the camps was fully coordinated with the British authorities, who saw the new settlements as additional bases to secure the territory, and the Jewish institutions updated British officials and the police on the future dates and sites for settlement in order to receive British assistance. The Mandatory authorities funded road paving and provided legal weapons for the protection of the new settlement points, and in many photographs from a camp's construction day, it is possible to identify the Jewish

Figure 2.10. Zionist "concurring troops," volunteers, help rapidly construct the wall and tower outpost of Kibbutz Ein Gev at the Sea of Galilee, 1937. Photograph by Zoltan Kluger, National Photo Collection of Israel, Government Press Office.

Figure 2.11. Aerial view of Beit Yosef wall and tower camp, Bet-She'an Valley, 1937. Unknown photographer, Central Zionist Archives, PHAL\1624342.

guards in the British police force *(notrim)* who supported the defense of the settlers during the action.[45]

A few basic conditions were considered necessary for the creation of a new wall and tower camp: an organized and trained force that, if attacked, would be able to hold the line until reinforcements arrived; the ability to quickly erect the so-called settlement point on a site within sight of another Jewish settlement, creating a sequence of camps that defined a territorial unit; and a road that would allow for the rapid arrival of other troops in times of trouble.[46] The communal kibbutz life was crucial for the intense life in the camp, as all the camp's members contributed equally to its construction, protection, development, and maintenance, just like soldiers, with the fortified camp enabling the settlers to cultivate the land and gradually build a permanent settlement (Figures 2.11 and 2.12). Thus, from a one-off initiative, the invasive wall and tower method generated an alignment of outpost camps whose visual and infrastructural connections created a ter-

Figure 2.12. Aerial view of Beit Yosef settlement, with what remained of the wall and tower camp at its center, 1939. Photograph by Zoltan Kluger, Central Zionist Archives, PHAL\1624343.

ritorial sequence of colonization whose meaning was much greater than a collection of settlements.

Major General Yosef Avidar, who managed the erection of the wall and tower camps on behalf of the Ha'gana, compared this settlement method to the appearance of the tank in World War I: just as the tank allowed for shielded movement that made the exhausting trench battles redundant, the quickly erected wall and tower camps allowed "for a rapid territorial break-through, which without this new weapon would not have been possible."[47] As a well-organized method, it adapted easily to improvisation to accommodate specific conditions: for example, the gravel for the Ein Gev camp near the Sea of Galilee was brought in sacks from the banks of the sea, and in the Hamadia camp, which was erected at night as it was near a Jordanian army camp, screws were used instead of nails to avoid the noise of hammers.

Facilitating Double Colonialism

In November 1936 the Peel Commission, formally known as the Palestine Royal Commission, began investigating the Arab uprising. In July 1937, it published the Peel Report, which, for the first time, recommended partition of the land between Jews and Arabs and provided a map of the partition plan. The Jewish Agency pushed the wall and tower project forward when it became clear that the country would be divided and it became necessary to enlarge the future territory by the establishment of new settlements. In June 1937, a few weeks before the partition plan was published, Moshe Shertok (later Sharett), head of the political department of the Jewish Agency and later the second Israeli prime minister, stated, "There is only one thing we can do in the current circumstances—to change the map of the land of Israel by establishing new [settlement] points. . . . Our role now is to grab and settle."[48] Settlement, then, became a territorial act aimed at creating a well-planned Jewish presence through a sequence of connected settlement points. This prefabricated invasive architectural instrument, which the Jewish institutions were initially reluctant to try, became a spatial and material method that had an unexpected formative capacity on the Zionist territorial and political project, with settlement needs creating new spatial forms that then constituted encompassing territorial endeavors to secure Zionist power over space.

This architectural instrument, which later became a core symbol of Zionist settlement, was already a symbolic icon when it was continuously re-created and documented as a reoccurring event across the territory, and a wall and tower model was chosen for the Land of Israel Pavilion at the 1937 World Exposition in Paris, only one year after Tel Amal was established.[49] During the course of the three-year campaign, fifty-two wall and tower outpost camps were erected throughout the country and were rapidly transformed into permanent settlements, significantly changing the map of Jewish settlements in Palestine. After the publication of the White Paper of 1939, which restricted the rights of Jews to buy and settle land, twelve new outposts were erected in one month, seven of them in one day. Some of these camps were erected at night, as they no longer received the consent and protection of the British authorities,[50] and the outbreak of World War II put an end to this territorial project. Zionist institutions continued to use similar territorial modes of instant settlements years after the wall and tower campaign was over. In 1946 eleven settlements were established in the Negev area in one night, known as "eleven points in the Negev," in order to enlarge the territory of the future state before Palestine's partition.

The wall and tower outpost camp made it possible to create pop-up territorial settlements by assembling, in a new way, British and Zionist institutions, people, and materials, such as prefabricated timber structures, barbed wire, a searchlight and guns for defense, agricultural equipment, and, importantly, a road infrastructure and motorized transportation that enabled the rapid movement of these com-

Facilitating Double Colonialism 79

ponents to their places. These new territorial "weapons," which acted as protective nuclei that rapidly grew out of their shells into permanent settlements,[51] were built and populated by recruited civilian soldiers who defined themselves as pioneers, with a strong ideology and institutions instead of an organized army. The blurred identity of both civilians and soldiers also characterized their settlements, which were created and managed in the area between civil and military action. As Israel Galili, a former Ha'gana commander, asserted, "Until the [1948] war it was the settlement [action] that conquered the land."[52]

This settlement method had some similarities to other contexts of settler colonialism, such as in the United States. "Look how absurd it is, the issue of timber forts," said Shlomo Gur, more than six decades after the invention of the wall and tower camps; "all the Wild West was made out of it. The outposts of the barbaric [white] Americans who went to the native Americans' territories were all built in the shape of [fortified] wooden cloisters with towers."[53] Described in Israeli historiography as a defensive system invented to cope with the violence of the local Arabs, here too, as in many other colonial contexts, "the settler is portrayed as surrounded by [violent] 'natives,'" as Stefano Harney and Fred Moten argue, and the role of the aggressor is inverted "so that colonialism is made to look like self-defense."[54]

Indeed, this invasive form of fortified outpost camps was used by colonial powers in North and South America and in other places around the world, creating protected entry points to hostile frontier territories. Like the camps of the Roman Empire, which sometimes became civil settlements, many colonial settlements also began as provisional outpost camps or, in the term of Paul Gilroy, as "fortified encampments of the colonizers."[55] These fortified camps created for territorial expansion prove the paradox of Zionism, which depicted Palestine as an empty land waiting to be redeemed yet had to invent an invasive spatial method to defend Jewish settlements from those who already lived there.

These provisional fortified frontier camps—like the improvised Spanish military nuclei in the Río de la Plata (today's Argentina), which later developed into cities, including Buenos Aires—were created as a response to constantly changing colonial boundaries: they could be rapidly built in strategic places to secure the conquered territory and then easily abandoned when occupation was advanced to new areas or when a permanent settlement was built.[56] The Australian settler camps, created in the late nineteenth century by and for European settlers and later deserted and wiped off the map or turned into permanent settlements, are another example of camps used as instruments of colonial expansion. But while in Australia such camps are currently studied as archaeological remnants, in Israel–Palestine they are still used, in their evolving versions, as active territorial instruments.[57]

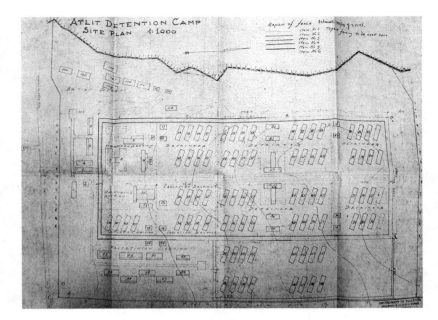

Figure 2.13. Site plan of the Atlit Detention Camp. Courtesy of Bintivey Ha'apala, Clandestine Jewish Immigration Information and Research Center, Atlit Detention Camp.

British Detention Camps

The nebulous distinction between the civilian and the military also characterized the British detention camps for illegal Jewish immigrants that were built in coastal Atlit and later in Cyprus. The organized illegal Jewish immigration to Palestine dates back to 1934, a year after Hitler came to power and the situation of Jews in Germany and other European countries deteriorated. Although tens of thousands of Jews were legally permitted to enter Palestine by a quota of entry certificates, this did not meet the need, and many decided to enter the territory illegally.[58] Between 1934 and 1939 more than twenty thousand illegal immigrants arrived in Palestine, and those captured by British forces filled the existing prisons. Following the publication of the White Paper of 1939 as a British effort to end the Arab uprising, the quota of Jewish immigrants was drastically limited, yet the number of illegal Jewish immigrants soared and the Atlit Detention Camp was opened in 1940 to serve as an internment camp for the captured illegal immigrants.[59] The camp was designed to hold 1,664 detainees, who were held there until they were awarded entry certificates in conformity with the new quota.[60] Camp plans, at 1:1,000 scale, were rapidly produced, and the structures, similar to those of the military camps, were quickly erected (Figure 2.13).[61]

Not unlike other detention camps created in British colonies, the camp was formed as a controlled space of containment, closely managing the lives of its civilian detainees.[62] Around the camp were two fences of barbed wire, between which armed guards patrolled. Inside the camp were seventy-seven numbered wooden huts with corrugated-iron roofs for the detainee's accommodation, with thirty-two

Figure 2.14. Within barbed-wire fences, nurses play with Jewish immigrant children at the Atlit Detention Camp, 1944. Photograph by Zoltan Kluger, National Photo Collection of Israel, Government Press Office.

beds in each hut. The larger structures were the cookhouse and the disinfection structure, composed of a timber frame and panels of corrugated iron, intended to provide for the basic needs of the men, women, and children detained there (Figure 2.14). After arriving at the camp, detainees were vaccinated and used the showers, and men were separated out and sent to twenty days of isolation. Despite the heavy security—which included daily roll calls, head counts, and camp lockdown from sunset to sunrise—the detainees were active in improving the living condition in the camp; they worked in the communal kitchen and grew vegetables on a small allotment, and the hospital in the camp was managed by detained doctors and nurses.[63]

During World War II, the illegal migration almost stopped because of the impossibility of traveling through and sailing around Europe, and the camp was shut down. It reopened immediately after the war following the massive waves of Jewish illegal migrants/refugees who had escaped Europe. During the three years between 1945 and the establishment of Israel in 1948, approximately seventy-thousand Jewish immigrants arrived in Palestine by sea on sixty-five ships, of

Figure 2.15. Nissen huts accommodate unaccompanied Jewish immigrant youth in a British detention camp in Cyprus, 1947. Unknown photographer, Central Zionist Archives, PHPS\1333355.

which only thirteen small vessels managed to bring their passengers to shore without being caught.[64] Ships sailed from Italy, France, and Greece carrying migrants/refugees from all around Europe, and the passengers caught by British forces were detained in the Atlit camp until, usually after weeks or months, they were provided with permits for legal immigration. In the summer of 1946, as the flow did not slow and the detention camps in Palestine were filled to capacity, passengers were forcibly transferred to newly established designated camps in Cyprus.[65]

From August 1946 to the end of the British Mandate in May 1948, about fifty-six thousand Jewish migrants/refugees were deported from Palestine to Cyprus.[66] Sixty percent of them were Holocaust survivors who arrived from Europe's displaced persons camps.[67] They were kept in Cyprus for a few weeks to more than a year and released according to a monthly quota of 1,500 permits. Consisting mostly of tents, the first camps were established near the city of Famagusta and were called "summer camps"; a few months later the "winter camps" were established, consisting of Nissen huts (Figure 2.15). Like the Atlit camp, they were surrounded by double rows of barbed wire and watchtowers.

The Jewish Yishuv in Palestine and Jewish organizations from around the world provided assistance in the camps, in the form of organized delegations that included doctors, teachers, and childcare workers, with the motto "Cyprus is also

Eretz Yisrael," and the camps were teeming with social and political activity.[68] The fact that the camps were self-managed by the detainees and supported by Zionist emissaries helped ease the tense atmosphere caused by the rough conditions, the desire to be released, the difficult life stories of the detainees, and their uncertainty about their future. On the day the state of Israel was declared, there were more than twenty-two thousand detainees in the camps. Nearly ten thousand were still imprisoned there a year after the state was established because the British refused to release young people who could be drafted to the new Israeli army, claiming that their immigration to Israel would tilt the balance of power in the Arab–Israeli war.

Whether located within or outside Palestine, the British detention camps for Jewish immigrants created zones of complex relations with the desired territory. While the detainees in Atlit camp in Palestine were held as if they were outside the territory they were trying to enter, the Cyprus camps were perceived by the detainees as being part of Eretz Yisrael despite their location. These detention camps created temporary spaces where people were suspended until they were included in the entry quota or until the political situation changed with the establishment of Israel, when their status also changed.

Like most camps created by British powers in Palestine, the Atlit camp was not dismantled after the establishment of Israel; rather, it was retained, to be used as a detention camp, this time by Israeli powers. During the Arab–Israeli war, Atlit served as a POW camp and a civil detention camp for local Palestinians; it was then used as an immigrant camp and transit camp for Jewish immigrants; and after the 1967 war, Syrian, Jordanian, and Egyptian POWs were detained there. The camp continued serving similar functions, now serving the political and military interests of the population who had been detained there in the past, turning the oppressed into the oppressors. The camp still exists today as an Israeli heritage site and a museum of the illegal immigration of Jews to Mandatory Palestine (*ha'apala*), with its temporary structures rebuilt and preserved, manifesting that history is not only "written by the victors," in Walter Benjamin's words, but is also physically reconstructed by them.

A Colonial Tactical Instrument

The British military camps and detention camps and the camps created by Zionist settlers differ substantially from one another, serving contrasting objectives of containment and expansion. Yet these camps also share certain characteristics that explain their vast use in Palestine, during the years of the territory's double colonization, as spaces of population and territorial (re)ordering facilitated by modern materiality of industrialization and speed.

These camps were all frontier spaces, creating or facilitating a zone where one society penetrated the territory of another before a full hegemonic rule was reestablished. The different spread of the British and Zionist camps in Palestine shows, however, that during the Mandate period the two groups considered different zones to be a frontier. The British saw the whole of Palestine as a frontier territory in relation to their metropole and to Europe, and consequently they spread their camps relatively close to the coastline. The Zionist organizations, on the other hand, identified the frontier with the zones that were not yet inhabited by Jewish settlers, away from the coastline, and so that was where they erected their camps. As frontier tactical instruments, all these camps existed on the military–civilian continuum in different ways, creating instruments in which people were managed in order to achieve a particular goal.

Each of the camps was created as a temporary space for what was perceived as an urgent need. The military camps were formed following the British conquest of Palestine and the need to control the territory and its populations, multiplied and grew following increasing military requirements such as World War II, and later served civilian needs for immigrants and refugees. The Zionist settler tent camps were created to settle and cultivate what was considered frontier territories and to gradually gain control over them, and the later fortified wall and tower outpost camps were created to address security needs during the Arab uprising and the territorial need to spread and solidify the Jewish settlement before a future partition of Palestine. The detention camps in Atlit and in Cyprus were created to deal with the waves of Jewish immigration and to control the demographic balance in Palestine.

The materiality of these spaces—composed of transitory, transportable, and often prefabricated shelters and structures such as tents, timber huts, and Nissen huts—and the road infrastructures on which they were dependent for their quick creation and ongoing services were key to their rapid formation and continuing maintenance. Although some of these structures still exist, they were built from light and cheap materials that were not intended to last. The choice of materials and building methods was the result of the urgency to create them without investing in permanent (and expensive) structures for situations perceived as temporary.[69] This was also the reason for another recurring spatial feature of these camps: repetition—either repetition of the same settlement module, such as the wall and tower camps, or repetition of structures within the camps themselves, such as the prefabricated huts. These camps are a clear product of industrialization, measured by aspects of logistics and cost, and their spatial repetition and multiplication is indifferent to, if not deliberately invasive and offensive within, the local environment in which they were erected. As such, they create a "weapon of mass construction" recruited to establish control over a territory and/or a population.[70] It is a weapon whose threat lies in its quantity and mobility, which transform a place into an arena of struggle and imposed force. The repetition becomes the means of reaching vaster fields, a territorial mechanism that, in Paul Virilio's words, "deploys its forces by multiplying them."[71]

In addition to the transportability, temporariness, and repetition of the camp structures, two other related spatial features are common to these camps: the fence and the watchtower. Whether for reasons of self-defense, as for the wall and tower and the British military camps, or for internment purposes, as for the detention facilities, these camps are architectural instruments of containment and separation. They separate one population from another, and, being closed spaces, they separate their inhabitants from the outside environment in which they are located. The watchtower is the elevated "eye" watching inside or outside to verify this separation, whether between new settlers and the hostile local population or between immigrants or refugees and the country they wish to enter. Yet, while separated, these camps must also be connected by a substantial infrastructure that forms a lifeline that both creates and sustains them.

The spatial temporariness of these camps, their infrastructural connections, and the speed of their creation allowed them to be used as tactical instruments to solve specific problems, yet many of these camps have continued to serve other functions and powers long after their foreseen expiration date. These spaces were planned and developed ad hoc, neither according to the standard rules and regulations nor according to any approved master plan, and they appeared as part of military or quasi-military actions that created "facts on the ground," which were followed by a changing political reality. British troops, Zionist "pioneer" settlers, and illegal Jewish immigrants were all residing in these camps because of their specified identity and the need to emplace or contain them as such. These populations resided in the camps—either by will or by force—to prevent them from or to assist them in transforming the environment around them.

The architectural machine of the camp, with its industrialized and mobile components, can be rapidly assembled anywhere and create a site of conquest, containment, and separation, a machine that transforms either the land on which it sits or the people it holds into objects that will be easy to manage and control. The camp ignores architectural sensitivities such as relation to the surrounding landscape, suitable materiality, durability, and specific everyday human needs. As a machine used to achieve military or political objectives, it is expected to be removed when the change is complete. What this modern machine produces from the raw materials of land and people is a territory and a nation, and with them it also produces other potential camp residents, those who will be considered not qualified to be part of these new political products.

The end of the British Mandate in Palestine and the establishment of the State of Israel did not terminate the role of the camp in managing land and people and creating or maintaining nationhood and territory. The British camps were appropriated by the new Israeli government to absorb the waves of Jewish immigration and to detain resisting local Arab populations, and they were also used by other powers to shelter Palestinian refugees beyond the borders of the new state. The Zionist settler camps mostly became permanent settlements, and other frontier camps were created to continue dispersing the Jewish population over the territory; the camp continued to evolve in the area, responding to its ever-emerging political needs.

3

GATHERING, ABSORBING, AND REORDERING THE DIASPORA
Immigrant and Transit Camps of Israel's Early Statehood

Let nothing be called natural
In an age of bloody confusion,
Ordered disorder, planned caprice,
And dehumanized humanity, lest all things
Be held unalterable!

          —Bertolt Brecht, *The Exception and the Rule*

In the first few years after Israel was established, during the mass-immigration period (1948–51), camps were widely used to gather, absorb, distribute, and temporarily accommodate newly arrived immigrants. In formal Israeli history, the *mahanot olim* (immigrant camps) and the later *ma'abarot* (transit camps) are said to be improvised responses to the difficulties caused by mass immigration, makeshift yet resourceful solutions to an almost–force majeure problem.[1] This chapter questions that account, and with it, the perception of the role of the camp during the state-formation period, by examining the camp not as an inevitable response to an unexpected problem, but as a strategic modern architectural mechanism that was extensively used in different forms as an inseparable part of creating and populating the new state. Israel is investigated here as a state formed by two allegedly contradictory but in fact complementary conditions: on the one hand, a product of a chaotic state of emergency created by mass immigration, and on the other hand, a product of a comprehensive, tightly controlled modernist project combining modern physical planning and social engineering. This duality enables us to establish a view of the variety of immigrant and transit camps as temporal and spatial black holes that swallowed the contradiction between the historical rapid and radical transformation of population and territory and the utopian rational and humanist self-image of the Zionist nation-building project. This historical account also allows us to closely examine the camp as a multifaceted and versatile instrument that evolves according to changing needs.

The subject of the camp in the context of the creation of Israel is usually discussed in relation to the Palestinian refugee camps created by UNRWA in neighboring Arab countries following the Nakba (the Palestinian Catastrophe), as a result of the 1948 war.[2] While the Palestinian disaster reappears here mainly through the absence of the Palestinians both physically and mentally from the civil reality created in Israel in the early years of the state, this chapter focuses on illuminating the crucial role of the camp in the geopolitical changes in the Jewish population in Israel during the same period. These camps facilitated the profound demographic and territorial changes that were part of the ambitious Zionist project, often at the expense of their inhabitants. As such, the immigrant camps and the ma'abara transit camps could be looked at as a distorted mirror image of the Palestinian refugee camps: they appeared in the same years as the Israeli immigrant camps, the Palestinian refugee and Jewish immigrant populations were roughly the same size—around 685,000 Jewish immigrants entered Israel in the three years following the state's establishment in May 1948, while approximately 700,000 Palestinians became refugees—and for a few years they created very similar physical landscapes of squalid tent camps.[3] However, it is important to highlight the opposing political roles of these camps, and therefore the difference in their duration, spatiality, and meaning. While the Israeli state dismantled the temporary ma'abara camps after a few years and left no physical trace of them, as if the immigrants had always been part of their new land, the Palestinian refugee camps that still exist are a physical reminder of the Palestinians' suspended existence as people without a state.

The Hebrew term *ma'abara* (plural, *ma'abarot*) is etymologically derived from the word *ma'avar*, meaning "transit." The concept of the ma'abara has long been expropriated from its original meaning, however, accumulating other connotations such as neglect, poverty, discrimination, degeneration, and the experience of marginalization in the Israeli society.[4] The linguistic gap between the functional intention in the original concept and its acquired meaning indicates the difference between the camp's initial objectives and their social, economic, and cultural outcomes. This gap is inherent to the Zionist modernist project, which aimed to create a nation-state, a project that necessitated radical alterations, presuming these could be made while maintaining its humanist values.

The ma'abara transit camps, which physically disappeared from the Israeli landscape once the immigrants were settled, are usually acknowledged by Israeli geographers and historians as only a brief transitional stage, mainly in relation to the creation of the peripheral "development towns."[5] These camps are often dismissed as an inevitable by-product of an unexpected phenomenon: the unstoppable influx of Jewish people into their new homeland.[6] The camps abroad, which were used by Zionist organizations and later by Israel to gather immigrants before

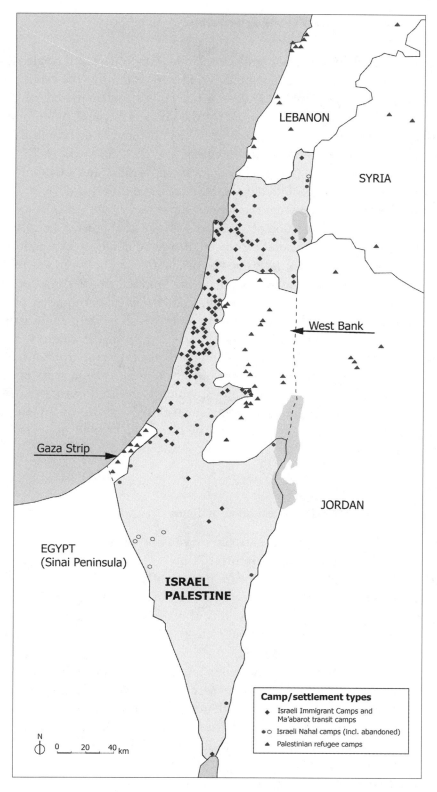

Map 3. Camps created in the first decade of Israel's establishment and of the Palestinian Nakba.

transportation to their new state, are also examined by others as a single isolated phenomenon related to specific sites and periods.[7] By examining the extensive role of the camp and its evolution during the prestate and early state periods, this chapter proposes a new analytical framework for the camp as a crucial modern mechanism that enabled the implementation of the Zionist and later Israel's national, demographic, territorial, and spatial strategies.

The close relationship between the Zionist movement and modernity, with the inherent contradictions of ideologies, practices, and ordering devices, are analyzed in this chapter to argue that the supposed messianic, uncontrolled mass immigration was actually a situation of "ordered disorder" that created a chaotic state of emergency that was very useful for the engineered emergence of a nation. This situation allowed the state to use camps to bridge the gap between the importation of masses of people to rapidly populate the emptied frontier territories and the completion and construction of the state's ambitious modern master plan and its development towns (or New Towns, as in their British model), while assuming that the dehumanizing effect of these temporary camp spaces would vanish together with their physical traces. The chapter also examines the frontier ma'abara camp as a hybrid camp typology that developed from two different types of camps: the prestate frontier Zionist settler camps, which were used during the British Mandate to settle in remote areas, and the Israeli closed and controlled immigrant camps. This typological evolution exposes the camp as a flexible and versatile instrument that evolves according to needs and available resources.

Camps and Modernity: The Zionist Realization of Utopia

Zionism developed as a modern national movement with a theological context: the messianic myth of the Jewish "return to Zion." The Zionist ideology appeared as part of the historical category of modernity at the same time as did other nineteenth-century revolutionary ideologies, representing a secular, universal attempt to achieve redemption from a reality of being an exiled minority by a rational effort to actively form a new Jewish collective identity. It was part of modernism as an aesthetic category, typified by the destruction of the past and the search for new cultural practices, and modernization, as a scientific, economic, and sociological category, was an inseparable aspect of its development.[8] As discussed in chapter 2, it has also developed as a settlement project, forming a settler colonial society with the idea of colonization (hityashvut) standing at its core. Colonialism and modernity were indeed expressed in all aspects of the Zionist enterprise, from its political and economic institutions to its technological projects. It was first and foremost exemplified in the gathering and transportation of masses of people and their subsequent resettlement in their new state according to a calculated plan.

Using modern technologies to manipulate and reshape populations and territories in what first seemed to be a utopian national idea, the modern instrument of the camp was widely adopted by Zionist and later Israeli organizations in order to carry out this ambitious task.

The social and technological changes of modernity led to the emergence of the genre of utopia, which imagines perfect modules of desirable communities. Social utopias, in which thinkers recruit science and technology for the realization of their cultural vision, arguably represent what Zygmunt Bauman suggests in *Modernity and Ambivalence* is the essence of modernity: the struggle for order against chaos. Edward Bellamy's *Looking Backward: 2000–1887* and Ebenezer Howard's *Garden Cities of To-morrow,* both published in the late nineteenth century, provide examples of social utopias that describe an alternative, well-planned, and reasoned perfect social order. Theodor Herzl's book *The Jewish State (Der Judenstaat)*, subtitled *An Attempt at a Modern Solution of the Jewish Question*, which appeared in 1896 and is considered one of the most important texts of Zionism, should also be considered in the context of modernism and utopia. Herzl, known as the "visionary of the state," transformed Zionism into an organized modern movement in what was written as a futuristic manual for nation and state building.[9]

The realization of the Jewish state was believed to be an unprecedented historical chance to establish an ideal preplanned society based on organized, logical thinking and on the most advanced innovative technologies:

> Everything must be systematically settled beforehand. . . . Every social and technical achievement of our age and of the more advanced age which will be reached before the slow execution of my plan is accomplished must be employed for this object. Every valuable invention which exists now, or lies in the future, must be used. By these means a country can be occupied and a State founded in a manner as yet unknown to history, and with possibilities of success such as never occurred before.[10]

Herzl's statecraft vision depended on systematic organization and order; it was a plan based on technologies and on future modern inventions that would enable it to be accurately executed. Spatial temporariness was embedded in his vision, which predicted that, after their use in the beginning for preliminary shelter, wooden "makeshift buildings" would be "replaced by superior dwellings."[11] In his utopian novel *Old New Land* (*Altneuland* in German, *Tel Aviv* in Hebrew), Herzl predicted the use of prefabricated structures transported globally for the temporary settlement of immigrants. "I ordered five hundred barracks from France—a new kind that could be taken apart like a tent and put together in an hour," he wrote, anticipating, in the spirit of settler colonialism and its mobile structures, the architecture that could be manufactured en masse in one place, then easily transported and rapidly erected in another to support its rapid settlement.[12] By the time Herzl's plans came into being, during the different stages of the colonization of Palestine, the camp was a modern invention ready to be employed.

Modernity and the Camps of State Formation

The camp has mostly been analyzed as a biopolitical "machine of ordering" of the nation-state, a space that appears and functions during a factual state of emergency, in which the sovereign excludes specific populations in order to "take care" of the "national body."[13] However, as the camps of Israel's stage of state formation show, the camp also allows the establishment of a completely new geopolitical order almost from scratch. This ordering instrument, which is mostly studied as a space that enables the exclusion of specific populations within a given territory, also facilitated the gathering of a globally scattered population in a specific territory and that population's distribution as a new nation throughout its new frontier. The evolution of the camp is therefore analyzed here in relation to two complementary genealogical roots: the first is related to the Agambenian camp typologies and their role in the concentration, exclusion, and sometimes expropriation of populations; the second is related to colonial camp typologies of territorial expansion of populations. Both typologies are inherently connected to the biopolitical role of the camp in managing populations and territories based on ethnoracial, social, and cultural categories and divisions.

While explaining that modern development's aims are to struggle against ambivalence and to achieve order, Bauman stresses the total dependency between the order and the chaos against which order constitutes itself. "Without chaos, no order," argues Bauman, explaining that chaos, "the other of order," is a product "of order's self-constitution: its side-effect, its waste, and yet the condition *sine qua non* of its (reflective) possibility."[14] The endless effort of ordering and classifying generates a process that is "both self-destructive and self-propelling . . . [and that] goes on with unabating strength because it creates its own problems in the course of resolving them."[15] Thus, the creation of order—such as the establishment of a new state in which the scattered Jewish Diaspora will gather—involves the production of a new chaotic reality, wherein the efforts to organize it may create a new chaos, and so on.

According to Bauman, the various intensities of the ordering process are influenced by the availability of force dedicated to control ambivalence and by the technologies applied to reduce it. Retracing the biggest catastrophes of the twentieth century, there is no doubt that the ordering mechanism of the camp, which uses violence to both control and forcefully rearrange specific populations, would appear as one of the main sites where horrific disasters have occurred. Nevertheless, in many realized utopian visions, such as the Zionist project, camps were employed as a central tool to establish and maintain themselves in an effort to transform an idea into a reality and a chaotic reality into an ideal order. However, while totalitarian regimes use force more easily to impose order, democratic states, as Israel portrays itself, often use different methods, such as consciously creating a chaotic state of emergency by bringing in a vulnerable population en masse, to achieve similar aims.

A Country of Camps: Creating and Absorbing Mass Immigration

In the first three years of Israel's existence, its Jewish population doubled to 1.2 million at a pace that reached record amounts of over 30,000 immigrants per month.[16] Jewish mass immigration to Israel was conceived of and presented as a natural, spontaneous, and almost-messianic event, the "Ingathering of Exiles," a miraculous leap in space and time—a myth that was also reflected in the Israeli Declaration of Independence as a collective aspiration of the Diaspora Jews to return and unite in their ancestral homeland. However, most immigrants did not arrive in Israel by their own genuine aspirations and means. Rather, an active operation of propaganda, transportation, and absorption was initiated, organized, and conducted by Zionist institutions and Jewish organizations both in Israel and abroad to bring Jewish immigrants to Israel.

The immigrants who arrived between 1948 and 1950 were assembled into immigrant camps, mostly located in former British military camps, until available housing was allocated for them. This new housing was mainly in Palestinian neighborhoods and towns that had been emptied during the 1948 war, while their original Palestinian residents became refugees and were prevented from returning to them. These immigrant camps did not appear merely as a result of a state of emergency caused by the increasing stream of immigrants; instead, they were also a product of an existing, detailed plan, the One Million Plan, consolidated between 1942 and 1945 as a way to absorb one million Jewish immigrants a few years before Israel's establishment.

The One Million Plan

In the period before the outbreak of World War II, David Ben-Gurion, the founding father of the Israeli state and its first prime minister, switched from the early Zionist utopian idea of a selective, ideological, and pioneering Aliyah (Jewish immigration to Eretz Yisrael) to the concept of mass immigration, an emergency rescue of the Jews in Europe, after recognizing the harsh reality lurking on their doorstep.[17] In November 1942, during World War II and following information about the systematic extermination of the Jews in Europe, Ben-Gurion gathered a team of experts to prepare a program for the rapid immigration and absorption of one million Jews in Eretz Yisrael, then Mandatory Palestine, in less than eighteen months. The postwar period was expected to be a crucial historical moment whose timing would allow the execution of a radical plan for the transfer of Jewish people in unprecedented numbers, which was then understood as vital for the Zionist project.[18] This ambitious project was a comprehensive plan that laid out what would be required for the task—such as food, water, housing, industry, and transportation—and consciously aimed to cross a demographic threshold. "The meaning of a million is making the Jews a majority" stated Ben-Gurion,[19] and a reliable scientific study was needed to convince the nations of the world that such a mission was indeed possible.

Camps were an integral part of the One Million Plan. The planners intended for these camps to provide the immigrants with their essential preliminary needs and suggested using vacated and repurposed British military camps. It was estimated that a total of 220,000 immigrants altogether would stay in the camps, and it was agreed that they would be employed in public works to build the infrastructure necessary for their further absorption, such as land preparation, road paving, and construction of housing, and that immigrants' time in the camps would be used for professional training.[20] The plan speculated that immigrants would come from both European and predominantly Arab countries and recommended that they be placed in camps according to their country of origin. The idea that the absorption of each immigrant group should be separately planned (including the geographical location of the camps, time spent in them, and training for specific future occupations) was broadly agreed upon by the planners.[21]

It is important to highlight that the camp's central role in this early prestate period was that of a technology for the management of the masses, part of a carefully planned scientific enterprise. As such, the camp was conceived as a two-layered biopolitical mechanism planned first, to absorb Jewish immigrants, and second, to divide them according to their ethnic origin. Thus, the camp was initially considered not only an absorption facility, but also a mechanism with the objective of creating an internal ethnically (or arguably racially) based order for the Jewish society in the prestate period of Mandate Palestine.

The Immigrant Camps: Between a Plan and a State of Emergency

The expected mass immigration did not immediately reach Palestine after the end of World War II owing both to the extent of the Jewish extermination in Europe and to the heavy restrictions on Jewish immigration imposed by the British Mandate. However, three years after its completion, the One Million Plan approached realization following the Israeli declaration of independence in May 1948 and the decision to open the state gates to Jewish immigration.

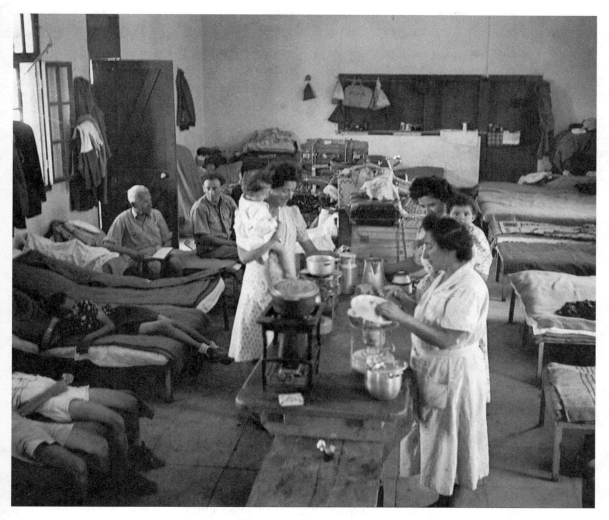

Figure 3.1. Immigrant women cook a meal inside one of the barracks of the Sha'ar Aliya immigrant camp, in the former St. Lucas British military camp, near Haifa, 1949. Photograph by Zoltan Kluger, National Photo Collection of Israel, Government Press Office.

As planned and anticipated, the camp gradually became a central instrument in the absorption process. Several small immigrant camps had operated before statehood in the center of the country, and in accordance with the One Million Plan, about thirty additional camps opened in former British military camps. This "kingdom of camps" was composed of distant facilities, closed and often surrounded by barbed wire, where entry and exit were strictly controlled.[22] While Sha'ar Aliya (Gate for immigration) camp, located not far from Haifa's port, functioned as the first arrival camp, from which migrants were directed to other camps and areas (Figures 3.1 and 3.2), in other cases, as in the One Million Plan, entire

Figure 3.2. Newly arrived immigrants line up outside the dining hall in the Sha'ar Aliya immigrant camp near Haifa, 1949. Photograph by Zoltan Kluger, National Photo Collection of Israel, Government Press Office.

camps were designated for immigrants from the same country of origin; Mahane Yisrael, for example, housed immigrants from Poland, and the British Ras el Ain RAF camp, which became Rosh HaAyin camp, housed Jews who came from Yemen (Figure 3.3). In the ways the immigrant camps were used to absorb the immigrants while concentrating and controlling them, they could be analyzed as being akin to other camps of containment, such as detention camps, refugee camps, and other similar formations driven by various mixtures of custody, control, and care that involve explicit and implicit forms of violence.[23]

In 1949, after a record number of 250,000 immigrants entered the country, all housing options were exhausted, and the immigrant camps were filled with increasing numbers of people who remained for indefinite periods of time. People of different sexes, ages, and cultures were densely crowded in halls, crumbling tents, or unsecured canvas huts in harsh weather with horrid sanitary conditions (Figures 3.4, 3.5, and 3.6). Poorly fed by the central soup kitchens of the financially collapsing Jewish Agency, many immigrants were also affected by worsening health problems.[24] At the end of 1949, more than one hundred thousand immigrants

Gathering, Absorbing, and Reordering the Diaspora 97

Figure 3.3. Immigrants from Yemen and Aden in Rosh HaAyin camp, circa 1949. Unknown photographer, Central Zionist Archives, NKH\408889.

lived in these camps, many for over six months, and the failure to settle them had become an impossible financial burden and a political problem that threatened the legitimacy of the new government. After repeated, violently suppressed demonstrations, state officials warned that the camps' inhabitants would create a counterrevolution: "In one day one hundred thousand of such people, . . . concentrated

Figure 3.4. Immigrant children in a tent of Beit Lid immigrant camp, 1949. Photograph by Zoltan Kluger, National Photo Collection of Israel, Government Press Office.

in the camps with no way out . . . will rise up against us, and cause an explosion that will blow away both the government and the Knesset [Israeli parliament] together."[25] A 1949 report by a foreign relief organization summarized, "Historically, the camps in Israel reflect one of the world's most ironic failures: Jews are holding other Jews in camps. It seems that they have learned nothing from their tragedy."[26]

In January 1950 Levi Eshkol, head of the Settling Department of the Jewish Agency, warned, "We have seen the death angel staring us in the face. . . . There will be hunger in the camps because there is no money. . . . We are standing on the verge of a catastrophe," and he suggested that it was necessary "to conduct the immigration according to a plan . . . satisfying both the needs of the immigrants and the needs of the state."[27] However, all suggestions to regulate immigration met a fierce front of political attacks, arguing that they contradicted the Zionist political spirit of faith and patriotism that glorified the state's messianic destiny as "a fight against all odds." Comparing mass immigration with the heroic biblical Israelite exodus from Egypt, Ben-Gurion stated, "As far as I know, there was no accommodation or occupation ready for the sixty thousand leaving Egypt, and nevertheless Moses did not hesitate for a moment over whether he should take them out."[28] But

Figure 3.5. Tents collapsed from the snow at the Rosh HaAyin immigrant camp, 1950. Photograph by David Eldan, National Photo Collection of Israel, Government Press Office.

despite this expressive remark, it seems that sometimes the state needed immigrants more than the immigrants needed the state; Ben-Gurion, following the UN decision on Israel's establishment, said, "The state lacks one fundamental thing, which is its most severe and serious scarcity: it lacks Jews, and as long as this scarcity is not minimally satisfied, there is no certainty to the existence of the state even after its establishment."[29]

Mass immigration was driven not only by Jews' sincere will to immigrate to the new state, but also by strong propaganda from Israeli Zionist emissaries, which combined intimidation, temptation, and deceit. Members of Jewish communities around the world were tempted by a promised life of wealth in Israel and warned that it could be impossible for them to leave their current countries in the future. "People were simply deceived," confessed a state official. "They lied to me," wrote an immigrant who came from Johannesburg to his mother; "I want to return immediately. If I do not return in one week I will starve. . . . This is a country with no god." His mother never received her son's letter; it was archived in one of the Mossad files with the label "Confiscated by the Censor."[30]

Figure 3.6. Light canvas huts toppled over in Beit Lid immigrant camp, 1949. Photograph by Teddy Brauner, National Photo Collection of Israel, Government Press Office.

Camps on the Way to the Promised Land

Around 90 percent of the prestate Jewish population in Palestine originated from Russia and eastern Europe, where Zionism had first developed. However, after the murder of six million Jews in the Holocaust, only one out of three European Jews survived, and while most of the remnant decided to leave the continent, they primarily emigrated to the Americas, South Africa, or Australia, with only around 370,00 survivors going to Israel.[31] As anticipated in the One Million Plan, during the mass-immigration period around half the immigrants were Ashkenazim (coming mainly from Europe), who mostly arrived first (86 percent of the 1948 immigrants), and about half were Mizrahim (from North Africa and the Middle East), who mostly arrived later (71 percent of the 1951 immigrants).[32] For neither population were the camps in Israel an unfamiliar reality.

Many of the European Jews had survived the Nazi camps and arrived in Israel

Figure 3.7. Hashed camp (also known as the Geula transit camp) for Yemeni immigrants in Aden, 1949. Photograph by David Eldan, National Photo Collection of Israel, Government Press Office.

from European displaced persons camps or British internment camps in Cyprus. Transit camps were also a common way in which the Jewish and Zionist organizations and later the Israeli absorption institutions gathered Jews from European, North African, and Asian countries before transferring them to Israel; the conditions were often far from satisfactory in these camps. The Hashed camp in Aden (also called the Geula—Hebrew for "redemption"—transit camp; Figure 3.7) was operated in 1949–50 by the JDC to gather the Jewish communities of Yemen before their transportation to Israel, providing them with food, shelter, and medicine. Around fourteen thousand people were crowded into the camp, which was designed to hold only one thousand people and thus failed to meet even basic needs. Consequently, more than four hundred people, many of them children, died in the camp before being transferred to Israel in Operation Magic Carpet.[33] A camp was created in Tehran for Iraqi Jews, and a camp was erected in Algiers for Jews from Morocco and Tunisia. As described by the Jewish Agency emissary, in the Algiers camp people were packed in "like animals":

Figure 3.8. Barracks and laundry hung between them in Camp d'Arenas near Marseille, France. Unknown photographer, Central Zionist Archives, PHG\1054716.

> From top to bottom, even on the stairwell, people sit with their belongings in their hands. They live, cook, fall ill, give birth, and die, men and women, young and old, everyone together. In a room of five square meters live more than fifty people.[34]

Jews from Libya were sent to a camp near the city of Brindisi in southern Italy, and tens of thousands of Jews from Europe and North Africa passed through Camp d'Arenas near Marseille in France, which locals called the "Jewish Camp" (Figure 3.8). This camp was leased by Jewish institutions between 1945 and 1962; in the prestate period, it was used as a displaced persons camp to gather European refugees before transferring them by boat to Mandatory Palestine. In 1948, after Israel's establishment, sixty-one thousand immigrants passed through this camp, around 60 percent of the immigrants who arrived in Israel that year; in later years, the camp was mostly used for North African Jews on their way to Israel.[35] These camps abroad, which assembled thousands of Jews and facilitated and later tightly controlled their immigration to Israel, were the distant threshold of the Israeli "open-gates" policy, which was altered according to the changing political needs of the state. The horrific descriptions of the reality in some of these camps show the negative side of this instrument, in which people are totally dependent on others for the most critical aspects of their lives.

From Immigrant Camps to the Ma'abara Camps

At the end of 1949, the Jewish Agency gradually began to transform the immigrant camps in Israel; it was decided that as "one hundred thousand Jews are sitting in the camps and live at someone else's expense," food would no longer be provided for the immigrants.[36] The camps were opened; immigrants could continue to live in them, as there was still a housing shortage, but they now had to work. Iraq's unexpectedly giving approval for Jews to leave and the deep financial crisis of the Jewish Agency led Levi Eshkol to suggest a "revolutionary proposal":

> to dismantle the immigrant camps in such a way that, all over the country, where there are any existing settlements, we will attach immigrant housing to them. . . . The immigrants will be employed in foresting works and orchard planting, preparation work, terracing and stone removal. . . . I see the government as a central partner.[37]

In the summer of 1950, most of the newly arrived immigrants were sent straight off the ship to the rapidly erected ma'abara transit camps, created to replace the closed immigrant camps, and by the end of 1951 more than 250,000 people lived in around two hundred ma'abara camps across the country.[38] Like the prestate Zionist wall and tower outpost camps, which were rapidly transformed from a one-off initiative to a mass-produced territorial system, the ma'abarot also quickly became a nationwide network of transit camps, repeatedly implementing the methods and systems of the same territorial and social mechanism. In the first camps, in which every family received its own shelter, either a tent or a hut, the layout was the dense, rigid grid of a military camp, and they were erected next to existing settlements in the center of the country to increase immigrants' chances of finding work (Figures 3.9 and 3.10). However, after 1951, many of the camps were constructed in less-developed areas according to the government's population dispersal policy (Figure 3.11). Thus, the ma'abara camps evolved as a combined solution to mass immigration and state-building; their population had to work and "build the country," and the camps allowed for immigrants' dispersal to frontier territories.

Mass immigration, then, was not a natural phenomenon; rather, it was a result of a political decision to dramatically change Israel's demographic balance, coupled with preplanned large-scale actions in which the camp was a central instrument. At best, the decisions and actions that brought the immigrants in the

Figure 3.9. Ma'abara transit camp near Tiberias, 1951. Photograph by David Eldan, National Photo Collection of Israel, Government Press Office.

Figure 3.10. Dense grid of corrugated-steel shelters in Talpiot ma'abara camp, Jerusalem. Unknown photographer, Central Zionist Archives, PHG\1012616.

Gathering, Absorbing, and Reordering the Diaspora

Figure 3.11. Frontier ma'abara at the foot of the hills of Nazareth, 1951. Photograph by David Eldan, National Photo Collection of Israel, Government Press Office.

camps to the verge of a humanitarian disaster could be seen as mere negligence, but they could also be seen as a calculated risk the government took to achieve its demographic and territorial objectives. In those days, as Israeli historian Tom Segev notes, planning was despised and improvisation highly valued,[39] and Israel saw itself as an improvised and improvising state acting "against all odds." The invention of the ma'abarot could indeed be explained through Alex Jeffrey's concept of "the improvised state," in which the state performs its resourcefulness through a process of "structured improvisation," as in Pierre Bourdieu's term, in which institutions and other actors are involved.[40] Yet this improvisation was based on previous Israeli camp experiments, such as the labor villages (kefarei avoda) established by the JNF in frontier areas (whose residents often lived in temporary structures and were employed in relief projects such as reforestation and construction), or other settlement constellations, such as Hosen moshav (which was established on the lands of the depopulated Palestinian village of Suhmata by immigrants who were members of the Herut right-wing political movement; Figure 3.12). The structured improvisations of the ma'abarot untangled the difficult situation in the immigrant camps and answered the new state's encompassing need to disperse the

Figure 3.12. Tents in Hosen moshav in the Galilee, with the stone houses of the depopulated Palestinian village of Suhmata in the background, 1949. Photograph by Zoltan Kluger, National Photo Collection of Israel, Government Press Office.

immigrants and make them earn their living. But in addition, the ma'abarot also enabled the facilitation of another institutional plan that would incorporate the immigrants in very particular ways and locations.

Dispersing the Immigrants, Populating the Plan

While immigrant camps in Israel and abroad were an essential aspect of the migration's organization and were used to gather immigrants before and after their transportation to Israel, the ma'abara camps developed a nearly opposite role: to disperse immigrants across the country. Only about 6 percent of Mandate Palestine's lands, 1.5 of 26.3 million dunams, were "Jewish owned" by 1948, while the borders of the new Israeli state surrounded 20.6 million dunams, of which only about 13.5 percent (2.8 million dunams) were under formal state or Jewish ownership.[41] (One dunam, a measure used in the Ottoman Empire and in Israel, is equal to a bit more than nine hundred square meters.) Israel's territorial expansion beyond the UN's 1947 proposed Partition Plan of Palestine had to be secured, and while various forms of legal land seizure began almost immediately after the 1948 war, immigration was seen as a necessary part of this task. Thus, around 50 percent of the ma'abara camps were scattered across frontier areas,[42] and the massive flow of immigrants, who in other countries tend to accumulate in urban entry gates, was directed by Israeli authorities to inhabit the frontier. The device of the camp, created to absorb the demographic flood of mass immigration, was therefore adapted to the planning and territorial needs of the new state; "civil conquest" of the frontier was also encouraged by the Israeli army (IDF), whose teams were involved in planning the civil space.

This was not the first time that Zionism used camps to quickly disperse Jewish populations to conquer and then consolidate control of territory. The Zionist settler camps of the prestate Aliyah waves, when temporary tent camps were used to colonize and cultivate desolate frontier areas, were the first demonstration of both the modernist Zionist attitude to land and people and the modernist mechanism for fulfilling it. The land needed to be "tamed," conquered, and controlled in order to turn it into a resource and a territory; the Zionist settlers needed to be formed as part of a modern Jewish nation; and the camp was the rapidly erected instrument that made these goals achievable. Another type of not dissimilar frontier camp that began to be created in the 1950s was the military–civilian Nahal outpost camp. The Nahal unit was initiated by Ben-Gurion in the first year of statehood, creating a method of settlement linking Israeli youth movements with the army while blurring the distinction between security needs and territorial settlement objectives. Each Nahal outpost camp was called *he'ahzut* (Hebrew for "holding on tightly") and combined military service with the creation of new agricultural frontier settlements.[43] The soldiers in the Nahal groups (called *gar'in*, Hebrew for "nucleus" or "kernel") erected camps in areas "too exposed, dangerous or difficult for normal civilian habitation" and divided their time between military and agricultural duties.[44] At the end of their three-year military service they became civilians, often remaining in the outpost and transforming it to a civilian settlement. More than ninety such camps were created in Israel's constantly changing frontier areas,[45] and many of them eventually became permanent kibbutz and moshav settlements.[46]

The inhabitants of the ma'abara camps, however, were not young, enthusiastic pioneers like those who volunteered to join the Zionist settler camps and the later Nahal camps. Rather, these were immigrants, men, women, and children, who were forced by the state to undertake the mission of settling the frontier. Additionally, most of the frontier ma'abara camps were erected to fulfill more ambitious goals, urban rather than rural. These goals had been defined in the framework of a preconceived National Plan that depended on these immigrants to both construct and populate new urban settlements as part of the internal colonization of the Israeli state's frontiers.

The National Plan

Only a few weeks after statehood, during the ongoing 1948 war, Arieh Sharon, then a senior Israeli architect, was invited to establish the Governmental Planning Department to prepare the National Plan that was often referred to as the Sharon Plan, or simply as the Plan, published in 1952 as *Physical Planning in Israel.*[47] The Planning Department, which was attached to the prime minister's office, was made up of professional planners, most of them architects and engineers who had studied in Europe and were committed to the humanistic ideals of modernism. The Plan was regarded as a mechanism to establish Israeli sovereignty over the new territory from a military and political point of view, but it was based on a modernist discourse that regarded society as a set of needs that had to be managed on the basis of "scientific" and "professional" knowledge. Modern urban and regional planning was a powerful method to advance development, spatial regulation, social and cultural assimilation, and a national modernist ideology, and mass immigration was perceived as an opportunity to implement it, as stated in the Plan itself:

> Since the establishment of the State of Israel a great proportion of land is in governmental and public ownership. This facilitates the possibilities of urban expansion and agriculture settlement, and of harmonious and well-balanced population distribution throughout the country. In Israel, however, with its mass immigration, the process entailed in the "distribution of population" does not involve a transfer of the existing population. . . . The directing of the incessant and ever-growing stream of immigration to undeveloped agricultural areas, and to new urban centers, is a relatively simple task.[48]

Thus, the ideal modernist "harmonious and well-balanced" Israeli settlement plan was intended to be achieved through the chaos of mass immigration. This chaos was both the problem and the solution, and the camp was the modern ordering instrument primarily applied to manage it. During the prestate period, Jewish settlements were based mainly on two polarized components: the three large cities of Tel Aviv, Jerusalem, and Haifa, and the kibbutz and moshav small agricultural settlements. Having full governmental support and equipped with newly conquered land and an endless stream of immigrants to settle there, the Planning Department intended to change this polarity and to "thicken" the frontier agricultural settlements with urban ones. The plan was designed for a "well-balanced disposition" of a population of 2,650,000 people (a number reached in 1966) that would change the "anomaly" created during the prestate period in which the ratio of urban to rural populations was the highest in the world. As Sharon explained, "When the state was founded the overwhelming majority of the population, totaling 82 percent, was concentrated in a narrow coastal strip extending from Haifa to Tel Aviv"; the Plan's aim was "to spread the population away from the Mediterranean seaboard into the country's empty areas" by directing the immigrants into the new regions.[49]

Needless to say, the data and aims of the National Plan relate to Israel's Jewish population alone. Dividing the country into twenty-four planning regions, each envisioned as a separate geographic and physical entity, the National Plan supported the creation of relatively small, balanced areas based on close interaction between regional towns and their rural environments. The Plan's desirable model was that of "small Central and West European countries, which are economically, physically and sociologically similar to Israel," in which a large proportion of the population (55–75 percent) inhabited small and medium-sized towns.[50] In order to colonize its territory with Jewish representatives and to realize what was thought to be an ideal European natural balance between town and country for the new country, the fledgling Israeli nation-state adopted a settlement pattern that had evolved in Europe over centuries.

The development towns program, named New Towns in the Sharon Plan as in the original British version, was one of the main instruments for the permanent population distribution policy. Eighteen towns were initially included in the plan; twenty-eight were eventually created according to European models such as Ebenezer Howard's Garden City, Walter Christaller's central place theory, and the later Greater London Plan of 1944.[51] When Sir Patrick Abercrombie, the author of the Greater London Plan, which envisioned the relocation of a million Londoners into twenty New Towns, met Ben-Gurion, the Israeli prime minister proudly remarked that "it was easier to do this in Israel, where we had only to direct the immigrants into the development areas and new towns."[52] The immigrants, of course, were not consulted about their anticipated role. They could be described here as what James Scott called a "shocked population," illustrating how, in situations of enforced planning actions, planners preferred "a 'shocked' population moved abruptly to the new setting" because such a population was easier to discipline to the new order.[53] Thus, although the planners believed in the humanist ideology of modern planning, according to which the "right" planning could create a better world and "serve the interests of the individual and the community," in Sharon's words, they also supported an aggressive population-dispersal policy.[54]

Eliezer Brutzkus, one of the National Plan's senior thinkers, compared the Plan's achievement to the new laborers' cities in the Stalinist Soviet Union, another relevant planning model, and admitted in retrospect, "To be honest, these results were similarly accomplished by us against the free will of the populating subjects."[55] Here, we begin to see the contradiction between the noble aims of modernism and the tragedies they produced, between designing a new, "better" order and then coercing weak people into it by utilizing a situation of chaotic disorder. By forcing immigrants to settle in a dispersed pattern, the planners were

Bridging the Gap

The National Plan opens with an outline that presents the "three-fold Basis for Planning: Land, People, Time," discussing the factor of time as one that does not coincide with the other two factors of land and people. The Plan's attitude to the factor of time is contradictory: on the one hand, it holds that "planning is by its very nature a slow process, demanding the basic survey of economic causes and careful research into physical and social conditions as a prerequisite condition," but on the other hand, it says, it is "urgently necessary for the State to treble its population within a few years." The "quickened tempo of development, and the resultant pressure," warned the planners, "combine to exert a great and sometimes negative influence on planning proper," which might result in irreparable architectural "blots on the landscape."[56] The ma'abara transit camps were a crucial device to avoid having to make compromises caused by the time factor; they bridged the gap between the desire to rapidly absorb and disperse as many immigrants as possible (the factors of land and people) and the time required for the proper planning and construction of their future settlements (Figure 3.13).

As far as the planners were concerned, the most important physical characteristic of these camps was their temporariness; their spatial layout was usually a dense grid of small, provisional units, and the planners avoided providing for any additional investment in them. However, in financial terms, the very creation of the ma'abara camps was a wasteful policy: the camps required imported prefabricated structures, which were paid for in foreign currency and were almost as expensive as permanent houses built from locally sourced materials and labor.[57] Nevertheless, the camps were seen as the best solution for the time factor dilemma: despite all the deficiencies of the temporary absorption, in aspects of the desired systematic creation of balanced settlement texture and its effective population dispersal, the camps gave planners a crucial extension of time for thinking and planning and prevented, at least partially, any hasty creation of permanent facts that were seen as impossible to change later. In *Kibbutz + Bauhaus: An Architect's Way in a New Land*, a book in which Sharon reflects on his own work, an aerial photograph captioned "A neighbourhood unit in the new town of Yokneam, being

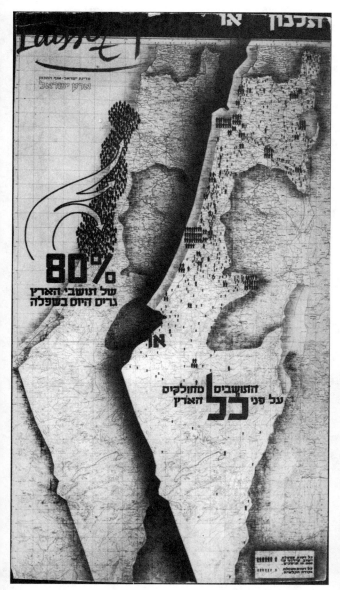
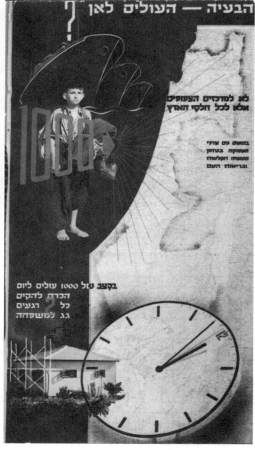

Figure 3.13. Panels exhibited in the town-planning exhibition, Tel Aviv museum, 1950. The panels read, "80% of the population live today on the coastal plain—the population [needs] dispersal" and "The problem—the immigrants—where to? Not to the overcrowded centers but to all parts of the country. According to the needs of work, security, industry, agriculture, and the health of the people. At a pace of 1000 immigrants each day—there is a necessity to build every two minutes a family dwelling unit." Yael Aloni Photo Collection. Courtesy of the Azrieli Architectural Archive, Arieh Sharon Collection.

Figure 3.14. An aerial photograph of Yokneam ma'abara and a neighborhood in the New Town built uphill from it. Yael Aloni Photo Collection. Courtesy of Azrieli Architectural Archive, Arieh Sharon Collection.

constructed by the immigrants living in provisional shacks along the road" (Figure 3.14) captures the temporary camp and the permanent settlement as being part of a single process of a rationalized spatial production. A close-up photograph of this temporary "settlement factory," however, shows the gap between the organized building blocks of the modernist settlement on the hill and the miserable camp where the captured labor force of immigrants was forced to live (Figure 3.15).

Being suspended in the camps meant that immigrants lost control over their

Figure 3.15. Yokneam's building blocks with one of the ma'abara inhabitants–laborers, with a view of the camp's shacks behind him and the neighborhood up the hill. Unknown photographer, Central Zionist Archives, NKH\402105.

own destiny; they were easily manipulated in favor of the dominant part of society and were stripped of ability to act as autonomous subjects. Modernity here served as the ideology, the goal, and the tool to shape chaotic mass immigration into an ideal new order, while sacrificing the well-being of the immigrants who served as the raw material for this grand project. While the early Zionist settler camps were formed by voluntary civilian pioneers, the frontier ma'abara camps, many of which were used to occupy and control Israel's newly conquered territories after 1948, were based on forced pioneering. As such, we can say that the ma'abarot were a hybrid of the closed immigrant camps, which were used for containment and social ordering, and the earlier Zionist settler camps, which were used for territorial expansion, combining camps that controlled people with camps that controlled the land. In addition, as the population in the ma'abarot was composed mainly of Mizrahi Jews and the established part of society was predominantly Ashkenazi, these camps continued the ethnic separation initiated by the immigrant camps and created an ethnically based division of the Israeli Jewish society. Consequently, the ma'abara camps have become the signifier of ethnically based inequality in Israel, representing the violence and humiliation that the Ashkenazi establishment inflicted on the vulnerable Mizrahi immigrants.

The Israeli government invited immigrants to Israel, arranging their transportation to and absorption in their new state so as to enhance Israel's image as "the ingathering of exiles," its demographic power, and its territorial abilities, yet the government excluded these people from Israeli society and resources once they got there, despite their role in forming Israel's image, territory, economy, and military power. In combining the two types of camp, the ma'abara seems to be a unique spatial phenomenon, an "invention" that under the disorder and state of emergency of mass immigration enabled the modern Israeli project to be realized.

American Jewish architect Louis Kahn was invited in 1949 by the Israel Housing Survey Committee to develop ideas for four hundred thousand housing units for immigrants. His plan shows an alternative model to the ma'abarot and development towns. From a quick look at Kahn's drawings, it is evident that his design did not stray far from a grid-laid plan of prefabricated shelters, similar to the curved Nissen hut, with palm trees adding to the Mediterranean (even Orientalist) imaginary (Figure 3.16). Yet Kahn's proposal, which included relatively generous plots containing semipermanent parabolic shell houses that could be rapidly erected and enlarged in the future, challenged the temporary aspect of the camp by allowing it to gradually develop into a permanent settlement.[58] Kahn argued that the creation of permanent homes would cost only one-third more than the temporary, disposable facilities, but his argument concerned more than economic solutions: "Kahn believed that such an approach was not only practical and cost-effective but profoundly human. Having been an immigrant himself in America, Kahn intuitively grasped the importance of privacy, stability, and roots for the olim [immigrants] in Israel."[59] Kahn's plan, however, was never realized; the planners preferred the rigidly planned modern towns with their "properly" designed housing blocks, a solution that required immigrants' suspension in the dispensable top-down created camps.

Ordered Disorder, Strategic Confusion: The Israeli National (Dis)order of Things

In *The Shock Doctrine,* Naomi Klein analyzes the ways certain leaders exploit crises in order to advance controversial policies while citizens are too busy recovering emotionally and physically to resist effectively.[60] It is implied that some crises may be created with the intention of pushing through unpopular reforms in their wake, enabling democratic regimes to undemocratically enforce certain policies. Although Klein discusses the method in the context of capitalism and free market policies over the last thirty years, it is possible to compare it with the reality and conditions created during Israel's mass-immigration period. While the strategic decision for the open-gates policy originated from the need for rapid growth in the country's Jewish population and from the utilization of a particular historical and political moment of fundamental global shifts that enabled the flow of Jewish immigrants to Israel, flooding the country with immigrants brought the state, in early 1950, to the "verge of a catastrophe," in Eshkol's words. Even though individual immigrants were put at real risk, the near catastrophe formed a humanitarian crisis, and with it the opportunity for the state to forcefully implement its population dispersal policy and its ambitious National Plan.[61] Democratic societies and laws could not allow people to be forced to live in frontier settlements to populate the Plan. However, the ordered disorder of mass immigration and its resultant chaos created a de facto state of emergency that allowed the ma'abara camps to be created, populated, and managed, suspending the "shocked population" of immigrants there until the frontier development towns were built.

Later informal Israeli state policies governing the form and function of various camps have been similarly analyzed as using disorder and confusion as a governance strategy that facilitated the management of specific populations outside the state's democratic order. Wendy Pullan uses the concept of "strategic confusion" to analyze Israeli governance policy in the occupied territories, saying the policy deliberately creates a "logic of disorder" and a system of confusing and deceptive conditions.[62] Yehouda Shenhav and Yael Berda also examine the mode of governance in the occupied territories as a deliberately irrational bureaucratic apparatus, whose effectiveness is achieved through its unpredictable mechanisms.[63] This is the juridical and governmental "state of exception" under which were formed the Jewish outposts in the occupied Palestinian territories and camps in other areas discussed later in this book. The concept of ordered disorder is used by Yonathan Paz to examine Israel's response to the influx of African asylum seekers, for whom the Holot camp, which will be discussed in chapter 7, was established.[64] It is in these "emergency" situations when camps flourish, even if these emergencies were deliberate and man-made.

During the 1990s, a second generation of immigrant camps appeared in Israel's periphery to accommodate the new wave of mass immigration arriving from

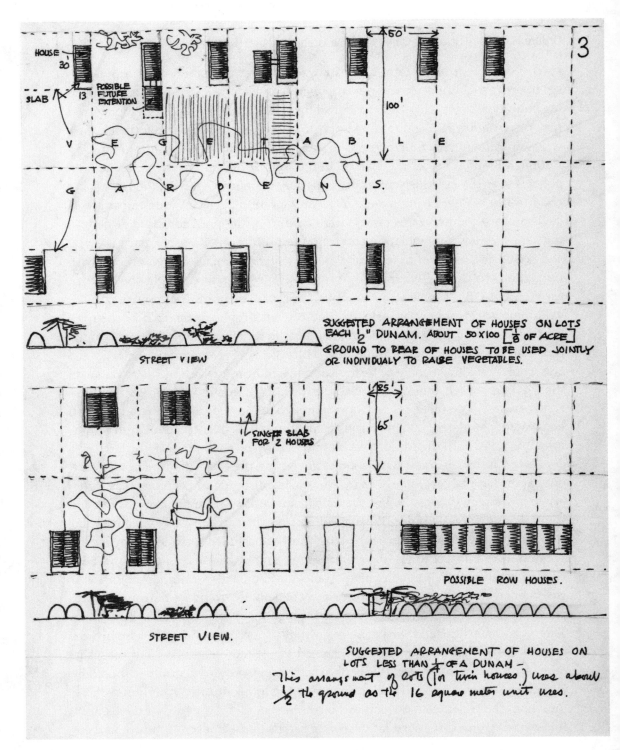

Figure 3.16. Louis Kahn's drawings, including site plans, views, and details for semipermanent dwellings for immigrants. Courtesy of the Architectural Archives, Stuart Weitzman School of Design, University of Pennsylvania.

1. Foundation poured.

2. House slabs laid. Slabs is made large enough to house all segments it takes to produce 1 house.

3. Segments poured - allowed to cure. and erected.

4. Segments completed.

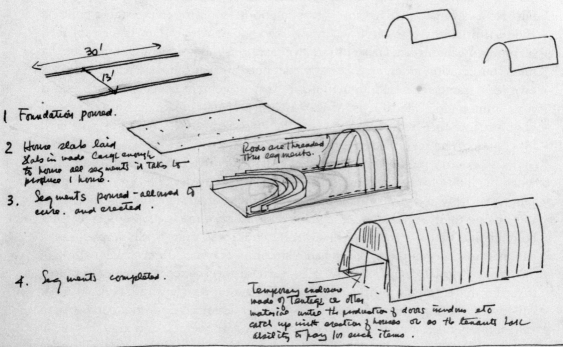

Rods are threaded thru segments.

Temporary enclosure made of Tentage or other material until the production of doors, windows etc catch up with creation of houses or as the tenants lose ability to pay for such items.

Ethiopia and the former USSR (Figure 3.17). It seems that in Israel–Palestine, ordered disorder is created whenever there is a drastic territorial and demographic change, and camps appear in these situations not only as an emergency solution but also as a way to manage specific populations according to the state's political and territorial interests, often according to ad hoc policies rather than established planning mechanisms. These different geopolitical situations are similar to the mass-immigration emergency of early statehood in that the state acts outside its own legal frameworks and regulations in its management of specific populations (e.g., immigrants, Palestinians, African asylum seekers), creating a blurred system of governance that frequently allows for the increased use of force and is sheltered by a "state of emergency" that enables legal exceptions.

This control method characterized all Israeli policies throughout the 1950s, when the multiple organizations (such as the Jewish Agency, the Planning Department, the army and government offices) and the unclear division of responsibilities among them created an ambiguous and informal mode of action.[65] It is not coincidental that the National Plan itself, which was almost fully implemented as a national megaproject, never had a statutory status and never went through any proper legislative procedures.[66] Hence, these governance strategies of ordered disorder and strategic confusion appear to be a pattern in the Israeli national (dis)order of things that repeats itself whenever actions that do not comply with the state's democratic order are required for its ethnocratic and arguably racial objectives. It is no wonder that different types of camps, whether created for the expansion of or for the exclusion of specific populations, tend to appear under this mode of governance.

The story of young Israel is often presented as a story of success, an almost-miraculous achievement obtained by a joint effort of the Israeli society, hiding not only the now well-documented displacement of the Palestinians, but also the resort to coercive methods to direct arriving Jewish immigrants. The instrument of the camp, which enabled the spatial and social implementation of the utopian modernist Zionist ideology, was also the instrument that allowed the state to use force on vulnerable populations, creating a difficult reality for many in the name of this ideology. "We can say that existence is modern," states Bauman, "as far as it is effected and sustained by design, manipulation, management, engineering";[67] the tragedy of modern mass-population projects, including the mechanism of the camp as one of their central features, lies in their dehumanizing effect on the human beings they manipulate, engineer, design, and manage.

Israeli mass immigration and its associated camps are usually presented as a necessary evil or an acceptable and unavoidable part of the labor pains of the new state, and of the new nation's inventive improvisation. The open-gates policy is presented as the only possible humanist response to the "natural" flow of immigrants, the rapidly erected camps are discussed as the only means of quickly

Gathering, Absorbing, and Reordering the Diaspora 119

Figure 3.17. A temporary camp of mobile homes (trailers) in Sderot before being populated by newly arrived immigrants, 1991. Photograph by Moshe Milner, National Photo Collection of Israel, Government Press Office.

absorbing them, and the improvisational spirit of the young state is celebrated. This, as we have seen, is only part of the story. Mass immigration was not only a mass-rescue operation and a response to a messianic call; it was also a mass appropriation of immigrants to the necessities of a young state coming into being, and its politically disputed effect was a man-made crisis that put immigrants at risk. This man-made crisis followed and enabled the implementation of two consecutive plans, the One Million Plan and the National Plan, with the first managing the arrival of mass immigration to Israel and the second administering their desired territorial dispersal, plans that both used the camp as a central instrument.

The story of mass immigration and the camps is first and foremost one of modernism and the nation-state with its related biopolitical and territorial practices; the masses of "right" (Jewish) people together with the device of the camp ensured that the territories conquered in the 1948 Arab–Israeli war would be immediately colonized in the "right" planned manner. The same instrument that was used to gather the Diaspora Jews by Zionist organizations abroad was used to absorb and disperse them across their new country, bridging the gap between the chaotic state of emergency (and the immigrants who were part of it) and the well-organized, modernist National Plan. However, these camps, which combined Israel's expansionist and exclusionist policies, were not only temporary spaces, planned to completely vanish from the landscape as soon as their role ended and the chaotic state of emergency was settled. These camps also entailed a specific mode of governance that deeply influenced their dwellers, who were essentially stored there until they were used as construction material for the modernist Zionist project, in all aspects of their life. Chapter 4 focuses on Tel-Yeruham, a ma'abara camp created on Israel's southern frontier, further investigating the ma'abara as a tool that was not only a physical form but also a social and governmental unit that enabled the state to temporarily suspend the autonomy of its new citizens in order to achieve its ambitious national goals.

4

FORCED PIONEERING
Settling Israel's Frontiers

If we were discussing settling the frontier today as we discussed it two years ago, we would not have sent even one family there. At the time we ourselves didn't know about the conditions in these areas, we did not know what the immigrants would go through.

—Giora Yoseftal, conference for ma'abara managers, 1954

At the heart of the Negev desert, cut off from the rest of the world, Tel-Yeruham ma'abara was established in 1951 as a transit camp for Jewish immigrants who had been sent to settle Israel's newly conquered territories. Surrounded by nothingness and struggling with harsh, arid conditions, most immigrants were placed in an environment very different from the cities and villages they had left and had to cope in their new state with an extreme situation they had never experienced before. The state, though, decided it was necessary to bring Jewish immigrants, men, women, and children, to this place in order to advance the central Zionist and later national mission to settle the frontier. The remote location, with very limited transport connections to the outside world, no regular work, and a severe shortage of basic supplies and services such as food, education, and health care, made the immigrants completely dependent on the authorities who had brought them there straight off the ship.[1]

Tel-Yeruham, located more than thirty-five kilometers south of Be'er-Sheva, then Israel's southernmost Jewish town, was a temporary camp for only a few years before it was turned into a development town named Yeruham. But although the government sent thousands of immigrants there according to its population-dispersal policy, erecting a second ma'abara camp in Yeruham in the early 1960s, the town grew very slowly, and still struggles against its label as one of the most deprived Jewish settlements in Israel.[2] Like other ma'abara camps created in frontier areas that later developed into peripheral development towns, Tel-Yeruham was

121

122   Forced Pioneering

not inhabited by keen immigrants who had gone there voluntarily like the Zionist settlers in the prestate frontier agricultural settlements.[3] Rather, these immigrants had had their mission imposed on them. They were left suspended in these camps until Israel's permanent frontier towns and villages had been planned and constructed, while being subjected to coercive measures that also suspended their status as free and autonomous citizens. These actions were justified by a powerful national ideology of advanced modern development that supported Israel's utopian and humanist self-image, although its goals were pursued on the backs of the immigrants.

Yeruham's ma'abara camps, which were part of Israel's nationwide ma'abara project, stand at the center of this chapter. The ma'abara is examined here as an instrument of territorial control and social engineering, and it is analyzed, through its spatial, governmental, and human aspects, as a temporary instrument allowing the control and management of a vulnerable population of Jewish immigrants under a coercive and centralized mode of governance serving the interests of the state. It is exposed as a device used by Israel to cope with the emergency situation of mass immigration while managing and exploiting immigrants according to the state's various territorial, ideological, ethnoracial, and economic interests, rather than according to its democratic laws and values.

There is no question that the ma'abara camps were spaces of neglect, subordination, and exploitation that left indelible marks on the immigrants and on specific sections of Jewish society in Israel, mostly Mizrahi Jews, who were the predominant group occupying these enduring camps. Yet the situation of the residents in these camps was more complex. The immigrants in the ma'abarot were not entirely passive; rather, they carried out actions of cultural resilience and political resistance, indicating that even in such terrible conditions people do not completely lose their power to act. A deeper understanding of the complexity of the camp and its prominent role in shaping Israeli spaces and society can be gained by examining how the camps in Yeruham, like many other ma'abarot, were erected and managed, influencing the lives of their residents while eventually becoming a permanent development town that partly reproduced the logics of the camp. Tracing the minor everyday spatial practices and political actions of the camps' residents can reveal the immigrants' efforts to recover their autonomy and agency in difficult conditions and can begin to reveal the camp not only as a spatial mechanism of control but also as a space of resourcefulness and transformation.

A Camp in the Desert

Tel-Yeruham camp was set up with the intention of establishing "a city in the Negev, in the desert, in a desolate area which offers passage for infiltrators and smugglers from the Gaza Strip to Jordan."[4] This was how Giora Yoseftal, head of the Absorption Department in the Jewish Agency, presented the reason for establishing Tel-Yeruham when he coincidently met Amnon Zair, a kibbutz member who immediately volunteered for the task of setting up and managing the camp.[5] Yoseftal's words, uttered less than two years after the Negev had been fully conquered by Israel in March 1949, indicate a desire to establish military and civilian control over Israel's new territories. The word "infiltrators" reflects Israel's perception and description of Arab populations as part of the state's postwar Emergency Regulations, which were designed to strictly control their movement into and within Israel's domains.[6] Following the war and the 1949 cease-fire agreements, Israel's territory had expanded far beyond what had been envisaged in the UN's partition plan. Although these were internationally recognized as Israel's borders, they were still not under full control, and many in the army considered them indefensible. The government and the IDF saw new civilian settlements, including dozens of immigrant transit camps, as an essential way of achieving a better hold over the new frontier territories.

The postwar cooperation among the IDF, the Jewish Agency, and the government's Planning Department in deciding on the location of new settlements is evidence of the tight relationship between the new civilian settlements and what were defined as Israel's military "security needs."[7] A document published by the IDF in September 1950, entitled "A Work Policy for Planning the Location of Settlements," states that the army's Planning Department would be involved in the location and planning of all types of settlements, including ma'abara camps, a territorial attitude reflected in other military documents:[8]

> It was clear to us that the war was not yet over, [that] as long as the whole country was not settled and cultivated we would not have control over its whole territory, that every area neglected by us would be invaded by an Arab.[9]

While the government's Planning Department, controlled directly by the prime minister's office, planned the territory from a professional viewpoint according to planning principles, such as a balanced population spread across various types of settlements, the IDF planning teams designed the civilian space from a military viewpoint, including the rapid creation of frontier "battlefront settlements" to quickly populate empty frontier areas.[10]

The strategy of providing civilian settlements with a military territorial role was a continuation of the earlier Zionist civilian–military practices discussed in the previous chapters. Such practices were adopted as a technique employed in other state-building and border-security enterprises around the world during that period. The frontier villages in the Demilitarized Zone established between South Korea and North Korea in the 1950s and 1960s, in which villagers were trained as both soldiers and farmers while living in a civilian environment surrounded by

124   Forced Pioneering

fences and watchtowers, is an example of such frontier settlements. The South Korean planners of these strategic settlements adopted, unsurprisingly, the Israeli kibbutz model, sharing the motto "Farming while fighting, fighting while farming."[11] The frontier military–civilian agricultural colonies created since 1960 in the Dominican Republic's borderland with Haiti, which were part of the state's nationalization process, are another example of settlements being used to fortify borders while gaining control over frontier regions.[12]

The Negev desert, an arid frontier area covering 60 percent of Israel's territory, had hardly been settled by the Zionist movement before statehood and was mostly inhabited by Bedouin tribes, who had lived in the area for centuries. The Israeli interest in conquering the Negev followed the strategic need for access to the Red Sea, and after statehood, settling the Negev was recognized by both the army and the government as a security necessity.[13] During the 1948 Arab–Israeli war, Prime Minister David Ben-Gurion stated that in the Negev, Israel had to "make every spot bloom with a bit of water . . . build a settlement near every wellspring," suggesting that a settlement plan should be established according to existing water sources.[14] Yet Ben-Gurion's vision of a blooming desert was not generated by agricultural ambitions or aesthetic aspirations; rather, it was an expression of a deep political anxiety:

> If you look at the map, you will see that in the south [of Israel] there are plenty of empty places. And nothing is as horrifying to me as this emptiness—not because nature does not tolerate emptiness, but because people do not tolerate it and politics does not tolerate the emptiness.[15]

With the conquest of the Negev, then, another frontier that needed taming had been created. Yet the 1949 government's Negev committee recommended that, instead of agricultural frontier settlements like those created before statehood, the state should promote the establishment of mining towns to utilize the Negev's unique natural materials rather than counting on the scarce water sources in the arid area.[16] Not only did this follow Israel's developmental and economic plans for extracting the new resources it now controlled, but, above all, it met the state's territorial demands for its empty southern region, which, according to Ben-Gurion, could suffer no void.

Architecture of Suspension

"There was nothing there," reflected Zair, writing in his diary about the desert area chosen by the Jewish Agency for the establishment of Tel-Yeruham; "not a path, nor a paved road, nothing—only one water hole called by the Arabs Bir Rakhma."[17]

The difficult conditions did not deter the settling institutions or the people sent on their behalf; after all, occupying the frontier had always been a central Zionist strategy. The exact location of the camp was selected for its proximity to three essential features: an existing road, the Oil Road that had been laid by the Iraq Petroleum Company in 1941, during the British Mandate; a well that provided two cubic meters of water per day; and the kaolin strip mines in the area, which were considered a potential source of extraction and employment.[18] These three essential material elements for the camp were in line with its function and location. Just as for the earlier Zionist outpost camps and other camps discussed in this book, a nearby transportation infrastructure was essential to the creation and maintenance of the isolated camp; with no water infrastructure in the area, the camp's location in an arid desert environment made a nearby water source a necessity; and given the difficulty of developing agriculture in the desert area, the ma'abara dwellers' dependence on labor demanded there be another form of employment.

An IDF reserve force was assigned to guard the ma'abara and its families, establishing a permanent military presence, and the press enthusiastically depicted the camp's establishment as a quasi-military operation:

> Within a few hours, with the speed of the wall and tower days, the new ma'abara in Tel-Yeruham was erected yesterday, in the heart of the wilderness. . . . With thirty trucks, utility vans and jeeps, workers, prefabricated timber and corrugated-steel huts, tent fabric, and all that is required for the seed of a settlement were brought to the site. . . . At 10:15 a.m. the corrugated-steel huts and first tents were already erected, the area was marked in order to be fenced, and a kitchen was installed. At 12 noon the Israeli flag was raised on the flagpole, . . . in a short formal ceremony three cypress trees were planted, . . . [and] a sprout of a settlement already protruded from the hill that three hours before was completely empty.[19]

This account of the particular material components for the creation of the camp—trucks and jeeps, tent fabric and transportable prefabricated structures, workers, three cypress trees, and an Israeli flag (as well as barbed wire, as in the wall and tower and immigrant camps)—illustrates how the camp became a modern technology integral to Israeli statecraft, combining speed, embedded temporariness, and national symbolism needed to settle the wilderness. The reference to the quasi-military wall and tower settlements is not coincidental; Tel-Yeruham was similar to those frontier outpost camps used as territorial mechanisms functioning between the military and the civilian. "It was like a military camp," described one resident who moved to Tel-Yeruham as a child; "there was a weapon shed with two Sten guns, three Czech rifles, and two hand grenades. . . . A fence surrounded the camp with smoke land mines, which the children enjoyed activating."[20] Indeed, expectations of security problems were met shortly after the camp was erected, as was immediately reported in the daily press:

> Tel-Yeruham, the new settlement in the Negev, established only ten days ago, has already managed to make "contact" with infiltrators [who] tried yesterday to steal a tent. . . . The guards noticed them and shot in their direction. The infiltrators escaped, leaving the tent behind.[21]

This minor security incident confirmed Tel-Yeruham's formal role as a frontier settlement, established to strengthen the territoriality of the new Israeli state. With the creation of the ma'abara that "protruded from the hill," a territorial void perceived as a potential security and political problem instantly became an active contested frontier zone in which the camp played a central role, with the military assuming the role of defending the civilians from the "natives" or "infiltrators." The mix of civilian and military systems in both planning and daily life was clearly an integral part of Israel not only before it was established but also afterward. Yet it is important to remember that Tel-Yeruham's inhabitants were neither soldiers nor ideological pioneers in the service of the new nation but immigrants who were compelled to live in these exposed, quasi-military conditions. The architectural and material characteristics of the camp, primarily its spatial temporariness and its multiple degrees of separation from the rest of Israeli space and society and from its immediate surroundings, were central to the camp's function as a spatial instrument that contained immigrants while using them for the state's territorial needs.

Temporary by Design

Tel-Yeruham was designed and created slightly differently from the other ma'abara camps owing to its exceptionally remote geographical location and the challenging desert conditions. Zair considered planning "a ma'abara which [would] be a bit nicer and more spacious," and the desert camp was supplied with dual-family Swedish timber huts, imported as ready-made kits. However, under pressure to absorb immigrants immediately, Yoseftal insisted that construction of the more comfortable huts should wait and that tents should be erected in the meantime, "the same as in every other place."[22] A few days after the initial Tel-Yeruham camp had been set up, more tents were added, providing the immigrants who arrived at the desert camp in mid-January with scant protection from the desert storms and freezing winter nights (Figure 4.1). Despite the good intentions to provide better conditions in the frontier camp, it was only in June 1951 that Tel-Yeruham's inhabitants celebrated their entry into the prefabricated huts, after six months living in tents (Figure 4.2).

Figure 4.1. Tents, kitchen hut, Romanian immigrants, and the surrounding desert in Tel-Yeruham ma'abara camp, 1951. Photograph by Fritz Schlesinger, Central Zionist Archives, PHG\1013051.

Figure 4.2. Immigrants assemble the prefabricated timber shelters in Tel-Yeruham, 1951. Photograph by Fritz Schlesinger, Central Zionist Archives, NKH\401977.

128   Forced Pioneering

Thousands of imported prefabricated temporary shelters, including tents and huts made from timber, corrugated steel, and canvas, functioned as the architectural instrument for the quick absorption of mass immigration. These were part of Israel's material assemblage for its ambitious demographic, territorial, and planning project, the ephemeral, transportable spatial "scaffolding" for the state's National Plan until it was set into its modernist cement blocks. However, these provisional structures were expensive compared to permanent housing built with local labor and material, and as they were bought from suppliers abroad, shipping increased the cost and payment was made in foreign currency. Yet these provisional structures were an integral part of the ma'abara project, with temporariness ensuring that no physical sign would remain of this brief distortion in space and time on the way to appropriate planning, and resolving the issue of ownership created by the principle of "possession through use."[23] Temporariness made it possible to deny the immigrants the right of possession and therefore made them displaceable if the state wished to send them to other locations, and it also ensured that the land could be vacated for the state's redevelopment projects, which were often awarded to companies aligned with particular political parties. In the opinion of the planners in the government's Planning Department, further investment in the camps might prolong their existence and turn them into permanent slums, and they were expected to be dismantled as soon as possible: "We are not flooring the huts not only because of lack of cement," explained Yoseftal, "but also because of budget issues. . . . I don't think it's worth spending these amounts on huts that will stand for only a few months."[24]

The spatial arrangement of the camps also guaranteed they would be provisional. Shelters were usually arranged in dense grids, even in vacant frontier areas, allowing the use of minimum infrastructure, thus making it easier to manage the camp and preventing residents from expanding their shelters and settling there permanently. While planners saw temporary absorption as essential, the dangerously poor conditions of temporary living, with the astonishingly high number of child deaths in the ma'abarot—doubling the national child mortality rate at the time—did not work as well for the immigrants: "We must draw your attention," wrote a regional doctor to the Jewish Agency about another frontier camp, "to the severe sanitary conditions in the ma'abara, and to the unsuitable sanitary toilet structures; tragedies have already happened, and it is a fact that two weeks ago a child fell into the toilet pit in the ma'abara and lost his life. This is the third case in this place."[25]

Although Tel-Yeruham was more spacious than other ma'abara camps, other conditions were more difficult because of its isolated location and difficult climate. Inhabitants drew water from the nearby well, and food was brought from Be'er-Sheva every few days. Although the camp was connected to electricity in its first year (Figure 4.3), there was no sewage system, and, as in the other ma'abara

Forced Pioneering 129

Figure 4.3. Connecting Tel-Yeruham to electricity, 1951. Photograph by Werner Brown, Jewish National Fund Photography Archive.

camps, educational and health services were poor: "In Tel-Yeruham there is no phone and the nearest doctor is 53 kilometers away," reported one of the participants in a Ministry of Labor committee overseeing ma'abara social services.[26] The camp's ex-residents remember this state of abandonment well: "It was a deserted place," described one immigrant who lived there; "you could have died there and no one would have known. There was a military communications link to

Be'er-Sheva police station, which most of the time did not work. There was no one to recharge its battery."[27]

Beyond the difficult everyday conditions, the situation of suspended temporariness was in itself a form of abandonment, denying the immigrants the autonomy to plan their own lives while undermining their sense of being: "Although people got shelter and employment (not always stable), the atmosphere in the ma'abara was one of enduring temporariness, temporariness that destroys family life, destroys the human being, and limits the will to make an effort," wrote an Israeli architect in the early 1950s.[28] Michael Biton, who was Yeruham's mayor and a second-generation ma'abara dweller, also reflected on the difficulties faced by his family in the temporary camp:

> The ma'abara dismantled the family cell, the community cell. [Protracted] temporariness makes people lose hope. People do not know their direction. . . . Temporariness hurts the community, one's strength, hurts the home as a place that delineates a proper orientation. The temporary house was a catastrophe. Temporariness cannot be praised.[29]

While Israel introduced the ma'abarot as an improvised relief-shelter project, the fact that they were planned as temporary spaces forced immigrants to deal with a difficult reality. While abandoning the immigrants in bad physical conditions was the most visible problem, suspending them in an in-between zone of protracted temporariness appears to have been even more destructive. The imposed temporariness of the ma'abara camp, which had no specific end date, could be described as a radical political space where the state not only directed immigrants to a particular place but also took hostage their ability to plan their own future. While this reality was part of Israel's chaotic situation in its early emergency years, it was also embedded in the adoption of the camp as an acceptable instrument for suspending immigrants in space and time until the frontier development towns had been properly planned and built and were ready to be populated.

Multilayered Separation, Unarticulated Spatiality

The ongoing temporariness of Tel-Yeruham and its geographical isolation separated the frontier camp from Israeli space and society. "They put people here like in a cage; the desert was the bars of the cage," described one of the camp's immigrants years later.[30] Yet the camp was not separated just from Israeli space and society by the bars of the desert; it was also physically separated from its immediate environment. A barbed-wire fence surrounded and protected the ma'abara, separating the "safe" internal area of the camp from the "dangerous" outside (Figure 4.4). Another aspect of Tel-Yeruham's spatial separation was the camp's posi-

Figure 4.4. A sign reading "Tel-Yeruham ma'abara" and indicating the camp, which is surrounded by barbed-wire fence. Unknown photographer, Central Zionist Archives, PHG\1078970.

tion on a hill as an all-seeing eye to overlook the threatening surroundings. Like the wall and tower watchtower, the camp's elevated location turned it into a panoptic observation point, transforming the land around it into an object of instrumental observation and seeking to control the surrounding landscape not by actual use but by territorial appropriation.

Yet other, more intangible modes of separation were created by the camp's physicality and materiality. The invasive spatial unit of the camp, with its provisional imported structures laid out according to a rigid plan, was alien to the area. Like other institutional camps, the ma'abarot were a clear product of industrialization, measured according to rational aspects of logistics and cost, and their architectural repetition was indifferent to the needs of their inhabitants and the local environment in which they were erected. Tel-Yeruham's temporary Swedish huts, designed for a cold climate, landed in the heart of the desert, where they were balanced on concrete blocks on a hill, with no foundations, ready to be dismantled and relocated at any time.[31]

Erected according to a 1:1,000 plan designed by the Jewish Agency's Technical Department and placed on top of the hill, the huts formed a pattern resembling a village street (Figure 4.5). In the architectural drawing, the ma'abara looks like a reasonably planned seed of a settlement, yet an aerial photo shows how deceptive the plan was. The clear, colorful division between private, public, and green areas

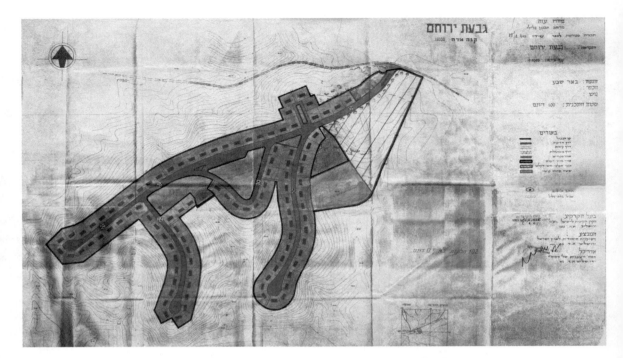

Figure 4.5. Tel-Yeruham plan titled "A Detailed Plan for the Labor Village Named Yeruham Hill," 1951. Private collection.

shown in the drawing disappears in the gray-scale aerial photo showing the vast arid environment surrounding the huts (Figure 4.6). The repetitive placement of huts on the scrappy desert landscape seems to lack substantial planning considerations. Although on paper the camp layout can be imagined to be a normal rural settlement, its actual space was very far from a standard village setting, more resembling a military camp, which was what it eventually came to be.

The ma'abara was separated from its surroundings, but the environment of the camp itself suffered from an unarticulated mixture of private and public realms that deeply influenced the lives of its inhabitants. The second ma'abara camp, erected in 1962 to house more than 150 immigrant families in densely packed prefabricated dual-family asbestos huts, reflects even more clearly the constraints of the limited and alienating instrumentality of camp planning. Like most of the ma'abarot, the camp was designed with no spatial flexibility to go beyond a strict, blunt, military-like binary grid of standardized anonymous structures, leaving no loose ends to be differently accommodated and utilized, and resisting any stamp of individuality (Figure 4.7).

"The sands were all the same and the shacks were all the same," wrote Israeli author Ronit Matalon in a novel on her life in a different ma'abara; "during the long dark nights people got lost in the dunes, knocked on strange doors, look-

Forced Pioneering 133

Figure 4.6. Aerial photograph of Tel-Yeruham, with the ma'abara camp at lower left, 1957. Yeruham Archive and Survey of Israel collection.

ing for their shack. People sometimes wandered lost in the moonlight until three o'clock in the morning."[32] The total order of the camps created by architectural uniformity and repetition formed what James Scott called a "mystifying disorder,"[33] an order that was legible to planners and administrators but not to the residents, who experienced problems of orientation in their confusing environment of indistinguishable units with no distinctive landmark, an environment they had to navigate daily.

Life poured out of these overcrowded huts into the space of the camp, blurring the separation between the camp's private and public areas: "In the ma'abara a person's life is uncovered and he does not have his own private corner. All the children are outside, all the families together. A roof alone cannot provide a feeling of privacy," reflected an Israeli architect at the time.[34] A planner in Yeruham who lived in the second ma'abara as a child remembers it as "a ghetto—everyone penetrated everyone's life. There was no privacy."[35] This condition, in which the unsatisfactory, minimal, private space of the shelters and the public realm of the camp are mixed with no clear distinction, was another form of the immigrants'

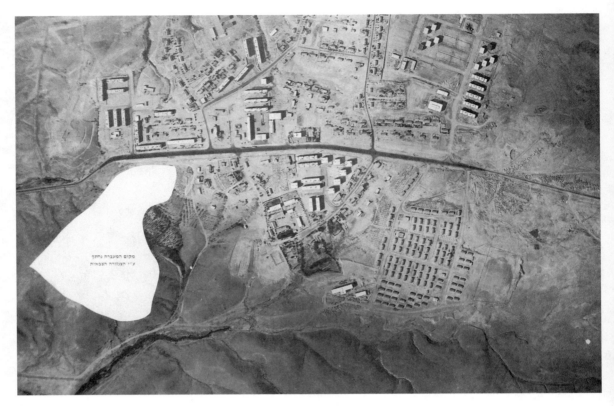

Figure 4.7. Aerial photograph of Yeruham, with the second ma'abara camp at lower right, 1964. The area of the first ma'abara, which became a military camp, was cut out by the censor. Yeruham Archive and Survey of Israel collection.

dehumanization and another way in which they were repressed by the state. Although Agamben's observation that "in the camp city and house became indistinguishable" relates to the camp's paradigmatic indistinction between the private sphere of life in the household (*oikos*) and the public political sphere of the city (*polis*), it also highlights the camp's de facto blurred public–private boundaries, where state power can either penetrate to or abandon every sphere.[36]

These multiple modes of separation and unarticulated spatiality in the camp, which disconnected its residents from their local environment and from the rest of Israeli society while blurring their private and public realms, interrupted immigrants' connection to their new landscape and becoming autonomous citizens of the state and society they had joined. Completely uprooted and prevented from putting down new roots, the immigrants of Tel-Yeruham camp were kept totally dependent on the authorities who had placed and suspended them there. The more centrally located ma'abara camps, established next to existing settlements, were also segregated both physically and socially from their environments: "All ma'abara dwellers said that life outside the ma'abara seemed to them to be part of a different world, a much better and more privileged world, to which they did not belong," reflected a state official during that period; "it is as if they are sitting in a closed ghetto, alien, psychologically distant from the city."[37] Whether located in the frontier of the country or in the frontier of the city, then, the ma'abara dwellers were disconnected from their surroundings, with the social separation reflecting the spatial one.

Instruments of Control and Abandonment

Israel's total control over immigrants at all stages of the immigration process, from their collection in camps abroad to their transportation to Israel and absorption in the ma'abarot, allowed the state to manipulate them according to its needs. The ma'abarot created an alignment of spatiosocial units managed by a specific mode of governance in which immigrants were completely dependent on institutions, exposed to their unmediated control, and subjected to various forms of violence.

The emergency situation in Israel's early years and the state's control over the immigrants' modes of arrival and dispersion not only allowed immigrants to be sent to underdeveloped frontier areas, but also permitted other means of subordinating them. The fact that the ma'abara camp was not a singular space but a countrywide alignment for tens of thousands of people allowed a parallel, coercive, and nationwide mode of governance to be created in the camps. Immigrants in the camps were manipulated by the Israeli ruling ranks to serve their territorial, political, cultural, and economic interests, using methods that were contrary to the democratic principles Israel was established on, inflicting real and symbolic violence on the state's most vulnerable population. Some of these oppressive practices—which were particularly aimed at the Mizrahi immigrants, who protested against their difficult living conditions in the camps—remain hidden in the classified archive files of the Israeli domestic security service (Shin Bet), where they are defined as the "prevention [practices] of political subversion in the ma'abarot."[38]

Lies, Deceit, and Manipulative Management Strategies

Sending immigrants to frontier camps straight off the ship was the first unofficial coercive strategy encountered by those reaching their new state. After the Tel-Yeruham tent camp was erected in January 1951, Zair traveled to the port of Haifa to bring immigrants—269 men, women, and children who had arrived from Romania—directly from their ship to the ma'abara. Although they were the first to leave the port in their two buses, the journey from Haifa in the north to the camp in the south was more difficult than expected, as Zair described in his diary:

> The road was long. . . . At the beginning they were all in a good mood, but after a while, when hardly any settlements were seen, the mood dropped. . . . After Be'er-Sheva we drove another half an hour on the road to Egypt, then we had to turn onto a dirt-track. No sign of a settlement, the buses continued in the dark, we couldn't see a thing, not a plant, not a tree, nothing. People started to become hysterical, pulling their hair, shouting at me, "You are Hitler! You are bringing us to a death camp." . . . Many refused to get off the bus and spent the night on it.[39]

Like the camp's first inhabitants, most immigrants did not arrive at Tel-Yeruham independently; rather, they were brought there, sometimes against their will. The immigrants who came to the isolated frontier camps and then settlements during the 1950s and early 1960s tell a recurring story about arriving after dark and refusing to get off the trucks and buses.[40] It was clear that nobody would move to Tel-Yeruham willingly, so lies were commonly used to bring in new settlers, as many testified:

> We arrived [from Casablanca] by ship to Haifa in January 1956. They asked us, "Where do you want to go?" My parents replied, "To Jerusalem." They said, "OK," but brought us all to Yeruham. We arrived at night; it was dark and freezing and my father refused to let us get off the truck. The driver said, "You all have to get down here but in a few minutes I will come back to pick you up." Years later, just before my father passed away, he said to me, "I am still waiting for that truck to return."[41]

Such experiences left immigrants with deep scars from being humiliatingly deceived, sometimes repeatedly, by official representatives of the authorities they had trusted. The strategy of transferring immigrants directly from the ship to the camp in the middle of the night started with the ma'abarot and remained an unofficial yet central state procedure for bringing immigrants to frontier settlements.

Forcing immigrants to go to the frontier ma'abara was not the only means of making them stay in the isolated camp. While Tel-Yeruham's managers were replaced after a certain length of time, the camp's inhabitants could not leave so easily: "When I [first] came to visit the place together with the representative of the Absorption Department of the Jewish Agency," testified one camp manager, "I found many families demonstrating and demanding 'approval' to be transferred to a different place."[42] Camp dwellers' pleas for "approval" to be transferred indicate another control practice of the settling institutions: there were strong restrictions on immigrants leaving the ma'abara where they were settled. When inhabitants of geographically isolated camps refused to accept their position in the national dispersal plan and decided to move independently to other camps in more central regions, the authorities imposed radical measures, preventing the transfer of ration cards and work permits—essential during that period of emergency and austerity—for immigrants who moved without prior approval.[43] Relocation approvals, however, were very difficult to obtain; in October 1951, over two thousand families asked to relocate, but only 5 percent received permission to do so.[44] This basic right, the freedom to decide where to live and settle, was denied to immigrants under the separate control framework of the ma'abara regime.

Organized Labor

In addition to providing shelter and securing a hold on territory, one of the main objectives of the ma'abarot was to relieve the Jewish Agency of responsibility for fully supporting immigrants in the closed immigrant camps: "The ma'abara differs from the 'immigrant camp' in that its inhabitants are self-sufficient; while those in the [immigrant] camps received bed and board for free . . . the inhabitants of the ma'abara live by wage labor."[45] Yet the immigrants who were settled in the frontier ma'abara camps could not reduce their economic dependency on national institutions: while residents in camps near existing settlements who could not find work were recruited as wage labor, relief projects based on manual labor were almost the only employment option for inhabitants of frontier camps.[46] This entailed a process of proletarianization of ma'abara dwellers, making them the most vulnerable category of workers.[47] Tel-Yeruham was initially created to supply a workforce for the kaolin mines in the Large Crater nearby.[48] Like residents of other ma'abara camps, immigrants were also employed in creating the new national infrastructure—for instance, laying the road to Be'er-Sheva (Figure 4.8) and later constructing the settlement's permanent houses.

Manual labor was not only the main work available for immigrants in the camps; it was also seen as an ideological and educational mechanism for altering the occupational structure of the new Jewish nation—from urban communities in the Diaspora relying on the labor of others to communities in the new state based on their own physical labor:

> In their countries of origin, most of the new immigrants were merchants, middlemen or engaged in other "Jewish occupations." Manual labour—the work of the farmer or the industrial workers—was considered low status. Our first task is therefore to change that attitude. We consider manual work not only the most important contribution to the construction of our country, but also a step towards the formation of a new Jewish man and character.[49]

Similarly, the Housing Ministry administrators stated, "Construction acts as a kind of natural vocational school for new immigrants. The majority of new immigrants

Figure 4.8. Constructing the road from Be'er-Sheva to Tel-Yeruham, 1951. Photograph by Werner Brown, Jewish National Fund Photography Archive.

come from the middle classes and are not accustomed to physical labour. . . . Under such circumstances the construction industry acts as an important and desirable transitional stage."[50] Not only did this approach rely on the early Zionist approach of the "conquest of labor" (kibbush ha'avoda), but Herzl, as part of his vision of the Jewish State, also scripted "relief by labor" as a means to transform immigrants into citizens with the right to their own housing, envisioning that "[Israel's] laborers [would] first mutually erect [their temporary] shelters; and then they [would] earn their houses as permanent possessions by means of their work"—not immediately, "but after three years of good conduct [in which] men will be practically trained for life."[51]

However, this career change was not well received by many immigrants, and it was especially difficult for the older ones, both physically and mentally, as remembered by Victor Na'im, who came to Tel-Yeruham in 1954 following his parents, who had gone there earlier from Tripoli:

> I got there [to Tel-Yeruham], looking for my father and I saw . . . I knew my father as a wealthy man, always smartly dressed, always wears a tie . . . I see him sweating, rolling stones. And each stone was a big one. It was difficult for him. I gave him a shout, told him to go home. He said to me "but it's a working-day." I said to him "I will finish your working-day."[52]

Manual labor in the ma'abarot was not only perceived as an educational tool to train immigrants in the new types of occupations required in the new country; it also forced immigrants to remain economically dependent on the established Israeli society. At the same time, the rapid growth of the population and the economy created by the influx of immigrants opened up many new positions in both the private and public sectors, which were mostly taken up by the more established population. The inhabitants of the ma'abara camps served as a reserve of seasonal agricultural labor for the kibbutzim and as provisional workers for the more privileged urban sectors and public works, contributing to the accumulation of value for the agricultural, urban, and national centers while remaining in substandard and precarious physical and professional conditions.[53] Thus, the ma'abarot created the scene for the most concentrated relationship of dependency between immigrants and the established Israeli population, allowing the latter to reproduce and reinforce its advantageous position in both economic and political power structures.

Centralized Governance

These coercive measures could only be enforced in the camps because the ma'abarot functioned as an almost-closed system under an oppressive state of emergency. While each camp was managed as an isolated unit, the entire ma'abara alignment was also managed separately by an institution working in parallel with the Israeli government system: the Jewish Agency. Like other significant Jewish institutions founded during the prestate Yishuv period, the Jewish Agency was an extraterritorial organization that was not subject to the same rules as the state's democratic institutions, nor was it supervised by them.[54] This allowed it to adopt a more centralized governance method for managing the camps, a method that originated from the socialist–communist legacy in which the Zionist leadership had its roots.[55] The camps' managers were in most cases not part of the ma'abarot; they were neither immigrants nor elected by them; instead, they came from the dominant group in Israeli society and promoted its interests. This arrangement also led to the active reproduction of the power of Mapai, then the dominant political party, which used its control over immigrants in the camps to increase its political strength with direct propaganda before Israel's elections.[56]

Importantly, the social divisions enforced by the ma'abarot were ethnically, even racially, based. Not only did the ma'abara camps separate established citizens from immigrants spatially and socially, but they also initiated a process by which the Jewish population of Israel became ethnically divided. By 1952, Mizrahi immigrants, who had arrived later from the Arab world, amounted to 82 percent of the camps' inhabitants.[57] "Most of the European families have already left the ma'abarot, and more than 90 percent of the ma'abarot inhabitants are Mizrahim" wrote the Jewish Agency's Absorption Department in Jerusalem in January 1953, and in 1956 Yehuda Berginsky, the head of the Jewish Agency's Absorption Department, stated, "We cannot send the Polish immigrants to small canvas and timber huts. For them we need acceptable dwellings."[58] Disempowerment of a specific population in the camps had to be somehow legitimized by the humanistic, democratic state. This was done through a powerful modernist and ethnoracial based ideology that not only justified the situation in the ma'abarot but also contributed to the development of discrimination between classes and ethnicities in Jewish Israeli society.

Designing a Modern Nation

Over half of the one million Jewish immigrants who arrived in Israel in the first decade after independence came from Muslim countries, transforming Israel's predominantly European Jewish society into a multiethnic one. The establishing group of the Israeli population, mostly composed of people of European origin (the Ashkenazim), was ambivalent toward the new immigrants, who were either Holocaust survivors or non-Europeans coming from the Middle East and North Africa (the Mizrahim), who did not match the new state's self-image.[59]

The central task of modern biopolitics and the camp, as seen by Agamben and many others, is the endless purification of the national body: determining who will be included and protected by the state and who will be excluded and abandoned. The ma'abarot, however, had a more complex role in forming and geographically arranging the Israeli national body. On the one hand, they facilitated the internal colonization of Israel's newly conquered and emptied territories by immigrants with the "right" (i.e., Jewish) identity, and on the other hand, they allowed the subordination and geographical distancing of Jewish immigrants on the basis of their ethnic origin while compelling them to be "reeducated" in order to transform their foreign character and make them "appropriate" and "modern" Israeli state subjects.

Modernism against Primitivism

Motivated by national and territorial goals, by anxieties provoked by mass immigration, and by the will to preserve the existing hegemony, Israel engaged in a large-scale project of cultural assimilation and subordination. While the "melting pot" was the common metaphor for national ethnic diversity, it was in fact a misnomer, as this project was cultural synthesis in neither ideology nor practice; rather, it was a process of forced cultural adjustment advanced by the dominant white Ashkenazi group, with the prestate Yishuv society as the model for the new state. The ma'abara camps were one of the mechanisms that facilitated this process, which was justified and supported by a powerful ideology in which certain identities of groups or individuals were erased in favor of the national project. This ideology was an integral part of the Israeli nation-building process, allowing its continuation, while pushing immigrants, mainly the Mizrahim, to the almost-total collapse of their previous cultural identity.

Ideology constitutes individuals as subjects by establishing an imagined reality whose pervasive "truths" serve the interests of the dominant group and its exploitative and repressive attitudes, which are enacted through particular apparatuses or practices.[60] It is important to consider the complex relation between ideology, identity, and state practices when attempting to understand the deep link between modernization and progress as inseparable parts of Israeli national ideology and its apparatuses, including the ma'abarot. The distinction between the (mostly Ashkenazi) establishing group, which saw itself as modern, advanced, and European, and the (mostly Mizrahi) immigrants in the ma'abarot, whose culture was presented as inferior, primitive, and underdeveloped, was emphasized by all the main channels of society, from politicians to academics to the media.[61]

"Many of these immigrants come to us without elementary knowledge, with no trace of Jewish and human education," stated Ben-Gurion in 1950, displaying the immigrants as a social and national challenge; "the spiritual absorption of the immigrants, molding them, turning this human dust into a cultured nation, creative, independent, and with a vision—is not an easy job."[62] This terminology, describing the absorption of immigrants as a national spiritual effort and immigrants as "human dust" with no clear identity worth preserving, reflects a national ideology to which immigrants should aspire. This ideology, which saw modernization and "progress" as part of the Israeli national identity, was embedded in every social aspect, including the Israeli media, which described the Jews immigrating to Israel as "a race we have not yet known in this country . . . people whose primitivism is at peak, whose level of knowledge is one of virtually absolute ignorance, and worse, who have little talent for understanding anything intellectual."[63] It is not difficult here to identify the deep racial aspects of this ideology, not only directing prejudice, antagonism, and discrimination against people based on their ethnic origin but also actively marginalizing them by containing and "educating" them away from society through coercive methods.

This attitude was also reflected in the way Zair recalled the day he brought the Romanian immigrants from Haifa: "I looked for young people who made a good impression and started to tell them about the desert. I used the example of America's Wild West. . . . But they were such primitive people; they didn't understand much of it."[64] The overwhelming gap between Zair's privileged position and cultural background, experiencing Tel-Yeruham as an adventurous Wild West–style frontier experience, and that of the post–World War II Jewish immigrants, who were terrified that he was taking them to a death camp, was quickly translated into a patronizing attitude that viewed immigrants as "primitive." This approach is also characteristic of other state officials, as documented in a publication concerning the Jewish Agency's camps outside Israel, on the route from North Africa:

> The major work of Israeli emissaries in the camps is to educate the immigrants . . . who don't know what is a fork or what is tooth paste. The education is most elementary. Beginning with the ABC in all spheres of life . . . they must teach them the most "simple" things such as: how to eat, how to dress and wash.[65]

Political scientist Henriette Dahan Kalev, who arrived in Israel from Morocco as a child, describes the patronizing attitude of state officials in the ma'abara from the immigrant's perspective, through the figure of a white-uniformed nurse "who came to our tent in the immigrant camp to tell my mother how she should raise me, my sister, and my baby brother, who was born in that tent. This nurse spoke of 'raising children' as if it was something Zionists invented."[66] Other immigrants have also identified the hierarchy that the Ashkenazi establishing group created, seeing Mizrahi Jews as racially inferior subjects with themselves at the top. "The European Jews who suffered tremendously from the Hitleristic Nazism see themselves as a superior race [geza' 'elyon] and the Sephardi [Mizrahi] as belonging to an inferior one [geza' nahut dargah]," reflected a soldier in the IDF in a letter to his family in North Africa; "instead of gratitude, they treat us like savages or unwelcomed elements. Bloodline rules here." Another immigrant explained to his family that "discrimination is so widespread that one can certainly compare it with the racial discrimination between black and whites in America."[67]

Like other projects that used education as a colonial tool to secure authority by conquering the nation's mind, pedagogy was perceived as the key to the immigrant's successful integration. "We cannot absorb in Israel without revolutionizing human lives," asserted a government report; "we need to break their way of life, change habits, language, clothes."[68] In the ma'abara camps, educational work with immigrants started, and the teachers sent to the ma'abarot were instructed to indoctrinate them in Zionist ideology. This educational program was designed according to the secular Yishuv model, disregarding the traditional religious life of most Mizrahi immigrants.

The ideology that rejected Mizrahi culture was driven by an additional fear based on Zionism's deep ethnoracial aspect: the Mizrahim were non-Europeans and were thus perceived as being too close to the Arab world, threatening to blur the boundaries of the "European," white, and "civilized" state that happened to be situated in the Middle East. "We do not want Israelis to become Arabs. We are duty-bound to fight against the spirit of the Levant," stated Ben-Gurion.[69] This negation of the culture of an entire group of people was in essence their dehumanization, allowing them to be perceived as material to be molded, changed, and used in the interests of the state. As long as it was possible to maneuver the immigrants from North Africa into enclosed and desolate areas such as frontier ma'abara camps, agricultural settlements, and, later, development towns and use them to seize control over former Arab territories, the "advantage" in the demographic struggle and the "advantage" from their "economic value" was stronger than the fear of them.[70] An academic paper by Samuel Z. Klausner entitled "Immigrant Absorption and Social Tension in Israel" summarized pontifically: "Eventually these Mizrahi immigrants will strengthen the Israeli economy by providing that class of 'drawers of water and hewers of wood' which is so sorely needed."[71]

Collapse of Identity

While the modernist national ideology justified the subordination of the Mizrahi immigrants' interests to those of the state, the practice of the ma'abarot was devastating to their identity. The enduring temporariness of the camps, the overcrowding, the blurring ambiguity between private and public realms, and the loss of control over one's own destiny brought the rapid collapse of significant cultural frames and values, as described by Yeruham's residents:

> The ma'abarot ruined the social frames of these families. They took a family cell with a clear hierarchy and put them in small boxes, devastating the father and [causing] quick deterioration. [In] a traditional family, modesty

is a very important thing, respect for the father and mother. And you find the father queuing for the shower behind his two daughters. This was a great humiliation for that father.[72]

Moroccan families, who came to Yeruham from a highly patriarchal culture, saw the respected father standing helpless and humiliated in the new country, unable to help himself or his family in the difficult conditions of hard work or unemployment in the isolated camps. The dense physical environment of these ethnicized camp spaces destroyed the hierarchical relations that had previously served as a basic frame. Yet for many immigrants in Yeruham, who often came from diverse and vivid urban environments, the bland, isolated desert environment they were brought to was even more difficult than the housing conditions in the camp:

> In Casablanca we lived in the *mellah*—the Jewish Moroccan court. It was a poor area, low rent, very dense. [But] as youths in Casablanca we used to go out in the city, to the movies, to the cafes. . . . In the ma'abara they gave us huts with running water, but around that was the desert, the sand. My mother used to cry, "Where have I brought my children to?" The problem was moving from a city to such a deserted place. It was traumatic.[73]

Yet it was not only the arid landscape, the isolation from the rest of society, and the loss of their unique identity as people from a particular place that traumatized the immigrants in the camp. The fact that they were treated in the ma'abarot as "Mizrahim," "Moroccans" or "uneducated immigrants" meant they had lost not only their previous lives and freedoms but also the opportunity to reform themselves as unique individuals in their new country. As a space separating people from the outside world and negating the development of private life and subjectivities within, the camp overrode similarities and differences: similarities between the camp's inhabitants and the "normal" citizens outside and differences among the immigrants within the camp, who were treated en masse according to a one-dimensional identity, leading to their disempowerment and dehumanization. Israeli author Shimon Balas came from Iraq in the early 1950s and lived with his family in a ma'abara for more than a year. In his novel *The Ma'abara* he gives voice to Iraqi immigrants' lived experience in the camp:

> It seems to me that since the Babylonian exile, the Jews of Mesopotamia were never inflicted with such a horrible holocaust as the holocaust that inflicts them in present days. All this enlightened and ancient Jewry was crushed to dust and scattered upon barren and squalid lands called ma'abarot.[74]

As one of the figures in the book recites:

> To Israel they hauled us like sheep
> And brought us to the black ma'abara
> Labour with [cement] blocks they taught us
> And we were blind like bats.[75]

With their images of a crushed society whose enlightened tradition is experiencing a Zionist-made holocaust after being scattered in the squalid "black" spaces of the ma'abara camps, these two excerpts expose the dehumanizing structures of Zionism. The apparatuses and spaces of Zionism, rather than only building "a new society," also destroyed, dispersed, and negated preexisting social and cultural structures and traditions. Rather than being redeemed in a promised land through the Zionist gathering of exiles, immigrants were brought to a disempowering, alienating, and exploitative ma'abara apparatus, where they were suspended in a liminal threshold, an in-between nonplace designed by the establishment as the immigrants' rite of passage in which they were stuck for an unknown period.

Spaces of Resilience and Resistance

Immigrants, however, were not completely passive about this difficult reality, and subversive actions were taken by ma'abara residents seeking to escape the total subordination imposed on them by the state. In November 1952, a woman from Emek Heffer ma'abara, who had allegedly stolen oranges from an orchard in the neighboring kibbutz, was attacked by the kibbutz guard, sparking violent clashes between camp dwellers and police. The clashes spread quickly, causing riots in other camps across the country. Thousands of protesters from other ma'abarot demanded that their desperate need for decent housing, services, and work be met, a response that emphasized the gap between the squalid camps and the wealthy kibbutzim—where many camp immigrants worked as wage laborers—that had become a symbol of the hegemonic privileged Israeli culture.[76] In the same year, Tel-Yeruham's immigrants threw stones at visiting clerks from the Jewish Agency, protesting against their imposed isolation; some demanded to leave, while others urged that the camp be developed into a permanent settlement.[77]

Between the Temporary and the Permanent

Although the ma'abara camps were planned as a temporary solution that would quickly disappear, the reality did not follow the plan; it was not until the end of the 1950s and the beginning of the 1960s that most ma'abara dwellers moved to permanent housing, sometimes having lived more than a decade in the transit camps.[78] In addition, the frontier ma'abara camps were supposed to be erected where future permanent settlements were planned, yet this was rarely the case. Like Tel-Yeruham, most ma'abara sites were allocated by the Jewish Agency, an organization external to the government, and their choices were not well coordinated with the government Planning Department's National Plan, which in 1951 was still a work in progress.[79] The immigrant absorption bodies acted ad hoc, whereas the planners at the Planning Department were reluctant to make decisions. A Jewish Agency worker claimed that government planners "did not want to give us land, so we said to them—if you won't give it to us—we will take it ourselves, and in fact we took every free area we could."[80] This split was also recognized by Arieh Sharon, who in May 1951 wrote,

> The location of the camps has been decided, in principle, according to the place where immigrant housing will be built in the future, but so far there has not been, unfortunately, any coordination between the Jewish Agency's Settlement Department, which constructs the ma'abarot, and us.[81]

These ad hoc responses, caused by the emergency of mass immigration and Israel's accelerated process of internal colonization, could be described by what Carl Schmitt refers to as constant "decisionism," creating a new geopolitical order in which the law is replaced by multiple and intersecting policies and authorities.[82]

This patchy mode of governance of the improvised state had a few clear advantages for the young Israeli government and the settlement organizations: it allowed quick and temporary solutions to be found and facilitated the rapid creation of facts on the ground while avoiding accepting future responsibility for them. Moreover, the criteria for allocating sites for temporary camps were different from those required for a permanent settlement. The exact location of Tel-Yeruham, for example, was chosen because it was near an existing road and a water well to supply the temporary minimal needs of the camp's inhabitants, and not because of the preferences of the Planning Department's planners, who had other considerations, such as proximity to future main roads. While funds and effort were invested in Tel-Yeruham by the Jewish Agency, which was thinking about establishing a city there, its primary role was to create camps and manage their immigrants temporarily until the state took over. For the planners, Tel-Yeruham was supposed to exist only briefly and then be liquidated, as a different city was planned to exist a few kilometers from the area. It seems, however, that these hypothetical settlement arrangements were disrupted by one factor that neither the Jewish Agency nor the planners ever considered: the immigrants themselves.

Resisting Temporariness, Changing the National Plan

Zair established Tel-Yeruham and managed it for six months. Before leaving the camp and going back to his kibbutz, he wrote a letter to Levi Eshkol, then head of the Jewish Agency Settling Department, stating, "There is no institution which is responsible for this place. . . . Nothing real is done in the Negev."[83] In contrast to the efficient and rapid erection and population of the camp, the development of Tel-Yeruham was vague and subject to a fierce dispute. In 1952, Michael Aberman, Tel-Yeruham's second manager, wrote that the immigrants were "making desperate efforts to leave the place. . . . The solitude, the hard and monotonous work, the lack of transportation and many other factors influence people here in their decision to leave"; he demanded the "*immediate* development of the camp."[84] Clearly, while the camp's suspended temporary situation suited the settlement and planning bodies, it was unbearable for the immigrants.

Shlomo Tamir, who arrived to manage Tel-Yeruham in August 1952, realized that "in the institutions there was no plan to develop the place. They saw it as a kind of transit camp that would soon disappear."[85] In a desperate letter to Ben-Gurion he wrote that Tel-Yeruham "should be demolished or strengthened. . . . Something needs to be done quickly in order to save the settlement from crumbling and degenerating."[86] In his response, Ben-Gurion promised that "this settlement should be strengthened, which is not above our capabilities."[87] Giora Yoseftal then wrote to the Ministry of Labor under the dramatic heading "Tel-Yeruham Cannot Die and Not Live," asking that a committee be appointed for the development of the settlement.[88]

In January 1953, two years after the camp had been established, a formal ceremony was held in the presence of Yitzhak Ben-Zvi, the second Israeli president, in which "the foundations for forty stone houses" were laid, meaning that the camp was "turning into a settlement; no more Tel-Yeruham, but Yeruham Village" (Figure 4.9).[89] Yet the construction of houses was suspended while negotiations over the future of the camp continued.[90] More than six months later a letter from Eshkol to Minister of Labor Golda Myerson (later Meir) asserted, "A number of times I have expressed my doubts in relation to permanent construction in Tel-Yeruham. . . . Who will take responsibility for the existence of this settlement? . . . The [Jewish Agency's] Department of Settlement hereby explicitly announces that we withdraw any responsibility for Tel-Yeruham."[91] Nevertheless, after lengthy correspondence, Tel-Yeruham was transferred to the responsibility of Amidar, Israel's national company for housing.[92] In an accompanying letter, Ben-Gurion stated that Yeruham "is not [only] one of the settlement points, but an 'outpost' of development in the southern Negev."[93]

In Tel-Yeruham's first days, it was the Jewish Agency that had invested in the camp in order to persuade immigrants to stay there, while the Planning

Figure 4.9. Israel's President Yitzhak Ben-Zvi visits Tel-Yeruham, 1953. Unknown photographer, Central Zionist Archives, PHPS\1337804.

Department's planners never included it in the National Plan. However, it was eventually owing to the immigrants, the camp managers, and Ben-Gurion—for whom settling the Negev was more important than "proper" planning—that Tel-Yeruham was further developed. Indeed, according to Eliezer Brutzkus at the Planning Department, the "reasoned" modernist National Plan and its temporary camp stage did not always work as expected:[94]

It would be an exaggeration to argue that all the urban centers which exist today in the Negev are an intentional product of precursory and comprehensive planning. There were also improvisations with no early planning. This is how Yeruham was established in 1951, as an initiative by the immigration department of the [Jewish] Agency. . . . This was done in contradiction to the plans of the planning department. . . . For long years the planning department and the housing department refused to recognize Yeruham as a permanent settlement, . . . but eventually Yeruham became "an existing fact" which could not be erased off the map.[95]

Yet the fact that Yeruham was created outside the National Plan had serious planning implications. For example, the ma'abara was built next to the existing old road to Eilat, but during the late 1950s the road was rebuilt next to Dimona, a preplanned development town, leaving Yeruham disconnected, far from the main route. Factories were also built elsewhere for planning reasons, and the town suffered severe economic difficulties.[96] The creation of temporary camps that were not always intended to become permanent eventually led to the establishment of unplanned settlements, causing predicaments that lasted for decades. Even after the authorities eventually acknowledged Yeruham as a town and sent thousands of immigrants there, the place developed very slowly: "150 thousand people have passed through this southern town, yet its number of residents remained the same as it was during the 1950s."[97]

Hybridizing the Camps and Tenement Blocks

Tel-Yeruham's residents had a subversive attitude not only to its continued existence as a temporary camp but also to its spatial character and function as a permanent settlement. When Yeruham became a development town in the early 1960s, tenement housing blocks were introduced, similar to other built environments in Israel during this period. Public immigrant housing had a dual role in early statehood: shaping both the national home and the personal home—that is, shaping Israeli territory and the immigrant's identity.[98] Israel's provision of public housing to hundreds of thousands of immigrants in need was not a welfare policy but an integral part of the Israeli nation-building process. It involved forced internal colonization and modernization carried out by a captive population of mostly Mizrahi immigrants, who were both the subjects and the agents of the process. The ma'abara camps and the later development towns were coercive tools of population management. Like the camps, public housing was an instrument used to permanently achieve much more than providing shelter for immigrants; it was used both to control the territory through its modern spatialization and to shape the cultural and social character of the residents' identity and social structure.

Figure 4.10. Social housing in Yeruham, 1968. Photograph by Dov Dafnai, Jewish National Fund Photography Archive.

The cultural and ideological reasons that the Zionist movement adopted modernism were based on a triple rejection: of the Diaspora, the bourgeoisie, and the Orient.[99] Yet modern architecture also became the tool that enabled Zionism to cope with the mass physical planning and construction the new state required. This was a very different modernism from that of the detailed design of the 1930s Bauhaus of Tel Aviv's private developers; it was more similar to the repetitive prefabricated, mass-produced architecture of the ma'abara huts (Figure 4.10). The housing types presented in the National Plan were limited to a few designs, and as suggested by Arieh Sharon himself, their "architectural monotony result[ed] from their mass-production" and from their "cheap building method, based on the use of standard modules," which were later changed to even more standardized housing blocks.[100] This repetitive architecture was a strategy of unification and standardization, rather than a lapse. As James Scott maintains of other highly modernist encompassing state projects, "The lack of context and particularity is not an oversight; it is the necessary first premise of any large-scale planning exercise."[101] The planning process for these modern housing blocks was not dissimilar to that of the camps. As described by Israeli architectural historian Zvi Efrat, these blocks were also "about a new beginning, a sheet of paper clean of any traces of an existing built environment . . . no style, no habits, no experience, no historic conditions . . . no *genius loci*, no view, no topography, . . . no time. There is only a raw composition which needs to be built, again and again."[102]

Unsurprisingly, the four distinct motifs of state practices that Kallus and Law-Yone identify in their exploration of public housing in Israel are very similar to those seen in the ma'abara camps:

> The *isolation* of the new living areas from the [Israeli] social, economic and political center; the *uniformity* which was imposed on the physical arrangements of the housing environment; the persistent aura of *transience* which continued to shadow the official spaces; the *ambiguity* . . . concerning the level of individual control over one's own personal space and between private and public spheres.[103]

In the isolation of the new development towns from Israel's social, economic, and political center, in the uniformity of their housing environment, in the transience that was part of the tenement dwellers' lives in their temporary contracts and their attempts to move, and in the ambiguity around the level of control over personal space and between the public and private spheres, the state's public tenement blocks continued the logic of the camp. Immigrants were enclosed in cement boxes in the name of modern efficiency, the ethnoracialized population-dispersal policy, and a progressive lifestyle ideology, ensuring that the repetitive modern aesthetics would characterize the new real and symbolic Zionist landscape.

While the temporariness of the ma'abara camps allowed the construction of permanent modern blocks in the development towns, these blocks carried the genes of the camp in them: a unified design for the masses, an ideological space detached from its specific place and specific inhabitants. As aptly put by David Kishik, who describes modernist public housing projects, "Cloaked in layers of moralistic and technocratic benevolence, all too many public housing projects cannot hide the fact that they are (dare we say) social concentration camps."[104] Thus, as spaces that both segregated the Mizrahi immigrants and attempted to reshape their identity, the ma'abara camps and later the development towns could be seen as disciplinary spaces in the Foucauldian sense. These camps and related towns were designed to form the Mizrahi immigrants into desirable modern, self-regulating Zionist political subjects, forming a threshold space by which a particular Jewish population group was morphed to fit its designated role in the Israeli national body.

Cultural Resilience between Huts and Blocks

Yeruham's residents, however, were not completely obedient to the spatial order the state imposed on them. They created their own spaces next to the modern housing blocks, including makeshift structures for farm animals and self-built Moroccan outdoor mud ovens (*frena*; plural, *frenot*; or *taboon*), which also appeared in the first ma'abara camp—described as "primitive" by those who documented

Figure 4.11. Moroccan immigrant bakes bread in a self-built *frena* in Tel-Yeruham's first ma'abara, 1956. Photograph by Fritz Cohen, National Photo Collection of Israel.

them—thus creating a more hybrid spatial reality than that imagined by the modernist professional planners (Figures 4.11 and 4.12). The *frenot* became a source of local pride for Yeruham's residents in the town's earliest days. They represented the immigrants' resourceful and symbolic spatial action, exemplifying their cultural resilience in highly modern spaces cleansed of any cultural relation to the Diaspora.

"I admit that I erased the *frenot* in Yeruham!" declared Haim Alalluf, who lived as a child in Yeruham's second ma'abara and later opened the first private bakery in town. "All the older women who came [to Yeruham] from the [Moroccan] suburbs and villages knew how to build *frenot*," he said, "and what wonderful bread they made! It was one of Yeruham's [most unique] experiences."[105] As opposed to the difficulties of social isolation, geographical remoteness, the poor supply of fresh food, and the general helplessness of the immigrants, the *frena* was described by Yeruham's residents as a triumphal initiative that created "wonderful," "fabulous," or "terrific" fresh-baked bread while also carrying a deep social meaning.[106] The *frena* was a shared space—first in the ma'abara and later near the town's housing block—that was highly gendered. It was created by and for women, allowing them

Figure 4.12. Makeshift structures—an animal enclosure and a *frena*—near Yeruham's modernist housing blocks, 1970s. Photographs by Saadia Mandel. Private collection.

not only to bake but also to socialize, as Saadia Mandel, Yeruham's town architect, reflected (Figure 4.13):

> Each *frena* . . . was built by a woman who had about five [female] friends; each Friday one of them, when it was her turn, came early and put some timber planks in the *frena* to heat it up. Then at around eleven o'clock all the other partners came with their [unbaked] bread and cakes and put them inside the *frena*. Then they took a few chairs, sat around, and chatted. The "event of the *frena*" was not only about the quality of the baking; . . . it gave the women a chance to meet and chat. It was not proper to sit in a café like in Tel Aviv. Their husbands would not allow them. You cannot demand that a Moroccan family change its tradition all at once.[107]

As modern architecture was an instrument used to restructure the identity of the newcomers, particularly Mizrahi immigrants, building the *frenot* could therefore

Figure 4.13. Moroccan women and children near a self-made makeshift structure of empty barrels built around a *frena* used for baking in Yeruham, 1968. Photograph by Moshe Milner, National Photo Collection of Israel, Government Press Office.

be seen as actions of continuous negotiation with these instrumental modernist spaces. The *frenot* created what Homi Bhabha calls "hybrid agencies" developing in colonial contexts, which "deploy the partial culture from where they emerge to construct visions of community, and versions of historic memory, that give narrative form to the minority positions they occupy."[108] The *frenot*, which were constructed with available materials such as mud and lightweight items (corrugated steel, barrels, wooden plates), have created the hybrid space of a common, semiprivate area, allowing women to gather in the traditional way. With this layer of self-made structures given to the camp and later the development town, their residents negotiated and resisted the modern functional culture imposed on them.

Late Institutional Regrets

"If we are talking about pioneers—this was a forced pioneership," concluded Zair, the first Tel-Yeruham ma'abara manager, in his diary.[109] Indeed, in contrast to official Israeli historiography, the ma'abara camps, mainly those erected on the frontier, were not merely an improvised response aimed at providing emergency shelter during the mass-immigration period; rather, they combined a specific spatiality, mode of governance, and modern ideology in order to manipulate the immigrants according to the state's territorial, economic, social, and cultural interests. These actions, carried out in the haste of Israel's early years, were conducted without full consideration of their implications for immigrants, as acknowledged by Yoseftal in the statement opening this chapter.[110] Nevertheless, thousands of unwilling immigrants were sent by the state to frontier camps and then settlements with only basic conditions many years after Yoseftal's statement from the early 1950s.

The ma'abarot allowed the young Israel to establish itself as a state by quickly absorbing and settling immigrants in its newly conquered territories. The temporary and centrally controlled camps bridged the gap between the rapid absorption of mass immigration and proper long-term planning, creating spatial patches that were adjusted according to the needs of the state and on the backs of immigrants. The story of the ma'abarot is similar in many ways to the story of other modern state-building projects in which new, encompassing, spatial and social orders were established while the needs of the people were ignored. In *Seeing Like a State*, James Scott identified several elements of the most tragic episodes that resulted from state-initiated social engineering projects. These elements—the ordering and simplification of society, a coercive power to implement the state's high-modernist designs, a strong modernist ideology, and a weak civil society[111]—are relatively easy to identify in Yeruham and the ma'abarot project as a whole, where they were all combined, allowing Israel to use the immigrants as pawns in its demographic and territorial struggles while excluding them from the more established parts of society. These elements and the ways they are expressed in the ma'abara camps, which then transferred to the development towns, are linked to the nation–state–territory triad through their exceptional governmental and spatial forms and actions aimed at the particular population of the mostly Mizrahi immigrants.

The ma'abarot were not only isolated camps with horrible conditions; for the immigrants they were black holes in space and time, where their past culture was negated and their future was unclear. As such, the ma'abarot had a devastating effect on their inhabitants, as is well expressed by a social services inspector who worked in the camps:

> The very fact that people were directed—to here, to there, that they were told "do this" . . . this meant that they were deprived of the possibility to determine their own lot, and this was a great humiliation to them. We brought them to extreme passivity. . . . The whole public had been crushed . . . and we, actually, had crushed them. . . . That was the damage we caused by our paternalism, by this whole project of direction, of another ma'abara and another one. It broke them down, and the effects are still with us generation after generation. . . . We thought that if we don't give them our values

Figure 4.14. Housing blocks at the outskirts of Yeruham, 2012. Photograph by the author.

in all respects, they'll be lost. We felt so arrogant and superior, as if we knew everything and they—nothing.[112]

Although created as temporary camps, the ma'abarot had a long-term influence on immigrants and Israeli society, generating an enduring ethnoracial discrimination against the Mizrahim, who continued to be marginalized on the state's periphery. Many scholars argue that this discrimination was deliberately generated.[113] They point to development towns like Yeruham, which started as ma'abara camps, as the main instrument of this engineered social marginalization: "Yeruham, maybe more than any other 'development town' in Israel, has become a synonym in the Israeli discourse for desolation, backwardness and wretchedness."[114] As a town of around ten thousand people today (Figure 4.14), Yeruham still struggles to change this image.

The deep discontent of Mizrahi immigrants erupted later in several pivotal events for Israeli society, including the Wadi Salib riots in Haifa in 1959 and the Israeli Black Panthers protest movement of the early 1970s, which called for social justice for the Mizrahim and contributed to dramatic national political change in the 1977 elections, when the right-wing Likud Party came to power. The majority of Mizrahim continue to vote against the left-wing parties that were historically in charge of excluding and discriminating against them in the ma'abarot and the development towns.[115] While the temporary architectural instrument of the ma'abara has long been physically erased from the Israeli landscape, it influences Israeli society and politics to this day.[116] Israel still uses Judaization, via the creation and expansion of Jewish settlements, to extend its control over the Negev, but it does so even more through the militarization of the area, including the "Military Training-Bases City" located about twelve kilometers from Yeruham.[117]

The government Planning Department did not intend Tel-Yeruham to become a permanent settlement, and there was no sign of Yeruham in Israel's National Plan. Yet one mark, quite easy to miss, appears on the plan in the place where Yeruham is located. This mark clearly reflects the frontier as a contested landscape that is being actively conquered, and it is related to a very different way in which the instrument of the camp and spatial temporariness were and still are used in Israel's territorial and political struggles, a way that will be discussed in the next chapter. The only mark showing on the 1952 National Plan in the almost-empty frontier desert area where Yeruham was created—is a Bedouin encampment.

5

UNRECOGNIZED ORDER
The Imposed Campness of the Negev/Naqab Bedouin

In 1951, the army came . . . and asked us to leave temporarily to the enclosed zone. We were promised by the army and some officials that we could return to our land soon after. . . . By using this tactic, the majority of the Bedouin were exiled from their land, and were not allowed to return.
> —Sayah al-Tori, al-'Araqib, quoted in Mansour Nasasra, "The Ongoing Judaisation of the Naqab and the Struggle for Recognising the Indigenous Rights of the Arab Bedouin People"

How can we be called intruders if we and our ancestors have been living in the Naqab for thousands of years?
> —Ismael Abu-Saad, "The Bedouins' Complaint"

While we wait, we also suffer.
> —Rakhma resident, reflecting on its unrecognized status

From a quick glance at Google Earth at the desert area around Yeruham or judging by an examination of Israel's official maps, Rakhma does not seem to exist.[1] While Yeruham is clearly defined on the satellite view by its ordered housing layout, tightly bound by the town's road infrastructure, Rakhma's houses merge into the arid land and can barely be seen. Viewing the two settlements from the main road also exposes their very different realities: while Yeruham's housing blocks rise firmly from the arid landscape, Rakhma's makeshift houses seem to be an accumulation of temporary structures with no clear connection between them (Figure 5.1). For a stranger, it is quite difficult to find the entrance to Rakhma; no signs or paved roads lead to the settlement, and its dirt tracks, branching off the main paved roads, can hardly be recognized and are easily missed as one drives past them (Figure 5.2).

Rakhma is an unrecognized Bedouin village of about 1,500 people, located

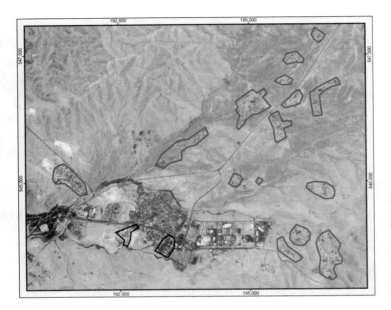

Figure 5.1. Google Earth image of Rakhma and Yeruham. The clusters of Rakhma's structures and the areas of the former Yeruham camps have been emphasized by the author.

around Yeruham, mostly within the town's municipal boundaries. The term "unrecognized" indicates that although the settlement physically exists, it is not acknowledged by the Israeli authorities; it does not appear on official maps and does not enjoy access to modern infrastructures like water, electricity, sewers, and paved roads and to other state and municipal services like health care, education, and garbage collection. Rakhma's situation is not exceptional among Bedouin settlements in the Negev (*Naqab* in Arabic) desert. The 1948 war had a drastic effect on the Negev Palestinian Bedouin; during and immediately after the war only thirteen thousand Bedouin remained in the Negev after most of the Bedouin, who had numbered around ninety-five thousand during the late years of the British Mandate, fled or were expelled to neighboring countries by the Israeli army. The Israeli approach to the fraction of the tribes that remained in the Negev was based on two basic colonial practices. The first was the expulsion of most of the tribes from their land and their concentration under military rule in a limited security zone called the *siyag* or *siyaj* ("fence" or "enclosure" in Hebrew and Arabic, respectively). The siyag, occupying around one-tenth of the Negev and known for its low agricultural fertility, was declared a restricted zone.[2] Heavy limitations were imposed on movement and other aspects of life in the siyag, including a ban on the construction of permanent buildings, with the overall aim of controlling the population through surveillance, administration, and systems of segmentation, dependence, and co-optation.[3] The second practice was the declaration that all the Negev was unregistered land that therefore belonged to the state.[4] Guiding this policy was a Zionist cultural–political vision accord-

Figure 5.2. A view of one of Rakhma's clusters from the main road, 2013. Photograph by the author.

ing to which the Negev desert was an uninhabited area, and the Bedouin were a primitive culture that would soon disappear.[5]

The siyag was part of the southern closed military zone that included the Negev as a whole, and it worked similarly to other military zones created in Israel after the 1948 war to control the Palestinian populations under martial rule, a situation that ended only in 1966.[6] The aim of the southern military zone was to block any contact between the Negev Bedouin and their related tribes across the Egyptian and Jordanian borders, to prevent a cross-border economy or "infiltrators," *(muhajareen),* and to maintain border security. It also prevented the expelled Bedouin from returning to their lands. The displaced Bedouin have nevertheless traveled to cross the newly established borders and to visit their ancestral lands, while adopting other modes of resistance to the new imposed order.[7]

Five tribes already living in the area of the siyag were joined by fourteen other tribes who were relocated by the army, a fact that divided the Negev Bedouin into two main groups: those who remained on their ancestral lands and those who had been displaced from their original territory.[8] From being a population who had inhabited the Negev almost exclusively for almost four centuries of Ottoman rule followed by the British Mandate, seminomadic pastoralists who also had a strong sedentary base that included stone houses, the majority of the Palestinian Bedouin

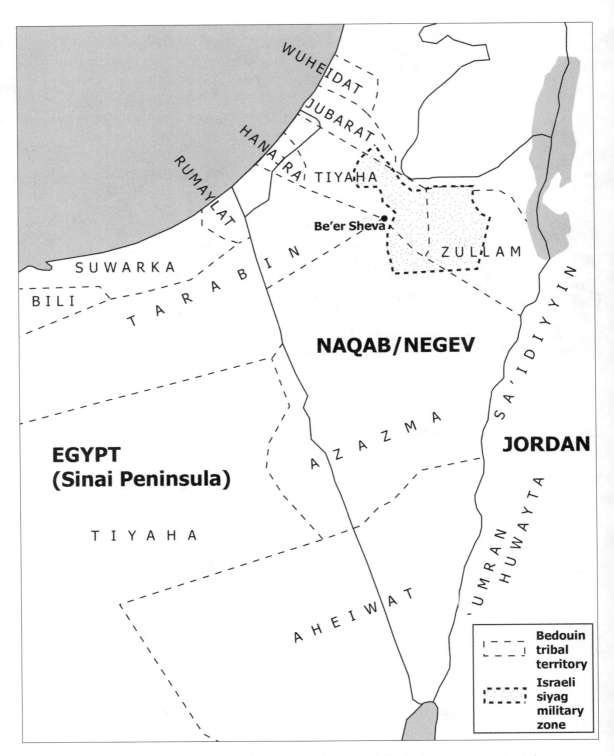

Map 4. The Negev desert and neighboring countries, with Bedouin prestate territorial divisions and the post-1948 Israeli military siyag zone.

Unrecognized Order 163

Figure 5.3. Houses in the then newly established Tel Sheva, the first Negev Bedouin township, 1969. Photograph by Fritz Cohen, National Photo Collection of Israel, Government Press Office.

became either refugees or IDPs under military rule for almost two decades, and their spatial temporariness was used by the state as an instrument of expulsion and expropriation. This happened even though the Bedouin who remained in Israel, whose tribes had had friendly relationships with the prestate Negev kibbutz settlements, became Israeli citizens who were also encouraged to volunteer for the army.

From the late 1960s, seven purpose-built townships were established within the siyag, to which Israel hoped to transfer all the Bedouin to further concentrate them and turn them into city dwellers (Figure 5.3).[9] The Bedouin who refused to relocate to these towns and by doing so refused to give up their culture and lands, to which they were struggling to return, have continued to live in their own settlements. The residents of these unrecognized villages face a range of pressure tactics used by the state to coerce them to migrate and concentrate in the towns: they are forbidden to construct permanent houses; they are deprived of many basic rights, such as the aforementioned access to state infrastructure and services provided to all other citizens; their houses are declared illegal and penalized by fines and demolitions; and they face increasing environmental restrictions on grazing and agricultural practices. In addition, they are governed separately from all other Israeli citizens by ever-changing bodies, ad hoc policies, and aggressive state actions.

By examining Rakhma and the wider issue of the unrecognized Bedouin villages, in which around ninety thousand of the Negev Bedouin population live today, this chapter analyzes an additional form of "campness" created by Israel and the ways it is resisted. While the Bedouin villages have either been situated in their location for generations or were placed there by Israel, they are controlled as de facto camp spaces whose population is suspended in temporary conditions and which are administered through specific modes of governance. The Bedouin unrecognized villages are not formally defined as "camps," and there is no intention here to impose a concept over a contested reality. Rather, by reflecting on the Bedouin's enforced temporariness and institutional abandonment compared to other forms of encampment produced in Israel–Palestine over the last century, this chapter aims to illuminate spatial and political connections between them in practices of power and in resistance carried out in and through their spaces.

Indeed, various degrees and mechanisms of campness functioned as versatile tools in Israel's double act of internal colonial settlement. They were used for colonial *expansion* and dispersal of the Jewish population over frontier territories, as shown with the ma'abara camps such as the one that created the neighboring town of Yeruham. In contrast, they have also facilitated the colonial *expulsion* of native populations from their ancestral land and the *expropriation* of those lands, as seen in relation to the Bedouin and other Palestinians. The campness situation of the Bedouin makeshift spaces aims to force their inhabitants to surrender to the government's spatial policy and further concentrate in designated spaces, giving up their lands and traditional way of life and submitting to Israel's efforts to reduce Bedouin space to a minimum in its ongoing attempt to de-Arabize its territory.

The Bedouin's situation of imposed campness enables us to examine the predicament of many of the Arabs who managed to remain within the newly established state after the 1948 war, and the Israeli policy of concentrating and abandoning them. Based on the postcolonial critical approach adopted to analyze the realities of the Negev Bedouin, this chapter shows how the exclusionary mechanism of the camp allows the territorial and cultural goals of Israel's settler society to be imposed on this indigenous population, which makes up part of the Palestinian population in Israel, continuing the colonial ethnoracial legacy of expulsion, segregation, suspension, and expropriation.[10]

Israeli policy did not systematically inflict the lingering, precarious reality of dislocation, followed by institutionalized, long-term temporariness and neglect on the displaced Negev Bedouin alone. Most of the approximately twenty-five thousand internally displaced Palestinian populations were forced to live in makeshift

Map 5. The unrecognized Bedouin villages in the Negev.

localities after they were torn from their original villages following the Nakba, villages to which they were prevented from returning by the Israeli emergency regulations. Legally defined by Israel as "present absentees" while their lands and original villages were confiscated and expropriated by Israel to expand the internal Jewish settlement and territory, the Palestinian IDPs were forced to live in provisional tents, shacks, and other temporary spaces, often located on the outskirts of Arab villages, mostly in the Galilee, for more than a decade.[11] The population of these suspended spaces was left out of sight, out of contact, out of history, and out of the state's future, becoming, as aptly described by Malkit Shoshan and Bert de Muynck, "a phantom people dwelling on ghostly ground."[12] At the same time, as this chapter shows, the Bedouin were and still are persistently resisting their ongoing limitation, expropriation, and state abandonment. Like other indigenous groups around the world, they struggle against the state's structure of domination while attempting to modify its governmental control system as part of their everyday life and activities and through well-focused spatial and legal actions.[13]

Suspended Encampments

The Bedouin call the unrecognized Negev settlements villages, while the Israeli authorities call them *p'zura*—the Hebrew word for dispersion or scattering. This term implies spontaneous and uncontrolled spatial dispersal, delegitimizing Bedouin actions by creating an image of Bedouin territorial grabbing.[14] It also implies that Bedouin space is chaotic, as if their villages are arbitrary settlements and as if the Bedouin's past nomadic culture was rootless and placeless.[15] However, the history and the current reality of the Negev Bedouin and their unrecognized settlements tell a very different story. By the time the State of Israel was established, the Negev Bedouin were already only seminomadic, and their economy was very much based on agriculture and landownership. Their current temporary status, however, was and still is created by the state.

The Negev Bedouin: From a Nomadic to a Sedentary Society

The Arabic term *badawi*, from which "Bedouin" is derived, describes a nomadic inhabitant of the desert—*badiyah*—whose livelihood is dependent on herds of sheep, goats, and camels. The Bedouin are organized on a tribal basis, with an extensive structure of kinship networks in which communities are based on a well-defined value system that monitors behavior and interpersonal relations.[16] Until the mid-nineteenth century, the Negev Bedouin were primarily pastoral nomads who largely migrated according to their need for pasture. Under Ottoman rule and during the British Mandate, the Negev Bedouin went through processes of sedentarization.[17] They adopted a seminomadic system of pastoral production combined with farming, a change that tremendously influenced their territoriality, as reflected in Aref Al-Aref's description of the 1930s Negev—mainly its northern parts—as primarily an agricultural district (Figure 5.4).[18] Tribal grazing lands were transformed into agricultural land, parceled into family land units and private plots, and other spatial formations related to fixed locations were created, such as agricultural facilities for storing crops.[19] The estimated area cultivated by the Bedouin before the 1948 war was around 1.8 million dunams, of which 140,000 were cultivated by the Azazma tribe, which also forms the majority of Rakhma's population.[20]

The influx of capital, labor, and knowledge increased the demand for land suitable for dry farming, and Bedouin ownership laws became increasingly important. The Bedouin began to trade in the land under their control, selling it mostly to buyers from Gaza and Hebron but also to representatives of the Zionist movement. Land sales increased during the British Mandate, and land brokerage became a primary occupation for a number of Negev Bedouin. While the traditional pastoral encampment was still common (Figure 5.5), it slowly disappeared as permanent houses began to appear in the 1930s, and a number of wealthy sheikhs

Figure 5.4. Bedouin of the Hazaili tribe plow in the Negev, 1951. Photograph by David Eldan, National Photo Collection of Israel, Government Press Office.

built large estates that included homes, flour mills, barns, and even mechanically pumped water wells used for irrigated agriculture (Figure 5.6).[21]

From a society with a culture based on nomadic life in the arid desert landscape, the Negev Bedouin became a seminomadic pastoralist society with a strong sedentary base, in which landownership was an important social, cultural, and economic factor. While these processes were respected by prestate Zionist settlers and organizations, they were ignored and denied after the Israeli state was established. Before the 1948 war, many Bedouin tribes and Zionist settlers in the Negev enjoyed good relations; the kibbutzim that were established in the northern Negev during the 1940s adopted a peace-seeking approach toward the Bedouin, advocating mutual respect for interests and lifestyles. But the state seems to always be the enemy of minorities who move around, and after the war Bedouin sedentarism was indeed desirable for Israeli rule. Yet the Bedouin spatial and territorial formations did not suit Israel's territorial agenda, which was aimed at limiting and reducing Arab space while enlarging Jewish space.

Rather than being the result of a nomadic life and culture, the Bedouin current spatial temporariness is the outcome of various Israeli territorial practices and

Figure 5.5. Part of a Bedouin encampment in the northern Negev, 1956. Photograph by Fritz Cohen, National Photo Collection of Israel, Government Press Office.

policies, which deny the Bedouin's claims of landownership while using a number of coercive methods to forcibly reduce their space. As in other settler societies, these methods, including the camp, form part of Israel's encompassing ethnoracial regime. Comparing Israel and other settler societies reveals the similarity of the territorial incentives, the cultural ideologies, and the biopolitical devices by which indigenous populations are managed, allowing the governance methods of which the camp is a significant part to be exposed.

Settlers and Natives: The Biopolitics of Settler Societies

While indigenous populations vary substantially, the UN has developed principles to define them. These principles reflect the exclusive connection between a distinct ethnic group and its territory, a connection disrupted when others create a new political reality that marginalizes, dispossesses, and/or excludes this distinct population.[22] The relation between population, land, and legal order, which forms the basic foundation of the nation-state, is inherently different in settler colonialism, which is based on a strategy of immigration and settlement that aims to

Figure 5.6. The permanent Bedouin house of Sheikh Suleiman in the northern Negev, 1951. Photograph by David Eldan, National Photo Collection of Israel, Government Press Office.

change the country's ethnic structure.[23] "Territoriality is settler colonialism's specific, irreducible element," writes Patrick Wolfe, arguing that access to territory is the primary driver of relations between settlers and indigenous populations: "Land is life—or, at least, land is necessary for life. Thus contests for land can be—indeed, often are—contests for life." Unlike in other forms of colonialism, argues Wolfe, settler colonizers come to stay, and therefore "invasion is a structure, not an event." This structure bears "the logic of elimination," with "elimination" here being not the genocide of the indigenous people but an entire range of spatial limitations and biocultural assimilations performed by varied practices. "Settler colonialism destroys to replace," writes Wolfe, and as long as the natives stand between the colonizers and their desired territory, they will be threatened in one way or another, in a structure that is not homogenous and can take on diverse forms according to the specific conditions that created it.[24] As such, settler colonialism involves various degrees of ethnic cleansing, which is focused at emptying a space of specific populations in an act in which the spatial dimension is central.[25]

Expelling, enclosing, and separating indigenous populations from the rest of society, including from society located on the other side of the state's territorial border, such as the creation of the military-controlled Israeli siyag zone, was part of this practice. As Harney and Moten argue, the settler is "enclosing what it cannot defend but only endanger."[26] Like those in other colonial projects, the elimination actions Israel undertook against the indigenous Bedouin and their culture were accompanied by a modern ideological vision. This ideology allowed both the extraction of land and the "domestication" of the Bedouin, who were designated as part of the local labor force. Modern planning and architecture were an inseparable part of this vision, as reflected in the words of Moshe Dayan, a military leader and politician who was the agriculture minister in the early 1960s:

> We should transform the Bedouins into an urban proletariat—in industry, services, construction, and agriculture. . . . Indeed, this will be a radical move which means that the Bedouin [person] would not live on his land with his herds, but would become an urban person who comes home in the afternoon and puts his slippers on. His children would be accustomed to a father who wears trousers, does not carry a Shabaria [the traditional Bedouin knife]. . . . The children would go to school with their hair properly combed. This would be a revolution, but it may be fixed within two generations. . . . This phenomenon of the Bedouin will disappear.[27]

This imagined elimination of the Bedouin culture through urbanization is a clear expression of a settler colonial attitude toward indigenous people typical of Israeli leaders, which was inseparable from Israel's territorial ambitions. As in other colonial settler states, this imposed change was effected by direct violence and various other necropolitical mechanisms, many of which were and still are enacted in designated spaces such as the siyag zone and the Bedouin unrecognized settlements, outside Western democratic laws and modes of governance.[28]

Terra Nullius, Nomadism, and the New Nomos

The deep connection between land and life was part of both violent colonial territorialization and the way Western law was incorporated and implemented by colonizers. European settlers, whether they settled in Australia, New Zealand, the Americas, or South Africa, exploited the lack of indigenous land documentation and the legal principles of the nineteenth century, declaring vast territories, sometimes entire continents, *terra nullius*, empty land owned by no one. By this colonial legal–geographical Schmittian "*nomos* of the earth," European powers disregarded the legal systems and property rights of entire native populations, drove them off the most fertile or mineral-rich lands, displaced them from their ancestral homelands, and concentrated them in reservations, camps, military zones, or other forms of enclavic spaces. At the same time, settlers created a new network of white settlements in most rural regions.[29] As one of the notorious hallmarks of the colonial period and practices, *terra nullius* enabled colonial settlers to class their occupation not as invasion but as a "peaceful settlement," with no agreements, compensation, or legal recognition of the property rights of indigenous populations. *Terra nullius* is not only a legal but also a cultural, historical, and political concept; on the one hand, it legitimizes dispossession and expropriation by presenting the land as empty, and on the other hand, it strips indigenous people and their cultures of their position as rightful owners of land and political power.[30]

In contrast to settler colonial states mentioned above, at the beginning of the Zionist settlement of Palestine, the "frontierness" degree of the territory was very low, because until 1948, although the country was represented as *terra nullius* waiting to be redeemed, land that was transferred to Jewish control had to be purchased.[31] However, this situation changed after Israel's establishment and the 1948 war, when a large territory was acquired by military force, creating new internal frontiers to control and settle, and providing the setting for major Jewish land seizures.[32] During the first decade of statehood, over 96 percent of the state's landmass was Judaized through extensive confiscation of Arab land: land belonging to Palestinian refugees was transferred to public or Jewish ownership, approximately 40 to 60 percent of land belonging to Palestinian Arabs who remained in Israel was expropriated, and Bedouin-held land was classified as *mawat* (dead land), enabling the state to claim ownership, while the myth of "empty land" was promoted.[33]

Indeed, the Negev desert was easily imagined as the ideal *terra nullius*, and the presence of Bedouin there was not recognized as legitimate but, rather, was seen as a threat. Under the Emergency Regulations that followed the 1948 war, the criminalizing term "infiltrators" included every Arab person entering the state without permission, and other laws were designed to strictly control the movement of Arab populations, including the Negev Bedouin tribes, into and within the state. Before the state's establishment, Bedouin traveled along legitimate trade routes among their territories, which extended between Jordan and the Sinai and across the future state borders. After statehood, such travel was redefined as illegal movement and invasion, and hence a security threat that needed to be blocked. In addition, as part of the strict martial law that was imposed on all Palestinian citizens of Israel during these years, those seen outside their designated martial-law zones were immediately suspects.

The geographical dispossession of the colonized and the reorganization of the emptied land by settlers were accompanied by various combined cultural, legal, and spatial practices. The settlers' land rights were secured by an imported legal system that was a matrix of values, ideologies, and ideas that were not debated but were assumed and imposed, such as the right of private property. In contrast to the settlers, who were seen as having protected land rights, natives were typically represented as nomadic, unsettled, and rootless in the settler colonial discourse.[34] Although Native Americans taught whites how to grow corn and Bedouin sold land to Zionist settlers, settlers regarded the natives' relation to the land as vague and unstable; the characterization of Bedouin as nomads made their land claims invisible to the Israeli legal system, even though it had been recognized by previous sovereigns.[35]

The charge of being nomadic "renders the natives removable," argues Wolfe; "moreover, if the natives are not already nomadic, then the reproach can be turned into a self-fulfilling prophecy through the burning of corn or the uprooting of fruit trees."[36] The well-established indigenous Bedouin legal system by which they had preserved law and order in accordance with their culture for hundreds of years—including landownership laws that are still respected by the Bedouin—was never recognized by Israel.[37] "The whole question of ownership of the land is seen by the Bedouin as a kind of paradox," argues Ismail Abu-Saad; "'How is it possible,' ask the Bedouin, 'that in the 1920s and 1930s, the Jewish National Fund and the Jewish Agency purchased land in the Naqab from its Bedouin owners, and today they're suddenly not the owners? What has changed?'"[38] Like other settler colonial states, Israel used nomadism to make the Negev Bedouin displaceable; this was and still is accomplished by an enforced and protracted situation of campness, including the temporariness imposed by their suspension outside the grid and by extensive demolition of their houses, wells, and crops.[39]

The violence inflicted on the Bedouin as part of the Israeli military rule was based on the 1945 Mandatory government's Emergency Defense Regulations, which were originally created to suppress the Jewish and Palestinian revolts and allowed the authorities of the British army the free use of power without the restrictions of any body of law. They were adopted by the state for use against the Arab minority in 1948, and some of these regulations remain in force to this day. Violence, as sociologist Ronen Shamir shows, was also used in the civil, legal, and cultural approach of "historians, geographers, reporters, engineers, policymakers, and educators [who] describe[d] the Bedouin as lacking the fundamental bond with the soil that marks the transition of humans in *nature* to humans in *society*." This approach redefined the Negev as empty by constituting Bedouin culture as part of nature awaiting civilization, treating the Bedouin encampment "as if it is no more than another element—alongside vegetation—in the wilderness."[40]

The way Rakhma was formed is an example of Israel's deep influence over the territory of the Bedouin and their distribution across the Negev. Before the state's establishment, the land around Rakhma was used for pasture by the Azazma–Sawachana Bedouin clan, which had lived in the area since the Ottoman period.

Most members of the clan escaped or were expelled to Jordan and Egypt during and after the 1948 war, but a minority remained in the area and lived from pasturing and seasonal agriculture. However, the majority of Rakhma's families are IDPs who belong to the Azazma–Sarachin clan, originating from an area closer to the Israeli–Egyptian border, from where they were transferred by the Israeli army in the late 1950s as part of Israel's policy of concentrating and further controlling the Negev Bedouin.[41] Today, most of Rakhma's population belongs to the transferred clan, though a few families belong to the original clan and a minority belong to other clans—all part of the Azazma tribe. This tribe, which before the war numbered tens of thousands of Bedouin spread across extensive areas of the Negev, was completely scattered after the war; most of its members were displaced outside Israel's borders, and others were internally displaced and subject to strict martial law.[42]

Rakhma was never recognized by the authorities and was left almost unnoticed for years. Although its residents were displaced to the area by the state and are all Israeli citizens, they were abandoned with no infrastructure, services, or economic resources, while their traditional sources of livelihood were constantly reduced. Like other currently unrecognized Negev Bedouin settlements, Rakhma is not a "natural" or "spontaneous" settlement of nomadic people who arbitrarily decided to settle in the area; rather, it is a reality of temporary makeshift-ness imposed by the state, affecting all aspects of their lives.

Expulsion, Exclusion, Expropriation: Israel's Governance Strategies

While Israel takes pride in being a democracy granting equal rights to all its citizens, since the state's establishment the Negev Bedouin have not been managed as regular Israelis. Rather, they are controlled through an administrative and legal patchwork of policies and often-violent practices that enable the state to suspend them in space and time while using varied forms of pressure to force them to give up their lands and culture and cluster in designated urban settlements. The relation between the Bedouin and the state is not based on direct access to regular government institutions or democratically elected local officials. Instead, the Bedouin are managed through an ever-changing assemblage of authorities that have been created only for their affairs according to the state's interests.[43]

The martial law imposed on Bedouin and Palestinian citizens after the 1948 war stated that nobody may enter or leave any military-controlled area without the military governor's approval. This allowed Israel to control the Bedouin population within the siyag zone while trying to prevent displaced Bedouin tribes from returning to their original locations.[44] This was a mode of governance based on fear, combining limitation of movement and prevention of settlement; it was managed by military courts and punitive practices and, as happened in the ma'abarot, also by lies and deceit. Israel used temporariness as an instrument of expulsion and expropriation, as the transferred Bedouin had been promised their relocation would only be "temporary," but although they repeatedly approached the authorities demanding to be allowed to return to their lands, they were constantly met with refusal.[45] To lessen their distress in their new location, the government allowed them to lease lands for agriculture. But only small and divided plots could be leased, and only for short periods, to avoid future claims of ownership. In addition, during martial law, Bedouin in the siyag were forbidden to build using stone or concrete, forcing most tribes to erect only temporary structures.[46] These instructions were based not on plans and laws but on policy and the military governance.

As Harney and Moten write, "Policy's chief manifestation is governance [which] should not be confused with government or governmentality" but should be seen as "a new form of expropriation."[47] Indeed, at the same time the military governance concentrated the Bedouin and restricted their movement, the Israeli government erected around fifty new Jewish settlements on the fertile lands previously cultivated by the Bedouin in the northwestern Negev, expropriating Bedouin's land after expelling them from it.

Rakhma, located south of the siyag, was initially managed by the army much as were other unrecognized Bedouin villages. Although no documents specifically dealing with Rakhma could be found in the IDF's archives, documents relating to other tribes show that the population was closely controlled both geographically and demographically by intrusive methods of surveillance: the Bedouin were counted and their communities were monitored, including the specific location of their encampments (at waypoints), the area of land they cultivated, the specific locations of their wells, the number of animals in their herds, and the number of radios they owned.[48] While all other Israeli citizens are governed by the state as individuals, the military governors did not discuss anything with Bedouin citizens individually, dealing only with sheikhs.[49]

No settlement policy followed the Bedouin's concentration in the siyag zone, and no funds were allocated to improve their living conditions. The area was neglected by planning authorities for more than twenty years, and the growing unrecognized Bedouin settlements appeared on no maps. The martial law period started the double abandonment of the Negev Bedouin in a campness situation: many of them could not practice their traditional form of life because they lacked sufficient land to support rain-watered agriculture and their herds in the siyag zone, and the state provided them with no supportive infrastructure or services, while banning them from building permanent housing and ignoring them in government planning, effectively excluding them from modern society.

Once martial law was over in 1966, Bedouin issues were transferred from the responsibility of the army to that of ever-changing special government committees. Townships were the second phase in the concentration of the Negev Bedouin; Tel Sheva, the first town, was established in 1968, and by 1990 another six townships had been created. Bedouin who agreed to relocate to the townships had to renounce any claim to land elsewhere in return for subsidized plots with access to infrastructure and state services. This further concentration of the Bedouin in the siyag townships was accompanied by new state laws allowing Arab lands to be transferred into Jewish hands. The 1965 Planning and Construction Law pulled the rug out from under the legal status of the Bedouin settlements, which were now labeled "unrecognized." None of them were included in the new state plans, and all their lands were marked as agricultural, creating an absurd situation in which all Bedouin settlements were considered illegal, even those that had existed for generations or that the state itself had created.[50] This law transformed the Bedouin into criminals, and all new construction was rendered illegal.[51] Bedouin who did not agree to withdraw all land claims have remained in unauthorized and unserviced settlements, suspended, as Oren Yiftachel argues, in a gray space between the lightness of recognition/legality/safety and the darkness of expulsion/demolition/abandonment.[52]

The efforts to force the Bedouin into townships, however, had the opposite effect, encouraging them to further establish settlements as a way to protect the lands they considered their own. This reaction is also described by the practice of *sumud* (steadfastness), an Arabic term denoting patience, perseverance, and determination and a political strategy of staying on the land to prevent its occupation by others, a practice of nonviolent resistance widely adopted by the Negev Bedouin. Despite harsh and consistent state pressure since 1960, only 55 percent of Negev Bedouin have actually moved to the designated towns.

During the early 1970s, Bedouin were allowed to prosecute ownership rights, but as most of them lacked landownership documents for various reasons, the state argued that the Bedouin could not prove ownership.[53] In 1975, a government committee recommended that all the Negev land be declared *mawat*, transferring it to state ownership and denying the Bedouin any right to land they had held for generations.[54] Following the peace agreement with Egypt, which necessitated the transfer of Israeli military bases from Sinai to the Negev and created a need for vacant lands, the Peace Law of 1980 recognized for the first time the Bedouins' relation to their land and their related property rights. However, compensation was meager, and the evicted Bedouin were still required to urbanize. Over the years, dozens of government committees and teams have been created to deal with the "Bedouin issue," with the Israel Land Authority (ILA, previously Israel Land Administration) battling against Bedouin land claims, and the Bedouin Authority in charge of the Bedouin day-to-day "management" on behalf of the state.[55]

Bedouin Authorities, Patrols, and Police Units

Salem Ubu Mariam, the manager of Adalah, a human rights NGO and legal center (*adalah* means "justice" in Arabic), describes the Bedouin Authority as "a state within a state."[56] Resembling specific governance bodies in charge of native issues in other colonial situations, this authority manages all Bedouin matters, from the development of townships to the allocation of land for pasture, yet almost none of its workers are Bedouin.[57] The Bedouin are the only community in Israel with a specific body in charge of their "development," and the Bedouin Authority is in charge of all budgets related to the Bedouin, as well as of decisions on issues such as water and health care. This authority is also ever-changing in its names and affiliations; in 1999, the government established the Authority for the Regularization of Bedouin Settlement in the Negev, under the Construction and Housing Office, and in 2014 this body was moved to the Agriculture Office and given a new name, the Authority for Development and Settlement of the Bedouin in the Negev.

"Not much has changed since the establishment of the state; only the means have changed," says one of the managers who has worked as an inspector in the various Bedouin authorities for the last twenty years. While the general attitude of the authorities is clear—to settle the Bedouin on the smallest area possible—government policies and their related regulations change constantly:

> There is not a single clear policy that I can point to on the Bedouin issue. The treatment is sporadic. . . . In an ideal world I would have had a clear law which would give me the authority to act . . . but there is no clear plan—one person is doing this, the other is doing that . . . and I am deliberately confusing you now, because that's how it is! The confusion! . . . I want you to leave this place [the Bedouin Authority] feeling confused—because this is how we are managed.[58]

It seems that we can identify here the repeating Israeli utilization of strategic confusion and ordered disorder discussed in chapter 3, which is also the way the state manages the Bedouin, using specific bodies to enforce their violent suspension in space and time. These words could be easily linked to other forms of colonial [dis]order that is "divided into compartments," in Fanon's words, in which different populations are separately managed, or, as Shenhav and Berda put it, to colonial rule that is "characterized by a tapestry of multiple sovereignties, as well as by a collection of rules and abrupt decrees, both of which challenge the unified concept of sovereignty."[59]

As well as being in charge of the Bedouin Authority, the ILA is also the main body financing the Green Patrol. The Green Patrol, officially the Supervision Unit in Open Areas, was established in 1976 by the Agriculture Office to "supervise and guard state lands, water sources, the landscape and the environment in open areas."[60] It also acts in relation to the Bedouin on the behalf of other authorities, such as the Agriculture Office, the Israel Nature and Parks Authority, and the Ministry of Defense, with Green Patrol inspectors working under the auspices of several bodies. One officer states, "The primary goal of the unit is to guard state land . . . to prevent incursions, and possibly expel intruders."[61] The Green Patrol uses excessive force, including using physical violence against the Bedouin, killing animals, destroying crops, blocking wells with sand, and using their jeeps to demolish tents and houses. Rakhma's residents have experienced repeated incidents with the inspectors that have substantially reduced their pasture areas.[62] In addition, a special and highly militarized police force, the Yoav Police Unit, was established in 2011 to "assist in the enforcement and implementation of policy regulating Bedouin localities in the Negev." The unit is tasked with enforcing construction regulations and land use in the communities of the Negev Bedouin, creating another part of the law enforcement apparatus dedicated to controlling them as a specific population group.[63]

Like populations in other camps discussed in this book, the Bedouin are also managed in a mode of governance that is different from the way other Israelis and Israeli spaces are governed. The temporary and precarious status of the Bedouin is enforced by a form of colonial state apparatus that directs real and symbolic violence against them. According to this strategy, unrecognized Bedouin settlements have developed into camp-like spaces where inhabitants are suspended and exposed to violence until they comply with the requirements of the state.

A History of Forced Necropolitical Changes

The livelihood of Rakhma's residents, like that of the other Bedouin in the unrecognized villages, depends mainly on the balance between social security benefits on the one hand and rain-watered agriculture and their herds on the other.[64] "We need an area for agriculture. . . . We have goats, camels—this is our livelihood," says one of Rakhma's residents,[65] and indeed almost all families in Rakhma own herds. In total there are more than three thousand sheep and goats and 130 camels, yet the herds are constantly shrinking due to lack of pastureland. The herds are kept mainly for everyday livelihood, but they are also very significant to the Bedouin culture; the whole family is involved in managing the animals, including women and children, who take them out to pasture. Although some residents work in other occupations, such as teachers or as career soldiers in the army,[66] agriculture is seen as the most sustainable livelihood and as inseparable from their form of life.[67]

Active military firing zones cover approximately 90 percent of the Negev,[68] and pasture areas, located on the margins of these firing zones, have been the subject of great dispute between Rakhma residents and the state in recent years.

178 Unrecognized Order

"There is almost no pasture; it is impossible to graze," said one of the residents, echoing others' statements.[69] While in the past there were arrangements between the military and the Bedouin, today most pasturing is done illegally, since the movement of Rakhma's herds is currently very limited because of the mosaic of military firing zones, protected natural reserves, and Yeruham's municipal areas:

> Twenty years ago . . . we went out to pasture. But today it is impossible to wander about. Today they push you from every side—natural reserves, firing zones, you can't graze. . . . If I take them [the herds] down to the [Large] Crater—there are fines from the Natural Reserve Authority—an inspector comes and tells you—you cannot be here, and they take you to court.[70]

Rakhma residents cultivate an area of about fifteen thousand dunams, mainly growing wheat and barley for both human consumption and fodder,[71] and the shrinking areas of agriculture and pasture tremendously affect the culture and economy of the residents that are fundamental to their identity: "The most important thing for me is my form of life. I am not willing for it to change. I was born with it; I live like this—this is who I am. I am proud of it; I cannot and I am not willing to change it," said one resident of Rakhma, expressing views similar to those of other residents.[72]

Like other Negev Bedouin, Rakhma residents were, and still are, subject to active, passive, and symbolic forms of necropolitical state violence that combine direct and unmediated control with neglect and abandonment. They were transferred to the area from their original territory during the 1950s, they were abandoned by the state with no infrastructures and no services, and their traditional sources of livelihood were severely restricted. Their persistent resistance to this violence has had considerable success, yet it also faces the state's ever-evolving violent methods, including new threats of further displacement to state-created camps.

Resisting Exclusion, Suspension, and Expropriation

Bedouin resistance, as Mansour Nasasra shows, began in the very early years of statehood against Israel's military rule and its practices. The continuous government pressure and clear discrimination have led the Bedouin to persist with their struggle and to initiate bottom-up actions aimed at influencing planning in Bedouin areas, including drafting local plans for unrecognized settlements and presenting them to the public as an alternative to demolition. In 1998, the Bedouin established the Regional Council for Unrecognized Bedouin Villages (RCUV), a voluntary organization representing most of the villages, which submitted a plan for the recognition of and long-term planning for over forty settlements. The Bedouin have also started to take proactive legal action; finding cracks in Israel's legal structure, they have challenged discriminatory Judaization policies, forcing the government to include Bedouin representatives and acknowledge their concerns about disputed plans.[73]

In October 2007, a government committee, chaired by former Israeli Supreme Court judge Eliezer Goldberg, was appointed to recommend a policy for "regulating Bedouin settlement in the Negev" and was given a broad mandate and extensive authority. The report of the Goldberg Committee declared in its opening note that "the Bedouin are residents of the state and its citizens, and as such they are not 'invisible' with no status or rights," thus acknowledging that the Bedouin had not been treated as citizens with equal citizenship rights but had been abandoned by the state. When reflecting on the Bedouin's continuous precarious reality, the report stated that "the factor of time is not neutral; it is pressing and has critical meaning," acknowledging for the first time that the campness situation, in which a population is suspended, has cumulative implications and is no longer acceptable.[74]

The Goldberg Committee recommended the recognition of most unrecognized settlements and compensation for those that would need to relocate, and Rakhma is one of forty-six villages included in the report as settlements that should be recognized.[75] However, the report declared that until the settlements' full recognition, the "law enforcement [on unauthorized construction] must be very strict and vigorous."[76] Spatial pressure was again adopted to deal with unrecognized settlements, and building restrictions were rigorously enforced almost immediately through a strict building freeze. However, most of the settlements for which the committee recommended acknowledgment, including Rakhma, were omitted from the area's master plan, which as a result received many objections. Since the year 2000, the government has slowly recognized eleven villages, yet the rest remain unrecognized, including Rakhma.

The Prawer Plan, also known as the Bill for the Arrangement of Bedouin Settlement in the Negev, approved in September 2011, was declared to be based on the Goldberg report, although its spirit was very different.[77] It was very vague about the promised recognition of the unrecognized settlements, and at the same time it called for the relocation of around thirty thousand Bedouin to existing townships and municipalities.[78] The draft law was condemned by the UN and the European Parliament, but it was approved by the Knesset in June 2013, leading to heated demonstrations by thousands of Negev Bedouin, following which the government decided to halt the plan. In 2014 the law was shelved.[79]

The state's pressure tactics, however, are still in heavy use, with the camp unsurprisingly reappearing as a ready-to-use Israeli mechanism for spatial (re)ordering, including for expulsion and expropriation. In October 2019, Israel's Southern District Planning and Building Committee convened to discuss two plans, both entitled "Temporary Residential and Public Building Solutions for the

Bedouin Population in the Negev."[80] The plans, currently halted, specify the use of "temporary camps of transportable structures," which will be created as part of the existing recognized Bedouin townships.[81] These displacement camps, according to the plans' notes, are intended to facilitate the "urgent" transfer of thirty-six thousand Bedouin residents of the unrecognized villages for a period of up to six years for "economic development projects," such as the Trans-Israel Highway, railway plans, phosphate-mining plans, and the expansion of military training zones. In effect, these plans, as a report by Adalah notes, "constitute another step by the State of Israel to forcibly transfer the Palestinian Bedouin population of the unrecognized villages in the quickest possible way, despite the lack of adequate and appropriate housing solutions for them." The report further notes that "the plans' sole concern is to clear the land without regard for the displaced population"— thousands of families, including children and the elderly, who will be devastatingly affected. With yet another threat of encampment on the horizon, the Bedouin makeshift built environment, including Rakhma's, continues to be formed through its residents' tactics of resilience and resistance, struggling with the state to create the everyday spaces they need.

Unrecognized Bedouin Spatial Order

In both an aerial photo and preliminary site observations, Rakhma seems to have no identifiable spatial pattern whatsoever. The settlement's general spatial arrangement, the layout of the built units, and the way they are constructed all seem to be the consequence of arbitrary rather than conscious decisions. However, what seems at first to be random and chaotic turns out to have a clear order, following specific rules and creating a distinctive architectural pattern based on the Bedouin form of life and its related spatial order, as influenced by the restrictions of the Israeli governance.

Rakhma, like other Bedouin unrecognized settlements, is constructed according to a specific sociospatial form influenced by kinship relations and other local social connections. As with Bedouin who are still firmly attached to tradition, the way the settlement is organized and governed is closely related to social norms and retained customs. But it is also linked to the rapidly changing Bedouin society. Rakhma's spatial pattern is divided into three main spatial units: a clan/social cluster, an extended family (*hamula*) cluster, and a family cluster. Each family cluster is used by a nuclear family, usually composed of a married couple and their children. If a man has several wives, each woman and her children live in a separate family cluster. The extended family cluster includes the houses and common spaces of the whole hamula, which often includes a man, his wife or wives, his married sons and their families, his unmarried sons and daughters, and additional family members. The clan/social cluster is composed of several hamula clusters; in most cases relations between them are based on kinship, but there may also be other connections, such as strong social relations formed during long years of being neighbors. Rakhma's approximately 220 families are organized in about 114 hamula clusters, and those are organized in 14 clan/social clusters in three main areas around Yeruham.

Family clusters usually accommodate the residential functions and include the *shig* (the traditional external structure or tent used, mostly by men, for hosting guests); the family's internal living room and bedrooms; a separate kitchen structure and courtyard, often containing a small garden for vegetables and fruit trees; and animal enclosures for basic household milk and meat production. The various structures in the family cluster are usually built in the same spatial order and in the same orientation: the shig and the entrance are usually at the north of the cluster, the shig being open to the east; separating the gate and the enclosed family structures is a courtyard or garden, and the kitchen structure is separated from the family structures, usually to the south. This spatial arrangement is similar to the layout and position of the traditional Bedouin tent, and similarly it has a gendered division: it is erected on the north–south axis; when facing its front, the men's section (the shig) is to the right (north), the women's section (the *mah'rame*) is to the left (south), and the kitchen and store are further to the left (south) side, sometimes outside the tent; the main opening of the shig is to the east, and when guests are present the women's section is entirely closed.[82] It is clear that the form of the family cluster is not arbitrary at all but is, rather, a repeating pattern that closely follows traditional Bedouin culturally based spatial forms, orders, and functions.

The different family and social ties that define the different clusters and the relations between them are well-known to all Rakhma residents, and they have deep social and cultural meanings associated with privacy and movement, meanings that are also gender-based. Residents and neighbors will not enter or pass through another family's cluster before first going to the shig, and women's movement is also related to the family cluster and is usually completely free only within its private section. The hamula clusters are also physically defined by assorted boundaries created by varied spatial means such as fences, roads, and physical distances. Family clusters are usually well-defined and protected by a closed fence surrounding the cluster's private section, and outside the fence is the shig, open to guests.

The family clusters and the structures within them are quite crowded and have relatively small habitable structures. However, the distances between family and hamula clusters are relatively large (50 meters on average), and the distances between the clan clusters are larger, varying from 250 to 1,500 meters. While the distances themselves are the most obvious separation between the different clusters, Rakhma's makeshift road system is also structured according to the placement of the clusters; roads usually pass between clusters, and there are almost no cases in which a road passes through a hamula cluster. These spatial relations, although they are very hard to identify from the outside, or at all for unfamiliar visitors, are created following strict Bedouin cultural codes requiring maximum privacy for family clusters, especially in the women's area.[83] As one resident explained, "Bedouin, from their roots, always lived separately. They never lived too close to each other. If there is a problem between them—it always turns into a violent fight. . . . It takes time for them to let it go."[84]

The distances between the houses are very important and give the Bedouin a crucial layer of protection. In their well-defined and well-controlled levels of privacy, the large open area around each house works like an additional skin, and residents express their strong embodied experience of distance as protecting them as much as their fenced cloister, a protection that also allows them a safe, free, and homely feeling. Even for an outsider, the large open spaces between houses do not feel neutral; rather, they feel as if they are highly controlled by the clusters' residents; once a car leaves the main road and joins a village track, it enters a highly supervised area.[85]

Relations between neighbors seem to be an even more important aspect of Rakhma's built environment than the distances between houses. "For us [the Bedouin], the neighbor is more important than the house itself," reflected one of the residents. If they had to relocate, all the interviewees stated, their first condition would be to have the same neighbors, so that the settlement would maintain the same spatial and social relations: "It is very, very important that if we move, the clusters stay," the same interviewee said.[86] And another stated, "If we move, my neighbor will stay my neighbor. If you have a good neighbor, you want to keep him as a neighbor."[87] The morphology of the landscape also has a crucial role in the location of the houses, which are built on relatively flat areas above the wadi (waterway) and below the hilltops in order to avoid the winter floods and the strong winds.

In recent studies, scholars researching the spatiality of unrecognized Bedouin settlements have also recognized their spatial order, based on the traditional Negev Bedouin way of organizing space, including the hamula clusters, the road system, the division of family houses, and the adaptation to desert morphology and climate.[88] What seems to be a chaotic spatial arrangement implied by the terms *p'zura* (scattering) and "spontaneous settlements" is in fact a distinct spatial order following spatial traditions based on well-defined cultural and social codes and environmental factors. "Familiarity brings an apprehension of implicit structure: as recurring features and rhythmic repetitions are recognized, a seemingly random environment becomes 'readable,'" writes architect John Habraken, confirming that such forms "typically conform to a socially determined framework."[89]

Arguably, in relation to Israel's hegemonic Western space and its planners, Bedouin space forms what Jean-François Lyotard has described as *differend*—a

Figure 5.7. A makeshift storage unit built of reused doors, 2013. Photograph by the author.

situation in which the speakers of one discourse do not recognize as meaningful or valid statements by speakers of a different discourse.[90] Israeli authorities make no effort to read the organized form in which the Bedouin inhabit the land. In their "typically modern practice," as Bauman puts it, they only try to exterminate ambivalence rather than see beyond it, overlooking Henri Bergson's definition of disorder as the "order we cannot see."[91]

Temporary Spaces: Between Tradition and State Restriction

Like that of other unrecognized Bedouin villages, Rakhma's built environment was meant to be temporary; its houses, stores, garages, fences, and animal enclosures all employ various forms of provisional construction using light building materials such as plastic sheets, corrugated steel, reused building parts, and prefabricated structures (Figure 5.7). The reasons given for this makeshift temporary materiality are varied. One explanation is that temporary encampments turned into temporary houses as a stage of the Bedouin's modernization. During the late 1950s, sheds and shacks made of timber and tin started to appear as a rapid and cheap solution for the younger generation, who wanted to abandon the traditional tent. A contribution to this process came from an unexpected direction: the gradual liquidation of the ma'abara camps made available tin and timber shacks that the Bedouin either purchased or just transported to the Negev for their use.[92] "When I passed by [a Bedouin] tribe [years ago]," a senior worker at the Bedouin Authority reflected enthusiastically. "I saw the huts we once lived in, in the ma'abara; the Bedouin have bought them!"[93]

The prohibition against building permanent structures (e.g., of concrete or stone) in the siyag zone during the military rule also explains the Bedouin's use of temporary structures,[94] and a report by the NGO Bimkom suggests that in an unrecognized settlement, where it is impossible to get building permission, temporary structures are built to answer the immediate and minimal needs of the population, using the cheapest construction methods in case of future demolition.[95] Attitudes about the subject can be related to a person's age: for the older Bedouin, a timber or tin shed has the right balance between comfort and the traditional tent, while the younger people wish to move into permanent stone or concrete houses, avoiding them only because of the demolitions policy.[96]

Rakhma's residents also recognized that the materiality of their houses was a reality imposed by the authorities: "It is impossible to build with blocks; the Ministry of Interior does not allow it," explained one resident.[97] "From the beginning blocks were forbidden," reflected another; "you could build only sheds."[98] Legal uncertainties also limit monetary investment: "[Light construction] does not cost much—one knows the state will come one day and demolish it," explained one of the Bedouin activists; "with no other solution, one builds a temporary structure."[99] It is also possible that the fact that temporary structures are erected rapidly is a reason to prefer them, both as a way to address urgent need and as a part of the effort to avoid interference from building inspectors, as it is legally easier for them to order the demolition of an unfinished building.[100]

While light and temporary structures were possibly first adopted as part of a transitional phase from nomadic life to permanent living, spatial temporariness soon became an Israeli policy imposed on the Bedouin, depriving them of the option of living in appropriately built houses while enforcing their temporary status. Like the ma'abara camps, Bedouin campness is used by the state as a mechanism to suspend the population until its desired territorial and cultural order is achieved. While the state partially justifies the Bedouin's current temporary spatiality by citing their nomadic past, it is clear that nomadism alone does not explain it.

This view is particularly challenged by the houses' materiality: while the outsides of the houses, with their temporary materials, look quite similar, the internal materiality of some of them is quite different, using permanent materials such as plaster boards on the walls and ceramic flooring. This significant difference between external and internal materiality, one being of a temporary nature and the other permanent, strengthens the impression that spatial temporariness is a form of existence imposed on a modernizing population, as one of the residents explains:

Figure 5.8. A shig outside one of Rakhma's family clusters, underneath the trees, 2013. Photograph by the author.

> [We put] corrugated steel on the outside [and] plaster boards inside [or] timber.... Sometimes it's insulated, sometimes not. There is ceramic flooring, electricity, water.... Tents are a problem, [as] every few years you have to change the tent [because] the sun destroys it; so [the Bedouin] moved to houses. Today the Bedouin are different. There is a fridge, a TV in every house.[101]

While from the outside family clusters look like neglected spaces, viewing internal courtyards sometime reveals the opposite picture: the protected internal open space is often carefully looked after, with paved surfaces or flourishing gardens, a striking difference from the arid surroundings. In addition, Rakhma's residents' intimate, special relationship with their current place appears in other forms: "My mother got married here, in this place, twenty-seven years ago," said one of Rakhma's women, explaining her close relationship with her mother's house while being with her own young children.[102] Rakhma's residents proudly showed both modern and traditional details in their houses: from blooming rose gardens, to modern electrical systems connected to solar panels, to delicate tapestry in the shig, to the animal enclaves and other structures made creatively from reused materials (Figures 5.7–5.12). "I built this house myself," one of the residents

Figure 5.9. A view from outside one of Rakhma's family clusters, 2013. Photograph by the author.

explained proudly; "it's very easy. You buy the materials—timber structure, corrugated steel panels. No engineers, nothing. I decided where to build it."[103]

These spatial practices and emotional attachments, which give an important value to the specific place of dwelling rather than to mobility and movement, show again that Rakhma's temporary materiality and status is very much the result of state policy rather than the inhabitants' form of life. The Negev Bedouin's material realities and cultures act here in a dual way, both physically and politically. On the one hand, this materiality is constituted by a political reality of imposed temporariness generated by Israeli territoriality. On the other hand, this materiality has strong aspects of permanence and continuity, and therefore is constitutive to the political reality of the Bedouin *sumud* and related claims on land rights. The self-built houses and infrastructures show an everyday resilience that is also a form of active resistance by indigenous people who resist their further displacement and spatial limitations and are struggling for their right to stay put.

In recent years, under the enforced building freeze, the spatial distress of Rakhma's population has drastically increased, as a resident reveals:

Figure 5.10. Solar panels to produce electricity are seen in many of the family clusters in Rakhma, 2013. Photograph by the author.

> Today it is impossible to build, to extend. They look down here from the satellites, and that's it.... All these house demolitions... so many of them.... They came with a large number of police and demolished the [neighbor's] house... like we are in Gaza! So many soldiers came—it was a total mess. And for what? Why? It creates a very bad feeling. A man serves thirty years in the Israeli army and then they demolish his house. They came and demolished everything. Everything. They came with tractors, their special units, soldiers. They are doing too many horrible things.... They push you into a corner.[104]

The current enforcement of the building freeze, accompanied by tight surveillance and house demolitions, deeply affects all aspects of the Bedouin's everyday

Figure 5.11. Blooming roses in one of Rakhma's family clusters, 2013. Photograph by the author.

lives: marriages are postponed, and houses become overcrowded with children. This is another level of violence enforcing the Bedouin's temporariness. While the Bedouin have managed to cope with the former version of spatial suspense through creative spatial and material practices, spatial actions were rearticulated and became even more complex in resisting the new imposed situation.

Resisting Oppression: Political Action in Rakhma

The environments of the unrecognized Bedouin villages can be compared with other current makeshift camp spaces created or reappropriated by their own dwellers. While these camp spaces are violent and repressive, they are also analyzed as assemblage spaces that produce different tactics and values, and evolving forms of political subjectivities based on their particular materiality, spatial forms,

Figure 5.12. One of Rakhma's residents shows his goat pen, 2013. Photograph by the author.

and modes of creation.[105] Similarly, the spatial actions of Rakhma's residents can be interpreted as practices of cultural survival and resilience, but the practice of construction without legal permission referred to as *sumud* is also an explicit form of political mobility and resistance: residents stay on land the state has declared its own and build despite the state's objections, and in so doing they collectively resist its policies. The temporary materiality of the structures, which can be erected quickly and with relatively low investment, is part of the way this political resistance is constituted, acting as the "*matters* that matter," in Latour's words, to this spatiopolitical action.[106]

This materiality matters not only because it enables the particular political action of *sumud* by allowing residents to build quickly and cheaply, but also because it creates a particular landscape, visible from almost every road in the Negev, that exposes the particular form of exclusion that stands at the base of the dominant Israeli political order. By their visibility and particular form and materiality, the

Bedouin settlements work against this order that marginalizes them by making them invisible. As Jacques Rancière notes, "The essential work of politics is the configuration of its own space," adding, "It is to make the world of its subjects and its operation seen."[107] Equality is Rancière's point of departure and the catalyst for politics, and politics is about the demand for equality by those who are unequal and the emergence of a subject, a collective subject of action, that imposes itself on the dominant political order and its scene. Politics here, for Rancière, is the resistance by an unrecognized group to unequal recognition in the established order, and aesthetics is part of this battle, as it takes place over the image of society in which every political community has a distinct form, such as the unrecognized Bedouin villages.

In addition to the Bedouin's individual acts of construction, which are manifestations of a collective political problem, Rakhma's residents act in other ways to claim their rights as equal citizens, including forming unexpected allegiances. In recent years Rakhma's residents and their leadership have acted together with activists and municipal officials from Yeruham, both spatially and politically, to alter their reality and resist the state's attitude to Rakhma. In January 2011, residents of both Rakhma and Yeruham, including the then Yeruham mayor, participated in a ceremony celebrating the official opening of a kindergarten for Rakhma's children. This was a happy ending to a combined local grassroots struggle that resulted in a district court ruling ordering the Ministry of Education and Yeruham's local council to establish a kindergarten in Rakhma. This decision was made in response to a petition submitted to the Israeli court by the Yeruham civic action group Mirkam Ezori (meaning "regional fabric"), the Association for Civil Rights in Israel (ACRI), and Udah Zanun, the head of Rakhma's village committee, stating that the lack of an educational framework for Rakhma's young children constituted a violation of their right to education and equality.[108]

Two previous attempts had been made to establish the kindergarten. The first was a provisional tent erected in 2008, but given the tough environmental conditions, its day-to-day use was limited (Figure 5.13). The second was a corrugated-steel structure that was demolished by the authorities. After the court's ruling, the attorney representing the petitioners stated, "The Court ruled decisively today that the authorities cannot hold children hostage in the struggle over the [Bedouin] unrecognized villages."[109] Accordingly, with special approval, a kindergarten was built within Yeruham's statutory boundary but geographically close to the village.

The approach adopted by both Yeruham and Rakhma activists was to tackle a specific problem (children's education) and achieve an ad hoc solution (the kindergarten), rather than reaching an inclusive solution to the problem of the unrecognized settlement as a whole. While the problem was presented and manifested as the nonphysical issue of children's education, the specific spatial solution was one of its most important aspects, with the materiality of the first temporary

Figure 5.13. Rakhma's tent kindergarten, 2008. Photograph by the author.

structures—the tent and the corrugated-steel structure—enabling the creation of a kindergarten bottom-up while also manifesting the communal need for it. The new kindergarten, which formed the first recognized and legally approved structure in Rakhma, was conceived as a possible first step for recognition of the settlement as a whole.[110]

This legal action against the state was therefore also an act of political activism that resisted the situation imposed by the authorities, resourcefully using the legal system as a tool to achieve spatiopolitical objectives. While the state's practices of suspended temporariness in the camp relate to *national* objectives of ethnoracial territoriality, this *local* political action seeks to achieve a sustainable permanent shared locality. This includes the collaboration between Rakhma and Yeruham, a Jewish town that preferred to support its neighbors rather than to comply with the segregating approach of the state, an approach that creates a separation between Jews and Arabs. While the struggle takes place at the legal and governmental levels, it is first and foremost spatial, and the building of the kindergarten is symbolic as much as functional, creating Rakhma's first formal public institution (Figure 5.14). The residents from both settlements are now acting to create a primary school for Rakhma's children, yet they still face difficulties posed by multiple authorities, such as the army, the government, and the Bedouin Authority;[111] all control the institutional production of the Israeli space.

Figure 5.14. Rakhma's new kindergarten being placed by Israeli authorities and on its celebratory opening day, 2011. Photographs by members of Mirkam Ezori, Yeruham.

Complementary Frontier Practices

Article 26 of the UN Declaration on the Rights of Indigenous Peoples emphasizes that "indigenous peoples have the right to the lands, territories and resources which they have traditionally owned, occupied or otherwise used or acquired."[112]

As with other indigenous populations around the world whose territories were occupied and lands taken by others, the Negev Bedouin, similar to other Palestinians living in Israel, are a dispossessed population. Their situation of campness is the instrument used by the state to separate them from their lands through methods of violence, abandonment, and suspended temporariness within and outside the normal legal and governmental order. This is also a struggle over the Negev as a frontier area that the state still does not fully control. In 2018, Israel's Basic Law: Israel as the Nation-State of the Jewish People, informally known as the Nationality Bill, formalized the discrimination and exclusion of Palestinians in Israel as a constitutional pillar; Palestinian citizens of Israel continue to demand equality, not only vocally but also through spatial actions such as those conducted by Rakhma's residents.

There is an inherent relation between colonization and mobilities, through which settler colonialism is enforced or resisted. While immigrants were brought in as representatives of the settling society to settle the frontier and actively expel indigenous populations from their land, indigenous minorities were pushed beyond the state's borders, moved to other regions, or concentrated and suspended in limited geographical areas, where they are still rendered displaceable.[113] Yeruham and Rakhma camps were indeed created by these two complementary movements and for two complementary reasons: while the ma'abara was created in order to disperse and settle Jewish immigrants in frontier territories, the Bedouin settlement was created as part of the effort to concentrate and dispossess the Bedouin. However, Yeruham and Rakhma have many things in common: both populations were transferred to the area by the state; both settlements began as temporary spatial arrangements; the inhabitants of both settlements were specific populations, Jewish and mostly Mizrahi immigrants and Palestinian Bedouin; and both were managed in a specific mode of governance: Tel-Yeruham camp by the Jewish Agency and Rakhma by ever-changing governing bodies specifically created to rule the Negev Bedouin.

While the settling institutions created Yeruham as an instrumental space to settle the frontier without any consideration of immigrants' specific cultural and social needs, Rakhma was created by its own inhabitants according to their culture and traditions. Thus, the "ordered" space of the historical Yeruham camps created a very thin order that, like a military camp, drew its strength from the internal discipline of its inhabitants and from its relation to the national camp alignment of which it was part. In contrast, hidden at the base of the "chaotic" space of Rakhma is a very sensitive and specific order, based on defined social, cultural, and environmental principles to which the state is blind. The act of building houses in a particular materiality as an action of spatial survival, resilience, and resistance, together with the successful struggle to establish the kindergarten as Rakhma's first recognized structure, show that Rakhma's residents are not passive in relation to their difficult reality; rather, they resist and act politically in order to change it.

6

CAMPING, DECAMPING, ENCAMPING
Palestinian Refugee Camps and Protest Camps and Israeli Settler Camps in the Occupied Territories

The refugee camps. The very mark of our condition, the sign of the original deed which catapulted us all into this unending journey, the embodiment of what might have been, what was, what could be, the body which must be dismembered for so many to breathe lightly, rest back in comfort. The body within our body, the representation of our memory.
> —Lena Jayyusi, "Letters from the Palestinian Ghetto," 2002

For their Palestinian inhabitants, the territories became an enclosed camp. It is not the wall that has created the camp, but rather the strategy and reality of encampment which has led to the construction of the wall.
> —Adi Ophir and Ariella Azoulay, "The Monster's Tail," 2005

On Saturday 10 June 1967, the day the Six-Day War ended, Israel found itself controlling an area over three times its previous size after the occupation of the Gaza Strip, the West Bank, the Sinai Peninsula, and the Golan Heights. Israel's "accidental empire" did not only mean control over new territories. Alongside its 2.7 million citizens, most of them belonging to the Jewish majority, Israel now also ruled an estimated 1.1 million Arab noncitizens;[1] a significant part of them were Palestinian refugees from the 1948 war. In the days that followed the Six-Day War a new wave of around three hundred thousand displaced Palestinians from the Gaza Strip and the West Bank, about half of whom were second-time refugees, sought aid in existing and new refugee camps, primarily in Jordan, and Israel began to debate the future of the territories it had occupied. East Jerusalem, its boundaries extending deep into the West Bank, was annexed less than three weeks after the war, but the other occupied territories were subject to political hesitation. The evolving approach to controlling the new territories was not dissimilar to

195

Israel's territorial approach after the 1948 war: to Judaize as much land as possible by dividing it into alternating parcels of Jewish and Palestinian spaces, operating under different forms of governance.[2] Yet, while after 1948 Israel included geographical patches of martial law—including the Bedouin siyag zone—under which most of its Palestinian Arab citizens were managed until 1966, Palestinians in the occupied territories were not granted citizenship and the land was not formally annexed. Instead, a slow and less formal process of land encroachment and territorial expansion began.

Settler camps were soon adopted as a familiar tool within this political and legal uncertainty. This time, however, and very differently from the prestate Zionist settler camps, these camps were created by Israeli groups while their existence was being negotiated with the government, and they were eventually backed by the strong and protective Israeli state and army, which kept the local Palestinian population under harsh military occupation. Indeed, the political void left by governmental hesitation was soon filled by the spatial actions of various groups of Israelis, including ambitious political, military, and religious leaders, who for various reasons wished to settle the state's vast new frontiers. Civilian settler tent camps and paramilitary agricultural frontier camps were first created in the Golan Heights and the Sinai Peninsula, and later in the Gaza Strip and the West Bank.

Only three months after the war, contrary to government guidelines yet with a wink from Levi Eshkol, Israel's third prime minister, Kfar Etzion, the first Israeli settlement in the occupied West Bank, was reestablished by relatives of inhabitants of the original Zionist settlement, which along with others in the area had fallen to the Arab Legion in the 1948 war.[3] Over the years, this initial, hesitant, and often arbitrary post-1967 settlement reflux initiated by groups of Israeli civilians became a well-coordinated state project that responded to the changing political conditions in the area with decisive and often deceitful acts of construction. Not long after their creation, these Israeli settler camps became settlements. These were later densified by various versions of outpost camps (ma'ahazim) and their supporting infrastructures, and gradually evolved into a well-coordinated territorial mechanism, dividing the Palestinian territories and encamping them as small, controlled enclaves that slowly shrink as Israeli settlements expand.

In addition to the camps used for territorial expansion, camps that politically were rigorously debated but were familiar to the Zionist–Israeli spatial–territorial conduct, Israel also inherited a different type of camp with its 1967 territorial occupation: the Palestinian refugee camps, more than two dozen of which have existed in the Gaza Strip and West Bank since the 1948 war. With the occupation, the plight of the Palestinian refugees living in these camps exposed the other side of Israel's strength, confronting it with one of its main moral contradictions and deepest anxieties.[4]

For some Israelis, addressing the situation in the refugee camps was the state's chance to tune up its ethical compass. "We have a moral obligation," wrote *Ha'aretz* journalist Amos Eilon a week after the war, "because the road to Israel's independence was paved on the backs of these people, and they paid, with their bodies, their property, and their future, for the pogroms in the Ukraine and the Nazi gas chambers."[5] Addressing the harsh reality in the camps was also considered to be positive propaganda that would strengthen Israel's moral right to hold the occupied territories and demonstrate its enlightened occupation to the world.[6] It would also assist the state's aspiration to rearrange its new territories and populations.

For other Israelis, the refugee camps were spaces that sustained one of the deepest fears haunting the state since 1948, when new Jewish settlements, ma'abara migrant camps, and pine forests had rapidly covered the lands of more than four hundred demolished Palestinian villages and Jewish immigrants had inhabited the Arab houses of Haifa, Jaffa, Lod, Ramla, Jerusalem, and other cities emptied of many of their Palestinian residents during the Arab–Israeli war. "Everyone will want to come home and they will destroy us" said Ben-Gurion a few years earlier, and Eshkol feared that the refugees in Gaza would march together to cross the border with Israel, both expressing their dread of the Palestinian refugees' demand to return.[7]

The persistent existence of the refugee camps, rendering Palestinian refugees visible in these extraterritorial and internationally administered spatial enclaves, was the living embodiment of what undermined Israel's exclusivist claims to Eretz Yisrael or Palestine. In their very being they contradicted the famous statement by Israel's fourth prime minister Golda Meir that "there is no such thing as Palestinians."[8] The refugee camps were also seen as one of Israel's most pressing security threats, perceived as spaces from which the Palestinian *fedayeen* guerrillas or militants, considered freedom fighters by most Palestinians and terrorists by most Israelis, had launched actions against Israel since the 1950s.[9]

For Palestinians, the camps were the live manifestation of the 1948 Nakba catastrophe in which most Palestinian land was lost, the national Palestinian home was denied, and Palestinian society was displaced and shattered. Indeed, since their creation the Palestinian camps have gradually acquired a fundamental political and symbolic role beyond their initial humanitarian purpose, as the materialization of and advocacy for the Palestinian right of return recognized by the 1948 UN General Assembly Resolution 194, a right that Israel has consistently denied. The Egyptian-controlled Gaza Strip and Jordanian-controlled West Bank were regions of Palestine to which Palestinians escaped during the 1948 war. They found themselves stuck there as refugees after the establishment of Israel over 78 percent of the territory and the fortification of the 1949 cease-fire lines, forbidden to cross back to their homes across the border. As integration was rejected by the regions and countries to which Palestinians were displaced, for most Palestinians the refugee camps became central spaces of struggle in which the camps' built environment played a central role. Since the occupation of the camps in the Gaza Strip and West Bank in 1967, Israel has pursued their dismantling, through often-contradictory developmental and military strategies, while Palestinian refugees have developed strategies to maintain the camps as both spaces of everyday life and instruments of resistance.

As a humanitarian spatial tool that acquired a central position in the Palestinian struggle, particularly Palestinian refugees' fight to return, the Palestinian camps are inherently different from the Israeli settler camps designed to expand and deepen Israel's control over the occupied territories. The Palestinian camps, in which refugees have been suspended for decades and fell under Israel's control, function as an instrument in which space itself plays a pivotal and complex role on various entangled planes, whether as symbolic, tactical, or lived spaces. The invasive Israeli settler camps backed by a strong state and army, differently, have become settlement points that together create a linked network tightening around the shrinking Palestinian space as part of Israel's territorial quest. A comparison between the camps of the displaced and of those who are still displacing and expropriating them would be not only unhelpful but also offensive, and this is by no means the intention of this chapter. Rather, by reading these camps together as the main political spaces of the current Israeli–Palestinian conflict and as particular material environments, this chapter, by exploring first the Palestinian refugee camps, including the Israeli military and planning decamping actions, then the Israeli settler camps that slowly encamped the occupied Palestinian space, and the Palestinian protest camps formed against the Israeli occupation (Map 6), investigates the camp as a spatiopolitical instrument used and stretched by various powers to push for substantial political changes. Reading these camps together exposes the camps' enduring role as swiftly created temporary instruments formed, designed, and reshaped by continuously changing powers and interests and as mobile, versatile, and embodied spatial and material tools through which actions of power and resistance are invented, enacted, and reconfigured.[10] It also reveals these camps as contrasting (geo)political spaces, with the refugee camps persisting as spaces imbued with the Palestinian demand for justice, and the Israeli settler camps persisting as spaces that consume the Palestinian space while enhancing, deepening, and signifying the injustice of the Israeli occupation.

Spaces of Refuge and Political Becoming

Forced to seek a place of refuge during and after the 1948 war, Palestinians displaced beyond Israel's armistice lines realized they were unable to return home. Many Palestinian refugees, assuming their situation was only temporary, were forced by the basic necessity of survival to accept aid, quite unwillingly, from

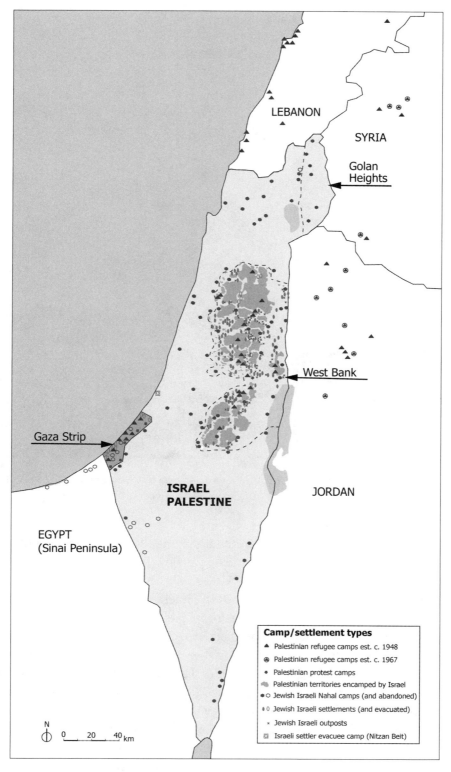

Map 6. Some of the Palestinian refugee camps, protest camps, and encamped territories; Jewish Israeli settler camps, outposts, military–civilian Nahal camps; and an evacuee settlement (only those within the map's boundary).

Figure 6.1. Tents in a camp for Palestinian refugees, Jericho, the West Bank, 1949. Photograph by and copyright B. E. Lindroos, ICRC Audiovisual Archives.

various humanitarian organizations in the disaster sites, aid in the form of makeshift tent camps that were scattered outside the new Israeli borders (Figure 6.1).[11] Around one-third of the more than 700,000 Palestinians who became refugees found themselves living in refugee camps in Israel's neighboring countries—that is, Lebanon, Syria, Jordan, including the Jordanian-controlled West Bank, and the Egyptian-controlled Gaza Strip—and others were scattered in villages and cities in the various Arab countries. The largest number of refugees were displaced to both sides of the Jordan River, with Jordan, which later annexed the West Bank, being the only country to provide the refugees with citizenship. In the small enclave of Gaza Strip, Egypt kept most refugees under military rule.

The several aid organizations already working in Palestine during the war were joined in the camps by the newly created UN Relief for Palestine Refugees (UNRPR).[12] In 1949, following Israel's continued refusal to allow the refugees to return, the UNRPR became the UN Relief and Works Agency for Palestine Refugees in the Near East (UNRWA), significantly adding "work" to "relief" as support for refugees' rehabilitation. Refugees, as anthropologist Julie Peteet argues, immediately suspected UNRWA of leading an unacceptable attempt to resettle them in their countries of refuge and resisted the agency's interventionist projects, especially those related to housing, worrying they might hinder their right of return.[13]

Hosted by four different states, the dozens of camps UNRWA was responsible for were very different from one another.[14] Some were preplanned and others were spontaneous;[15] some were established in rural areas, and others stood on the outskirts of cities; and like the camps created by Israel for Jewish immigrants during that period, Palestinian camps were also erected in former British military camps.[16] Yet, created as a combined action by UNRWA, the host countries, and the refugees, all camps similarly worked from the very beginning as extraterritorial, ever-changing spatial organisms of hybrid modes of governance and material and spatial actions, transforming according to the alterations of the political situation around them, which often echoed and collided within their spaces.

Shifting Camp Environments

From the time of their creation, the Palestinian refugee camps constantly shifted under the tapestry of the multiple, partial, overlapping, hybrid, and ambiguous sovereignties of UNRWA, the host states, and other powers.[17] Host governments designated and prepared suitable sites, compensated landowners for their temporary use, defined the camps' borders, and provided water and security. UNRWA leased the land from the host country, transferred payments for services, registered refugees, and provided them with food rations, health care, education, and other essential services. In late 1950, UNRWA's first director described refugee camps as "improvised quarters,"[18] but while the agency and the host countries attempted to stabilize the camps as controlled enclaves of humanitarian provision, the refugees resisted their imposed immobility, reshaping the camps as ever-changing assemblages in which material and human aspects were constantly reconfigured by one another. Camps grew when refugees who were scattered among Arab towns and villages relocated their tents to be near the humanitarian provision points, and although movement between camps was heavily restricted, many refugees moved between them until the mid-1950s to seek refuge near friends and family.[19]

The internal composition of the initial tent camps also changed continuously as a result of their mobile materiality and unstable social arrangements. Families moved their portable tents, pitching them next to relatives and forming clusters named after their original villages.[20] In some areas, the internal social and material layout of the camps re-created their residents' lost geographies, becoming spatial memory capsules of dispossessed places that could no longer be reached. Indeed, it was not only the refugees' sociospatial choreography that redesigned the camps, but also the camps' material ephemerality; harsh winter storms and a lack of

Figure 6.2. Hybrid of tent and stone walls in Jelazone camp for Palestinian refugees, the West Bank, 1950. Unknown photographer, ICRC Audiovisual Archives.

drainage that severely damaged tents, for example, prompted refugees to reinvent their shelters. By collecting stones or using cement blocks, camp residents built low walls to keep out drafts and stop rainwater from leaking into their tents, combining construction methods used in their home villages with the limited resources at hand. This ad hoc building technology created unique hybrid structures: while the masonry-built bottom imported from the past created the solid walls, the fabric tent forming the top, which could be quickly folded and packed, belonged to the ephemeral present (Figure 6.2).[21]

The prolonged period of living in tents and their expensive renewal demanded an eventual transition to more robust shelters, and by the early 1960s tents were a relic of the past.[22] In most camps, building more permanent shelters required the camp's thorough restructuring, a contested process that became politically explosive; many refugees resisted the replacement of their transient tents by more permanent shelters out of fear that improving their living conditions would jeopardize their chances of repatriation. UNRWA persuaded the refugees that such shelters were being built for economic reasons alone, naming them *malja* ("shel-

Figure 6.3. After years of living in tents since their exodus in 1948, Palestinian refugees of Aida camp in the West Bank enter their new concrete block shelter, 1959. Copyright Jack Madvo, UNRWA Archive.

ters" rather than "houses"), and occasionally threatening to stop issuing rations if refugees refused to move.[23]

Deterritorializing the Grid

Within a few years, the chaotic tent camps were replanned by British and French architects commissioned by UNRWA. Streets were laid out in a military-like grid, with plots of seventy to one hundred square meters on which simple modules of cubicle shelters, often with zinc roofing, were built according to family size (Figure 6.3). UNRWA tried to ground the refugees in a grid and uniform units, forbidding them to expand, sell, rent, or alter their temporary shelters, whose rigid form was repeated in the refugee camps created following the 1967 war (Figure 6.4). The controlled environment of the reconstructed camps, however, met persistent

Figure 6.4. Overview of Baqa'a refugee camp in Jordan, one of the six camps set up for Palestinian refugees displaced from the West Bank and Gaza Strip in the 1967 war, after UNRWA replaced the tents with prefabricated shelters, 1969. Copyright George Nehmeh, UNRWA Archive.

resistance. Soon after the refugees moved in, their new shelters went through a substantial process of transformation and informalization, and the strict technocratic spatial language was rapidly deterritorialized through an intricate mode of construction. Rooms and kitchens were added, floors were paved, windows were glazed, and walls were built around the designated plots, with spaces being added incrementally until plots were almost fully built up. The built areas were also often enlarged at the expense of the streets, blurring the boundaries between the original plots and the linear roads, creating a narrow labyrinthian public space of winding alleyways no wider than a meter or so with occasional dead ends and unexpected nodes of movement (Figure 6.5). These actions both redefined refugees' private and public space and gradually reshaped the layout of the camp, disintegrating the ordered grid through dense and ever-changing cumulative construction of ad hoc extensions built of different materials in varying heights and sizes. These spatial actions created illegible and seemingly chaotic environments for outsiders; one UNRWA director assessed as "unsightly" and "unhealthy" what he saw as the "mushrooming" construction in the camps.[24] These spaces, however, formed familiar environments for refugees, established by the spatial enactment of their needs, skills, resources, memoryscapes, and social and political identities.[25] Temporariness was maintained in the camps in other forms; trees were not

Figure 6.5. An alleyway between the dense houses developed by the refugees from their basic shelter units in Aida camp, the West Bank, 2007. Photograph by the author.

Figure 6.6. Open infrastructures in Beach camp, also known as Shati, in the Gaza City area, 1979. Streets and alleyways in the camp are often very narrow, and the camp is considered one of the most densely populated areas in the world. Copyright by unknown photographer, UNRWA Archive.

Figure 6.7. Exposed cement walls and urbanized dense fabric in Aida Palestinian refugee camp, the West Bank, 2007. Photograph by the author.

planted, and the minimal infrastructure was left exposed (Figure 6.6), enacting and symbolizing the rejection of permanence.[26]

In his "Assembling and Spilling-Over: Towards an 'Ethnography of Cement' in a Palestinian Refugee Camp," Nasser Abourahme traces the rapid increase in the use of cement-based concrete in Palestinian refugee camps after their occupation by Israel, looking at how the material transformed the pace and possibilities of building in the camps and enabled these dense environments to grow vertically, breaching built forms and topological boundaries (Figure 6.7).[27] This cemented change is not limited to the material and lived experience of refugees' quotidian life; rather, it is constantly spilling over to the symbolic–political in a variety of ways. Cement rapidly urbanized the camp, eroded the authority of UNRWA (which forbids the building of more than one floor), and created new associations out of the human assemblage of the camp (builders, popular and maintenance committees, neighborhood groupings), which enables construction. Here, refugeehood is not a fixed ontological marker, but, as Abourahme argues, "a contingent collective made and remade in the assembling of the camp;"[28] it is a composition in which the cement and concrete collide with and problematize categories and assumptions such as humanitarian management and aesthetics of temporariness and transience.

The camp is at once a lived space and a symbolic political space, and as such it is constantly re-created by the ever-changing practices (responding to new material and political realities) that are reworked through one another.

Agency here is immanent to the continuous interactions between the material and human factors and actors. Refugee subjectivities are formed not only through direct acts of resistance but also as everyday negotiations in which subjects both shape and are shaped by their material environment. Exposed concrete, which almost became an identifier of refugee camp houses, did not only become a political aesthetic of the unfinished and incomplete; it is also placed somewhere in the in-between: not the settledness of Palestinian traditional stone housing, nor the radical temporariness and exposed vulnerability of the tent or the zinc-roofed shelters.

With these ongoing changes, from moving tents to expanding shelters, it is clear that, rather than being a static architectural object, the camp is formed as a fluid, dynamic, and diverse space shaped by a variety of factors, including its everyday materiality, practices, and built structures through which matters and people, objects and subjects, create mutually constitutive relations.[29] Through these practices, the refugees deterritorialize the camps' institutional language—such as an easy-to-control humanitarian space crafted by aid organizations and the hosting states' political logic—and create an ongoing process of becoming that encompasses the camp environment and the refugees.

For sure, if we compare the materiality of the permanent-looking cement structures of the Palestinian camps, whose political essence is *return*, to the materiality of the temporary-looking light structures in the Bedouin imposed campness, whose reality and subversive political essence is the steadfastness of *staying on the land*, we can see the paradoxical realities of the camp. In these realities the materiality is often determined by a variety of forces and actors (governmental, military, humanitarian, the residents themselves), yet its meaning cannot be reduced to its physical attributes; rather, its meaning is determined by the unfolding subjectivities of those creating their environments with these materials. These paradoxes emerge out of the conflicting forces at work on and within the camp, where the needs of lived realities—or the power *of* life—collide with the needs of those trying to forcefully control reality, inflicting their power *over* life. The subversive pronunciations of these imposed spaces (Palestinian exposed concrete, Bedouin light structures wrapped around permanent-looking dwellings) register them as particular aestheticopolitical articulations that are not only the product of particular politics but also actively work against it.

Politicizing the Private Realm

Indeed, it was not only the grid and the repetitive shelter modules that were deterritorialized; so were the dictated societal and governmental structures that the camp attempted to shape. The well-defined domestic private sphere created by UNRWA's original shelters was also undermined by the refugees' actions, which destabilized the possibility of homemaking in displacement, turning the private sphere into one that is always intertwined with the political.

Rather than being calculated distances separating shelter units, as in UNRWA's camp design, the new spatial connections between the shelters evolved around the refugees' local social agreements, which made their private realms tightly connected and seemingly inseparable from one another, blurring differences between family units. These adjustments created fluid boundaries between the camp's private spaces and between them and the camp's public realm, making the personal place of the home an inseparable part of the camp's collective social and political meaning. In addition, because of the density of the camps and their overcrowded shelters, domesticity overflowed the confines of refugees' homes, merging into the entire environment of the camp. Food preparation spilled into the camp's public spaces, while front doorsteps extended domestic spaces, opening the cramped shelters to air and light. At the same time, the private realm also sheltered activities of political resistance, while the camp's incremental environment itself became a physical barrier, squashing intelligible order and uniformity into dense, winding, and dynamically changing clusters that defended residents and guerrilla fighters from external powers when camps became intensified sites of armed struggle. Here, the architectural object of the camp, including its private spaces, does not only represent resistance through its aesthetics but also facilitates it through its built form. This private/public obscurity formed the camps as large units of intimate spaces, working against the often-unwelcoming exterior environments.

The camp's blurred binary distinction between the public and private realms resonates with the Agambenian notion of the indistinguishability between city and house in the camp.[30] In modern political thought, at least before its feminist turn, the private realm (which maintains life) is often considered to be inherently separated from the political sphere and beyond the reach of the political, with politics limited to the public realm.[31] For Agamben, the paradigmatic indistinguishability of these realms in the camp as the "experimental laboratory of contemporary biopolitics" means that the ability to act politically is taken from those detained there, who now exist as stripped bare life.[32] In the Palestinian refugee camps, however, which Agamben himself identifies as "counter-laboratories," both spheres became inherently political and invaluable to the Palestinian struggle, in both practical and symbolic manners.[33] With the influence of Marxist ideology on the Palestinian Liberation Organization (PLO) in the 1970s, domestication was seen to work against the Palestinian revolution, which negated the home as a sign of bourgeois culture; "normal" forms of everyday domestic inhabitation, creating more comfortable living environments, were seen as betraying the Palestinian goal of return.[34] At the same time, the camp as a whole was adopted as a collective domestic realm in a shared reality of displacement; "camps were homes to be defended," Peteet argues, while the *fedayeen* guerrillas were referred to as "sons of the camp," presenting the camp as the site that collectively "gave birth" to militant resistance.[35] This private/public and domestic/political obscurity was enforced in a completely different way by the Israeli army when soldiers walked through the internal walls of the camps' Palestinian houses during military operations, violently penetrating and further blurring their boundaries.[36] From the initial Palestinian insistence that more permanent houses would not replace the temporary shelter, to the blurriness between the private and public that creates a collective announcement of a reality in which politics resides everywhere, the camp is again created as both a living environment and a political claim, where the threshold between the two is continuously problematized and reworked.

Assemblage Spaces of Political Becoming

Confined to the spatial framework of the camps, facing both the impossibility of building elsewhere and the impossibility of using the technocratic grid of the more permanent shelters that worked against social and cultural identity, needs, and political aspirations, refugees had to carve together lines of flight within the camp by altering their spaces, transforming impossibility itself into a tool of revolutionary spatial formation.[37] Rather than acting as individual builders or householders, or as helpless and powerless people of what Jennifer Hyndman defines as the "non-communities of the excluded," refugees constructed camps as agents who were all connected to a joint enunciation, reflecting the complexities of living in the camp.[38] The assemblage of materials, objects, people, and institutions, reshaped through processes of ongoing construction, has accumulated into a collective value through the actions and connections of the camp's heterogenous physical and human components. The distinct symbolic political expressions that became part of the spaces of Palestinian camps, such as murals and posters in the camps' public spaces or the symbolic key reflecting displacement and the right of return (Figure 6.8), became a more declarative part of the camp's assemblage.

Rather than conforming to the major power structures of international and national politics and technocratic humanitarianism, the refugees in the camp adopt minor practices as a radical liberating force mobilized from below within the structure of the camp. These assemblages of spatial creation often do not directly resist the spatial language of the major powers creating and running the camp but, instead, create lines of flight through the built environment itself and deterritorialize it in ways that often together announce broader political meanings. While "majority" implies a state of domination, not in quantity but in quality, these forms of spatial actions could be seen as what Deleuze and Guattari describe as *minoritarian becoming* that creates escape routes through the existing structures rather than confronting and resisting it altogether.[39] These are practices that do not resist the camp but that might use it as an instrument of resistance in the more substantial Palestinian struggle, while constantly re-creating the camp according to changing political, physical, and everyday needs and realities. They could also be described as creating what Harney and Moten call "the undercommons"—that is, the space of refusal that exists "always in the break," a space where planning "is not an activity, not fishing or dancing or teaching or loving, but the ceaseless experiment with the futurial presence of the forms of life that make such activities possible."[40] As such, the space of the camp rejects the nation as the basis of coming together and the condition of politics but creates a political terrain in itself that subverts the imposed situation of encampment by forming the unpredicted conditions of possibilities for its future change.[41]

In these ever-changing, seemingly chaotic, and materially intrinsic built fabrics, clear definitions and categorical divisions such as past/present, private/public, permanent/temporary, or containment/liberation are questioned, stumbled over, and subverted by the spaces in which politics is formed and enacted. These practices are not dissimilar to others enacted by refugees in other camps around the world in their efforts to inhabit an environment that was created as uninhabitable. Each of these spatial transformations also entails particular yet ever-transforming assemblages of materials, sets of skills, modes of construction, institutional limitations or support, and other components that create them in specific political formations, rejecting any reductive opposition between these material practices and symbolic political ones. As such, camp inhabitants are far from being a depoliticized "noncommunity" but, rather, are acting, as Silvia Pasquetti identifies, in ways that "routinely connect their day-to-day struggle against material deprivation" to their cultural and political struggles for recognition and participation as Palestinian refugees living in a controlled camp environment.[42]

In one of his reflections on Palestinian prose, Edward Said observes that its most striking aspect is its "formal instability," which, with its broken narratives and fragmentary compositions, creates the "elusive, resistant reality it tries so often to represent."[43] On a similar note, it is not only the camps' humanitarian or exclusionary function but primarily their radically transformative, fundamentally responsive, and intentionally incomplete, fractured, and unstable spatial forms, collectively created by their residents, that create their "formal instability" as spaces of continuous political becoming. Refugees in the camp face extreme ongoing violence precisely because of that uncontrolled instability that is both represented and enacted in it. Indeed, as soon as Israel occupied some of the Palestinian camps in 1967, it began working to dismantle these spaces, in which the refugees were perceived as a particularly troubling and subversive force.

Figure 6.8. Mural of life in Palestine before the Nakba; a flag-map of Palestine titled "We will return," with a list of the Palestinian villages left behind; and a gate with a key that symbolizes the return. Aida camp, the West Bank, 2007. Photographs by the author.

Decamping through Destruction and Development

After the 1967 war, the occupied territories became a contested frontier zone, creating an encompassing state of exception in which the Palestinian camps became focal points of Israeli intervention through both seemingly progressive and extremely violent spatial actions.[44] The ultimate objective of these actions was to liquidate the Palestinian camps and by doing so to eliminate the living–spatial testimony of Palestinian displacement and refugees' demand to return, as well as to demographically redistribute the Palestinian population of the occupied territories and control Palestinian resistance. While the ma'abara camps became part of history and the Jewish immigrants were now settled across Israel's frontiers, as if they had always been there, the refugee camps remained as a persistent disruption to the encompassing territorial and national reordering of the Zionist settler project, which the Israelis hoped to "sort out," at least in the Gaza Strip and the West Bank. The reorganization of the Gaza Strip's camps was of particular interest to Israel. Of the more than 700,000 Palestinians who became refugees following the 1948 war, over 200,000 fled to the Strip, tripling the local Palestinian population of 80,000 overnight and making the displaced the vast majority. The everyday reality in the Strip was particularly harsh, with Egypt's president, Gamal Abdel Nasser, actively encouraging the camps to become spaces of armed Palestinian resistance.[45] In addition, Israel aspired to eventually annex the Strip to create territorial continuity between its prewar southern region and the 1967 concurred Strip and Sinai, which Israel began settling shortly after the war.

The 1967 occupation was not the first time Israel had controlled the Gaza Strip's camps. In the 1956 Sinai Campaign (Operation Kadesh), Israeli, British, and French forces conquered the Sinai Peninsula. Israeli forces raided the Strip's camps after *fedayeen* attacked Israel from the Strip, killing hundreds of fighters and refugees; the massacres caused an exodus of over forty thousand refugees from the Strip.[46] This movement was actively prompted after the 1967 war, when Israel suggested the transfer of one hundred thousand refugees from the camps to the West Bank, Jordan, Iraq, Libya, West Germany, and even Brazil, setting up a secret unit to "encourage" refugees to emigrate.[47] The refugees' temporary status and the harsh realities in the camps seemed to provide the political opportunity and the humanitarian and moral justification for fulfilling Israel's territorial ambitions by liquidating the camps and actively transferring the refugees elsewhere. The Israeli perception of the camps as central to the Palestinian insurgency, with the entrenchment of Palestinian militant groups such as Fatah, the Popular Front for the Liberation of Palestine (PELP), and other Palestinian armed movements within the maze of the camps, served as a military incentive to eliminate what were seen as spaces of violent resistance.

The rage and misery of the refugees in the Gaza Strip camps and their armed struggle were fully comprehended by Israeli generals and existential philosophers alike. "What can we say against their terrible hatred of us?," asked Israeli Chief of Staff Moshe Dayan in a 1956 eulogy for an Israeli killed by a group of *fedayeen* in Nahal Oz kibbutz, only one kilometer from the Strip. "For eight years now, they have sat in the refugee camps of Gaza, and have watched how, before their very eyes, we have turned their land and villages, where they and their forefathers dwelled, into our home."[48] French philosopher Jean-Paul Sartre, who visited the Strip with Simone de Beauvoir and Claude Lanzmann a few months before the 1967 war, commented, "The refugee camps that I just saw in Gaza last week are realities that weigh very heavily on Israel's future," capturing what had haunted Israel since 1948.[49] Israel saw control of the camps as an opportunity to change this reality.

Eliminating the Camp

After the war, Israel embraced an open-door policy allowing free movement between Israel and the occupied territories, including the opening of a Gaza–Tel Aviv railway line using existing British-built tracks. Unsurprisingly, this approach, which enabled Palestinians to work in Israel yet did not allow them to return to their original homes or gain citizenship, did not appease Palestinian resistance to Israel. A wave of agitation swept the Gaza Strip in 1969–70, including demonstrations in refugee camps and increasing grenade attacks on Israeli vehicles.[50] Ariel Sharon, then military commander of the southern region, decided that the IDF's intensive raids on the camps were no longer sufficient. In what Eyal Weizman describes as the "Haussmannization of Gaza," the IDF decided to completely reconstruct the camps, which were perceived as a "habitat of terror"—not only the central physical location of Palestinian armed resistance, but also the labyrinthian spatiopolitical context that was perceived as breeding it.[51] In a campaign beginning in July 1971 and lasting seven months, the Strip's refugee camps of Shati, Rafah, and Jabalia were kept under prolonged curfews, while Sharon's troops raided houses, carried out mass arrests and planned assassinations, and systematically destroyed much of the camps' built environment.[52] Thousands were killed, and almost thirty-eight thousand refugees were displaced, many of them relocated outside the Strip, including to al-Arish in Sinai.[53] Army bulldozers damaged or destroyed about six thousand homes while clearing security areas around the camps and carving wide roads through their dense fabric, some 320 kilometers of which were made suitable for military patrols. This was accompanied by the isolation of the Strip as a whole, with a security fence eighty-five kilometers long erected around it.[54]

These actions, located within the framework of colonial urban counterinsurgency campaigns, did not only violently displace the refugees from their spaces

Figure 6.9. Israeli soldiers patrol one of the refugee camps in the Gaza Strip, 1972. Photograph by Moshe Milner, National Photo Collection of Israel, Government Press Office.

of refuge once more and destroy the carefully knit structures that supported and protected them in exile; they were also, as Nasser Abourahme and Sandi Hilal argue, a "war on refugees," whose violence was aimed "not only to cripple resistance and pacify the camp, but also to undo the refugee as a political category."[55] As Norma Nicola Hazboun aptly argues, "The aim behind the liquidation of the refugee camps and the refugees as a category was to negate their characteristics as refugees, which forms the hard nucleus of the whole Palestinian problem, and to attempt to promote the Israeli resettlement schemes in the long run."[56] Sharon's ambitious plan was, indeed, to eliminate the refugee camps entirely, with the intention of resettling the refugees in the towns of the Gaza Strip and the West Bank, allowing some to return to Israel, while, at the same time, creating new Jewish settlements that would divide the Strip into smaller, controllable sections, in what he called "the five-finger plan."[57]

For Sharon, eliminating the camps meant not only solving security issues but also destroying the refugees' unsettling spaces of dissent and resistance and with them the refugee problem as a whole, while reinforcing the meaning of the camp

Figure 6.10. Aerial photograph of "ground zero" in Jenin refugee camp, 2002. Photograph by David Silverman, National Photo Collection of Israel, Government Press Office.

as an exposed violent space where, in Agamben's words, "anything can happen" (Figure 6.9). It was assumed that Israel's measures against the Gaza Strip's camps and refugees would lessen the Palestinian struggle, yet instead of improving security, they resulted in stiffening hatred and resistance.[58] "If they want to transfer us from here they have to ask us where we want to be transferred," exclaimed a Palestinian refugee at the time, while another said, "I am ready to go from here but to Jaffa."[59] Indeed, when the first intifada broke out in December 1987, it was from Jabalia camp that it rapidly spread to the Gaza Strip and the rest of the occupied territories.[60]

While Sharon did not manage to pursue his "big plan" for the Gaza Strip, he later, as prime minister, continued what Stephen Graham calls "urbicidal" strategies when, in 2002 during the second intifada, about 170 square meters in the center of Jenin refugee camp in the West Bank were completely flattened under the claim that the area served as a launch site for terrorist attacks.[61] The operator of a D-9 military bulldozer proudly stated he had made "a stadium in the middle of the camp," an area later called "ground zero" by the residents (Figure 6.10).[62]

His testimony is another case exposing the colossal damage caused to the built fabric of Palestinian camps, perceived by the Israelis as a threat. Entire sections of the camps were flattened and became necropolitical spatial deathscapes, with no consideration of the lives of the refugees residing there. This form of destruction, as Graham argues, denies the Palestinians "their collective, individual and cultural rights to the city-based modernity long enjoyed by Israelis."[63] It also denies Palestinians the right to a core political space while creating new forms of displacement and with them new forms of encampments created by those who remained homeless in their exposed space of refuge. Indeed, "urbicide in Palestine is an ongoing story," reflects Nurhan Abuji as he compares Jenin's destruction to other urbicidal demolitions of Palestinian spaces.[64] Yet it is a very different Israeli strategy, aimed at eliminating the camps not by destruction but through development, that shows it is not only Palestinians' right to enjoy city-based modernity that Sharon (nicknamed "The Bulldozer" for his systematic destructive campaigns) was seeking to eliminate. Rather, he was mainly after the Palestinian's right to live in camps as refugees while continuing to struggle for their right of return.

Decampment by Design

Israel's violent military destruction and restructuring of the Gaza Strip's refugee camps during summer 1971 was not the only attempted method of liquidating the camps; the government also tried almost-opposite ways of achieving the same goal, producing multiple plans for the camps' liquidation through development. As Fatina Abreek-Zubiedat shows, these developmental efforts were based on Israeli architects' and urban planners' "professional knowledge" rather than on the often-contrasting military aims and actions.[65] In 1969, even before Sharon's bulldozers had entered the Strip, Israel's Ministry of Foreign Affairs suggested development projects as a way to dismantle the camps while economically "rehabilitating" the refugees, and in 1970, Shimon Peres, minister of immigrant absorption, created a secret Trust Fund for the Economic Development and Rehabilitation of Refugees.[66] With this, perhaps, Israel's experience with immigrant absorption (and with dismantling the ma'abara transit camps) has intersected with the state's attempts to liquidate the Palestinian refugee camps. In early 1971, the trust's mission was to relocate the refugees in the Strip's camps to new neighborhoods to be built adjacent to the dense camps or within the Strip's cities. Peres hoped that, by the resettlement of Gaza's refugees, UNRWA's works would be replaced by the military government, while undermining the Palestinian objectives. This was objected to by both the refugees and Palestinian leaders; Gaza City's mayor Rashad al-Shawa, for example, refused to cooperate with the Israeli attempt to integrate Shati camp into Gaza City, in order to not compromise the refugees' right of return.[67] Despite these objections, the trust managed to complete some of its planned projects, such as building 1,200 houses and infrastructure in the areas between the camps and their adjacent cities, beginning to blur the distinction between them.

Sharon's destructive actions in the Gaza Strip's camps in 1971, which were an attempt to decamp the refugees through violence, worked against the development and rehabilitation strategy initiated by Israel's development trust fund, which, as Abreek-Zubiedat argues, was developmental and "not urbicidal in nature."[68] The trust's actions were based on encouraging refugees to leave the camps willingly, countering the rise of Palestinian nationalism and the refugees' demand to return to their homes by turning them into homeowners in upgraded living conditions, while facilitating their integration in the Strip's cities. While the trust's strategy and Sharon's actions had the same purpose—to liquidate the camps—the trust's officials saw his destructive methods in drastic opposition to their developmental approach. The trails of destruction Sharon left behind forced the trust to move faster both to find housing solutions for a large number of Palestinian refugees who were again displaced and also to cope with the refugees' increased resistance to the Israeli government and distrust of the fund's plans.

Following Sharon's dismissal after his raids, IDF General Yitzhak Pundak, the Israeli military governor of the Gaza Strip, called for improving the living conditions in the Strip and was antithetical to Sharon in his approach.[69] He requested a new master plan from the Israeli Ministry of Defense to replace the trust's earlier plan, which envisioned an extensive design project of territorial continuity between Israel, the Strip, and the Sinai Peninsula. The plan presented long-term changes for the Strip, including the planning of Jewish settlements and Palestinian cities and villages, and also formulated the main principles for reorganizing the refugee camps, including integrating their built fabric into adjacent cities and relocating their residents into new housing projects. According to the plan, while refugees would be able to build their own houses subsidized by the Israeli government, any new construction within the Strip's refugee camps would be forbidden. In 1972, Pundak's area command created the Refugee Rehabilitation Unit, responsible for preparing housing programs and appointing refugees to senior positions in public institutes in order to improve their low social and economic status. These practices were reinforced by very specific policies that had a clear spatial dimension: in return for guaranteed employment and a new house, refugees had to relinquish their UNRWA refugee ID and give up their refugee status and the associated welfare benefits. They also had to destroy their own shelter in the camp and reuse or sell the materials.[70]

Israel attempted to turn the Palestinian refugees into ordinary urban dwellers in the Strip, receiving services from the municipality and new jobs in the Israeli or local labor market rather than from UNRWA, while the Israeli government would not be blamed for demolishing the agency's shelters. The new modern neighborhoods were intended to encourage refugees to leave the cramped camps, while

Figure 6.11. The repetitive units of the Israeli housing project for Palestinian refugees at Shaikh Raduan, a district in Gaza City that borders Shati camp, 1977. Photograph by Sa'ar Ya'acov, National Photo Collection of Israel, Government Press Office.

making the camps and their political meaning redundant. Israeli architects and engineers were recruited to plan and build thousands of units while developing experimental building methods. Dov Eisenberg, chief engineer at the Israeli Department of Public Works, for example, pursued what he called "expanding construction."[71] Refugees received a plot and a core unit connected to infrastructure that they could then expand themselves (Figures 6.11 and 6.12). In the camps' vacated areas, Israeli architects planned to build more housing, parks, and urban institutions, thus erasing the camps' deterritorialized material legacy. While the Israeli government showed off its enlightened housing schemes in the camps to foreign visitors, the true logic behind them was reflected in the words of then minister of defense Moshe Dayan, who exclaimed, "As long as the refugees remain in their camps . . . their children will say they came from Jaffa or Haifa; if they move out of the camps, the hope is that they will feel an attachment to their new land."[72]

Israeli plans to eliminate the Strip's camps and merge them into the cities continued until the Oslo Accords of the early 1990s. However, owing to strong opposition from local authorities, UNRWA, Arab countries, and the refugees them-

Figure 6.12. Palestinian refugees from Rafah camp expand their new house, part of the Rafah refugee housing project, 1973. Photograph by Moshe Milner, National Photo Collection of Israel, Government Press Office. See also in Abreek-Zubiedat and Nitzan-Shiftan, "'De-Camping' through Development," 150.

selves, only a few such plans were ultimately carried out, primarily owing to the function of the camps as core embodied political spaces needed for the Palestinian national objectives.

The Right to the Camp

Over the years, the Palestinian camps in the occupied territories, like those in Jordan, Lebanon, and Syria, have gone through continuous processes of urbanization and physical deterioration, many becoming dense enclaves within the expanding urban environments of their adjacent cities. These spatial processes, alongside the camps' persistent political role and increased exposure to violence, made the development or improvement of the camps an incendiary question. When the Israeli government and the PLO signed the Oslo Accords, the institutional landscape and spatial practicalities in the camps of the Gaza Strip and the West Bank changed significantly. Israel maintained military authority, while the Palestinian

Authority was now responsible for the population in Palestinian-controlled areas, and the political issue of the refugees was postponed until the final peace negotiations, creating a sort of a suspension within the camps' suspended status. Worrying about their future rights, camp leaders led a number of initiatives to secure the camps' status as temporary spatial entities hosted by the Palestinian Authority while being managed by Popular Committees operating under the PLO's Department of Refugee Affairs with continuing support from UNRWA's "phantom sovereignty."[73] This also influenced the institutional landscape in the camps; while in the pre-Oslo period the camps' few institutions were highly political, usually belonging to one of the main Palestinian political factions, the post-Oslo institutions were created by multiple local centers and NGOs. These spatial, political, and governmental transformations are part of the background to what eventually became inflammatory negotiations on the delicate relations between the political role of the camps and their everyday function as lived spaces.

In the aftermath of the dramatic collapse of the Oslo process during the 2000 intifada, UNRWA, managing what was by now one of the most overcrowded, poor, stigmatized, and marginalized environments in the world, was beginning to replace its traditional relief-centered mandate with a new developmental–humanitarian approach. While the goal of Israel's developmental projects during the 1970s was to liquidate the camps, UNRWA's approach endorsed both the refugees' right of return and their right to live in dignity. By establishing its Infrastructure and Camp Improvement Programme (ICIP) in 2006, UNRWA introduced a plan to upgrade the camps' physical and social environments through a participatory and community-driven planning approach.[74] Some refugees firmly resisted UNRWA's improvement of the camp with the claim that this might jeopardize the right of return, while others insisted that all rights should be maintained, arguing that the "frozen transience" of refugeehood, in Bauman's term, had, according to a community leader in Dheisheh camp, "prevented [the refugees'] societal development" because of their inability to plan the future in a state of transit.[75] "The tension between equalizing access and rights and maintaining some fundamental differentiation is extremely complex and immanently palpable," aptly argue Nasser Abourahme and Sandi Hilal, an architect who headed ICIP, because, clearly, the "political stakes whether real or imagined are high."[76]

Indeed, this complexity was reflected in the design and implementation of Jenin refugee camp after its aforementioned extensive destruction in 2002, which was already informed by UNRWA's new approach. Reconstruction of the camp, one of the main sites of radical Palestinian collective opposition, was furiously debated; the discussions included proposals to leave the camp's core of destruction untouched and a demand that the area be rebuilt in its previous shape as a testament to Palestinian political claims, struggle, and endurance.[77] Soon after Israeli forces withdrew, UNRWA introduced mechanisms to facilitate community participation, including a broad emergency committee representing the camp's community. Yet against the committee's position that the camp should be rebuilt as it had been, UNRWA argued that it was impossible to replicate its previous dense, interconnected, kasbah-like nature, suggesting instead that the camp's narrow alleys be widened to prevent their future destruction. Facing objections from the camp's committee that this meant surrendering to the occupying Israeli army by creating passageways for its tanks, Muna Budeiri, leader of the camp's urban design team, presented UNRWA's master plan to the camp's residents in March 2003.[78] While the plan's approval was followed by the resignation of a number of the committee's members, the camp's new houses were built according to the plan. In the following years, residents seemed to be satisfied with the improved movement within the camp, the better ventilation, and the increased sunlight reaching their houses, yet, as Linda Tabar shows, they also complained that the new roads made them more vulnerable to Israeli violence; in the camp's earlier labyrinthian fabric, "the Israeli jeeps and tanks could not enter the camp," reflected one resident; "now they have built the camp in such a way . . . that night incursions occur regularly."[79] Although the camp's residents eventually adopted UNRWA's developmental approach, Tabar argues, its professional position came at the cost of exposing refugees to greater insecurity and violence, while undermining the community's struggle for its rights against unjust political relations that were previously protected by the spaces they have created.[80]

The agency's new approach indeed led to thorough debates on the ever-changing nature of the Palestinian camps, encouraging their communities and leadership to rearticulate claims for a set of rights based not only on broader Palestinian politics but also on the refugees' lived experience. In West Bank refugee camps like Dheisheh and Am'ari, urban improvement was linked to the creation of new political spaces of agency, marking a significant change in how refugees and other Palestinians instrumentalized and interpreted their camp environments.[81] This attitude, similar to Henri Lefebvre's "right to the city," aimed to restore the collective power of camp residents to reconfigure the social and political relations that produce their space, an attitude that, as Dorota Woroniecka-Krzyzanowska suggests, could be called "the right to the camp."[82] This is not only about the right to maintain the camp as a central site of Palestinian political resistance; it is also, primarily, about challenging previous approaches that aimed to keep the camps' miserable environments while advocating for their residents' right to live life fully in their spaces of refuge while not compromising their right of return. A suggestion to "make the camp a heritage site" of the experimental educational program Campus in Camps is presented as another "way to avoid the trap of being stuck either in the commemoration of the past or in a projection into an abstract messianic future that is constantly postponed and presented as salvation."[83]

Through spatial initiatives, compromises, and ongoing acts of resistance, the

Palestinian camps are constantly reshaped as contradictory extraterritorial sites. While being spaces of humanitarian care, they also form deathscapes of unmediated violence; while they may take the shape of permanent urban environments, their temporariness is key; while they form memoryscapes of longing, they are also everyday spaces of belonging. They shift between unity and contestation, and their ongoing status as camps is met with contrasting and ever-changing practices of decampment or those facilitating their campness in a constantly evolving reality. While being symbols of the persistent Palestinian struggle for rights and justice, these camps also create spaces of becoming for their generations of residents, who constantly redefine the spatial and political meaning of living in a Palestinian refugee camp. This also includes living with Israeli violence that, with its invasive settler camps, puts pressure not on the refugee camps alone but on the entire Palestinian space.

Settler Camps, Splintering Infrastructures: Encamping Palestinian Space

From the early days after the 1967 War, Israeli efforts were invested not only in dismantling the Palestinian camps but equally in establishing new camps as nuclei for new Israeli settlements in the occupied territories. The nature and dynamics of these settler camps, including the methods and actors involved in their creation, transformed significantly over the years according to the shifting realities in the area. Yet while the link to previous Zionist and Israeli territorial settling practices is clear, this time the forces behind them were not an ethnic minority struggling to survive, but a strong state whose newly occupied territories included a vast majority of Palestinians, including refugees, to whom the state had no intention of granting equal rights and citizenship.

Only twenty-four hours after the occupation of the Golan Heights (Jawlan or Djolan in Arabic), Haim Gvati, minister of agriculture in Eshkol's government, met Ra'anan Weitz, head of the Jewish Agency's Settlement Department, who had replaced Eshkol in this position. This meeting followed the prime minister's request "to prepare material about the settlement possibilities in the administered territories [the former name for the occupied territories]."[84] In his tour of the Jordan Valley just after the war, Eshkol carefully examined the quality of the ground, stopping every few miles to "feel it and smell it and taste it," and on his first visit to the Golan Heights he delightedly exclaimed the landscape is "just like in the Ukraine!"[85] Yet in contrast to the enthusiastic annexation of East Jerusalem and its expanded boundaries just a few weeks after the war, no similar decisions were made in relation to the other occupied territories, which might threaten the Jewish majority Israel had worked so hard to achieve.

The void in the government's indecisive agenda, which avoided inconvenient political decisions, was soon filled by the sporadic actions of multiple Israeli organizations and agents: not only the familiar players working outside the state's ordinary governmental institutions such as the Jewish Agency, the JNF, and the army, but this time civilian initiatives as well. These actors erected ad hoc settler camps according to impulsive, multiple, and changing plans. These actions and decisions, made bit by bit, created facts on the ground that added up to a new policy, never agreed upon nor fully articulated, but with clear territorial purposes. In the Golan, on the "emptied land" created by the systematic destruction of over 130 abandoned villages and ethnic cleansing through the displacement of around 95 percent of the 128,000 Syrians living there, temporary outposts initiated by kibbutz members began to appear, and pressure to establish settlements throughout the new frontiers began to mount.[86] The Sinai Peninsula, the Gaza Strip, and the West Bank also rapidly transformed into an active frontier in which settlements, mostly initially formed by settler camps, again became a profound territorial tool, as Yehuda Harel, a founder of the Merom Golan kibbutz, stated to the *New York Times* in 1975:

> Israel is a country without borders. . . . What we have is where Jewish people have settled. The only solid thing is that in the last eighty years the Jewish people have never willingly given up a settlement. The people feel that by coming here [to settle] they have made this the [new] border.[87]

The occupied territories were politically presented as bargaining chips to be cashed in during future negotiations on peace agreements with the Arab states. New settlement tactics, therefore, had to be adopted, in which spatial temporariness was not only an operational and material instrument but also a political and legal key.

A Temporary "Framework of Camps"

Eshkol's government, while avoiding a clear approach and simply allowing things to happen, sought legal advice from the foreign minister's legal counsel Theodor Meron. Creating new "civilian settlement in the administered territories," Meron stated clearly, "contravenes the explicit provisions of the Fourth Geneva Convention."[88] But while insisting that the illegality of new Jewish settlements in the occupied territories was a categorical and unconditional contravention of international law, Meron also provided the government with a way to bypass it, to which camps were paramount, adding,

> If a decision is to be made to take steps for Jewish settlement in the administered territories, it is essential that the settlement be pursued by military

bodies, and not civilians. It is also important, in my opinion, that this settlement be *under the framework of camps* and be, in its external appearance, *of a temporary character* and not a permanent one.[89]

Meron's recommendation on military settlements within the framework of temporary camps was indeed adopted in the first years after the occupation. Familiar concepts and frameworks already in Israel's camp toolbox, such as labor camps and paramilitary camps, were used, and new ones, such as civilian outposts, were also created. All these ad hoc camps, encampments, and outposts had the potential for immediacy, mobility, flexibility, and the appearance of temporariness—creating ideal instruments for civilian–colonial and often militarily camouflaged expansion with clear genealogical links to the early Zionist military–civilian camps.

The military–civilian Nahal outpost camps that were created since the 1950s in frontier areas (discussed in chapter 3) were the perfect settlement instrument, one Israel already had in hand for its changing frontier, and they were indeed extensively used for this purpose. When the IDF asked the first settlement in the Golan, created by civilian kibbutz members, to disguise itself retroactively as a Nahal camp, Israeli general and politician Yigal Allon explained that this would make it politically easier for the government, noting, "Once [before statehood], we built an army camouflaged as settlement," and "now we'll build settlements camouflaged as an army."[90] Nahal camps were used extensively in Allon's settlement plan (known as the Allon Plan), presented to the government a few weeks after the war—a plan that was never officially adopted but that shaped Israel's settlement policy between 1967 and 1977, until the Likud Party came to power. The erection of Nahal camps followed the Allon Plan's suggestion of the fortification of Israel's borders along the Great Rift Valley, colonizing it from the northern Golan Heights through the Jordan Valley, including areas around Jerusalem, and down to Sharm el-Sheik on the southern tip of the Sinai Peninsula (Figure 6.13).[91] These paramilitary camps were also used to settle the Gaza Strip and northern Sinai, where local Bedouin were employed as day laborers in what later became Israeli settlements (Figure 6.14).

Another supposedly temporary form of Israeli settlement in the territories were the civilian camps in the West Bank's mountain region, often created against government protocols, primarily by members of Gush Emunim (Hebrew for "bloc of the faithful"), a movement that became a new national, religious, messianic, militaristic, and ultra-right-wing form of quasi-Zionism. It was founded to promote Jewish settlement in the post-1967 occupied territories, and mainly after the disastrous Israeli outcomes of the 1973 Yom Kippur War. Gush Emunim followers saw the territories as the God-given biblical "entire Land of Israel" (Eretz Yisrael Ha'shlema), a holy land that had to be redeemed. For them, the West Bank was an arena requiring a new form of "Israeliness": a tough and devoted way of

Figure 6.13. Prefabricated structures in Nahal El Al outpost on the Golan Heights, 1972. Photograph by Moshe Milner, National Photo Collection of Israel, Government Press Office.

life liberated from the government's stiff rule of law. The messianic sentiments that early Zionist leaders had used for their secular national struggle (described in chapter 3) burst onto the frontier of the occupied territories with strong religious backup and leadership while working against earthly legal and governmental constraints. And so, with and without agreement from the changing governments and using a wide array of temporary spaces and spatial objects, including military camps, work camps, Nahal camps, and civilian encampments and outposts, with a changing mix of tents, mobile homes (often referred to as "caravans" in Israel), and shipping containers, settlers struggled and negotiated with the government—physically on the hills, politically in the Knesset's corridors, and legally in court—settling territories while often not only ignoring the rule of law but also abusing the Palestinian populations around them.[92]

The Gush Emunim tactic was to settle sites rapidly without government permission, forcing the state to approve their actions retroactively to avoid the territories being evacuated in future political agreements. Initially, so long as a settlement could be presented to the Israeli High Court of Justice (HCJ) as a "temporary

Figure 6.14. Tents of the outpost camp Nahal Dekalim in the Rafah Plain region in northern Sinai, where Bedouin of the neighboring Shaik Zuaied tribe worked as day laborers, 1969. The military camp became a civilian settlement, relocated following the Egypt–Israel peace agreement to create Neve Dekalim, the largest Israeli settlement in the Gaza Strip, which was demolished in 2005 following Israel's withdrawal from the Strip. Photograph by Moshe Milner, National Photo Collection of Israel, Government Press Office.

intervention" meeting "pressing security needs" and helping in the struggle against Palestinian "terrorists," the settlement was approved, even if it was erected on private Palestinian land.[93] Yet in a 1977 court case concerning the settlement Elon Moreh, a Gush Emunim settlement established in Sebastia on private Palestinian land, when one of the settlers explained their ideological views that their right to the land was eternal, that they saw "Elon Moreh to be a permanent Jewish settlement," and that the settlement could then not be justified by urgent "security needs," the court ordered that the settlement be dismantled and the land be returned to its owners (Figure 6.15). Following the 1978 Camp David Accords and peace agreement with Egypt, Israel agreed to evacuate the Sinai settlements, including the city of Yamit, and the court was then convinced that even permanent places could be considered temporary. Since the Elon Moreh case, however, requisition of private land for settlements based on "security purposes" has not

Figures 6.15. Gush Emunim settlers in front of their tent camp in their attempt to establish the Elon Moreh settlement in Sebastia near Nablus in 1975, and the prefabricated mobile houses of the relocated settlement on Mount Kabir, 1980. Photographs by Moshe Milner and Chanania Herman, National Photo Collection of Israel, Government Press Office.

230   Camping, Decamping, Encamping

been permitted by the courts, yet "urgent and temporary military needs" have continued to enable settlements to be enlarged, and public land (rather than private Palestinian land) confiscated by Israel has been identified for the creation of new settlements.

The Encamping Encampments

By May 1977, when Likud came to power after a decade of Labor government control over the occupied territories, more than ninety settlements had already been established: twenty-five on the Golan Heights, twenty-two in the Gaza Strip and Sinai, thirty-six in the West Bank (mainly in the Jordan Valley), and a dozen residential quarters in East Jerusalem.[94] Although aside from East Jerusalem the number of settlers remained relatively small, ten thousand at most, the settlements raised fears among Palestinian residents that the land would be taken and alienated permanently and that they would be gradually squeezed out of the territories. Indeed, while 4,500 settlers lived in the West Bank in 1977, by June 1981, the end of Likud's first term in office, the number had quadrupled to 16,200.[95] The chaotic improvisation that had characterized the first years of the settlement project in the Palestinian occupied territories had begun to change to a more calculated and structured territorial approach.

From the early 1980s, the Israeli land grab was gradually regulated and legitimized, and settlements began to form according to a certain logic. Plia Albek, director of the civil department of the State Prosecutor's Office, who led the legal aspects of the nationalization of the Negev lands based on Ottoman laws, also led an encompassing mapping project in the West Bank that identified patches of unbuilt and uncultivated "public land" that could easily be claimed by the state to establish new Jewish settlements.[96] These patches, because of physical conditions, often existed on hilltops. In 1981, a Civil Administration was established to manage the West Bank and Gaza Strip, which, as in Israeli spatial policy thus far, operated along complementary lines of territorial expansion and expulsion through dispersal and concentration of the Jewish and Arab populations, respectively: promoting the construction of Jewish settlements and Israeli territorial expansion while limiting that of Palestinian towns and villages. Under the control of the Civil Administration, fast-track special planning committees could grant building permits to Israeli settlements, while the expansion of existing Palestinian settlements was severely restricted, with the "blue lines" delineating their boundaries often drawn as close as possible to their built-up areas.[97]

Jewish settlements were usually established through temporary nuclei of small outposts composed of tents, shipping containers, and mobile homes.[98] They were protected by their location on hilltops rather than fences, which allowed them to function as natural observation points with boundaries as fluid as those of the Israeli state itself. "If you put up a fence, you put a limit to your expansion,"

Ariel Sharon explained; "we should place the fences around the Palestinians and not around our places."[99] And so they have; while most Jewish settlements in the territories were surrounded by fences only in the second intifada, they were interconnected by a network of roads and barriers, created not only to link them and to connect them to the rest of Israeli space, but also to form territorial "fences" designed to encamp the Palestinian space.[100]

As Israeli historian Ilan Pappe shows, in the summer of 1963, following the growing unrest in Jordan and the experience of occupying the Gaza Strip for a few months in 1956, and based on its experience with the military closed zones described in chapter 5, Israel was already prepared with the administrative toolbox to run occupied Arab areas in the West Bank by dividing them. Officially named the Organization of Military Rule in the Occupied Territories, code-named the Shacham Plan, the plan divided the West Bank into eight districts to facilitate the imposition of organized military rule.[101] The linked Israeli settlements gradually created the expanding de facto barriers around the shrinking Palestinian space, and their initial temporary encampments eventually evolved to facilitate the plan of encamping the Palestinians.

In *Barbed Wire: An Ecology of Modernity,* Reviel Netz describes two very different yet complementary control mechanisms from early modernity—the mass-produced blockhouse and the concentration camp—both used by the British colonial powers in South Africa in their fight against the Boers at the turn of the twentieth century (as discussed in chapter 1). These two mechanisms had three alternative spatial roles: to prevent exit, or motion to the outside, to prevent entry, or motion from the outside, and to prevent movement across a plane. In concentration camps, barbed wire was used to confine the Boer population in order to "protect" a specific territory from them.[102] The blockhouse of the Boer War had the opposite spatial role; it was a mass-produced fort which was itself protected from the Boer guerrilla fighters. Constructing a network of blockhouses connected by barbed wire along British railway infrastructure, this system not only protected the lines from the Boers, but also parceled and controlled the areas divided by the infrastructure, limiting the movement of the Boers in the veldt with a minimum of manpower.[103] This system is similar in principle to the fortified prestate wall and tower outpost camps examined in chapter 2, which were not only protected by barbed wire from the threatening outside but were also built as minimal points relatively close to one another and linked by infrastructure and which eventually created a territorial sequence that enabled Zionist control over large areas.

Yet the territorial division plan in the colonized occupied West Bank was even more sophisticated than the prestate territoriality, as this time, similarly to South Africa, the territorial sequence of settlements/camps also encamped others. As geographer Ariel Handel shows, the system that was created consisted of settlement "points," whether these were small outpost camps or large settlements that had evolved from similar encampments, and protected and exclusionary infrastructure "lines," the roads connecting them. As such, they not only formed Jewish spatial enclaves of Israeli territorial expansion sustained by the state through infrastructure, subsidies, and military protection, but also created a network encamping the Palestinians in small territorial enclaves with highly restricted exit and entry points enforced by an ever-changing alignment of military roadblocks. This system, which divides the Palestinian landscape and functions as what Israeli political activist Jeff Halper calls the "matrix of control," consists of three main parts: the settlements (points), the road infrastructure (lines), and the moving military structures that supervise them (checkpoints), enabling the encamped Palestinian space to be closed and isolated by Israel at any time.[104]

The 1980 Gush Emunim master plan for settlement of the West Bank stated, "Our hold over a stretch of land does not depend on the size of the population inhabiting it, but on the size of the area on which this population leaves its imprint."[105] Accordingly, the broad dispersal of settlements over the entire territory is a consequence of a calculated design that heavily restricts Palestinian movement and expansion. Another plan, envisioned in the late 1970s by Ariel Sharon and Technion-based architect Avraham Wachman, consisting of a network of over one hundred settlement points across the West Bank organized in blocs and connected by major highways, embeds the same logic. According to that plan, the settlements would function as enveloping barriers that would fragment and contain the Palestinian space in the mountain region.[106] While the plan was never officially accepted, it was eventually more ambitiously pursued and implemented by various Israeli governments and settlers until it was entrenched in the 1990s in the interim Oslo Accords with the partition of the West Bank into Areas A, B, and C. Area C, which is controlled by Israel, encompasses 61 percent of the West Bank and connects settlements to one another and to Israel in a territorial web. Area A (full Palestinian control) and Area B (Palestinian civilian control and Israeli security control) are encamped within it as no less than 150 noncontiguous enclaves of various shapes and sizes. Movement within this archipelago can be rapidly restricted to a minimum, therefore making them easily controlled by Israel.

Since the Oslo Accords, Israeli control over Area C has been continuously entrenched by the creation of civilian outpost camps and by a severe restriction on Palestinian construction, among other means. The Unit for Strategic Planning of the Settlements Department of the World Zionist Organization, for example, a body that is not under the Israeli government yet is funded by Israeli taxpayers' money, created in 1997 a comprehensive master plan to enlarge the existing Israeli "settlement constellations" in the West Bank and to promise their future connectivity and development, while lending money to create illegal settlements.[107] Since 1967, Israel has created over 250 settlements and outposts in the West Bank; while Israel (but not international law) has legalized the settlements, dozens of outposts established without government approval since the Oslo Accords, which limited

Camping, Decamping, Encamping 233

Figure 6.16. The Israeli illegal settlement of Kokhav Ha'Shahar, established in 1979 on lands confiscated from the Palestinian villages Deir Jarir and Kafr Malik, West Bank, 2017. Photograph by Ahmad Al-Bazz, Activestills.

the Israeli settlement in the occupied territories, are considered by Israel to be illegal (Figures 6.16 and 6.17). These outposts are created for a variety of reasons and in response to a number of incentives, including revenge, and settlers have continued to use a range of tactics of transient materiality to bypass Israeli laws and military supervision—for example, constructing robust structures within tents or covering them with fabric, using the heavy machinery employed in the area for paving new roads to flatten the ground for outposts, or obtaining military authorization to build a sukkah (a temporary dwelling built for the Jewish holiday of Sukkoth), but creating it from a metal frame and later transforming it into the first semipermanent house in its settlement—ironically using the symbolic Jewish transient structure for territorial purposes.[108] Often, however, these ongoing settlement actions are supported by the Israeli army (Figure 6.18).

As Robert Young suggests, unlike imperialism, which is driven from the center, the practice of colonialism is composed of a set of activities on the periphery.[109] The method by which initial unauthorized settling actions in frontier areas are only later reinforced by the physical power of the state and its supportive

Figure 6.17. Inhabited and deserted mobile homes in the illegal outposts of Kida (established 2003) with Esh Kodesh in the background (established 2000) in the West Bank, 2019. Photograph by the author.

infrastructures could be linked to other settler colonial models such as those described by Cole Harris in "How Did Colonialism Dispossess?," where he reflects on other contexts and periods.[110] This temporary outpost camp phase has become a sought-after pioneer-like symbol, even if the settling projects are created inside Israel's official borders, forming a badge of honor of the spatial transience embedded deeply in Israeli culture, which became addicted to the adrenalin of territorial grabbing.[111]

The built-up area of these settlements is relatively small, as is their population: in 2021, settlers are only 14 percent of the West Bank's population (and 5 percent of Israel's entire population), and the built-up area of the settlements consists of less than 2 percent of the territory.[112] These relatively small settlements, however—too small to be self-sufficient like the other camps discussed in this book—together with their connecting road infrastructure form a highly coherent system that facilitates not only the territorial expansion of the Jewish population and its movement in the occupied territories, but also the exclusion and containment of the Palestinian population in their restricted territorial encampments. Palestinian movement between them, managed through a complex permit system, is highly compromised and often impossible. "I wasn't able to visit my sick uncle

Figure 6.18. An Israeli soldier protects a group of Israeli extremist hilltop youth settlers near their new revenge tent outpost erected in 2020 near the Palestinian town of Deir Jarir in the West Bank, as Israeli forces react to Palestinian protests against the outpost with heavy tear gas, rubber bullets, sponge bullets, water cannons, and live fire. Photograph by Oren Ziv, Activestills.

who is currently hospitalized in Nablus. . . . Many of our family members were stuck in the cities where they work, or at home," said Ramallah resident Fareed Taamallah after the Israeli army closed the city and shut major checkpoints between cities in December 2018, following shootings in the West Bank that killed and wounded Israelis. Zena Tahhan from Ramallah recounts how a strong sense of solidarity and enduring struggle emerged during one of the prolonged Israeli closures, when "across the West Bank, Palestinians opened their doors to strangers who were stuck on their commutes home," and "restaurants offered free meals until checkpoints were reopened."[113]

After more than five decades, this network of settlements and roads has effectively transformed into de facto annexation, with the State of Israel being declared by Israeli human rights organizations and Amnesty International to be an apartheid regime.[114] The latest so-called peace plan presented in January 2020 by President Donald Trump and Prime Minister Benjamin Netanyahu—Palestinians were not involved in its creation and immediately rejected it—is a direct continuation of the Israeli land grab and the fragmentation of Palestinian space.[115] The graphics of the plan's map, which uses different colors for "Israeli access road" and "Palestinian major road" and large symbols representing a "bridge or tunnel" connecting the Palestinian enclaves, shows how the Israeli territorial strategy of encamping the Palestinian space has materialized into an approach, recognized by the United States, that relegates millions of Palestinians to territorial islands enclosed by Israel. It was clear that the plan paved the road for unilateral (and illegal) annexation of significant portions of the West Bank that are controlled by Israel, including all settlements and the Jordan Valley, and Israel's territorial practices of encamping the Palestinian space received an unprecedented official recognition by a major political power. Ironically, the "peace plan" was rejected not only by the Palestinians and their supporters, but also by Israeli settlers. For them, the idea that some of their settlements were included in the plan "only" as enclaves within the pressed Palestinian space was intolerable.

Resisting Israel's Encampment

"What choice do the occupied have in this state?," asks Adi Ophir on the Palestinian situation, answering, "The liberal tradition of political thought in the West, the tradition upon which the Israeli legal system is also based, and the mainstream tradition of political action in the West—a tradition that Zionism, which defines itself as the Jewish people's liberation movement, wished to join—says that in such a situation the occupied have no choice: They have no choice but to resist."[116] Indeed, the regime of encampment, blockage, and closure of Palestinian space continuously disrupts everyday Palestinian life, yet it also encounters resistance. As in the refugee camps, the difficult restrictions unite Palestinians, who demand the right to move freely in the West Bank and resist their encampment in Area A, which instead of being the territorial seeds for Palestinian independence, as promised by the Oslo Accords, has become the beginning of their further division, concentration, and expropriation.

Among these acts of resistance, Palestinian protest camps were created to struggle against the ongoing Israeli land grab in the West Bank, such as the protest outpost of a portable structure erected as an action against Israel's land confiscation in Bil'in village in 2005, a structure that was later confiscated by the Israeli army (Figure 6.19). One of the most highly articulated Palestinian protests against Israel's settlement policy was the tent camp created in January 2013, accommodating around two hundred Palestinian and foreign activists (Figure 6.20). Named Bab al-Shams (Arabic for "gate of the sun") after the novel by Elias Khoury, this organized encampment of around twenty-five large steel-framed tents was erected on private Palestinian land in the E1 zone located between Jerusalem and the Israeli settlement of Ma'ale Adumim. The decolonial outpost protest camp was part of an

Figure 6.19. Israeli army confiscating a portable Palestinian structure that was part of a protest outpost created in 2005 in Bil'in against an Israeli separation wall on the village's lands. Photograph by Oren Ziv, Activestills.

effort to obstruct Israeli plans to build more than 3,500 housing units in the area, which would create an Israeli territorial continuity disconnecting the two major Palestinian northern and southern parts of the West Bank and also separating them from East Jerusalem. According to warnings from European diplomats, the construction could eliminate any hope of a contiguous Palestinian state. Mirroring the Israeli settlement material tactic of using temporary encampments for territorial purposes, this decolonial nonviolent popular resistance was described by Palestinian lawyer and writer Raja Shehadeh as a "countersettlement."[117] It emphasized the contradiction between the dozens of illegal Israeli outpost camps, protected by the Israeli army and nourished by the Israeli government, and the new Palestinian campsite, briskly dispatched by Israeli forces after only two days. Indeed, different from the violence of the Israeli territorial settlements, this protest camp could be seen here as a pure gesture, or what Agamben refers to as "means without end," the politics through which human beings emerge as such through their "communication of communicability" and its inherent ethical dimension.[118]

Figure 6.20. The Palestinian protest tent camp Bab al-Shams (gate of the sun), constructed in the E1 zone, West Bank, 2013. Photograph by Oren Ziv, Activestills.

Tunnels and Kites

Palestinian resistance to territorial encampment also developed specific spatial and material tactics in the Gaza Strip following the tight blockade enforced by Israel and Egypt, which gradually turned the Palestinian coastal enclave into one big camp.[119] This spatial resistance, operating at ground level as well as below and above ground, mostly confronts the fortified border fence erected around the Strip, which slowly isolated it in an almost-hermetic blockade. Israel tightly controls the Strip's land crossings as well as maritime and air space while frequently raiding it with drones and aircraft, keeping it for years on the verge of an unprecedented humanitarian crisis. The main form of Palestinian spatial resilience and resistance developed underground, with the creation of hundreds of smuggling tunnels between the Strip and Sinai to sustain the Strip's two million residents.

The hidden infrastructure of tunnels became an essential lifeline for the Strip, through which goods like food, medicine, concrete, fuel, car parts, and livestock, as well as weapons and people, were delivered from the other side of the border. The tunnels, dug from the basements of houses primarily around Rafah city and refugee camp and surfacing on the Egyptian side of the border, first appeared in the mid-1980s after Israel's withdrawal from the Sinai Peninsula and the subsequent division of Rafah. The number of tunnels increased following the Oslo Accords in the 1990s, when Israel tightened the restrictions on the movement of people and goods into the Strip, building a barrier around it. The barrier was closed periodically, which led Gazans to seek alternatives.[120] These needs increased following the militarization of the Strip and the frequent lockouts during the second intifada in 2000 and when Israel pulled out from the Strip in 2005, and they reached their peak following the ongoing tight blockade imposed by Israel and Egypt after 2007, when the Palestinian Islamist movement Hamas seized power, completely cutting the Strip off from the rest of the world. With access above ground barred, Hamas initiated an industrial-scale scheme of burrowing underground, creating a sub-economy of diggers and smugglers, whom it also regulated and taxed.[121]

The by-product of these spatial actions of digging was also used spatially; the poverty of the refugees and the lack of construction materials such as cement and metal in the Strip led residents to build their homes, some of which had been badly damaged by Israeli air raids, using bricks molded from mud excavated from the tunnels connecting them to the world outside.[122] Later, a warfare tunnel system was also created, connecting the Strip's cities, towns, and refugee camps and branching to cross-border tunnels under the Israeli border fence, from which armed attacks against Israel were launched.[123] These actions of counterencampment, this time creating real lines of flight, have continued to form the spatial minoritarian language that utters the particular meaning of an enduring existence in the hermetically closed "Gaza camp." Egypt and Israel continued to fight the tunnels, systematically destroying hundreds. Egypt sprayed toxic gas into them, flooded them with sea water and sewage, constructed a subterranean barrier, and created a five-kilometer buffer zone; Israel built an underground wall and blocked tunnels along its border in a continuous attempt to keep the Strip a disconnected enclave.

The struggle against Israel and its blockade also continued above ground. Hundreds of missiles were launched from the Strip at Israeli cities, mainly S'derot, only fourteen kilometers northeast of Gaza City, but also Ashkelon, Tel Aviv, and beyond.[124] These were followed by violent Israeli responses, such as the 2014 Gaza War, also known as Operation Protective Edge, in which more than 2,250 Gazans were killed, more than 10,000 Gazans were injured, and more than 100,000 Palestinians were displaced, taking shelter in makeshift tents and encampments (Figure 6.21). Such actions of urbicide and domicide and the resulting displacement, when occurring in refugee camps (as they often do), create a situation of a camp within a camp for refugees who are displaced again and again.[125]

More direct demonstrations against the Israeli border fence began in March 2018, seventy years after the Nakba, when protests by tens of thousands of Palestinians were launched from five tent camps along the fenced border in a campaign

Figure 6.21. A makeshift tent created by displaced Gazans in the Shejaiya quarter in Gaza City was heavily damaged by Israeli attacks in the summer of 2014. Photograph by Basel Yazouri, Activestills.

called the Great March of Return, highlighting the fact that the majority of people living encamped in the Strip are Palestinian refugees (Figure 6.22). During the protests, originally planned to last from 30 March (Land Day) to 15 May (Nakba Day) but continued until June and renewed again later, Palestinians launched "fire kites" bearing incendiary devices or Molotov cocktails across the fence. The kites caused hundreds of fires in the vast agricultural fields and woodlands on the Israeli side, thus creating a makeshift Palestinian weapon of protest against the encampment in the Strip. In the Israeli army's response to these mass demonstrations, 146 Palestinians were killed and over 15,000 were injured.[126] Here, the protest tent camps are used again as part of the material inventory of transient spaces to resist the ongoing situation of a prolonged encampment, supporting the march of the Gazan refugees toward Israel, the march that Eshkol, decades earlier, had feared so much.[127]

The Palestinian refugee camps still function as extraterritorial spaces within the Palestinian territorial encampments or the enclaves created by Israel in the Gaza Strip and the West Bank, yet the tightening restrictions on the entire population mesh them together as densifying and controlled campscapes. These

Figure 6.22. Palestinian women sit near a tent at the Return camp, Eastern Gaza Strip near Shejaiya, in front of the Gaza border fence, as part of the Great March of Return, and a photograph taken from the Israeli side of the Israeli–Gaza border shows the camp near the city of Beit Hanoun, 2018. Photographs by Mohammed Zaanoun and Oren Ziv, Activestills.

Figure 6.23. Prefabricated "caravillas" (part caravan, part villa) in Nitzan Beit, the temporary settlement/camp of the Israeli settlers evacuated from the Gaza Strip, 2005. Photograph by Amos Ben Gershom, National Photo Collection of Israel, Government Press Office.

islands of refugee camps within the shrinking and segregated Palestinian territorial archipelago surrounded by the expanding Israeli territory are the reversal of the Zionist archipelago of settler camps and settlements of the first half of the 1900s (discussed in chapter 2). This evolving process of settler colonialism, in which a struggling Jewish minority became a strong regional player, now continues to consolidate while crushing Palestinian territory and national ambitions into fenced pieces.

It is important to remember that temporariness is still embedded in the Israeli settlements in the occupied territories, which occupy a history of being disassembled and sometimes physically relocated, with new types of camps being involved in these movements of people in space. Israel's disengagement from the Gaza Strip, for example, in which around eight thousand settlers living in twenty-one settlements were relocated, included the creation of the temporary site Nitzan Beit for evacuees until permanent settlements were built for them within Israel proper (Figure 6.23). Some of the temporary settlement's residents ironically dubbed it a "refugee camp," in what could be seen as poetic justice embodied in this decolonial camp.[128] The encompassing reality in the occupied territories, with the Palestinian refugee camps and territorial encampments and the expanding network of Israeli settlements and outpost camps, could perhaps still be seen as a temporary reality that could potentially be undone, as Israel–Palestine's never-ending story of encampments continues to unfold.

7

IN THE DESERT PENAL COLONY
Holot Detention Camp for African Asylum Seekers

This place is doing everything it can to break us, but we've already been through hell.
> —Tewalda, a week before being released from Holot

You've seen yourself how difficult the writing is to decipher with your eyes, but our man deciphers it with his wounds.
> —Franz Kafka, *In the Penal Colony*

About a year before the Holot detention camp for African asylum seekers was opened in December 2013 in the Negev desert, its architectural illustrations were published in the Israeli media. The colorful renderings—of women in headscarves cheerfully playing on a basketball court under a softly clouded sky, black men relaxing in the shade of vines climbing on trellises, with green areas surrounding the buildings—almost managed to camouflage the purpose of this facility and its harsh arid environment.[1] Located at the heart of an isolated, closed military-training fire zone near the Israeli–Egyptian border, Holot (Hebrew for "sands") was designed for the prolonged mass incarceration of no less than eleven thousand people as a state instrument to deal with the arrival of asylum seekers, mainly from Eritrea and Sudan, for whom Israel has been a primary destination country since 2006.[2] The contrast between the inviting images of the facility—presenting it as resembling a leisure center—and its purpose and function, as a distant camp where asylum seekers would be concentrated and contained away from society, was striking.[3]

The descriptions that accompanied the vivid illustrations of the Holot Residence Center, to use its full title, added to the contrasts and ambiguities around it. It was depicted as a generous facility, with a budget of 250 million Israeli new shekels (ILS) for its construction and covering 750 dunams (185 acres), designed to care for, support, and advance those who would "reside" there, while carefully considering their unique social and cultural needs; the publication highlighted the fact that "a social adviser [had] accompanied each planning stage in order to thoroughly examine and understand the population that will stay in the facility" and would respond to each and every aspect of life there. The vocabulary used implied openness, freedom, and even empowerment, with the text reading like a brochure for a holiday resort rather than a description of an isolated desert detention camp:

> The residence facility will be planned and operated as a "campus" model . . . allowing it to be populated according to communities of origin, with the creation of specifically designated public and religious structures that will enable community life. . . . Normal clinics, emergency clinics, dental clinics and expert clinics will be built . . . near dining halls, kiosks, classrooms, a club, a library, a prayer room, a playground and sports facilities. . . . Because of its proximity to the Gaza Strip, shielded structures will be built, protecting against Quassam rocket launches. The two-floor buildings will be U shaped to create a feeling of a community's residential neighbourhood, with a lawn at the centre. In addition, the plan is to provide the residents with agricultural training . . . in case they choose it as an occupation after they move back to their countries of origin or if they later return [sic] to Israel.

This overly positive description did also mention that the facility would be supervised by the Israeli Prison Service and would be fenced and equipped with closed-circuit television and biometric surveillance systems, implying that it was designed to form a "total institution" of strict control.[4] The fact that those detained in Holot would either move on or "return" to Israel implies that the facility was perceived as an extraterritorial site, a camp par excellence, which despite being located within Israel's territory was seen as its detached outside. While Holot was defined as an open facility, which detainees could leave in the morning and return to in the evening, its isolated and remote location made it a de facto detention camp where the detainees' freedom of movement was severely limited. At the same time, the images and description of Holot to the public reveal that those who created the facility were not only interested in presenting its carceral role to Israeli society, part of which was already protesting against the African "outsiders" living in its cities, but were also inclined to emphasize the large investment in the project and its "humane" aspects. Indeed, the hundreds of online comments on this news report describing the camp reflected both sides of the political debate around it. Many complained about so much taxpayer money being invested in a place "for invaders" that "looks like a hotel" instead of being "invested in Israelis." Others stated that Holot was no different from a horrific concentration camp, expressing shame about its very creation, "especially considering the Jewish past of persecution and searching for refuge."

Holot was initiated as a border reception facility, the first formal entrance point to Israel for asylum seekers who were trafficked or smuggled through the Sinai desert, often after paying large sums. The thousands who crossed to Israel went through arduous journeys, with many reports of starvation, sexual assault, and other forms of violence en route, including being held in torture camps operated by traffickers trying to extort ransoms from their families. Those who took the risks and survived the journey were hoping to receive protection in Israel, which was perceived as a democracy that would assist them and where their human rights would be respected.[5] The scope and scale of the phenomenon was unprecedented in Israel, which for the first time in its history became a destination country in what Matthew Gibney calls the "globalisation of asylum seeking."[6] More than fourteen thousand African asylum seekers entered the state in 2010, and more than seventeen thousand in 2011, the years when the camp was conceived and planned, and this was where new asylum applications would be processed to determine whether the newcomers would be allowed to stay in the country legally or should be deported.

Yet when the camp was opened in December 2013, it was given a quite different role as a result of another grand national project that accompanied its creation: the construction of a secure fence running along the Israeli–Egyptian border, tasked with putting an end to irregular migration from the Sinai to Israel.[7] The fence and camp projects were designed together to stop unauthorized movement, both by physically blocking it and by deterring it through the intimidating prospect of prolonged detention, creating "a 'normative barrier' to potential infiltrators,"[8] together materializing the idea of the territoriality of the state (Figures 7.1 and 7.2). The construction of the fence, however, changed the meaning of the camp altogether, from a border facility to a detention camp. In 2012, when Holot's design and construction was still in its early stages and the fence project was progressing, the number of crossings began to drop to under 10,500, and they fell dramatically to only 43 crossings in 2013 and 21 in 2014.[9] Holot was therefore no longer needed as a border processing camp.

Nevertheless, at the end of 2013 Holot was opened as planned to detain thousands of African asylum seekers, who were described by the state as "infiltrators." The camp's opening was accompanied by the approval of a draconian amendment to the 1954 Anti-Infiltration law, which was originally written, based on 1945 British Mandatory emergency regulations, to secure Israel's borders from Palestinian "infiltrators" who attempted to enter (or return to) the country after the 1948 war (see chapters 4, 5, and 6). The amendment classified the African asylum seekers as "infiltrators" because they entered Israel "illegally" rather than through the Israelis' formal border-control apparatus, and the state initially planned to administratively detain them for a minimum of three years, and potentially longer. Many Israelis condemned the long detention of asylum seekers as a

Figure 7.1. A view of Holot with its prefabricated structures and arid surroundings, 2013. Photograph by Oren Ziv, Activestills.

moral disgrace,[10] and it was later altered by the Israeli High Court of Justice (HCJ). However, although newcomers were no longer arriving in 2013, asylum seekers were nevertheless sent to Holot from places in Israel where they had already settled, significantly changing the camp's role and meaning. Instead of functioning as a border camp where new detainees arrived immediately after crossing, and unlike other detention facilities across the globe, which usually serve as a transition point before asylum or deportation, Holot became a place to which asylum seekers already living in Israel were banished. The facility, paradoxically described as an open camp, concentrated them in a remote desert area for an unlimited time (later limited to one year), functioning as an isolated spatial instrument that contains African asylum seekers away from Israeli cities and society while intentionally inflicting misery and despair on them in an attempt to "persuade" them to leave the country.

This chapter illustrates how, from its opening until its eventual closure, Holot functioned as a large Kafkaesque penal colony, to which the destitute population of African asylum seekers in Israel was expelled en masse without choice and

Figure 7.2. View of Holot's entrance gate and sign, which reads "The Prison Service, 'Holot' Residence Facility," 2014. Photograph by Yotam Ronen, Activestills.

without trial. The rapid architectural design of the facility was informed by socially aware approaches and standards, yet those who were sent to the isolated camp entered a grim and violent world where their familiar everyday configurations and future plans fell to pieces in the hands of an arbitrary power. This power, orchestrated by the state, followed no explicit logic other than the stated intention to hold asylum seekers away from Israeli cities. While the camps discussed so far could be seen as part of colonial and nation-building territorial processes of expansion and expropriation, and its resulted refuge, with glimpses of decolonial actions of resistance, Holot is part of the postcolonial shift to camps created as part of the border politics of the reinscription of territorial and national control against transnational human movement. The impact of these camps is not limited to national borderlines; rather, it penetrates deeply to everyday environments in inner cities, where racialized black bodies are filtered out through the reinforcement of territorial border control. These politics of asylum seeking and their carceral border spaces are underpinned by the logics of race, othering, and colonial legacies of empire.[11] In colonial spaces, as Mbembe reflects, slaves and other colonized bodies were "kept alive but in a *state of injury,* in a phantomlike world of horrors and intense cruelty and profanity."[12] In Holot, as in other camps worldwide, these wounds and states of injury were inflicted on the racialized detainees through the difficult conditions in the desert camp, where control and neglect physically and mentally damaged them during and after their stay. Holot could therefore be seen as part of the current global penal colony where refugees and other "people on the move" are suspended and circulated. However, the role of the remote desert camp, designed to detach a particular group of people from their everyday urban life, marks it as a space of pure banishment to which they were sent for the undeclared goal of breaking their spirit until they "voluntarily" agree to leave Israel for good.

"Flooding the Country"

The violent breakup of Sudanese protests in Cairo at the end of 2005, which resulted in many people being sent to detention centers in Egypt and others being deported, initiated a major movement of asylum seekers to Israel, more each year until 2013. By that time, a total of around sixty thousand had arrived.[13] The issue of asylum seekers in Israel was a rather neglected policy area until 2006, and no Israeli refugee law was drafted. The influx of refugees that year, however, focused public attention on the matter, awakening demographic fears over the composition of the state's population.[14] Because of international nonrefoulement obligations, Israel is legally unable to deport asylum seekers to their home countries. At the same time, Israel's formal recognition rate of asylum requests is close to zero.[15] The state has thus embarked on endless efforts to stop asylum seekers from entering its territory while actively "encouraging" those who had already entered to leave. Politically, African asylum seekers' entry into Israel and their settlement in central Israeli cities was—and still is—seen as threatening the state's sovereignty by jeopardizing its ability to manage people according to its institutional and ethnoracial logic and as exacerbating its ongoing demographic collective anxiety.

Initially, Israel incorporated a range of accommodating procedures and deterrence measures while projecting an atmosphere of nonpolicy, otherwise described as "chaotic bureaucratic ambiguity," "governmental unruliness," "a refusal of any long-term responsibility," or a deliberate approach of "ordered–disorder" shaped by a "consistent logic intended to make asylum claims unsustainable" through the constant production of inconsistencies.[16] Unsurprisingly, this is similar to other situations and camp spaces analyzed in this book, in which a policy of no clear policy becomes an ever-changing tool for managing a situation separately from, yet within, the state's stable, recognized, unified, and publicly and legally agreed laws and governmental systems. During the early years of arrival, African asylum seekers were usually picked up by the army when they crossed the border and were detained in Ktzi'ot, a detention facility located within a prison complex adjacent to the Egyptian border in the area where Holot was eventually located. The facility, created to accommodate only 1,000 people, was later enlarged to accommodate 2,500, including an encampment of temporary tents where African women and children were also detained, while the increasing pace of arrivals required the relatively rapid release of detainees in order to make room for new ones.

Following a 2008 government decision to give some asylum seekers work permits, many were discharged from the desert facility and taken on state-designated evening buses to Lewinsky Park in south Tel Aviv, near the main bus station.[17] While some NGO activists, friends, and relatives would occasionally gather to meet those arriving in the big city, often with only the clothes they wore, many had nowhere to go and slept rough in the park for days or weeks.[18] Tel Aviv municipality began to provide basic shelter services to asylum seekers, who later moved to often-overcrowded rented flats in the area. While some began working formally and informally in the city, others opened small businesses such as restaurants, mobile phone services, and barber shops, mainly in and around Neve-Sha'anan Street in south Tel Aviv, transforming the area socially and culturally.

Israeli NGOs and some south Tel Aviv residents supported asylum seekers in the city, while others protested against their presence, objecting to the changing spatial, social, and cultural character of the area's streets, public parks, and playgrounds. While asylum seekers also moved to other cities, such as Eilat and Jerusalem, the majority stayed in south Tel Aviv, where the state had initially sent them. Like displaced people in other countries, the asylum seekers themselves also preferred to live in Tel Aviv, where they hoped to find housing and employment, relying on existing though exhausted social networks of care and support formerly established by African foreign workers in the city.

South Tel Aviv was already a neglected area, forming part of what Sharon Rotbard has called the "black city" of poverty and marginalization, as manifested in these southern urban quarters intentionally populated mainly by Mizrahi Jews and later by other marginalized groups such as foreign workers and African asylum seekers.[19] This destitute and exposed urban area, created through government planning and other social engineering practices as a ghetto for those Loïc Wacquant terms "urban outcasts," is seen as contrasting with Tel Aviv's affluent "white city," with its well-maintained European Bauhaus-style architecture and its confident and secure attitude and conditions that dismiss and displace everything that is not white.[20] With the constant stream of new arrivals, south Tel Aviv became even more overburdened with people sent there without adequate support, and its already poor institutional and infrastructural systems struggled to cope.

Not long after the Israeli government placed the asylum seekers on Tel Aviv's margins, many who had already managed to find their footing in the city found

252 In the Desert Penal Colony

themselves living on borrowed time. Following 2008 publications on the over-crowded Tel Aviv shelters, then prime minister Ehud Olmert declared all asylum seekers to be "infiltrators," who therefore must be imprisoned. A campaign of arrests began in the city, aimed at evicting three hundred people a day.[21] Another way to push asylum seekers outside Tel Aviv was to limit their work permits to peripheral locations described as "north of Hadera and south of Gedera"—cities that frame the Tel Aviv metropolitan area to its north and south, respectively.[22] These actions turned Tel Aviv into a site of policing and border control, and the streets became hunting grounds that penetrated the city's everyday life.[23] Israeli politicians gradually began referring to African asylum seekers racially, describing them as a national danger who posed, in the words of Interior Minister Eli Yishai, "an existential threat to Israel."[24] The increasingly volatile mood on the subject was manifested in a 2012 demonstration in Tel Aviv and a claim by then prime minister Benjamin Netanyahu that "illegal infiltrators [were] flooding the country" and threatening Israel's "national security," "national identity," and "the social fabric of society." The city, declared Netanyahu, had been "invaded by Africans," and he promised that it would "be returned" to its Israeli residents. Around one thousand demonstrators waving signs saying "Infiltrators, get out of our homes" were told by Israeli Member of Parliament Miri Regev that the "infiltrators" were "a cancer in our body," and the event escalated to violent attacks on Africans and their shops in Tel Aviv.

Holot, planned as the world's largest detention center and already approved by the Israeli government in November 2010, was created as a direct instance of this approach, initially preventing asylum seekers from entering Israeli spaces and society by stopping them at the border and later preventing them from settling and establishing themselves in Israeli cities. Planned and coordinated by Israel's Ministry of Defense with the involvement of the IDF and run by the Israel Prison Service (IPS), Holot embodied a particular mélange of security and carceral bodies that collaborated to encamp those seen as threatening outsiders. But as is clear from the way the facility was architecturally conceived and presented to the public, Holot functioned neither as a refugee camp nor according to the logic of reception and processing centers. Rather, it was primarily planned as a residence center or holding facility to detain thousands of people banished there from Israeli cities, preventing them from "contaminating" the Israeli national body from within.

Adrenaline Architecture

Holot's design process started in early 2011, when Israel's Ministry of Defense commissioned Israeli architect and planner Thomas Leitersdorf to plan the facility. Educated at London's famous Architectural Association School of Architecture,

Leitersdorf has worked on diverse large-scale projects worldwide. His portfolio includes residential, institutional, and urban architectural and planning schemes, from U.S. military bases to hotels in the Ivory Coast capital Abidjan, in Israel's Caesarea, and at the Dead Sea, a fact that was considered central to the project. Leitersdorf is also the architect and planner behind the Israeli city Ma'ale Adumim in the occupied West Bank, and Holot's design can be seen as a continuation of his involvement in politically controversial state projects.

The brief, recalled Leitersdorf in an interview in his office in north Tel Aviv, was to create a "residence facility." He emphasized that while it was intended to be run by the Israeli Prison Service, it was "certainly not a prison."[25] The design precedents shown in the presentation for the project, however, include planning proposals for prisons in the United States and Europe that inspired Holot's planning. The project was called "Ktzi'ot custody" in the initial architectural documents and a "detention facility" in later ones, but Leitersdorf emphasizes the differences between Holot and a prison.[26] He explained that its users, planned at the time of its design to include women and children, "are not criminals in the ordinary sense of the word."[27] Leitersdorf highlighted the fact that it was not clear until the very end of the design process whether the "open" camp would be bounded by a fence, and the state's brief asks for a facility designed on a "campus" model, meaning a site divided into sections that can be built separately and controlled "at different levels of openness."[28] Holot's chosen location, however, a derelict military site next to other military facilities and the state prisons Ktzi'ot and Saharonim in one of the most remote and isolated parts of the Negev desert, was located an hour's drive from the nearest town. Palestinian security prisoners are mostly detained at Ktzi'ot, and Saharonim is the first or last stop for irregular migrants and asylum seekers entering Israel. Holot was a new addition to this detention complex surrounded by a military zone, which in the past had also included the Antzar 3 mass-detention camp for Palestinians detained during the first intifada (discussed in chapter 6).

As well as presenting the camp's design logic, Leitersdorf's planning document is concerned with justifying the facility as a whole, specifying "the influence on the public of the infiltrators staying in Israel." The design document says that "the infiltrators grab the simple jobs that do not require training, pushing Israelis out of these jobs and increasing unemployment among Israelis"; that they create a feeling of insecurity, as "a multiplicity of foreigners" inhabit certain areas of cities, causing a feeling of a "lack of security for citizens"; and that they overwhelm local social services. This planning document does not only show a position aligned with the ethnocratic and xenophobic approach of the state; it also demonstrates that from the very beginning Holot was intended to be not just a border camp but, rather, a facility designed to change the reality of asylum seekers living in Israeli cities, which was seen as a disturbance to the Israeli public. "Israel did not know how to treat them," reflected Leitersdorf, explaining that Holot was established as a place where "infiltrators" would stay until their status was determined by the state. But, rather than in a prison environment created as a place of punishment, they would stay in the state's custody "in a nicer facility," in Leitersdorf's words, created for their administrative detention.

As in many other camps discussed in this book, time and speed were a core aspect in Holot's creation. The brief, Leitersdorf recalled, specified a tight time frame for "a very rapid project," and, in his view, it was the role of the architect to explore solutions to what was seen as an unfolding emergency situation. "We had to invent the program brief and standards ourselves," he reflected, explaining that he investigated European and U.S. federal authorities' approaches to "disaster areas" facilities for this task. As an expedited initiative responding to a changing situation, the facility's brief was a work in progress, according to Leitersdorf, developing in parallel with its design, so that many of the camp's substantial aspects—such as the specific location of the site, the living standards offered, the nature of the spaces included, the number of people detained there, and whether it would have a perimeter fence—were determined during the design process itself. This was an "insanely rushed project," said Leitersdorf, "like erecting a city in one go; everyone worked together. . . . Fifteen construction crews worked in parallel on site." This recalls Leitersdorf's reflections on his design of Ma'ale Adumim, another rapid architectural enterprise conducted both within and outside the state's normal planning.[29]

Temporality and temporariness were embedded in the design of the camp in various aspects, from its rapid creation to detainees' temporary yet enduring stay there. It was also planned to be used as a detention camp only temporarily, until the "problem" of the asylum seekers was solved. In order not to waste the state's investment in the camp, Holot was designed to be later transformed into a military facility and was therefore built according to IDF standards. Like many other camps examined in this book, therefore, Holot also shifted between Israel's civilian and military needs. As stated in Leitersdorf's website, the "politically uncertain conditions required the preparation of a strategy that would allow changes in the use of the complex in order to allow its fast transition to an army base," and "in light of recent Supreme Court decisions [to close the camp], this transition may indeed occur."[30]

Yet while the camp was conceived as a swift project, the time element crucially affected its meaning because of how long it took to complete it and the critical changes along the border during that time. The project spanned almost three years from the day it was commissioned until the day it was opened; during that period the flow of asylum seekers almost completely stopped. During its design and planning, the project therefore evolved from a border custody facility into a detention camp to which displaceable, detainable, and suspendable people would be banished from their everyday urban living environments.

Holot's design is presented as a rushed, adrenaline-fueled architecture responding to what was seen as a threatening emergency situation, the asylum seekers arriving in Israel. Yet whereas the designs for disaster areas, such as those the architect consulted, are usually produced to support the people displaced by the disasters, in this case it seems that the asylum seekers themselves were seen as the disaster disturbing Israeli society and cities. This emergency architecture was not created to support the most destitute but, rather, to further displace them by forcibly removing them from everyday Israeli environments, joining other accelerated Israeli projects of drastic territorial and demographic shifts adopting emergency-like violent spatial actions of displacement and emplacement, to which the camp is central.

Hotel Panopticon

Beyond its rapid creation, "the main difficulty with the design of Holot," Leitersdorf reflected, was that the facility had to be designed for "young, capable people," who would inevitably be bored in a camp that was essentially isolated from civilization. The social adviser assigned to assist in developing the design recommended that the grounds include not only accommodations for the residents but also classrooms and sports facilities; as in detention or refugee camps around the world, the asylum seekers in Holot were deemed to be "helpless and passive" individuals who could be artificially "activated through special programmes," in a way that recognizes the human need for a meaningful life yet isolates this life away from society to avoid contested political implications.[31]

Gradually, the architects came to understand "what the product [was] and how much it [would] cost the state." Costs, however, were related not only to the construction of the facilities Holot required but also, particularly, to the maintenance of the thousands of people whose lives would become dependent on the camp's provisions. It was clear from the very beginning, reflected Leitersdorf, that "running costs would be enormous; 10,000 meals three times a day—these were numbers that nobody was familiar with." At this point, Leitersdorf's hotel-designing skills came in handy. His familiarity with calculating food provision per capita, for example, enabled him to determine that the creation of designated kitchens in the camp would be cheaper than daily delivery of meals from Be'er-Sheva, and his knowledge of Israeli tourism guidelines led him not only to adopt IDF standards but also to consult the Ministry of Tourism standards. Holot was therefore designed as an architectural hybrid based on precedents and guidelines of disaster areas, detention camps, prisons, hotels, and military facilities, most of which function as total institutions designed to administer the life of those cut off from the wider society.

In this context, the links between tourism hospitality and the incarceration of those seen as unwanted guests must be understood as part of the Foucauldian understanding of the efforts to discipline through space those considered outsiders.[32] This is not surprising, as hotels are considered to be closely related to camps, where custody and care go hand in hand. With their space–time encapsulation and management of temporary guests, both represent spatial biopolitical techniques designed to answer every aspect of the basic biological lives of the populations they host, such as shelter, food, hygiene, and security, providing the human body displaced by will or force with a temporary space and basic sustenance. This close similarity enables hotels to be transformed from spaces of tourist hospitality into improvised emergency shelters, refugee camps, or detention camps, while at the same time the confined geographies and spatialities of leisure have enabled carceral spaces to be transformed into sites of tourism.[33] Indeed, the spaces and mechanisms of both hotels and camps enable the needs of custody, care, protection, and control to be met, often concurrently. As Orvar Löfgren argues, "Summer camps, auto camps, nudist camps . . . baseball camps, holiday camps" and "other, more menacing, kinds of camps," such as "correction camps, military camps, POW camps, refugee camps," have elements of a common structure—the idea of "large scale, detailed planning and control, self-sufficient communities with clear boundaries," while the "management experiences, as well as blueprints of Tayloristic planning, are in constant circulation between the different kinds of camps."[34] Architecturally and logistically speaking, then, as tourist and carceral facilities interchangeably discipline both welcome and unwelcome guests, it's no wonder Leitersdorf found his experience with the hospitality industry relevant.

Thus, the colorful architectural illustrations discussed at the beginning of this chapter, while seemingly only publicity materials in media reports portraying a detention site as an enlightened investment by the state, are presented by Leitersdorf not as a mere propaganda but as a comprehensive design philosophy of hospitality comfortably coupled with hostility. Beyond the hotel–camp connection, it is also galvanized by the belief that designing a facility that isolates the population of African newcomers from Israeli society is a national necessity pursued to the highest national standards of both the Israeli tourist industry and the IDF. The fact that people did not arrive at this isolated facility of their own free will but were banished to it from where they had settled was not considered disruptive in the design process.

While Holot's architectural design took its logistical cue from the world of leisure, the facility's role as a site of direct Foucauldian disciplinary control is unmistakable. Physically composed of the familiar portable shipping containers and other light structures, sometimes colored for easier identification among the repetitive characterless rationalized architecture, the facility was planned as an octagon after a search for the "perfect form" that would permit the camp's personnel and senior staff maximum control over the detainees. The intention, reflected

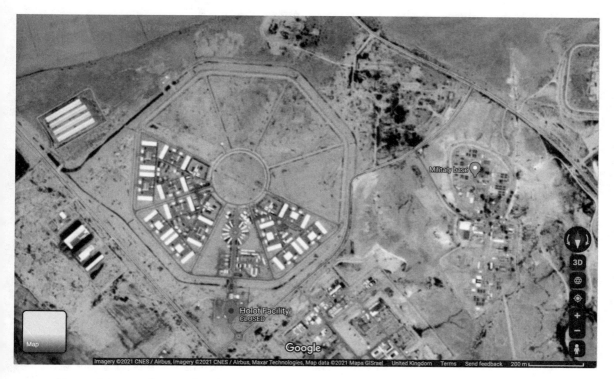

Figure 7.3. Aerial view of Holot, with its half-constructed octagon-shaped plan. Google Earth.

Leitersdorf, was to "shorten the distances" for personnel, enabling them to "be in control" over the camp's eight triangular sections, planned as separate from one another.

At first sight, the site plan looks like a giant panopticon, Jeremy Bentham's iconic institutional building and control system invoked by Foucault not only as an architectural tool of self-regularization but also as a substantial metaphor for how modern disciplinary societies normalize their members. Yet in Holot the panopticon was not designed as a building to discipline detainees individually in their cells through a hidden and constantly present all-seeing eye. Rather, Holot was designed as an entire site containing thousands in their masses, and its center was not an elevated structure for concealed guards but an open area, planned as green yet inevitably bleak and arid. Here, the disciplining eye of the panopticon was replaced by an empty space, mirroring the desert around the camp, disciplining detainees to the desert as an isolating border, as if spelling out the inability of those detained there to be included in the world they wished to be part of.

In the octagon-shaped facility of the distant Israeli penal colony—only half of which was ultimately constructed as a first phase to detain three thousand people, while the other half was only marked out by unpaved roads (Figure 7.3)—despair was designed into the camp as a disciplinary tool used to persuade those detained there to relinquish any hope of achieving formal asylum status and becoming part of Israeli society. The ability to design a desert camp to detain people away from the cities they once inhabited, while simultaneously imagining it as a green hotel-like space that supports community living, was possibly attained by the sheer un-bridgeable double distance between the leafy, quiet, affluent area in the "white city" of north Tel Aviv, where Leitersdorf's architectural practice is located, and two distant sites. The first site is located in the architect's own city, the destitute "black city" of south Tel Aviv, only a short drive away. From there, people could be easily expelled to the camp as part of their already exposed reality. The second site is the isolated and isolating Negev desert, whose vast expanses could easily be colored, from a distance, in endless shades of green.

The camp, designed by architects from one side of the city and to which people from the other side were forcefully displaced, could be understood as the city's constitutive outside and as an inherent part of unequal urban systems and citizenships, a space that violently reshapes the city while being shaped by its marginalizing structures and by the professionals employed to design spaces for the state's exclusionary objectives. Its desert location could be seen as another degree of the marginalization of the Negev, which again appears here as a site of encampment. Ben-Gurion envisioned the redemption and Judaization of the desert, seeing it as a political void but also as site of potentiality. Instead, it became a place of peripherality, neglect, and eventually exile. The state's forced pioneering inflicted on the Mizrahi Jews and the abandonment of the native Bedouin population, as discussed in chapters 4 and 5; the continuous militarization of the Negev, which Holot is designed to be part of; and the banishment of asylum seekers to the area—all mark the campization of the Negev as an isolated space of exception, where those who are seen as undeserving of settling are placed in an area deemed undeserving of settlement.[35]

Banished to the Isolated Penal Colony

With the dramatic decrease in entries into Israel by asylum seekers, Holot was transformed into a desert penal colony to which African asylum seekers were banished. There were two main reasons for this: to separate and remove them from Israeli cities, and to intimidate, pressure, and coerce them to go to a third African country through a "voluntary programme."[36] Israel's interior minister, Eli Yishai, stated publicly in 2012 that he would "lock them up to make their lives miserable," revealing Holot's main aim a few months before its completion. "The infiltrator threat is just as severe as the Iranian threat," he added, while ordering the

Authority for Immigration and Population to begin mass arrests of asylum seekers from Sudan and Eritrea.[37]

As with many other camps and temporary settlements discussed in this book, the legal and governmental actions and modes of operation around Holot were also debated in and shaped by the Israeli court, which blocked and altered laws and government decisions about how the camp should function, who should be detained there, and for how long. Indeed, the camp was regulated through a long process of hearings and negotiations; while the government acted as the defender of Israel's ethnoracial character, the court acted as the appointed guardian of the state's democratic values. The court found that the camp "disproportionally violates the [detainees'] rights to liberty and dignity and must therefore be annulled."[38] Both authorities eventually agreed on a maximum of twelve months' "open detention" in Holot for single men—excluding women, children, the elderly, men with extreme disabilities, and parents of minors. During that time they had to check in twice a day.

The fact that Holot was defined as an "open facility" allowed the HCJ to approve its function, seeing it as "softer" detention that was less harmful to asylum seekers' freedom of movement—which the court cherished as a central liberal–democratic value while ignoring the fact that Holot's "openness" lacked real meaning. The camp's isolated location tens of kilometers from any significant settlement, supplied only by infrequent and expensive public transport, caged by the desert and by a military fire zone, made it a de facto closed carceral concentration and containment facility and prevented detainees from exercising this freedom. While detainees were free to leave the facility between 6 a.m. and 10 p.m., their freedom of movement was curtailed by the remoteness of the camp, even when its gates were open.

Holot functioned as a nonprison that was nevertheless managed by the IPS, a controlled, overcrowded, poorly equipped, and poorly run isolated facility, adding to the distress of the thousands who were sent to it without trial. Surrounded by two tall fences, it had three wings where detainees were accommodated. Each wing contained four cell blocks divided into twenty-eight rooms, each with five bunk beds to sleep ten people, with a living space of around 4.5 square meters per person. That density deviated from the Israeli National Outline Plan, which sets a maximum legal limit of six persons per room. Other compromised basic amenities made Holot an even more miserable place: the food was extremely low quality and came in very small portions, and detainees were not allowed to bring food in from outside; though winter temperatures in the rooms dropped close to zero degrees Celsius, winter supplies from the IPS, including radiators and blankets, were insufficient; and although social life in the camp was planned in advance, there was a lack of leisure and educational activities. In addition, detainees were surveilled through biometric gates located at the entrance and between the different cell blocks, making it a highly supervised facility. "The conditions for animals in the zoo of a Third World country are better than what you see here," exclaimed one of the volunteers supporting the asylum seekers in Holot; "it is terrible what we are putting these people through."[39]

Being detained in Holot had an immense effect on the detainees. "This doesn't feel like an open camp at all, this is a real prison," wrote Ahmad on his first day in Holot in a photo diary documenting the boredom, the poor food, the humiliation of waiting in long queues for modest allowances, and the general neglect in the facility.[40] Like other instances of irregular migration, Holot produced manifold situations of waiting (in queues, to be released from detention), along with an unanswered need to fill up the time.[41] Other detainees told of long days in which "we lie in bed 24 hours" because "there is nothing to do," remembering that before their detention they had been employed in Israel in demanding jobs in hospitals, care homes, restaurant kitchens, and the construction industry. Yet, unlike other situations of waiting in processes of asylum determination, which are followed by either a confirmed or denied asylum status, staying in Holot did not entail the possibility of a confirmed asylum status, but only that of an imposed "voluntary" deportation.[42] Arbitrary acts of punishment were another component of the harsh and Kafkaesque reality in Holot. Camp officials could punish detainees for violations like failing to check in at the required times, and detainees did not know why, when, or how they would be punished, as the process was neither clear nor externally supervised. While officials were instructed to act fairly, in some cases detainees were punished severely, with deductions from their allowances or imprisonment in Saharonim prison, for minor violations.

Asylum seekers engaged in a number of actions and protests against their detention, including making solidarity visits and bringing homemade food from Israeli cities to the camp, arranging large strikes and demonstrations in Tel Aviv against incarceration in the camp, protesting in Holot in the call to close the camp, and going on "marches for freedom," first from Holot to Jerusalem and later from the facility to the Israeli–Egyptian border in protest of Israel's asylum policies, calling on the Red Cross and the UN to intervene (Figures 7.4–7.7). In order to improve their everyday reality, in 2015 the detainees created a makeshift area of restaurants and other businesses outside the camp to support themselves and each other socially, culturally, and physically, helping them kill time and compensate for the camp's isolation and miserable conditions. Sudanese and Eritrean restaurants with traditional sweets became packed with diners, who maintained that "eating the same food every day [in the camp] makes you crazy; a person needs something to remember their home and culture."[43] Improvised stalls and shops, around thirty structures in all, sold everyday products like soft drinks, soap bars, packs of cards, and blankets, while a makeshift gym with weights imported from

Figure 7.4. A solidarity visit to Holot by asylum seekers living in Tel Aviv and Israeli activists, serving traditional food to the detainees outside the camp's fences, 2014. Photograph by Yotam Ronen, Activestills.

Figure 7.5. Approximately thirty thousand African asylum seekers demonstrate in Tel Aviv's Rabin Square, calling for all those detained in Israeli prisons and the Holot detention center to be freed and for the recognition of all refugees' rights, 2014. Photograph by Yotam Ronen, Activestills.

Figure 7.6. Detainees in Holot protest behind the prison's fence, calling for the camp to be closed and for the refugee rights of the African asylum seekers living in Israel to be recognized, 2014. Photograph by Oren Ziv, Activestills.

Tel Aviv was opened, charging fees of fifty Israeli new shekels per year—the detention period at the time (Figure 7.8). By forming their own personalized spaces, the asylum seekers created a world to replace the one taken from them, acting against their dehumanization and reclaiming lost agency through specific practices. The temporary materiality of the institutionalized camp, with its shipping containers, corrugated-steel hangars, and barbed-wire fences, was supplemented by the ad hoc structures of its detainees, who used materials brought from remote urban and cultural worlds to re-create what they had been forced to leave behind.

These spatial acts of world building could be considered instances of Arendt's notion of natality as the ontological condition of people as beginners who realize their freedom by creating something new through which their distinctiveness as human beings is reflected. They could also be examined through the lens of what Deleuze and Guattari imagine as minoritarian becoming, when lines of flight are created within and through existing structures, or as Harney and Moten's "undercommons," enabling detainees to survive Holot together rather than surrendering to the state's attempts to "persuade" them to leave. The detainees' spatial actions of

Figure 7.7. More than eight hundred African asylum seekers march from the Holot detention center to the Israeli–Egyptian border, 2014. The group was stopped by the Israeli army and spent the night a few hundred meters from the border. Photograph by Yotam Ronen, Activestills.

endurance and "agency-in-waiting [in] everyday time" could be theorized and politicized by highlighting the asylum seekers' ability to resist the power apparatuses controlling and limiting their daily life in the camp.[44] These makeshift structures, however, should not be overly celebrated. Unlike the Bedouin and Palestinian broader alignments of spatial actions that maintain an exposed yet enduring form of resistance, these structures created in one site were extremely vulnerable to state power, and indeed, they were demolished by the authorities a few months after their creation, putting an abrupt end to this resourceful initiative.[45]

The Opposite of City

Israel's unofficial yet clear intention in creating Holot was to make the lives of asylum seekers so desperate and miserable that they would leave the country "voluntarily." However, the camp's official aim, as explained to the HCJ by the state, was

Figure 7.8. Restaurants and bars in the makeshift leisure area self-built by the detainees outside Holot to compensate for the poor-quality food and lack of activities in the camp, 2016. Photograph by Oren Ziv, Activestills.

to prevent asylum seekers from settling in Israeli urban areas: Holot was intended to "serve distinct social interests relating to Israel's sovereignty and its ability to deal with the consequences of the settlement of tens of thousands of infiltrators in its cities."[46] In turn, the HCJ stated that while the "Israeli [detention] model is unique, as in fact it was not created to *disperse* the infiltrators' population . . . but to *concentrate* it in one distant facility," Holot's "objective of preventing the settlement [of asylum seekers in cities]" in order to "'alleviat[e] the burden' of cities, especially south Tel Aviv . . . [is] a legitimate one."[47] With this ruling, the court legitimized the state's coercive policy of urban expulsions, making Holot the official space to which noncitizens were banished from the civic space of the city to pacify the rage of other urban residents. This state action denied asylum seekers not only the Lefebvrian "right to the city," that is, the right to cocreate the city as its inhabitants by shaping it according to their needs and preferences, but also the ability to exist in the city in any form.[48]

While not all asylum seekers were detained, when Holot closed in March 2018 more than thirteen thousand had been held there for various periods of time.

The possibility of either detention or deportation created an urban existential threat that became a central defining feature of asylum seekers' lives in Tel Aviv and elsewhere; although the camp was many kilometers away, it became a constant shadow looming over their urban life. As those detained in Holot were not allowed to resettle in cities like Tel Aviv and Eilat, and as asylum seekers detained in the camp were sometimes persuaded to leave the country, Holot often became the black hole into which people were sucked from their particular everyday urban life, never to return. When detainees were released after a year or more in the camp, they had to reconstruct their lives almost from scratch.

The court recognized the camp's influence on asylum seekers even when they were not detained there:

> The current law adopts the system of "centrifugal circulation" as its way of removing infiltrators from city centers, spinning them in a centrifugal motion to the outskirts of the desert . . . then back to the city centers, while at the same time, taking others out of city centers "to fill their places" in the [Holot] Residence Center. This distorted path of a constant change of infiltrators, "revolving doors," . . . raises concerns as to whether behind the declared objective of preventing settlement in urban centers lies the objective of "hazing" the infiltrators and breaking their spirit [and their "encouragement" to leave Israel].[49]

Detaining asylum seekers in an isolated camp was therefore acknowledged by the court not only as an act of segregation and social engineering but also as an act of banishment and torture in a distant Kafkaesque penal colony that stretched its long arms to the everyday urban lives of an entire population, reshuffling them whenever it pleased. As Tewalda, an asylum seeker from Eritrea, reflected, Holot is designed to break the spirit of asylum seekers after their already-difficult experience:

> This place is doing everything it can to break us, but we've already been through hell. Many of us have experienced torture and imprisonment, and here we're united and support one another. Yes, there are those who break and return to Africa. They're ashamed to tell us about it; these are usually people in despair. We talk to them, explain that their lives are in danger and that it's better to stay imprisoned but live.[50]

The camp's revolving-door system had an immense effect on detainees who had already developed a life in their cities. Consequently, not only was detention in the camp intolerable during the time spent there, but it also created a devastating rupture in asylum seekers' already-fractured lives. As another asylum seeker from Eritrea, who was detained in Holot for a year, testified:

> When I was released from Holot I couldn't move, I tried to understand what had happened to me in those twelve months, what am I doing now. I lived in Israel for six years before I was sent there. I worked in restaurants, I translated, I had friends, I drew. . . . But after a year in Holot you forget everything. All you know is the facility's routine, you no longer know what to do outside. It is as if you have arrived in Israel again from Sinai. . . . I cannot get myself together to overcome the detachment and loneliness.[51]

When asylum seekers were released from the camp, forbidden to settle in certain cities, many had to move to unfamiliar places, increasing their feelings of disconnection. "There is no reason to detain us here but to break us and make us leave [Israel]," said one of the asylum seekers; "this is abuse as the year here emptied us and now we need to get back on our feet, and it's harder. Why did it really have to be this way? We are refugees, not criminals."[52] Holot also caused the dismantling of the urban mutual-support and aid mechanisms created by asylum seekers in cities, such as a Sudanese community center in Tel Aviv and the kindergarten it operated, both of which were closed after those who maintained it were detained.

Looking at the sheer numbers, detaining asylum seekers in Holot worked well for the state, as after the camp opened there was an increase in the number of those leaving Israel. In 2014, when people could be detained in Holot for an unlimited time, 6,414 asylum seekers left the country. A year later, when detention was limited to one year, the number who left dropped to 3,381 but was still significant. While around 2,400 of those who left were resettled in safe countries such as the United States and Canada, others left to an unclear and often-dangerous future in Uganda or Rwanda. These forms of resettlement and abandonment followed earlier unofficial Israeli attempts to create agricultural farms and temporary transit camps in unstable countries such as South Sudan, "dump[ing] African refugees in blood-drenched dictatorships" and abandoning them to their fate.[53] Of the sixty thousand asylum seekers who had entered Israel, around thirty-six thousand remained in the country.

The court's decisions limiting the state's actions to encourage the "voluntary" departure of asylum seekers met increasing rage and protest among some south Tel Aviv residents. If the camp was a place of concern for the court, for the urban protesters the facility, detaining only some of the asylum seekers who settled in their part of the city, was not efficient enough to deal with their transformed urban reality. At the end of 2017, the government approved a plan to close Holot and begin a systematic deportation of asylum seekers to third countries—namely, Rwanda and Uganda. Those who did not agree to be deported would face indefinite imprisonment. Yet, in contrast with the earlier protests, now the city showed its protective side in a wave of protests and petitions against the deportations, and large demonstrations of civic solidarity, some with over twenty thousand participants, were held in Tel Aviv and other cities.

Holot was indeed closed in mid-March 2018. The government intended to begin mass deportation in April, but that plan was eventually halted by the Israeli court and a failed deal with the UN High Commissioner for Refugees (UNHCR). A few months after the camp was closed, while the government was considering reopening it, Holot's former detainees who had returned to live in Israeli cities still could not understand why they had had to spend months and sometimes years in the camp. "In other countries, when they put you in such a place," explained one of those detained there, "they must decide—either you need to leave the country or they give you documents allowing you to stay. Here, I spent months and months in the camp, and for what? Nothing has changed. The government is still chasing us."[54] For many of them, the arbitrariness and pointlessness of this violent and oppressing act of banishment was the most disturbing, as an asylum seeker from Eritrea reflected:

> I was in Holot, got released, and now what? I lived eight years in Israel, two more years in Holot, but where are the results? Give me a refugee status, at least that! When I came back from Holot, it was like starting from scratch. . . . If you leave a dog in the house for the entire day, what do you think will happen? It will lose its mind. They took me from here after eight years in Tel Aviv, to be locked . . . [in] a closed place, in the middle of the desert. It makes you crazy. You allowed me to live here for eight years, why [are you] taking me away? Why [are you] taking me like a dog, like a chicken, to a cage in the middle of the desert? This is what disturbs me the most.[55]

The uncertainty created by the constantly changing state policies and the enduring physical presence of the camp continues to haunt asylum seekers in Israel even after its closure.[56] Holot is still there, and even if it is waiting in the heart of the desert as a closed and empty space, its mere existence is still seen as a threat by its potential detainees.

The Global Infrastructure of Camps

Unlike many of the camps discussed in this book, Holot was not part of an alignment of similar spaces in Israel–Palestine. Yet although only one such designated detention camp for African asylum seekers was created, Holot should be examined not as an isolated case relevant only to the Israeli context but, rather, as part of the global context of a worldwide alignment of camps, in which, in the words of sociologist Michel Agier, the "undesirables" are "managed."[57] Camps form an expanding infrastructure that facilitates the global geopolitical order of territorial fortification and increased control over transnational movement, whether created on remote Pacific islands on behalf of the Australian government, on the outskirts of European capital cities, or near national borders around the world, and Holot, while not hiding its particularities, should be examined in this context.

This global alignment of camps, whose terrain is constantly navigated by irregular migrants and asylum seekers, should not be seen as just a collection of unrelated spaces established within state territories or offshore. Rather, these camps should also be perceived as part of a global infrastructure of encampments, a "carceral archipelago," to use Foucault's term,[58] which is connected through the bodies of knowledge, power, practices, and interests of those who create them and through the transnational flows of those whom they circulate. Similar to "global cities," which function not only within and in between countries but also as part of one single global entity encompassing those countries, this global "infrastructure of camps" extends beyond the framework of the single state.[59] Unlike the well-connected global cities, this camp infrastructure is part of a system of what Harsha Walia refers to as the global apartheid enforced by "border imperialism," which encapsulates the overlapping and concurrent structuring of mass displacement and securitization of borders in certain areas. This postcolonial global division, part of the legacies of empire, is reflected by the asymmetrical relations of global power, the criminalization and incarceration of illegalized migrants, and the racialized hierarchies of citizenship that often come together with the exploitation of migrant labor.[60]

This is what Didier Bigo has identified as the current "differential freedom of movement (of different categories of people),"[61] which is grounded in all scales of population management, from international frameworks of geopolitical ordering to state facilities and urban bordering actions that penetrate people's everyday lives. These camps often form part of the ever-growing international border apparatuses of walls, barbed-wire fences, and biometric identification systems that heavily fortify some of today's national territories and regions and their constantly "shifting border[s]" that push these apparatuses either to the heart of cities or to offshore territories.[62] These borders and camps are violently connected to what Nandita Sharma describes as the current "postcolonial new world order" in which people are defined, identified, and managed through the racialized apparatuses and infrastructures of nation-state sovereignty, international bodies, and global flows and capital.[63] They expose the current tension between an ideology of free movement and open borders, and between the exponential fortification and technological "protection" of borders and their expanding restrictions of movement. These camps and the fortified borders they relate to also paradoxically mark, as Wendy Brown argues, the waning relevance and cohesiveness of nation-state sovereignty, which no longer exclusively defines or monopolizes the field of global political relations and the powers organizing it. Rather, they are "part of an ad hoc global landscape of flows and barriers both inside nation-states and in the surrounding postnational constellations," including those dividing "richer and poorer parts of the globe."[64]

In recent decades we have increasingly heard the testimonies of refugees, asylum seekers, and other "people on the move" who find themselves trapped in this global infrastructure of camps, transferred from one detention camp to another, where they are suspended for weeks, months, or even longer during their long odysseys within and between states. The ever-expanding vocabulary that describes these camp spaces—detention facilities; reception, registration, and accommodation centers; holding sites; hubs; hot spots; emergency temporary shelters—fails to camouflage their rise as part of the framework within which people's freedom and rights are restricted. Because many camp spaces are temporary and ephemeral owing to their materiality, political and governmental objectives, and relevant legal definitions, this global infrastructure itself is constantly changing while also maintaining its detainees as mobile, circulated, and displaceable people, as seen in Holot's revolving-door practice.[65] Yet like other global infrastructures, the infrastructure of camps constitutes an inseparable part of today's interstate relations: it is a built network that reproduces the uneven global divisions between territories, populations, and resources; it makes up the architecture of circulation that processes the mobility of unwanted people; and while most of it is created and functions as part of an encompassing institutional arrangement, it, like other infrastructures, is also informal in parts, such as the makeshift "Jungle" camps that appear next to bottleneck border spaces of blocked movement or the makeshift area created outside Holot.[66]

These unstable and moving spaces, which themselves form junctions of human and material movement, relate to the conditions of encampment and the variety of practices through which asylum seekers and refugees contest or escape the state techniques of bordering, policing, and provisioning.[67] This flickering reality makes unprotected people even more vulnerable, and Holot adds another example to the global spectacle of the "illegality" of migrants and to the related stream of alarming reports from camps in Western countries—from Australia through Europe to the United States—where vulnerable people are contained and circulated without the minimum of provisions and protection.[68]

Each of these camps, surely, is a particular case in its legal, spatial, and other specifics. Holot is a specific case not only in being part of the ongoing use of camps in Israel–Palestine as part of the coercive and often ethnoracial organization of people in space. It is also specific in its function as a space of banishment to which asylum seekers were sent to remove them from the Israeli cities where they already lived and to push them out of the country altogether. At the same time, Holot should be considered as part of the global infrastructure of camps, which together with refugee camps and state and offshore processing facilities, contain and suspend certain people away from society. The human and physical context of Holot is therefore simultaneously the cage of the Negev desert and the proximity of the border, the Israeli cities from which its detainees were displaced, and the global infrastructure of containment, suspension, and despair where "people on the move" are circulated as excess humanity.

CONCLUSION, OR TOWARD AN EVER-EMERGING THEORY OF THE CAMP

Define, on the two-dimensional surface of the earth, lines across which motion is to be prevented, and you have one of the key themes of history. With a closed line (i.e., a curve enclosing a figure) and the prevention of motion from outside the line to its inside, you derive the idea of a property. With the same line, and the prevention of motion from inside to outside, you derive the idea of prison. With an open line (i.e., a curve that does not enclose a figure), and the prevention of motion in either direction, you derive the idea of border. Properties, prisons, borders: it is through the prevention of motion that space enters history.

    —Raviel Netz, *Barbed Wire: An Ecology of Modernity*

Spatial form can alter the future course of the very histories which have produced it.

    —Doreen Massey, "Politics and Space/Time"

It is not easy to devise a nation-state. Control needs to be established over a territory, a nation assembled and managed, an agreed legal and governmental order formulated, and a national identity shaped through an ideology that gives the nation-state meaning and form. State creation and nation building are not easy tasks, especially if one starts almost from scratch, as in the case of Israel, whose path is quite different from that of states formed gradually over time. State creation and management are particularly challenging if they are a consequence of the divestment of colonial holdings and the creation of a new postcolonial world order; many states in the Middle East, Africa, and elsewhere are examples of this. State creation and management are also notably challenging in settler colonial states, where an order shaped and dictated by a dominant settler ethnic group is introduced to multiethnic societies. In addition, in the face of growing global flows of refugees and migrants whose mobility is more heavily controlled and hindered than that of most state citizens, state governance is also becoming increasingly in dispute, presenting a fundamental inequality and violence similar to some of their colonial legacies, violence that stands at the core of liberal citizenship. Israel, although unique in many ways, including the persistent colonization project that consistently expands over Palestinian lands, is to some extent a product of its time.

The camp has been widely analyzed as a spatial and political formation adopted by modern states as well as colonial and postcolonial global powers over the last century to order and contain unwanted, resisting, and displaced populations. The camp, however, is also tied to the seizing and creation of colonial spaces and of the modern state itself, functioning as a central means of beginning and carrying out this territorial, national, and juridical project. Thus, "the common camp"—that is, the camp as a versatile and common spatial instrument of control over people and lands—is central to the way modern populations and territories were and still are reshaped, organized, and controlled. Camps, although sometimes presented as marginal spatial episodes, are common because they frequently appear in relation to drastic yet prevalent geopolitical changes; the various populations who are part of these changes often share the camp as something in common, yet the ways they experience it are very different. Occasionally, camps create new common grounds among the populations contained together in them, and their embodied and sometimes flexible spaces are used to enact and articulate political claims for rights and justice.

This characterization of the camp as common is something that extends well beyond the boundaries of Israel–Palestine, because the camp is a phenomenon intertwined with modern materialities and technologies, modern politics, and the modern state, both in its internal ordering and in its relation to the ever-changing global order and postcolonial order. In these times, when states around the world are experiencing crises, the camp seems to be more prevalent than ever; it is used both by states to contain and exclude the displaced populations who find refuge in them, and by displaced and resisting populations as temporary makeshift spaces that they themselves create, sometimes on their way to a better future.

Israel–Palestine has an undeniably strong camp legacy that is still unfolding. The camps explored in this book expose the common role the camp played in reshaping and manipulating the lands and populations of this contested territory over the last century, yet in multifaceted forms and manners. This variety of camp functions and types is not coincidental; rather, it is an outcome of the political and territorial logics that correspond to the very basic conditions of modern biopolitics, functioning in different ways as mechanisms of control in the service of nationalistic and state-building enterprises. However, the development of camp spaces over the years has itself influenced various factors that do not always work according to the interests of the powers that initially created these camps. While too often being dehumanizing spaces of exposed life, camps also appear as temporary flexible platforms where spatiopolitical actions of power struggles and resistance may be conducted and where new political subjectivities can emerge.

The various types of camp discussed in this book served and still are serving in various ways as the physical in-between space wherein one had either to be molded according to the needs of the national machine and its colonial ambitions, or to be contained away from it, absorbed into a spatial void where enduring suspension and imposed mobility prevail. These different camps indeed show multiple perspectives that expose the varied spatialities and functions of the camp, but in the end this book can be crystallized in five main complementary arguments and their related understandings about the common camp.

The first argument is that *the camp is a multifaceted spatiopolitical mechanism of modernity that may serve, through its containment and inherent connectivity, very different, even opposite, objectives, but that nevertheless has distinct commonalities and genealogy.* These commonalities are connected to camps' particular material aspects and political roles in facilitating and contesting colonial and nation-state projects. They primarily include the camp's specific populations, its legal and governmental exceptionality, and its embedded temporariness; these three aspects are inherently linked to the nation–state–territory triad. These commonalities are also all related to modernity in its governmental forms that seek to (re)order populations, often according to ethnoracial categories embedded in colonial, national, or postcolonial regimes, frequently through unmediated forms of violence on the military–civilian nexus. These commonalities are also linked to modernity in its technological innovations of speed and flows, which enable the camp to rapidly appear and then to function as a suspended and separated space, which is nevertheless based on mobility: while camps are often detached from their immediate surroundings to separately contain people, they are also dependent on modern systems of movement and connectivity to be created and sustained as machines of circulation and ordering.

These modern attributes of order and technology are inherently linked to the reoccurring specific material elements of the camp that facilitate im/mobility, including its initial prefabricated transportable structures, the barbed-wire fence that often surrounds it, and the infrastructures and vehicles that enable its logistical creation and function. This materiality of a spatial machine dependent on other machines and their associated assemblages is then inherently connected to, and arguably generative of, the political function of the camp as a highly flexible and adaptable modern instrument of governance. Such an instrument could be transported, erected, and then changed according to political needs to facilitate the modern desire to rapidly expand over new spaces and to divide, categorize, reorder, and channel particular populations there, and it sometimes facilitates the resistance of these populations and their subversive actions against such processes.

274   Conclusion

The second argument makes a related claim that goes beyond the prevailing understanding of the camp as a space of separation and exclusion, contending that *the camp may be an instrument of restrictive containment but may also be used, in colonial contexts, for expansionist human movement*. While camps are indeed used for enforced immobility, including that related to expulsions and expropriations, other camps facilitate voluntary movement and colonial territorial expansions. While this versatile role of the camp is tightly connected to the formation and development of the space and territory of Israel–Palestine in particular, it is deeply rooted in colonial history and in the ongoing creation of controlled lands and bodies. In this context, the camp is an instrument that facilitates territorial conquest while containing the displacement and emplacement it causes. It functions as a tool in struggles over mobility, territory, and related rights, struggles common in what are described as frontier areas. This new understanding of the camp allows it to be examined as a complex instrument that also belongs to other radical spatiopolitical dynamics and practices, including those of active resistance and protest.

As spaces of both expansion and expulsion, of both movement and containment, created to control people and land, camps are often created not only as isolated and isolating spaces, as they are usually examined, but also as nodes of highly connected alignments of similar camp spaces. Such a sequence of camps often evolves from a particular type of camp formed as a response to specific geopolitical realities such as radical territorial and demographic changes. A network of camps connected and served by the same logistical and governmental apparatuses might be created to exclude and to maintain particular populations, such as the Palestinian refugee camps and the Jewish immigrant camps managed by UNRWA and the Jewish Agency, respectively. Alignments of camps, however, might also form a well-coordinated territorial instrument, as did the wall and tower camps of the Zionist settlers in Mandatory Palestine, the frontier ma'abarot camps used for Israel's internal colonization, and the neocolonial settlements in the occupied Palestinian territories. Infrastructures here are important not only for the creation and provision of camps, as explained in the previous argument, but also for their connection to one another as a system of points (camps) and lines (roads) that parcel out and control particular spaces and territories.

The third argument is related to the spatiality of the camp, claiming that *the camp's embodied and multifaceted spatiality is an outcome of the various and often conflicting forces that influence its swift creation and alteration*. This spatiality is therefore often much more complex that it initially seems, with the camp's "ordered" institutional layout frequently disguising a superficial and violent rational order, and the camp's "chaotic" informal layout is in some cases an expression of a much deeper social and cultural order. In addition, institutional and makeshift spaces are strongly linked in camp settings; they are either created next to one another as complementary spaces, or they develop from one to the other in processes of formalization and informalization—an indication of the dynamic forces that not only create and use camps but also work within and around them. These include everyday spatial actions of inhabitation, which significantly change and sometimes urbanize camp environments.

These complex spatial relations are also at the heart of the spatiopolitical entanglement between the city and the camp, spaces that are differently configured and reconfigured over time and that emerge from one another depending on both the types of camps and their related urban environments. As such, the camp could be seen as an ever-evolving versatile space that responds to a variety of external and internal factors that create, stretch, compress, and eliminate it as a hyperresponsive tool. The camp's elasticity and versatility are linked to its particular modes of governance and shifting materiality, and to the turbulent politics that reshapes it. The camp, therefore, is not only a space that facilitates and contains movement; it is also a "moving space" in its own right, changing and transforming through actions of rapid creation, appropriation, and demolition performed by the different powers that work on and within it.

In line with these findings, the fourth argument maintains that *the camp is not only a biopolitical and necropolitical space of desubjectivation, dehumanization, and death, but it can also be a space where new political actions, subjectivities, and identities emerge.* The camp's spatial, governmental, and inherently versatile dimensions allow it to be rapidly erected, redesigned, and transformed for new tasks and alignments, and it can thus be a space of radical political potentiality. As such, camps are embodied spatial tools that are often created, adopted, and adapted when the geopolitical reality is in flux, and they can also be used by their inhabitants to negotiate with and strive to influence or subvert their political reality in pursuit of visibility, rights, and justice, through their own spatiopolitical actions, resistance, and protest. Camps are therefore not only mobile mechanisms formed to meet political needs to control people and territories; they are also spaces that might themselves generate new forms of political power with those contained in them. With the broad understanding of the political as the domain of power, the camp, through its versatility and elasticity, might enable new political forms and practices to materialize and act for the creation, reinforcement, or destruction of new, emerging, and existing powers.

The camp is a space that can either be used for bio/necropolitical ethnoracial control or be seized as an instrument of a political agency and self-emancipation, an undercommons that disrupts dominant forms of power. As such, it may indeed enable the reconsideration of politics by spatial actions forming new realities on the ground, with new intersections between people and materials consolidating into a more encompassing geopolitical reality. This can happen through changes within camps, such as in the Palestinian refugee camps, or through their multiplication for territorial endeavors, such as in the wall and tower camps, creating broader constellations of power. With their particular material and governmental attributes, camps could be formed as tactical spatial instruments designed to achieve specific political ends. And at the same time, they could also be spaces constituting and representing a particular political logic, creating an end in itself that might nevertheless be turned away from the path its history had created for it and change the course of that history. This politics is usually conducted not through organized forms of political representation or clear military occupation but, rather, through embodied and sometimes contingent spatial actions that are crafted and accumulate into new realities on a variety of scales, from a particular site to regional transformations.

Last, the fifth argument intertwined in the structure of the book and in the spatial genealogy it presents is that *the camp could be identified as the spatiopolitical hidden gene of Israel–Palestine and the reemerging way the territory has been reshaped and negotiated over the past century*. As such, the camp allowed for the extreme territorial and demographic changes in the region, for the suspension and containment of some populations, and for the movement and expansion of others. The adaptable instrument of the camp and its versatile spaces were used by actors from all sides of the political spectrum to change, negotiate, maintain, and resist very different, and sometimes contradictory, political objectives. The incorporation of the camp as a central spatial and political instrument to reshape and control populations and territories has worked in other national and colonial settings in general and in relation to the geopolitics of settler societies in particular. Israel–Palestine has gone through rapid, abrupt, and dramatic demographic and territorial transformations in its history and is still a contested territory. The camp has a central and ongoing role in working across populations and sovereignties to destabilize certain geopolitical realities while creating and reinforcing others.

The colonial and racial underpinnings of the camp are still shaping populations and territories in the area: camps are still being used to seize control over Palestinian territories by the neocolonial project of Israel's settlers and government; at the same time, camps are still the spaces where Palestinian refugees and IDPs are suspended and where, and with which, they resist their situation, while other camps are used to hold African asylum seekers away from Israeli cities. Over the last century, in many ways, Israel–Palestine as a whole has been reshaped and managed as a large camp, mostly disconnected from its immediate surroundings while being politically and economically supported from afar, with its populations and lands reordered en masse and its territorial, demographic, and political future still unknown. Whether it is or will be Israel–Palestine, Israel/Palestine, or Israel and Palestine, as political entities that are intertwined, overlapping, or separated, is still a subject of an ongoing political dispute.

I will now examine these arguments more closely in order to draw a clearer picture of what the camp is, in all of its spatial, political, and human complexities.

The Mechanism of the Camp

Camps, as seen throughout this book, take various forms and have different purposes. Nevertheless, they share a genealogy and commonalities that enable them to be perceived as a distinct spatial instrument related to particular modern material and political constellations. Whether they are constructed from prefabricated components transported to their specific location or from available materials cobbled into makeshift structures, this light and transportable materiality enables the creation of camps with great speed in both inhabited and uninhabited environments. This swift creation forms the camp as a highly versatile "moving" instrument that enables fast, intense, and unexpected geopolitical and spatial maneuvers and changes. As the spatial unit of the camp is often separated from its surroundings, either to protect those inside from the threatening outside (such as in the case of wall and tower camps), or to isolate the outside from their presence (such as in the case of detention camps), the use of barbed wire is prevalent in both cases. Yet while the camp is often separated from its immediate surroundings, it is nevertheless highly connected to infrastructures and other logistical mechanisms beyond its immediate environment in order to be formed and sustained as an embodied yet detached space. Trucks, buses, and ships, together with their infrastructures of roads and ports, continued to reappear as background yet crucial material actors needed for the creation and population of the camps discussed in this book and for their ongoing maintenance. Camps are therefore both separated and connected spatial instruments whose existence is highly dependent on related logistical apparatuses.[1]

These material elements of the camp as a modern mechanism of rapid movement and control are linked to the understanding of the camp as a temporary space or as a space where people are held temporarily, although such temporariness may linger for an unknown period of time. We have very different examples of this spatial temporariness, in aspects of the camps' materiality, territorial objectives, and durability. As spaces created ad hoc and at great speed, from prefabricated structures (tents, huts) transported from elsewhere, and from light materials (fabric, timber, corrugated steel), they do not last long and can be dismantled and cleared easily. These camps can therefore be created as "meanwhile" spaces until more permanent structures are built in the same location, or until the particular situation that requires their creation changes and the camp can be dismantled altogether or given a different function. Importantly, the definition of the camp as a temporary space could allow territorial and political transformations to take place on the promise that these are only temporary, creating realities that are then very difficult to change or resist.

Some camps in this book, such as the Zionist pioneer settler camps, the ma'abarot, the Nahal camps, and the settler outposts in the occupied Palestinian territories, were created as temporary spaces, constructed from prefabricated units, as part of the Zionist and then Israeli project to spread Jewish populations to frontier territories and suspend them there until governmental mechanisms and political realities would allow them to be formally and permanently included. Other camps, such as the Palestinian refugee camps and the Bedouin campness reality, were also created as temporary arrangements, with temporariness itself being used as a governmental tool for facilitating abrupt changes and unmediated control, yet they still exist until in a lingering but also highly political reality of waiting. While these examples of spatial temporariness are very different in their form and purpose, they both show the role of the camp as a space erected ad hoc only to later be suspended until a permanent spatial and political arrangement is achieved.

The camp is also created and managed as an exceptional space in a specific mode of governance. Many of the camps discussed in the book were created as part of the state of exception or emergency years of the Mandate period and Israel's early statehood and the Nakba, after the 1967 Israeli occupation, during the influx of immigrants from the former USSR and Ethiopia during the 1990s, or during the flow of African asylum seekers to Israel. These camps were managed under distinct and often hybrid institutional, governmental, and juridical arrangements, working both within and outside the democratic state order and often involving increased use of direct and indirect violence as part of their control methods.

Camps are also spaces created by or for specific populations. Whether formed by or for immigrants, refugees, or settlers, camps are often inhabited by people with a specific identity: either one inherent to a population, like Zionist settlers ("pioneers"), or an external identity defined or imposed according to their specific situation, like "immigrants" or "refugees." The ma'abarot were created for and inhabited by Jewish immigrants from various countries, later mostly for and by Mizrahi Jews, while Holot was created for African asylum seekers. The camp overrides similarities and differences, and it may impose on its residents a simplistic identity based on prejudice, ignorance, and often ethnocratic and racial hostilities, ignoring cultural, spatial, and other crucial differences between its individual inhabitants and thus stripping them of their humanity, turning them into a group of anonymous, identical, and easy-to-manage people.

These salient common attributes of the camp relate to the functional nexus of the modern nation-state and to the way the nation–state–territory triad (or population/subjects–law/governance–space/land) is recalibrated in it.[2] The camp is used to achieve the maximum overlap between the state's territory and its desired nation, facilitating the expansion of the state by spreading one population and concentrating and suspending the other. To decide who will be included and protected within the state order and who will be excluded and abandoned is the central task of modern biopolitics and necropolitics. In the camps examined, the different populations were excluded (or excluded themselves) from the central state order, and in some cases they could be included within it under specific conditions, only after certain political, educational, and cultural processes were completed and the state's ethnoracial *nomos* enforced.

The camp is therefore a spatial tool of sorting and separating, the prevalent approach, in the context of Israel–Palestine, of first British and then Israeli authorities, both socially and spatially, toward different populations. While territorial and ethnoracial segregation is a common phenomenon in world history,[3] Israel's active role in generating segregation was inscribed in the Zionist movement's basic ambition: to establish a national home for the Jewish people in a country inhabited by an Arab majority. In this manner, the camp continues the legacy of other ethnoracial projects of colonial and national expansion and segregation, functioning as a device of biopolitical ordering that facilitates the sovereign decision over who is in, who is out, and who is suspended for decades. As instruments of territorial struggle, these camps are spaces related to mobility and violence, conditions that also facilitate the struggle over the frontier, where indigenous and new populations fight to control the land.

The Territorial Instrument of the Camp

Understanding the camp as an ever-changing spatiopolitical mechanism allows us to trace its genealogy in all its various forms and functions and grasp the conditions of possibility for this multifaceted space. This perspective on the camp goes beyond the more usual examination of coercive camp typologies (such as the detention camp, concentration camp, or refugee camp), suggesting a new conceptual framework to examine the camp's complex political and territorial role in Israel–Palestine and beyond.

The camp is often perceived as a biopolitical machine where specific people are contained, excluded, and often transformed into controlled, suspended, cared for, and/or exposed bodies. Such a space is tightly related to the camp's early use as a colonial instrument to manage disastrous realities such as famine, plagues, and wars.[4] That function was later incarnated in the World War II concentration camps of the United States, Nazi Europe, and elsewhere and linked to the refugee camp and to the actual or metaphorical camp spaces of today, created each time a state of exception is materialized. We have already seen, however, that the camp has various political and territorial uses that are much broader than the exclusion of unwanted populations. The understanding of the Zionist frontier settler camps and ma'abara immigrant transit camps, for example, whose main role was to expand the Jewish population across the territory, requires a different approach. This approach, I argue, is also deeply grounded in colonial history, when camps were used not only for territorial containment and exclusion but also for transnational mobility and territorial expansion.

In *The Origins of Totalitarianism*, Hannah Arendt examines the central role played by European imperial expansion in the development of totalitarianism. Arendt writes about the dichotomy between expansionism and the principles of the nation-state, explaining that expansion, as the central political idea of imperialism, could not bring national laws with it and impose them on other peoples. "The inner contradiction between the nation's body politic and conquest as a political device," writes Arendt, "has been obvious since the failure of the Napoleonic dream."[5] Indeed, colonial *expansion*, as history tells us, leads quickly to *expulsion* and *expropriation*, creating a laboratory where new modern forms of power mechanisms, including the camp, were tested. However, the camp had a crucial role long before it was used as a space of containment and expropriation by colonial occupiers to enclose weak, yet sometimes resisting, local populations. This role is inherent in colonial expansion itself as an immediate means of moving to, invading, and inhabiting what became frontier territories. While "camps of expulsions" enabled the containment and expropriation of populations within the colonial matrix and later within the national territory, "camps of expansion" allowed the territory to be penetrated, conquered, and colonized in the first place, and they later facilitated control over the occupied territory. This points to symbiotic, complementary relations between mobility and expansion and between immobility, exclusion, expulsion, and expropriation, with one action often leading to the other.

In Israel–Palestine, camps and temporary architecture were used by Zionist settlers from the early days of Zionist settlement. The first Zionist communal settlements were composed of small agricultural groups which tended to work and erect tent camps in remote, desolate, and temporary locations. This form of temporary camp was enhanced, improved, and changed during the prestate, early state, and later periods, becoming more and more territorial. One of the most famous types is the wall and tower camp, adopted during the Arab uprising, which allowed prefabricated fortified outpost frontier camps to be constructed in one day, significantly changing the map of Jewish settlements in Palestine. Like prestate settler camps, the semi-military Nahal camps also blurred the distinction between military needs and territorial settlement objectives, with their surroundings perceived as a potential threat against which their residents were protected, either by a wall or by barbed wire, and always by weapons. Thus, while other types of camps were used to exclude specific populations from society, these camps of expansion excluded themselves from their surroundings, which were still not entirely in their control. In addition, while violence is usually inflicted on the inmates/dwellers of other camps, these camps of territorial expansion inflict violence on their exterior by their invasive territorial actions.

The complementary side of these camps can be seen in concentration camps, detention camps, and refugee camps, where specific populations are confined, often also within a fence, in order to "protect" a specific territory and other populations from them. The threatening outside is enclaved and surrounded by barbed wire—this time to keep people inside, coercing them into a specific controlled area, making them "passive recipients of violence."[6] These two types of camp could be seen as working in tandem not only in Israel–Palestine but also in other colonial settings, such as in South Africa during the Boer War, when the colonial blockhouse and the concentration camp appeared as two complementary spatial practices. In Foucault's terms, and admittedly in quite a simplified manner, we could describe the "camps of expansion" as ones that "make live" and the "camps of expulsion" as those that "let die," creating inverse spatiopolitical reality.[7] In the colonial permanent state of exception marked by "random and unaccountable violence," camps of expansion create "colonizing islands" linked to one another and nourished by the legal protection and material support of the states of origin.[8] In contrast, within the national order, camps create an archipelago of containment to which (often racialized) people who are deemed undesired are channeled only to be excluded, circulated, and suspended. The specific hybrid case of the ma'abara camps emerged from the combination and reinterpretation of two types of camps that had already been adopted by the Zionist/Israeli institutions in that historical period: settler camps (used for territorial expansion) and immigrant camps (used for containment), in order to force the immigrants to colonize the Israeli frontier.[9]

Both types of camps, for expansion and expulsion, are created as enclaves of isolating spaces within a given territory, separating specific populations from the rest of their society and from their immediate surroundings, whether to protect the population outside the camp from those in it or to protect the population in the camp from those outside it. Yet camps are often created not as isolated installations but, rather, as part of a spatial sequence, an archipelago or alliance formed as part of a particular situation. Often, camps are not individual spaces but, instead, are part of encompassing schemes, policies, and material apparatuses, interconnected spaces that form or maintain a territory and/or a nation. The spaces of these "networks of camps" should be studied not in isolation from one another, but as parts of broader systems that generate new political geographies.[10]

The Camp's Multifaceted Spatiality

The examination of the camp as a temporary and isolating yet connected space and the identification and definition of camps created for expulsion or for expansion have enabled an understanding of the camp as a versatile spatial tool facilitating territorial and biopolitical (re)ordering. However, within these distinctions there is still a need to understand the multifaceted spatialities of the camp. After all, the camp is not a mere technology but is a space in itself, one whose varied forms are linked not only to its function in the colonial and modern state spaces but also to the various ways it is created, used, and altered. Within each category, there are camps with very different spatial features; camps of expulsion, for example, include rigidly built institutional detention camps, self-built makeshift IDP camps, and in/formalized refugee camps, with very different spatial formations that needed to be analyzed separately.

The camps examined in this book not only play the complementary territorial roles of expansion and expulsion but also represent almost-opposite architectural types. While some are rigid spaces formed of repetitive structures placed in a functional and rational order, others evidence an inherently different spatiality: at first glance they look arbitrary and chaotic, yet they are often built according to specific social and cultural rules reflecting a deep order and meaning. The extremely rigid or chaotic spatialities of these camps seem to reflect, respectively, control over or abandonment of the camp dwellers: camp rigidity suggests that camp dwellers were subject to strict and total control; camp chaos suggests that the inhabitants were completely abandoned. The reality, however, is more complex; most camps were exposed to radical relations with the ruling power involving violent forms of both control and abandonment, which, along with additional factors, created their very different spaces.

The way camp spaces are formed, managed, and altered is crucially influenced by a combination of multiple factors. As with any built environment, factors related to the location of the camp—such as climate, topography, and proximity to other built environments—may have a significant influence on its spatiality, as can factors related to scale, the duration and nature of its temporariness, the character of its legal exclusion and mode of governance, and the culture, needs, habits, and skills of the specific populations suspended in it and its political situation. The ma'abara camps, for example, differed substantially in their location and scale, as well as in the services and public institutions they possessed, such as schools and synagogues. Another significant factor influencing the spatiality of the camps is the nature of their basic structures, whether they are tents, huts, or barracks. The relation between private and public also varies between camps: in some there is no private or family space and inhabitants are completely exposed in their most intimate moments, which affects both the level of control in the camps and the human identity of those who live there.

Hence, the creation and evolution of camps as "formal" rigid spaces or as "informal" makeshift spaces is dependent on multiple factors. The Israeli ma'abarot and the Palestinian refugee camps were both composed, at some stage, as rigid spaces of repetitive prefabricated units placed in a rational order. While in the ma'abarot, except for minor spatial actions by camp dwellers such as building *frenot* ovens, the spatial form did not change significantly during their several years of existence, while the Palestinian refugee camps changed significantly over time through multiple actions by their residents, UNRWA, and other forces, including violent military destructions. In makeshift camps, while it looks as if shelters are assembled and scattered across the landscape with no apparent order, their "chaotic" spatiality is often organized according to specific cultural and social orders, memoryscapes, traditions, and customs, constrained by limitations imposed by the authorities. For example, the Bedouin situation of campness seems to create arbitrary spaces, yet their houses have been constructed and developed over time according to traditions and modernization processes specific to the Bedouin, practices that nevertheless were and still are violently restricted by the state.

Thus, the rigid order of camps, such as the second Yeruham ma'abara, was in fact a very thin order covering the violent disorder of immigrants' lives in their new location, where they inhabited a strange, alienating, and confusing "total order" with others who were often from different countries and cultures. In contrast, behind the chaotic disorder of makeshift spaces such as Rakhma, it is possible to identify a deep spatial order, based on slowly evolving cultural and social order. We may return here to Zygmunt Bauman's theory of modernity's violent quest for order and its dialectic relations with chaos and disorder,[11] or we can use the words of modernist poet Wallace Stevens, who expresses this accurately in his poem "Connoisseur of Chaos":[12]

> A. A violent order is a disorder; and
> B. A great disorder is an order. These
> Two things are one.

Importantly, these "ordered" and "disordered" environments often penetrate and reshape one another. The makeshift environment created near the institutional Holot camp by the detainees is an example of the way such environments might intersect.

That camps' ordered and chaotic spatialities reach such extremes is due to the radical modes of governance of control and abandonment imposed on them during their rapid creation and continuous inhabitation. However, once created ad hoc, either as makeshift or institutional environments, camp spaces might be significantly transformed by the powers that inhabit and control them from within or from the outside in a process of ongoing negotiation of sovereign authority. There is a need, therefore, not only to discuss the camp in general but also to discuss particular camps and understand their situated spatial and political dimensions in their historical and geopolitical contexts.

The need to understand camps in their particular contexts is also pertinent in discussing the relationship between camps and cities. The city and the camp are often perceived as a dichotomy, corresponding to Agamben's argument that the camp, and not the city, is the West's fundamental biopolitical paradigm, as space where the ideal Aristotelian division between the public and political sphere of the *polis* and the private sphere of the *oikos*, where the needs of life are provided, becomes indistinguishable. While cities are seen as highly connected spaces of heterogeneity and plurality that incrementally develop over time, camps are depicted as temporary and isolated enclaves formed ad hoc as the city's (and state's) "constituting outside" for particular needs and populations. Yet camps and cities, as indicated in this book, have multilayered and complex relationships, which are specific to their geopolitical contexts. Camps might create the initial temporary nucleus of the spatial frameworks from which cities emerge, as in the case of the British military camp that later became an immigrant camp that formed the foundation of the Israeli city of Rosh HaAyin, or many of the Zionist settler camps and the ma'abara transit camps that evolved into kibbutz and moshav settlements, or development towns that later became cities, similar to other colonial camps of territorial expansion.

Camps can also urbanize while remaining defined and administered as camps for humanitarian and political reasons; the Palestinian refugee camps are such an example, including those that later became de facto parts of adjacent cities that grew and absorbed them. Such camps could be related to what sociologist Michel Agier identifies as the "city-camp" *(camps-villes)*. He asks whether, as a refugee camp becomes an increasingly permanent, heterogeneous, and complex space, it might "become a city in the sense of a space of urban sociability, an *urbs*, and indeed in the sense of a political space, a *polis*," but concludes that the camp remains a potential "city-to-be-made."[13] While some scholars still suggest reimagining the camp as the city, others argue that we must reject the "rigid dichotomy between camps and cities."[14] Indeed, more complex city–camp relations are identified, such as urban camps of refugees that are seen as "increasingly becoming 'slumlike' or mimicking cities," as "campscapes" of refugees and other urban outcasts, or as an "improvised dispositif" of invisible urban planning.[15] Yet the camp is also considered, following Agamben, as inherently different from the city; the makeshift or informalized camp is seen as distinct from other "slum" and "squatter" situations in that it questions the normative relations between space and citizenship on a biopolitical basis.[16] This could be also relevant to camps created in relation to urban situations, such as Holot camp, which formed as the other side of Tel Aviv through state-initiated acts of expulsion. Camps are therefore created next to cities, within cities, and by cities, and they also urbanize as camps or eventually transform into cities. The questions, importantly, are not mainly spatial but, rather, inherently political, and they relate to issues of rights and national citizenship.

Between Spaces of Necropolitics and Spaces of Natality and Political Emergence

So far, investigation of the camp as a versatile spatiopolitical instrument has deepened our understanding of the meanings of its various forms and functions. However, if we look at the spatial actions of appropriation and inhabitation that urbanize the camp, another significant argument on the camp's political role arises. This argument stands at the core of the understanding of the camp as a complex space that goes beyond its Agambenian conception as a biopolitical machine spinning around an "empty core" that constantly needs to be filled with "biological substance," "bare life" stripped of any human and political existence.[17] While some camps are indeed dehumanizing spaces of desubjectivation and thanato- or necropolitics, in Mbembe's words, creating black holes that suck in all those who are deemed unentitled to enjoy freedom and other rights, other camps appear as spatiopolitical mechanisms of resistance, subversive power, and mobilization where new political subjectivities emerge.

Camps were and still are indeed often initially created as sites for the control and management of populations according to colonial, national, and postcolonial interests. However, in many camps, at different levels, spatial actions were conducted by residents that contradicted the ideologies, policies, and political practices that created them. Yeruham's inhabitants built outdoor mud ovens, and in so doing contradicted the highly modernist ideology that rejected their traditional culture. Rakhma residents gradually created a built environment with a profound connection to its specific place, society, and culture, despite the state's efforts to enforce their temporary status. Their creation of the kindergarten and related spatial–legal actions were clear acts of spatiopolitical struggle in their efforts to achieve recognition by the state. The political existence of the Palestinian refugee camps and the politicized everyday spatial actions in them are another example of active resistance not only *within* but also *by* the camp. The accumulated spatial actions of everyday life are part of a way to escape the imposed situation of the camp itself, not by actually leaving the space but by transforming it into a new reality, which might spill over beyond the quotidian and become a political action conducted by its residents.[18] While these political spaces were initiated and enacted within and using camp spaces, other camps form, by their very creation, spaces of political mobilization assembled by those who form the weaker side of the political map, such as the Palestinian protest camps in the occupied Palestinian territories.[19]

The camp here becomes not only a space that is part of the colonial and state biopolitical apparatuses but also a space of nonrepresentational politics, or what Arendt calls *natality,* that is, the ontological condition of political actors as beginners who realize their human freedom through acting together to create their world anew. "Because they are *initium,* newcomers and beginners by virtue of birth," exclaims Arendt, "men take initiative, are prompted into action," an action that could be seen in the political subjectivities that sometimes emerge through the re-creation of the camp's own spaces.[20] Here, the camp could become a space of political emergence or "minoritarian becoming," in the language of Deleuze and Guattari, or subversive "undercommons," in the language of Harney and Moten.[21] People escape the space of the camp itself and the situation that created it by using its structures rather than resisting it completely, and at the same time work to create a new world for themselves within and by the camp. As such, the camp is seized and changed, from a humanitarian or a detention space where helpless people are contained, or a territorial space created by the strong, into an instrument that generates new forms of power and realities through resistance, deterritorialization, and spatial enactment. This could be possible because of the exceptional spatial form of the camp, which could be rapidly created, even by the weak, and emerge as a visible political call, such as in the case of the Palestinian "countersettlement" camp.[22] Or it could be possible because of the way certain camps are governed, such as in the case of the Palestinian refugee camps whose residents act to disrupt the very powers that created them.[23] By these disruptions, negotiations, and subversions of sovereign powers *through* the versatile space of the camp, the camp's own space has the potential to be one of the factors that changes its own initial trajectory of imposed subordination predicted by those who created it.

The Spatial "Hidden Gene" of Israel–Palestine

Interpreting the vast multifaceted mosaic of camps in Israel–Palestine revealed in this book required various keys, including a genealogy that identifies the emerging, evolving, deviating, continuing, and shifting attributes and meanings of the camp as a spatiopolitical mechanism, an understanding of its territorial role in the expansion and expulsion of specific populations, a comprehension of its "ordered" and "chaotic" spatial manifestations, and an acknowledgment of its use as a platform for political struggles. These keys reflect the camp as a mechanism that, following its ad hoc appearance, often resonates as an ongoing event and an in-between space until it is either stabilized as a permanent settlement or demolished and erased completely. On the one hand, we can see some of these camps as the temporary scaffolding on which Zionist settler society built Israel's nation and territory; on the other hand, we can see many of them as the unyielding bars that limit and suspend the Palestinian populations who lived and still live on the same land, while also being re-created as the tool for their ongoing resistance.

We can look at the camp as a spatial mechanism that allowed Zionism to enter history through territory, also allowing it to suspend others from history by including them within the state (and territory) only through their exclusion, expulsion, and expropriation. As this research continued to discover more and more camp varieties in Israel–Palestine, the camp was exposed as one of the hidden genes of this contested territory; history shows that every time drastic territorial or demographic changes occur in this territory, camps are constructed. It seems that spatial temporariness can be regarded as one of the most permanent phenomena in this region, where the constitution of nations and the struggle over territories seems to be a never-ending story.

Many of the camps discussed in this book no longer exist. This is of course inherent in their spatial role: as in-between spaces and as constitutive instruments, camps may be erased, change function, be suspended for generations, or develop into permanent spaces, either rural or urban. Yet camps, even if completely erased, often leave indelible marks, not only through the national territory they create or the subversive political role they assume, but also through their particular narratives and implications. The frontier settler camps, many of which developed into rural settlements, are an integral part of Israeli pathos and its celebrated national story. By contrast, the frontier ma'abara camps, some of which turned into development towns like Yeruham, and the suspended Bedouin spaces, which could potentially develop into permanent settlements like Rakhma, may bear the damage of the imposed camp situation for many years afterward. Thus, the spatial, social, and political story of the camp does not end with the termination of the situation of ongoing spatial temporariness; sometimes it forms part of a larger story of how neighborhoods, settlements, towns, cities, and of course states are formed and develop.

Camps were used as the spatial generators of and receptors for profound geopolitical alterations and reorganizations in Israel–Palestine. They were used to put specific populations in "their proper place," which in many cases meant suspending them and thus giving them no place at all. They were also used to create, with the blink of a camp, a new political reality as if the previous one had never been there. There is some historical irony in these ordering and suspending actions used by Israel and intimately related to its creation as the "national home" for the Jewish people, if we think about them in relation to past perceptions of Jews around the world. In *Modernity and the Holocaust,* Zygmunt Bauman describes the anti-Semitic European figure of the "wandering Jew," a concept constructed by the practices of the Christian Church that marked Jews as a frightening force, "an image construed as compromising and defying the order of things," visualizing "the horrifying consequences of boundary-transgression, of not remaining fully in the fold." For the order narrated by the church, "the conceptual Jew," which was separate from actual living Jewish people in European society, "was a most reliable frontier-guard of that order [by carrying] a message; the alternative to this order here and now is not another order, but chaos and devastation."[24] Is it the playfulness of history that the New Jew—the Zionist Jew—escapes this conceptual chaotic identity and its related anti-Semitic violence by frantically ordering his own domain while transferring this metaphorical "chaoticness" to others, such as the

Bedouin in the unrecognized villages and the Palestinians in the camps?[25] The use of the camp to create the utopian Zionist order in Israel–Palestine can be seen as a syndrome brought from Europe involving the imposition of a new colonial, national, and territorial order by and for those who were persecuted for being "out of place," an order that also includes the constitution of the chaotic expelled and expropriated others and their embedded continuous spatial temporariness.

Israel–Palestine is indeed an extensive laboratory of camps, and their multifaceted appearance there has allowed the various spatial and sociopolitical meanings of the camp to be unpacked. However, as we have seen throughout this book, the camps created in Israel–Palestine over the years reflect similar camp spaces created worldwide in comparable colonial, state-building, and global-ordering postcolonial projects, facilitating the movement and flourishing of some people while restricting that of others based on the ever-present ethnoracial categories and legal and spatial practices of the exception.

For the Camp Yet to Come

As an instrument of (im)mobility and (re)ordering, the story of the camp is also the story of modernity and of the way lands and people are utilized and classified, with control over them being concentrated in a few dominant centers. This is where "the undesirables" and the most vulnerable are still circulated, suspended, and kept away from society, often in facilities offshore or in uninhabitable desert environments. In this manner, the camp is inherently linked to colonial settler societies, to national creation and state building, and to the current global order of things in the way spaces and populations are controlled, managed, shifted, reshaped, and manipulated on a large scale for social engineering and bio/necropolitical ordering on local, regional, and global levels. This is also why camps are so common in Israel–Palestine: they are a crucial instrument of the constant geopolitical transformations that this contested territory has been through over the last century, changes that are inseparable from global geopolitical attitudes and events.

The examination of various camp types and their meanings in this book allows us to view the global proliferation of camps from a new angle. This perspective—which is not limited to seeing the camp only as a space of exclusion, expulsion, expropriation, and separation, but also considers it as a networked space of expansion, reordering, and movement—may assist in interpreting the camps being currently constructed across the globe as part of a spatial mechanism that, like the city, preceded core political constellations such as the nation-state and may possibly continue beyond them. This interpretation must engage the much broader horizon this book opens in relation to the camp, which views it not only as an instrument used by major dominant political actors to control life or to make significant demographic and territorial changes, but also as an instrument that might permit, through its creation and spatial alterations, processes of undercommoning or minor becomings of new emerging political powers and identities.

As has been seen throughout the history of Israel–Palestine, camps are spatial entities inherently related to the movement of people in space: to the suspension and limitation of that movement and to its facilitation, absorption, and ordering. The story of the camp is the story of mobility and its restraint, of change and of the fear of change. Thus, the camp can be regarded as a shadow that constantly follows modern politics, as a space where people are dehumanized by other people and that as such should be abolished; but it could also be looked at as a beam of light that indicates where new political subjectivities and changes may emerge. These changes would also entail alterations in the camp's spatiality and political meaning and would therefore also mean an ever-emerging theory of the camp.

"The meaning of politics is freedom," Hannah Arendt reminds us, arguing that it is "the freedom of movement" that is "the substance and meaning of all things political."[26] While the movement Arendt refers to is that of speech and its diversity, physical movement from place to place and the material movement and change of space itself are also crucial to freedom. The camp, as a space that in some cases limits mobility and in other cases enforces or facilitates it, is a crucial mechanism related to the practices and policies of movement and thus of politics as a whole. In a world where the movement of people between spaces and territories is heavily supervised and restricted, and where the ability to settle in a different place is dependent on what documents and money one possesses, camps signal not only a reinforcement but also a rupture in this tight order. Studying the camp therefore means studying changes as they happened and currently happen, and its concrete manifestations may suggest the emergence of alternative political forms and new geopolitical orders that we still cannot fully imagine.

NOTES

Introduction

1. On war on terror camps, see, for example, Judith Butler, *Precarious Life: The Powers of Mourning and Violence* (London: Verso, 2004); and Derek Gregory, "The Black Flag: Guantánamo Bay and the Space of Exception," *Geografiska Annaler* 88, no. 4 (2006): 405–27; on the proliferation of camps, see, for example, a variety of chapters in Irit Katz, Diana Martín, and Claudio Minca, eds., *Camps Revisited: Multifaceted Spatialities of a Modern Political Technology* (London: Rowman and Littlefield, 2018); on the return of the camp, see Claudio Minca, "The Return of the Camp," *Progress in Human Geography* 29, no. 4 (2005): 405–12.

2. Zygmunt Bauman, "A Century of Camps?," in *The Bauman Reader*, ed. Peter Beilharz (Oxford: Blackwell, 2001), 230–66.

3. Liisa H. Malkki, "Refugees and Exile: From 'Refugee Studies' to the National Order of Things," *Annual Review of Anthropology* 24, no. 1 (1995): 495–523.

4. Walter Benjamin, "Thesis on the Philosophy of History," in *Illuminations,* ed. Hannah Arendt (New York: Schocken Books, 1968 [1940]), 256. On "spatial violence," see Andrew Herscher and Anooradha Iyer Siddiqi, "Spatial Violence," *Architectural Theory Review* 19, no. 3 (2014): 269–77.

5. A subject would establish her *"khaima"* in a territory to claim a living space, for undefined duration, on a particular plot. Other words used are *ma'wa* (مَأْوَى), relating to finding shelter in a situation of emergency or urgency, and *malaja'* (مَلْجَأ), meaning finding protection in an emergency situation. I thank Aya Musmar for the conversation about the terminological meaning of the camp in Arabic.

6. Thomas Hobbes, *Leviathan* (New York: Oxford University Press, 1998 [1651]), 7.

7. See Stefano Harney and Fred Moten, *The Undercommons: Fugitive Planning and Black Study* (Wivenhoe: Minor Composition, 2013).

8. Ironically, many of the German World War II work and concentration camps in Europe were transformed into refugee "assembly centers" when the war ended. Malkki, "Refugees and Exile," 499–500; and Aidan Forth, *Barbed-Wire Imperialism: Britain's Empire of Camps, 1876–1903* (Berkeley: University of California Press, 2017). See chapter 1 for camp genealogies in more detail.

9. Hannah Arendt, "We Refugees," in *Altogether Elsewhere: Writers on Exile*, ed. Marc Robinson (Boston: Faber and Faber, 1994 [1943]), 111.

10. Hannah Arendt, *The Origins of Totalitarianism* (Cleveland: Meridian Books, 1962 [1951]), 284.

11. Silvia Pasquetti, "Negotiating Control: Camps, Cities, and Political Life," *City* 19, no. 5 (2015): 702–13, 702.

12. Such a camp was called a *castrum,* a word anglicized as "chester" (a camp), a trace that appears in many other names of cities in England, such as Winchester. As architectural historian Joseph Rykwert shows, Roman military camps not only developed into cities but were themselves created *as cities,* being the diagrammatic evocation of the city of Rome, "an anamnesis of *imperium.*" See Joseph Rykwert, *The Idea of a Town* (Cambridge: MIT Press, 1988), 68. On the camp as an improvised city, see Flavius Josephus, "Description on the Roman Army," http://www.historymuse.net/readings /Josephusromanarmy.html.

13. Paul Gilroy, *Between Camps: Nations, Cultures and the Allure of Race* (London: Allen Lane, an imprint of Penguin Press, 2000).

14. Giorgio Agamben, *Homo Sacer: Sovereign Power and Bare Life,* ed. and trans. Daniel Heller-Roazen (Stanford: Stanford University Press, 1998), 181. The concept of biopolitics is discussed in chapter 1.

15. Also see Giorgio Agamben, *Remnants of Auschwitz: The Witness and the Archive* (New York: Zone Books, 1999); and Agamben, *State of Exception* (Chicago: University of Chicago Press, 2005). These and related writings were published together in *The Omnibus Homo Sacer* (Stanford: Stanford University Press, 2017).

16. Arendt, quoted in Agamben, *Homo Sacer,* 170.

17. See Nasser Abourahme, "The Camp," *Comparative Studies of South Asia, Africa and the Middle East* 40, no. 1 (2020): 35–42.

18. For example, see Gregory, "The Black Flag."

19. Arendt, *Origins of Totalitarianism,* 440.

20. Wendy Brown, *Walled States, Waning Sovereignty* (New York: Zone Books, 2010), 14. The term "shifting borders" comes from Ayelet Shachar, *The Shifting Border: Legal Cartographies of Migration and Mobility* (Manchester: Manchester University Press, 2020).

21. See, for example, Adam Ramadan, "Spatialising the Refugee Camp," *Transactions of the Institute of British Geographers* 38, no. 1 (2013): 65–77; and Romola Sanyal, "Urbanizing Refuge: Interrogating Spaces of Displacement," *International Journal of Urban and Regional Research* 38, no. 2 (2014): 558–72.

22. For more on Agamben's analysis of the camp as paradigm, see Abourahme, "The Camp."

23. See Charlie Hailey, *Camps—A Guide to 21st-Century Space* (Cambridge: MIT Press, 2009), for a broad inventory of camp types and formations.

24. Zygmunt Bauman, *Modernity and Ambivalence* (Cambridge: Polity Press, 1993); Gilles Deleuze and Félix Guattari, *Kafka: Toward a Minor Literature,* trans. Dana Polan (Minneapolis: University of Minnesota Press, 1986).

25. Friedrich Nietzsche, *On the Genealogy of Morality* (Cambridge: Cambridge University Press, 1994 [1887]), 51.

26. Michel Foucault, "Nietzsche, Genealogy, History," in *Language, Counter-Memory, Practice: Selected Essays and Interviews,* ed. Donald Bouchard (Ithaca, N.Y.: Cornell University Press, 1977), 140, 146.

27. In 1850, of a population of 340,000, only 13,000 were Jews, mostly Orthodox Jews living mainly in Jerusalem, Safed, Tiberias, and Hebron. See Gudrun Krämer, *A His-*

tory of Palestine: From the Ottoman Conquest to the Founding of the State of Israel (Princeton: Princeton University Press, 2011), 135.

28. See, for example, the projects discussed by James Scott in *Seeing Like a State* (New Haven: Yale University Press, 1998).

29. On Zionism as a self-described colonial project, see Nur Masalha, *The Palestine Nakba: Decolonising History, Narrating the Subaltern, Reclaiming Memory* (London: Zed Books, 2012), and chapter 2. See also Gershon Shafir, *Land, Labor and the Origins of the Israeli–Palestinian Conflict, 1882–1914* (Cambridge: Cambridge University Press, 1989); and Daiva Stasilius and Nira Yuval-Davis, *Unsettling Settler Societies* (London: Sage, 1995). While traditional colonial structures are based on exploitation by major powers for economic gain, Oren Yiftachel and Avinoam Meir suggest that Israel is an "ethnic-survival" form of colonization, based on a particularly national and then territorial, rather than economic, colonization, with a specific ethnic character because it was established a priori as an ethnonational project. See Oren Yiftachel and Avinoam Meir, *Ethnic Frontiers and Peripheries: Landscapes of Development and Inequality in Israel* (Boulder, Colo.: Westview Press, 1998), 7; and Oren Yiftachel, *Ethnocracy: Land and Identity Politics in Israel/Palestine* (Philadelphia: University of Pennsylvania Press, 2006), 53–54. Importantly, however, Zionist settling institutions were initially highly selective in giving permits to those who wished to come, rejecting requests of pogroms survivors begging to find refuge if they were not "productive elements" capable of "building and being built by" the Land of Israel. See Gur Alroey, "'Between the Straits': Jewish Immigration to the United States and Palestine, 1915–1925," *East European Jewish Affairs* 47, nos. 2–3 (2017): 150–68, 165.

30. Yiftachel, *Ethnocracy*, 14.

31. *Aliyah* (meaning "ascent"), a basic notion of Zionist ideology, is the immigration of Diaspora Jews to the Land of Israel. The opposite action, emigration from Israel, is referred to as *Yerida* (descent). Anti-Jewish laws, persecutions, and economic problems were the main causes of Jewish immigration from eastern Europe during the late nineteenth and early twentieth centuries. There were six Aliyah waves before Israel was established.

32. See Forth, *Barbed-Wire Imperialism*.

33. The historical studies for this book rely on literature and on data gathered in Israeli and other archives, housing relevant historical documents, such as photographs (including aerial photography), construction plans and planning documents, newspaper articles, and formal letters and official documents. These archives include the Yeruham Archive; a variety of kibbutz and private photo collections; the Zionist Archive (Jerusalem); the Israel State Archives (Jerusalem); the Israeli National Photo Collections; the Haganah Archive (Tel Aviv); the Yad Tabenkin Archive of the Kibbutz Movement (Ramat Ef'al); the Israeli Defense Force Archive (Tel Ha'shomer); ActiveStills archives; ICRC Audiovisual Archives; UNRWA's online photo and film archive; and the British National Archives.

34. The research for this book includes more than sixty interviews conducted with government and municipal officials, planners, local nongovernmental organizations (NGOs), and residents of current and past camps.

35. Jacques Derrida, *Specters of Marx* (New York: Routledge, 1994).

36. Frantz Fanon, *The Wretched of the Earth* (London: Penguin Books, 2001 [1963]), 40.

294 Notes to Introduction

37. Achille Mbembe, "The Power of the Archive and Its Limits," in *Refiguring the Archive*, ed. Carolyn Hamilton et al. (Dordrecht: Kluwer Academic Publishers, 2002), 20.

38. See, for example, chapter 4 on the classification of Israeli documents from the 1950s immigrant transit camps. During recent processes of digitization of archives, documents that were open to the public are being actively concealed to hide evidence on actions conducted by the Israeli army and other militant groups, including massacres of Palestinians during the 1948 war and the Nakba. See Hagar Shezaf, "Burying the Nakba: How Israel Systematically Hides Evidence of 1948 Expulsion of Arabs," *Ha'aretz*, 5 July 2019, https://www.haaretz.com/israel-news/.premium.MAGAZINE-how-israel-systematically-hides-evidence-of-1948-expulsion-of-arabs-1.7435103.

39. Ariella Azoulay, *The Civil Contract of Photography* (New York: Zone Books, 2008), 22.

1. The Camp Reconfigured

1. Forth, *Barbed-Wire Imperialism*, 1; Agamben, *Homo Sacer*, 174–75; Michel Agier, "Between War and City towards an Urban Anthropology of Refugee Camps," *Ethnography* 3, no. 3 (2002): 317–41, 332; and Claudio Minca, "Geographies of the Camp," *Political Geography* 49 (2015): 74–83, 74.

2. On the regulation of human movement, particularly in relation to Israel–Palestine, see Wendy Brown, *Walled States, Waning Sovereignty* (New York: Zone Books, 2010), 40–47; and Hagar Kotef, *Movement and the Ordering of Freedom: On Liberal Governances of Mobility* (Durham, N.C.: Duke University Press, 2015).

3. Zygmunt Bauman, *Liquid Modernity* (Cambridge: Polity Press, 2000), 9–10, 112–14.

4. Bauman, *Modernity and Ambivalence*, 3–7.

5. Arendt, *Origins of Totalitarianism*, 281–82. The state–people–territory triad has also been adopted by other scholars (though sometimes in different words), such as Agamben, as discussed in the introduction, and Swiss geographer Claude Raffestin, who sees "population, territory and authority" as the three elements of the state, saying, "The entire geography of the state derives from this triad." Quoted in translation from French in Stuart Elden, *The Birth of Territory* (Chicago: University of Chicago Press, 2013), 5.

6. See Max Weber, "Politics as a Vocation," in *From Max Weber: Essays in Sociology*, ed. Hans Heinrich Gerth and Charles Wright Mills (Abingdon: Routledge, 1991 [1919]), 77–128, 78.

7. Agamben, *Homo Sacer*, 174–75.

8. For more on sovereignty and its paradoxes, see Brown, *Walled States*, 65–66.

9. Hobbes, *Leviathan*, 82.

10. Hobbes, *Leviathan*, 84.

11. Hobbes, *Leviathan*, 114.

12. Jean Bodin, *On Sovereignty: Four Chapters from the Six Books of the Commonwealth* (Cambridge: Cambridge University Press, 1992 [1576]), 46.

13. Michael Foucault, *Society Must Be Defended: Lectures at the Collège de France, 1975–1976* (London: Penguin Books, 2004), 241; see also in Foucault, *Discipline and Punish: The Birth of the Prison* (New York: Vintage Books, 1995).

14. Claude Lefort, *Democracy and Political Theory* (Cambridge: Polity Press, 1988).

15. See Thomas Blom Hansen and Finn Stepputat, *Sovereign Bodies: Citizens, Migrants, and States in the Postcolonial World* (Princeton: Princeton University Press, 2005).

Notes to Chapter 1   **295**

16. See Jean-Jacques Rousseau, *Of the Social Contract and Other Political Writings* (London: Penguin Books, 2010 [1792]).

17. Rousseau, *Of the Social Contract*, 7.

18. This paradox is discussed in Jacques Julliard, *La faute à Rousseau: Essai sur les conséquences historiques de l'idée de souveraineté populaire* (Paris: Editions du Seuil, 1985).

19. Carl Schmitt, *Political Theology: Four Chapters on the Concept of Sovereignty*, trans. George Schwab (Chicago: University of Chicago Press, 2006), 5.

20. Schmitt, *Political Theology*, 5.

21. Julia Reinhard Lupton, "Creature Caliban," *Shakespeare Quarterly* 51, no. 1 (2000): 1–23, 5–6.

22. Schmitt, *Political Theology*, 7; Agamben, *Homo Sacer*, 15. See also Agamben, *State of Exception*, 35.

23. Agamben, *Homo Sacer*, 17, 17–18, 168–69; emphasis in the original. All emphases are original unless otherwise noted.

24. Agamben, *Homo Sacer*, 170, 171, 109.

25. See Jenny Edkins, "Sovereign Power, Zones of Indistinction, and the Camp," *Alternatives* 25, no. 1 (2000): 3–25.

26. Agamben, *Homo Sacer*, 136–43.

27. Benjamin, "Thesis on the Philosophy of History," 257

28. Agamben, *State of Exception*, 2.

29. See Noam Leshem, *Life after Ruin: The Struggles over Israel's Depopulated Arab Spaces* (Cambridge: Cambridge University Press), 79–90.

30. Michael Foucault, *Security, Territory, Population: Lectures at the Collège de France, 1977–78* (Basingstoke: Palgrave Macmillan, 2009), 286–87.

31. Foucault, *Security, Territory, Population*, 353, 354, 107.

32. See, for example, Lucas Oesch, "The Refugee Camp as a Space of Multiple Ambiguities and Subjectivities," *Political Geography* 60 (2017): 110–20; Adam Ramadan and Sara Fregonese, "Hybrid Sovereignty and the State of Exception in the Palestinian Refugee Camps in Lebanon," *Annals of the American Association of Geographers* 107, no. 4 (2017): 949–63; and Gaja Maestri, "The Contentious Sovereignties of the Camp: Political Contention among State and Non-State Actors in Italian Roma Camps," *Political Geography* 60 (2017): 213–22.

33. Alex Jeffrey, *The Improvised State: Sovereignty, Performance and Agency in Dayton Bosnia* (Chichester: John Wiley and Sons, 2013), 16.

34. Kirsten McConnachie, "Camps of Containment: A Genealogy of the Refugee Camp," *Humanity: An International Journal of Human Rights, Humanitarianism, and Development* 7, no. 3 (2016): 397–412, 399.

35. Forth, *Barbed-Wire Imperialism*, 2–3.

36. Hansen and Stepputat, *Sovereign Bodies*, 19–20.

37. Arendt, *Origins of Totalitarianism*, 440.

38. Agamben, *Homo Sacer*, 166. Concentration camps for anti-insurgency, however, had already appeared in colonial countries before this period—for example, those used in the United States from the first half of the nineteenth century to hold Native Americans resisting land occupation, or similar mechanisms used in Australia to hold Aborigines. See Scott Lauria Morgensen, "The Biopolitics of Settler Colonialism: Right Here, Right Now," *Settler Colonial Studies* 1, no. 1 (2011): 52–76, 69; and Alan Gray, "The Formation of Contemporary Aboriginal Settlement Patterns in Australia," in *Population*

296   Notes to Chapter 1

Mobility and Indigenous Peoples in Australasia and North America, ed. John Taylor and Martin Bell (London: Routledge, 2004), 201–22, 202

39. Forth, *Barbed-Wire Imperialism,* 5, 15.

40. Josef Goebbels, Hitler's propaganda minister, traced the term "concentration camp" to the British internment camps of the Boer War, attempting to locate an architectural and political precedent in British imperial rule. See Elizabeth Stanley, *Mourning Becomes . . . : Post/Memory, Commemoration and the Concentration Camps of the South African War* (Manchester: Manchester University Press, 2006), 7. As Hans Frank, the Nazi governor of Poland, proclaimed, "The region shall be treated like a colony [in which] the Poles will become the slaves of the Greater German Empire." See Benjamin Madley, "From Africa to Auschwitz: How German South West Africa Incubated Ideas and Methods Adopted and Developed by the Nazis in Eastern Europe," *European History Quarterly* 35, no. 3 (2005): 429–464, 438, quoted in Lindsay Weiss, "Exceptional Space: Concentration Camps and Labor Compounds in Late Nineteenth-Century South Africa," in *Archaeologies of Internment,* ed. Adrian Myers and Gabriel Moshenska (New York: Springer, 2011), 21–32, 30.

41. African workers in South Africa's diamond industry were held in labor camps for six-month periods in order to prevent theft; see Weiss, "Exceptional Space."

42. Erving Goffman, *On the Characteristics of Total Institutions* (New York: Holt, Rinehart and Winston, 1961).

43. Racial tropes that transformed the Dutch-speaking Afrikaner Boers from "virile Anglo-Saxons" into "the lowest stock of European Humanity," "nothing more nor less than a low type of the genus homo," and suggestions that "verminous" Boers be ruthlessly "exterminated" as "a plague-infected rat" highlight the flexibility of the racial categorization and ideology that dominated the colonial and Western discourse. Quoted in Forth, *Barbed-Wire Imperialism,* 137–38.

44. See Stowell V. Kessler, "The Black Concentration Camps of the Anglo–Boer War, 1899–1902: Shifting the Paradigm from Sole Martyrdom to Mutual Suffering," *Historia* 44, no. 1 (1999): 110–47; also in Forth, *Barbed-Wire Imperialism,* 172.

45. In this evolution of the camp as a genocidal weapon, it is a troubling historical link that the first commissioner of the German camps in Namibia was Heinrich Goering, father of Hermann Goering, founder of the first concentration camps in Germany. See McConnachie, "Camps of Containment."

46. See, for example, David Atkinson, "Encountering Bare Life in Italian Libya and Colonial Amnesia in Agamben," in *Agamben and Colonialism,* ed. Marcelo Svirsky and Simone Bignall (Edinburgh: Edinburgh University Press, 2012); Stephen Morton, "Reading Kenya's Colonial State of Emergency after Agamben," in Svirsky and Bignall, *Agamben and Colonialism;* and Samia Henni, *Architecture of Counterrevolution: The French Army in Northern Algeria* (Zurich: gta Verlag, 2017).

47. Ann Laura Stoler, "On Degrees of Imperial Sovereignty," *Public Culture* 18, no. 1 (2006): 125–46.

48. George Fredrickson, "Colonialism and Racism: The United States and South Africa in Comparative Perspective," in *The Arrogance of Race: Historical Perspectives on Slavery, Racism, and Social Inequality,* ed. George Fredrickson (Middletown, Conn.: Wesleyan University Press, 1988), 112–31.

49. See Neve Gordon and Moriel Ram, "Ethnic Cleansing and the Formation of Settler Colonial Geographies," *Political Geography* 53 (2016): 20–29.

50. Shafir, *Land, Labor, and the Origins of the Israeli–Palestinian Conflict,* 10.

Notes to Chapter 1   **297**

51. See Stasiulis and Yuval-Davis, *Unsettling Settler Societies,* 5; and Patrick Wolfe, "Settler Colonialism and the Elimination of the Native," *Journal of Genocide Research* 8, no. 4 (2006): 387–409.

52. Baruch Kimmerling, *Politicide: Ariel Sharon's War against the Palestinians* (London: Verso, 2003), 214–15.

53. Yiftachel, *Ethnocracy,* 13.

54. Agamben, *Homo Sacer,* 178.

55. Adi Ophir, "State," *Mafte'akh: Lexical Review of Political Thought* 1 (2010): 67–96.

56. Hannah Arendt, *The Human Condition* (Chicago: Chicago University Press, 1998 [1958]), 321.

57. The term "biopolitics" was originally conceptualized by Michel Foucault in *The History of Sexuality* (London: Penguin, 1978) and was developed in his lectures at the Collège de France—mainly in *Society Must Be Defended*; *Security, Territory, Population*; and *The Birth of Biopolitics: Lectures at the Collège de France, 1978–79* (Basingstoke: Palgrave Macmillan, 2008).

58. Foucault, *Society Must Be Defended,* 245.

59. Foucault, *Society Must Be Defended,* 241, 247.

60. These efforts to improve life included the development of medicine and infrastructures to advance public hygiene, vaccinations, coordinated medical care, and the elimination of accidents or random elements. Foucault, *Society Must Be Defended,* 244, 248.

61. Foucault, *Society Must Be Defended,* 257.

62. Foucault, *Society Must Be Defended,* 254.

63. Michel Foucault, *Dits et écrits*, vols. 3–4 (Paris: Gallimard, 1976), 719; quoted in Agamben, *Homo Sacer,* 3.

64. Walker Connor, *Ethnonationalism: The Quest for Understanding* (Princeton: Princeton University Press, 1994), 95–111.

65. Declaration of the Rights of Man and of the Citizen, quoted in translation in Connor, *Ethnonationalism,* 95.

66. Benedict Anderson, *Imagined Communities: Reflections on the Origin and Spread of Nationalism* (London: Verso, 2006 [1991]), 3.

67. Eric Hobsbawm, *Nations and Nationalism since 1780: Programme, Myth, Reality* (Cambridge: Cambridge University Press, 1987), 144–47.

68. Gilroy, *Between Camps,* 68, 82, 84.

69. Arendt, *Origins of Totalitarianism,* 269.

70. Arendt, *Origins of Totalitarianism,* 297.

71. Hobsbawm, *Nations and Nationalism since 1780,* 161.

72. Judith Butler and Gayatri Chakravorty Spivak, *Who Sings the Nation-State? Language, Politics, Belonging.* (London: Seagull Books, 2007), 33–35.

73. Agamben, *Homo Sacer,* 177. On Arendt's reflection on the camp, see the Introduction. Importantly, residents in camps are differently categorized as "refugees," "asylum seekers," "immigrants," "infiltrators," and other titles by different actors, and are referred to in this book according to the specific context. On this problematic and changing categorization, see Heaven Crawley and Dimitris Skleparis, "Refugees, Migrants, Neither, Both: Categorical Fetishism and the Politics of Bounding in Europe's 'Migration Crisis,'" *Journal of Ethnic and Migration Studies* 44 (2018): 48–64.

74. Agamben, *Homo Sacer,* 182, 171, 9.

75. Agamben, *Homo Sacer,* 181, 9.

76. Butler, *Precarious Life*, 98, 67.

77. Achille Mbembe, "Necropolitics," *Public Culture* 15, no 1 (2003): 11–40, 26. See also Mbembe, *Necropolitics* (Durham, NC: Duke University Press, 2019), 79.

78. Agamben is criticized for his shortcoming in adequately relating to colonialism and race in their various aspects. See Simone Bignall and Marcelo G. Svirsky, eds., *Agamben and Colonialism* (Edinburgh: Edinburgh University Press, 2012), 1–14.

79. See for example Edkins, "Sovereign Power"; and Minca, "The Return of the Camp."

80. See, for example, Kim Rygiel, "Bordering Solidarities: Migrant Activism and the Politics of Movement and Camps at Calais," *Citizenship Studies* 15, no. 1 (2011): 1–19; Nando Sigona, "Campzenship: Reimagining the Camp as a Social and Political Space," *Citizenship Studies* 19, no. 1 (2015): 1–15; Ramadan, "Spatialising the Refugee Camp"; and Sanyal, "Urbanizing Refuge."

81. One pertinent example showing how the human spirit prevails in the cruelest camp realities is the story of the Zhehnnerchaft ("group of ten"), which illustrates the phenomenon of "camp sisters": A group of young Jewish women survived three camps during the Holocaust, including the Auschwitz death camp, through mutual support and assistance. See Judith Tydor Baumel, "Social Interaction among Jewish Women in Crisis during the Holocaust: A Case Study," *Gender and History* 7, no. 1 (1995): 64–84. Also see Richard Carter-White, "Communities of Violence in the Nazi Death Camps," in Katz, Martin, and Minca, *Camps Revisited*, 177–95.

82. See Patricia Owens, "Reclaiming 'Bare Life'? Against Agamben on Refugees," *International Relations* 23, no. 4 (2009): 567–82, 577; and Michel Agier, *On the Margins of the World: The Refugee Experience Today* (Cambridge: Polity Press, 2008).

83. Two examples mentioned by Agamben are the stadium in Bari where, in 1991, Italian police concentrated Albanian illegal immigrants before deporting them and the *zones d'attentes* in French international airports where foreigners are detained if they are asking for asylum. See Agamben, *Homo Sacer*, 174.

84. This mutability was seen in the African Boer camps and black camps discussed above and will be revealed throughout this book.

85. Martin Van Creveld, *The Rise and Decline of the State* (Cambridge: Cambridge University Press, 1999), 332.

86. Elden, *Birth of Territory*, 10.

87. See Andreas Osiander, "Sovereignty, International Relations, and the Westphalian Myth," *International Organization* 55, no. 2 (2001): 251–87; and Benno Teschke, *The Myth of 1648: Class, Geopolitics, and the Making of Modern International Relations* (New York: Verso, 2003).

88. Teschke, *The Myth of 1648*, 11.

89. Christopher Rudolph, "Sovereignty and Territorial Borders in a Global Age," *International Studies Review* 7, no. 1 (2005): 1–20, 5.

90. Henri Lefebvre, *State, Space, World: Selected Essays* (Minneapolis: University of Minnesota Press, 2009), 226.

91. Robert David Sack, *Human Territoriality: Its Theory and History* (Cambridge: Cambridge University Press, 1986), 19–22.

92. Joe Painter, "Rethinking Territory," *Antipode* 42, no. 5 (2010): 1090–118, 1093–94.

93. Michel Foucault, "Questions in Geography," in *Space, Knowledge and Power: Foucault and Geography*, ed. Jeremy W. Crampton and Stuart Elden (Aldershot: Ashgate, 2007 [1972–1977]), 173–82, 176.

94. Elden, *Birth of Territory*, 17.

95. Kal Raustiala, "The Geography of Justice," *Fordham Law Review* 73 (2004): 2501–60, 2513. The camps created in Guantánamo Bay in Cuba by the United States after 9/11 for "war on terror" detainees are probably among the best-known examples of camps established by a state outside its territory; their use allows the United States to ignore international conventions to which it is committed. In his work on Guantánamo, Derek Gregory argues that the camps there involve political and juridical aspects that fold "between the national and transnational" rather than being framed and contained by a single state. Other countries also replace inland camps with offshore ones to avoid legal and other moral constraints—for example, the Australian "Pacific Solution" of notorious camps where refugees and asylum seekers are detained on remote islands in the Pacific Ocean such as Manus Island and Nauru. Europe also sponsors camps on the far side of the Mediterranean in order to keep refugees and migrants away. Gregory, "The Black Flag," 407. See also Ayelet Shachar, *The Shifting Border: Legal Cartographies of Migration and Mobility* (Manchester: Manchester University Press, 2020); and Luzia Bialasiewicz, "Off-Shoring and Out-Sourcing the Borders of Europe: Libya and EU Border Work in the Mediterranean," *Geopolitics* 17, no. 4 (2012): 843–66.

96. Doreen Massey, *For Space* (London: Sage, 2005), 10–11.

97. Henri Lefebvre, *The Production of Space* (Oxford: Blackwell, 1991 [1974]), 280.

98. Neil Brenner and Stuart Elden, "Henri Lefebvre on State, Space, Territory," *International Political Sociology* 3, no. 4 (2009): 353–77, 374, 362.

99. Foucault, *Society Must Be Defended*, 252–53.

100. See also Scott in *Seeing Like a State*.

101. Adi Ophir, "Moral Technologies: Managing Disaster and Forsaking Life" [in Hebrew], *Theory and Criticism* 22 (2003): 67–104, 85.

102. Fanon, *The Wretched of the Earth*, 40.

103. Stoler, "On Degrees of Imperial Sovereignty," 128, 137.

104. Nezar Alsayyad and Ananya Roy, "Medieval Modernity: On Citizenship and Urbanism in a Global Era," *Space and Polity* 10, no. 1 (2006): 1–20, 13.

105. See Irit Katz Feigis, "Spaces Stretch Inward: Intersections between Architecture and Minor Literature," *Public Culture* 22, no. 3 (2010): 425–32.

106. Carl Schmitt, *The Nomos of the Earth in the International Law of the* Jus Publicum Europaeum (New York: Telos Press, 2003); Agamben, *Homo Sacer*, 19–20, 30–38, 175.

107. Schmitt, cited in Agamben, *Homo Sacer*, 19.

108. It also means "to distribute, to possess (what has been distributed) and to dwell." Arendt, *The Human Condition*, 63.

109. Schmitt, *The Nomos of the Earth*, 70.

110. Gary L. Ulmen, "Translator's Introduction," in Schmitt, *The Nomos of the Earth*, 9–34, 10.

111. Ulmen, "Translator's Introduction," 10–11.

112. Schmitt, *The Nomos of the Earth*, 94.

113. Mbembe, "Necropolitics," 24.

114. Agamben, *Homo Sacer*, 20, 175.

115. Agamben, *Homo Sacer*, 175, 176.

116. Howard Roberts Lamar and Leonard Monteath Thompson, *The Frontier in History: North America and Southern Africa Compared* (New Haven: Yale University Press, 1981), 7, 8.

117. Yiftachel and Meir, *Ethnic Frontiers and Peripheries*, 3, 5.

118. Yiftachel, *Ethnocracy*, 61.

119. Stephen Graham, *Cities under Siege: The New Military Urbanism* (London: Verso, 2011), xiii.

120. Ariel Handel, "Frontier" [in Hebrew], *Mafte'akh: Lexical Review of Political Thought* 4 (2011): 143–66, 156.

121. See Georgine Clarsen, "Introduction: Special Section on Settler-colonial Mobilities," *Transfers* 5, no. 3 (2015): 41–48, 42. Some of these ideas are discussed in Irit Katz, "Spreading and Concentrating: The Camp as the Space of the Frontier," *City* 19, no. 5 (2015): 722–35.

122. Agamben, *Homo Sacer*, 169.

123. Adi Ophir, "A Time of Occupation," in *The Other Israel: Voices of Refusal and Dissent*, ed. Roane Carey and Jonathan Shainin (New York: New Press, 2002), 60.

124. Yousif M. Qasmiyeh, "The Camp Is Time," Refugee Hosts Project, https://refugeehosts .org/2017/01/15/the-camp-is-time/.

125. David Bissell, "Animating Suspension: Waiting for Mobilities," *Mobilities* 2, no. 2 (2007): 277–98, 282. See also Rebecca Rotter, "Waiting in the Asylum Determination Process: Just an Empty Interlude?," *Time and Society* 25, no. 1 (2016): 80–101. See also Christine M. Jacobsen, Marry-Anne Karlsen, and Shahram Khoravi, eds., *Waiting and the Temporalities of Irregular Migration* (London: Routledge, 2021).

126. Cathrine Brun, "Active Waiting and Changing Hopes: Toward a Time Perspective on Protracted Displacement," *Social Analysis* 59, no. 1 (2015): 19–37.

127. On Palestinians' and Jews' relationship with time and temporariness through history, see Amal Jamal, "The Struggle for Time and the Power of Temporariness: Jews and Palestinians in the Labyrinth of History," in *Men in the Sun*, ed. Tal Ben-Zvi and Hanna Farah-Kufer Bir'im (Herzliya: Herzliya Museum of Contemporary Art, 2009), http:// www.men-in-the-sun.com/EN/amal-jamal-part-1.

128. Jamal, "The Struggle for Time and the Power of Temporariness."

129. Arendt, *The Human Condition*, 18–19.

130. The characteristics of duration are its "pure heterogeneity"; its continuous emergence as something that did not exist before, because for Bergson "duration means invention, the creation of forms, the continual elaboration of the absolutely new"; and the fact that its emerging changes and new forms of existence are unpredictable and "could never have been foreseen." This simultaneous existence of conscious human temporalities exists as an ongoing process of transition with a constant potential for change and transformation, affecting the creation of space as a fluid, time-dependent process. See Henri Bergson, *Time and Free Will: An Essay on the Immediate Data of Consciousness* (London: Routledge, 2014). The creation of space by the residents of refugee camps, for example, could be seen as an action of world building that brings back the human time to the camp and reaffirms its duration through space, after the appearance of the camp as a mere humanitarian space for sustaining mere biological life after the space-time rupture of displacement.

131. Elizabeth Grosz, *Time Travels: Feminism, Nature, Power* (Durham, NC: Duke University Press, 2005), 94.

132. See Katherine Bermingham, "Time for Arendt: Political Temporality and the Space-Time of Freedom," 29 March 2019, Hannah Arendt Center, https://medium.com /quote-of-the-week/time-for-arendt-political-temporality-and-the-space-time-of-freedom -995cefae8f69; Bergson, *Time and Free Will*; and G. Watts Cunningham, "Bergson's Conception of Duration," *Philosophical Review* 23, no. 5 (1914): 525–39.

133. See, for example, Anna Feigenbaum, Fabian Frenzel, and Patrick McCurdy, *Protest Camps* (London: Zed Books, 2013).

134. Bruno Latour, *Reassembling the Social: An Introduction to Actor-Network-Theory* (Oxford: Oxford University Press, 2005).

135. See Irit Katz, "Mobile Colonial Architecture: Facilitating Settler Colonialism's Expansion, Expulsions, Resistance and Decolonization," *Mobilities* 17, no. 2 (2022), https://doi.org/10.1080/17450101.2021.2000838.

136. Benjamin Meiches, "A Political Ecology of the Camp," *Security Dialogue* 46, no. 5 (2015): 476–92.

137. Meiches, "A Political Ecology of the Camp," 477.

138. See Irit Katz, "Adhocism, Agency and Emergency Shelter: On Architectural Nuclei of Life in Displacement," in *Structures of Protection? Rethinking Refugee Shelter*, ed. Tom Scott-Smith and Mark E. Breeze (New York: Berghahn Books, 2020), 235–46.

139. Nasser Abourahme, "Assembling and Spilling-Over: Towards an 'Ethnography of Cement' in a Palestinian Refugee Camp," *International Journal of Urban and Regional Research* 39, no. 2 (2015): 200–217.

2. Facilitating Double Colonialism

1. See this chapter's second epigraph, in which M. Shweiger, a member of the Labor Battalion, a Zionist group created for Jewish settlement, labor, and defense (on its settler camps, see later in the chapter) depicts a younger generation gazing back at them, the settlers, from the future. He predicts that a century hence, a teacher will lead his pupils to the area of Zionist settlements and show them scenes, with a "magic lantern," from the lives of their forefathers in their settler camp. Published in *MeHayeynu* (From our lives), the newspaper of the Yosef Trumpeldor Labor Battalion. Quoted in Boaz Neumann, *Land and Desire in Early Zionism* (Waltham, Mass.: Brandeis University Press, 2011), 178.

2. Cited in Krämer, *A History of Palestine*, 145.

3. Cited in Krämer, *A History of Palestine*, 149.

4. Colonial expansion into the Arab territories of the Ottoman Empire intensified from the mid-nineteenth century onward: France occupied Algiers in 1830, Aden was ruled by Great Britain from 1839, and, following the Russo–Turkish War (1877–78), Cyprus was leased to the British Empire. The British strategic concern to secure its lines of communication to the oil in Iran in the beginning of the twentieth century was followed by an immediate attack on Iraq after the outbreak of World War I; see Krämer, *A History of Palestine*, 139–41.

5. Allenby entered the Old City of Jerusalem on 11 December 1917 to proclaim an allied military government. Krämer, *A History of Palestine*, 152.

6. Krämer, *A History of Palestine*, 162, 164.

7. Article 22 of the Covenant of the League of Nations; quoted in Krämer, *A History of Palestine*, 164–65.

8. Jacob Norris, *Land of Progress: Palestine in the Age of Colonial Development, 1905–1948* (Oxford: Oxford University Press, 2013), 64–66; see also Krämer, *A History of Palestine*, 165.

9. Krämer, *A History of Palestine*, 156.

10. Krämer, *A History of Palestine*, 154.

302   Notes to Chapter 2

11. Amiram Oren and Rafi Regev, *Country in Khaki: Land and Security in Israel* [in Hebrew] (Jerusalem: Carmel, 2008), 23.

12. Eliyahu Biltzky and Mordechai Amster, *In the Years of Emergency: The "Camps" Period, 1937–1947* [in Hebrew] (Tel Aviv: Histadrut Poaley Habinyan, 1956), 18.

13. See the discussion in chapter 1 on the materiality of the camp.

14. See Arnon Golan and Amiram Oren, "The Use of Former British Military Bases during and after the 1948 War," *Israel Affairs* 24, no. 2 (2018): 221–39, 223.

15. Amiram Oren, *Drafted Territories: The Creation of Israeli Army Hegemony over the State's Land and Its Expanses during Its Early Years (1948–1956)* [in Hebrew] (Givatayim: Madaf, 2009), 20.

16. This hut design is exemplified in the specifications for "New Construction of Camps" in "Chief Engineer—Technical Instructions No. 36," 28 September 1940. See War Diary of Chief Engineer Palestine and Transjordan, vol. 13, September 1940, WO 169/152, British National Archives.

17. Jean-Louis Cohen, *Architecture in Uniform: Designing and Building for the Second World War* (Montreal: Canadian Centre for Architecture; Paris: Hazan; distributed by Yale University Press, 2011), 258; Sari Mark, "Nissens Were Seen in the Country: The Industrialized Hut in the Service of the British Army" [in Hebrew], *Israel* 24 (2016): 143–61.

18. Chris Chiei and Julie Decker, *Quonset Hut: Metal Living for a Modern Age* (New York: Princeton Architectural Press, 2005), xvi, 6.

19. Paul Francis, *British Military Airfield Architecture: From Airships to the Jet Age* (Cheltenham: History Press, 1996), 209–10.

20. Between 1827 and 1829, a small group of British settlers came to West Australia equipped with small wooden houses manufactured in sections in England. The Manning Portable Colonial Cottage for Emigrants was "specifically designed for mobility and ease of transportation" and could be easily carried to and erected in distant frontier areas. See Gilbert Herbert, "Portable Colonial Cottage," *Journal of the Society of Architectural Historians* 31, no. 4 (1972): 261–75. See also Katz, "Mobile Colonial Architecture."

21. "Chief Engineer—Technical Instruction No. 37—Building Materials," September 1940, British National Archives, WO 169/152, Kew, UK.

22. Monthly Report by S. S. W., September 1940, WO 169/152, doc. C1-1, British National Archives, Kew, UK.

23. Monthly Report by S. S. W., September 1940, WO 169/152, doc. C1-1, British National Archives, Kew, UK.

24. The elimination of the Nazi threat together with the continuation of the immigration quota policy and the land-purchase restrictions of the White Paper of 1939 led to a surge in Jewish anti-British resistance after the war, including organized illegal Jewish immigration to Palestine and construction of new Jewish settlements. See Krämer, *A History of Palestine*, 304–7.

25. Krämer, *A History of Palestine*. Also see Oren, *Drafted Territories*, 18; and Golan and Oren, "The Use of Former British Military Bases," 223.

26. See Golan and Oren, "The Use of Former British Military Bases," 230; and chapters 3 and 6.

27. Between 1949 and 1950, around thirty-five thousand immigrants passed through this camp, which was one of the largest immigrant camps in Israel. While most of the

immigrants were put in tents, the British structures were used for the camp's public institutions, such as the kitchens, hospital, and staff accommodations.

28. See Masalha, *The Palestine Nakba*, 35.

29. Maxime Rodinson, *Israel: A Colonial–Settler State?* (New York: Monad Press, 1973), 91; also see Edward W. Said, *The Question of Palestine* (New York: Vintage Books, 1979).

30. Yiftachel, *Ethnocracy*, 54. On the Zionist limitations on Jewish migration to Palestine to only capable individuals, see Gur Alroey, "'Between the Straits.'"

31. Freddy Kahana, *Neither Town nor Village: The Architecture of the Kibbutz, 1910–1990* [in Hebrew] (Ramat Efal: Yad Tabenkin Press, 2011), 261; see also Gabriel Schwake, "Settle and Rule: The Evolution of the Israeli National Project," *Architecture and Culture* 8, no. 2 (2020): 350–71, 354.

32. Quotation attributed to Trumpeldor in Schwake, "Settle and Rule."

33. See Baruch Kimmerling, *Zionism and Territory: The Socio-Territorial Dimensions of Zionist Politics* (Berkeley: University of California, Institute of International Studies, 1983).

34. Yosef Trumpeldor (1916), quoted in Neumann, *Land and Desire in Early Zionism*, v.

35. Shlomo, one of the first settlers, quoted in English in Amia Lieblich, *Kibbutz Makom* (London: Deutsch, 1982), 25.

36. Eyal Amir, Arza Churchman, and Avraham Wachman, "The Kibbutz Dwelling: Ideology and Design," *Housing, Theory and Society* 22, no. 3 (2005): 147–65, 149.

37. Neumann, *Land and Desire in Early Zionism*, 1, 50.

38. Davar newspaper, 1924, quoted in Yael Allweil, *Homeland: Zionism as Housing Regime, 1860–2011* (Abingdon: Routledge, 2016), 134, as part of her discussion on the importance of the children's house in the kibbutz.

39. Allon, quoted in Gershom Gorenberg, *The Accidental Empire* (New York: Times Books, 2006), 67.

40. In three years (1933–35), with the rise of Nazi Germany, the Jewish population in Palestine had almost doubled from 175,000 to 370,000 people, reaching nearly 30 percent of the entire population owing to the flow of immigrants from Europe, mainly from Germany. This expedited the breaking of the nationalist uprising of Palestinian Arabs against British colonial rule, and mass Jewish immigration and land purchase. The uprising started as strikes and other forms of political protest directed by the elitist Higher Arab Committee, but later it became a violent resistance led by peasant movements that aimed at British forces and Zionist targets and was suppressed by the British army and the Palestine police force. See Jacob Norris, "Repression and Rebellion: Britain's Response to the Arab Revolt in Palestine of 1936–39," *Journal of Imperial and Commonwealth History* 36, no. 1 (2008): 25–45.

41. See Sharon Rotbard, "Wall and Tower *(Homa Umigdal)*: The Mold of Israeli Architecture," in *A Civilian Occupation: The Politics of Israeli Architecture*, ed. Eyal Weizman and Rafi Segal (New York: Verso, 2003), 39–58.

42. Gabriel Tzifroni, "The 'Trojan Horse' of the Jewish Settlement" [in Hebrew], *Ma'ariv*, 17 December 1976, Ha'hagana Archive, Tel-Aviv.

43. Ratner later became a general in the IDF and served in the 1950s as head of the Faculty of Architecture in the Haifa Technion.

44. Kibbutz Tel Amal was not the first prefabricated settlement erected by Zionist settlers. In the summer of 1898, almost forty years before the first wall and tower camp,

304   Notes to Chapter 2

the settlers of Ha'dera wanted to move to a new settlement away from the swamps and mosquitoes. In order to erect the settlement quickly to avoid obstruction by the Turks, they built twenty huts in Jaffa, transported them secretly by boat to Ha'dera, and erected the new settlement within two days while avoiding the Turkish soldiers. See Mordechai Naor, "Tower and Stockade in the Nineteenth Century" [in Hebrew], *Ma'ariv,* 31 December 1976, Ha'hagana Archive, Tel-Aviv.

45. "Settlement points" was the term used to describe the wall and tower outposts, implying that a territorial "point" on the map had more importance than the "settlement" itself. Elhanan Oren and Shlomo Gur in an interview with Mark Ariel, "Wall and Tower–A Dream and Its Fracture," *Ba'mahane—IDF Journal,* February 1977. The Israeli myth is that the wall and tower camps were all erected at night as they were not supported by the British authorities, and were based on Turkish law by which it is impossible to demolish a roofed structure. However, the method of erecting roofed structures at night was used only during the days of the first (1882–1903) and second (1904–14) Aliyah (the migration waves of Jews to Palestine) during the days of the Ottoman Empire, and after the publication of the "White Paper of 1939" after which twelve new settlements were erected at night.

46. However, when there was an urgent political need to settle as many points as possible, it was sometimes necessary to abandon one or more of these principles. See Yehuda Ariel, "Tirat Zvi's Night of Courage" [in Hebrew], *Ha'aretz,* 6 July 1977, Ha'hagana Archive, Tel-Aviv.

47. Yosef Avidar, "The Days of Wall and Tower: Memories and Appraisals" [in Hebrew], in *The Wall and Tower Days, 1936–1939,* ed. Mordechai Naor (Jerusalem: Yad Ben-Zvi, 1987), 145–50, 145, 147.

48. Shertok, quoted in Shalom Raichman, "The Creation of the Yishuv Map during the Mandate Period" [in Hebrew], in *The History of the Jewish Yishuv in Eretz-Yisrael since the First Aliya,* ed. Moshe Lissak (Jerusalem: Mosad Bialik, 2008), 248–99, 263. "Grab and settle" was later referred to as "the settlement strategy," which emphasized territorial control of the settlements and establishment of new settlement points, and preferred security and political considerations to civil and economic ones.

49. Rotbard, "Wall and Tower," 37.

50. The British response to the first unauthorized camp when it was discovered in the morning was to demand that it be dismantled. When the settlers refused, the British presented an ultimatum, stating that the camp would be attacked by British forces, who were already aiming their weapons at the camp. The incident was solved diplomatically, and the wall and tower method continued to be used. See Avidar, "The Days of Wall and Tower," 146–47.

51. See Roy Kozlovsky, "Temporal States of Architecture: Mass Immigration and Provisional Housing in Israel," in *Architecture and Politics in the Twentieth Century: Modernism and the Middle East,* ed. Sandy Isenstadt and Kishwar Rizvi (Washington: University of Washington Press, 2008), 140–60, 156–57.

52. Elhanan Oren, "The Security–Settlement Offensive in the Years 1936–1939" [in Hebrew], in Naor, *The Wall and Tower Days,* 13–34, 33.

53. Gur, quoted in Ariela Azoulay, *How Does It Look to You?* [in Hebrew] (Tel Aviv: Babel, 2000), 35. For other transnational comparisons between the American and Zionist frontier actions, see Ilan Troen, "Frontier Myths and Their Applications in America and Israel: A Transnational Perspective," *Journal of American History* 86, no. 3 (1999): 1209–30.

54. Harney and Moten, *The Undercommons*, 17.

55. Gilroy, *Between Camps*, 71.

56. Luis Maria Calvo, Adriana Collado, and Luis Alberto Müller, "Colonial Settlements in the Río de la Plata: Between Transference and Development of Spanish Urban Models," in *Repenser les limites: L'architecture à travers l'espace, le temps et les disciplines*, ed. Alice Thomine-Berrada and Barry Bergdol (Paris: INHA, 2005), http://inha.revues.org/pdf/359.

57. Shane Burke, Peter Di Marco, and Simon Meath, "'The Land Flow[ing] . . . with Milk and Honey': Cultural Landscape Changes at Peel Town, Western Australia, 1829–1830," *Australasian Historical Archaeology* 28 (2010): 5–12.

58. Between 1920 and 1936, more than 280,000 registered Jewish immigrants legally entered the country. Krämer, *A History of Palestine*, 241. *Ha'apala* is a term describing the illegal Jewish migration to late Mandatory Palestine.

59. In 1939 close to 40 percent of Jewish immigrants arrived in Palestine illegally. Krämer, *A History of Palestine*, 300. The British also opened detention camps for Palestinian Arabs during the Arab uprising. Between 1936 and 1938, nine thousand Arabs were detained in prisons and camps. See Norris, "Repression and Rebellion," 40.

60. Yehoshua Kaspi, "Prisons in Eretz Yisrael during the British Mandate Period" [in Hebrew], *Cathedra* 32 (1984): 141–74, 152.

61. Tal Freidman, the conservation architect of the Atlit camp, interview, 6 January 2013.

62. See Forth, *Barbed-Wire Imperialism*.

63. Personal testimonies of detainees in Mordechai Naor, *Atlit: "Illegal Immigrant" Detention Camp; A Story of Time and Place* (Mikveh Israel: Yehuda Dekel Library, 2010).

64. The *Exodus*, the most famous ship used by the Mossad, brought 4,554 Holocaust survivors to Palestine. The ship was intercepted and its passengers were deported back to the displaced persons camps in Europe. This case symbolizes the difficulty faced by the British authorities in fighting illegal migration, on the one hand, and, on the other hand, dealing with global public opinion, which showed sympathy for Holocaust survivors' struggle to reach Palestine.

65. The establishment of the camps in Cyprus was part of an intensification of the British struggle against the Jewish immigrants. This was following the Palestinian question, which, at that time, was referred to the United Nations, and the bombing in Jerusalem of the King David Hotel, headquarters of the British general staff, on 22 July 1946 by the militant right-wing Zionist underground organization, in which ninety-one people were killed and dozens more injured.

66. Israel Karmi, *In the Routes of Immigration and Absorption, 1938–1950* [in Hebrew] (Tel Aviv: Karmi, 1992), 81.

67. Dalia Ofer, "Holocaust Survivors as Immigrants: The Case of Israel and the Cyprus Detainees," *Modern Judaism* 16 (1996): 1–23.

68. An education system was established that included nursery classes and schools for the thousands of children in the camps. During the two and a half years the camps operated, more than two thousand babies were born. Naor, *Atlit*, 32. Among the eight thousand young people aged twelve to sixteen were six thousand who had lost both parents. Ofer, "Holocaust Survivors as Immigrants."

69. This is in contrast to the massive Tegart forts—dozens of fortified police stations

306   Notes to Chapter 2

built around the country (1940–43) following the Arab uprising. See Richard Cahill, "The Tegart Police Fortresses in British Mandate Palestine: A Reconsideration of Their Strategic Location and Purpose," *Jerusalem Quarterly* 75 (2018): 48.

70. See Brian Carter, "The Quonset Hut: War, Design and Weapons of Mass Construction," in Chiei and Decker, *Quonset Hut*, 47.

71. Paul Virilio, *Speed and Politics* (Cambridge: MIT Press, 2006), 90.

3. Gathering, Absorbing, and Reordering the Diaspora

1. See Alex Bein, *Immigration and Settlement in Israel* [in Hebrew] (Tel Aviv: Am Oved, 1982); Miriam Katchensky, "The Ma'abarot" [in Hebrew], in *Olim and Ma'abarot: 1948–1952; Sources, Summaries, Selected Affairs and Supporting Materials*, ed. Mordechai Naor (Jerusalem: Yad Yitzhak Ben-Zvi, 1986), 69–86.

2. These and other related camp spaces of Palestinian refugees and IDPs are discussed more broadly in chapters 5 and 6.

3. Kozlovsky, "Temporal States of Architecture," 154.

4. Batya Shimony, *On the Threshold of Redemption: The Story of the Ma'abara; First and Second Generation* [in Hebrew] (Tel Aviv: Kinneret Zmora-Bitan, Dvir, 2008), 10.

5. See, for example, Erez Tzfadia and Haim Yacobi, *Rethinking Israeli Space: Periphery and Identity* (London: Routledge, 2011), 17.

6. Eliezer Brutzkus, "The Dreams That Became Cities: On the Experiments to Plan Settlement and Immigrant-Absorption Regions in the Years of 1948–1952" [in Hebrew], in Naor, *Olim and Ma'abarot*, 127–40.

7. For example, see Esther Meir-Glizenstein, "Operation Magic Carpet: Constructing the Myth of the Magical Immigration of Yemenite Jews to Israel," *Israel Studies* 16, no. 3 (2011): 149–73; and Avi Picard, *Selective Immigration: The Israeli Policy towards the Immigration of the North-African Jews, 1951–1956* [in Hebrew] (Jerusalem: Bialik, 2013).

8. David Ohana, *Modernism and Zionism* (London: Palgrave Macmillan, 2012).

9. Kozlovsky, "Temporal States of Architecture," 154.

10. Theodor Herzl, *The Jewish State*, trans. Sylvie D'Avigdor (MidEastWeb, 1946 [1896]), 41, http://mideastweb.org/jewishstate.pdf.

11. Herzl, *The Jewish State*, 19.

12. Theodor Herzl, *Old New Land* (New York: Herzl Press, 1987), 205.

13. Bulent Diken and Carsten B. Laustsen, *The Culture of Exception: Sociology Facing the Camp* (London: Routledge, 2005), 17.

14. Bauman, *Modernity and Ambivalence*, 7.

15. Bauman, *Modernity and Ambivalence*, 3.

16. Brutzkus, "The Dreams That Became Cities," 129.

17. Ari Barell and David Ohana, "'The Million Plan': Zionism, Political Theology and Scientific Utopianism," *Politics, Religion and Ideology* 15, no. 1 (2014): 1–22, 7. On the earlier selective Zionism, see Alroey, "Between the Straits."

18. Dvora Hacohen, *From Fantasy to Reality: Ben-Gurion's Plan for Mass Immigration, 1942–1945* [in Hebrew] (Tel Aviv: Ministry of Defense Publishing, 1994), 13–14.

19. Ben-Gurion, quoted in Barell and Ohana, "'The Million Plan,'" 13.

20. Hacohen, *From Fantasy to Reality*, 129–36.

21. Hacohen, *From Fantasy to Reality*, 125.

22. Bein, *Immigration and Settlement in Israel,* 59.

23. This violence included what has become known as "the Yemenite children affair," in which around one thousand babies and infants were abducted from mostly Yemenite families in the immigrant camps. The children were taken from their parents, sometimes forcibly, and taken to infants' homes in the camps for "hygiene reasons" or to hospitals for treatment, and soon after, the parents were told that the children had died. The bodies were never returned to the families, and "dead" children were found by their parents after they were put up for adoption. The story has been denied for years by Israeli authorities; a recent historic decision is admitting the role of the Israeli Health Ministry in the children's disappearance. See Tamar Kaplnsky, "Israeli Health Ministry Report Admits Role in Disappearance of Yemenite Children in 1950s," *Ha'aretz,* 8 December 2021, https://www.haaretz.com/israel-news/.premium.HIGHLIGHT.MAGAZINE -health-ministry-report-admits-israel-s-part-in-disappearance-of-yemenite-children -1.10450266.

24. Tom Segev, *1949: The First Israelis* [in Hebrew] (Jerusalem: Domino Press, 1984), 125–28.

25. Segev, *1949,* 139.

26. Segev, *1949,* 130.

27. Segev, *1949,* 143.

28. Ben-Gurion, quoted in Segev, *1949,* 144.

29. Ben-Gurion, quoted in Hacohen, *From Fantasy to Reality,* 235.

30. Both quoted in Segev, *1949,* 112–16.

31. Ofer, "Holocaust Survivors as Immigrants," 1.

32. Moshe Sicron, "The Mass Immigration: Its Numbers, Characteristics and Affect on the Population Structure in Israel" [in Hebrew], in Naor, *Olim and Ma'abarot,* 31–52.

33. Meir-Glizenstein, "Operation Magic Carpet," 150–53.

34. Segev, *1949,* 166.

35. Moshe Lissak, "The Mass Immigration in the Fifties: The Failure of the Melting Pot Policy," in Lissak, *The History of the Jewish Yishuv in Eretz-Yisrael,* 16–17.

36. Segev, *1949,* 153.

37. Eshkol, quoted in Dvora Hacohen, *Immigrants in Turmoil* [in Hebrew] (Jerusalem: Yad Yitzhak Ben-Zvi, 1994), 205.

38. Different sources give different numbers for how many ma'abara camps there were, but there seem to have been between 129 and 200, some of which were immigrant camps that had been transformed to be open ma'abara camps.

39. Segev, *1949,* 142.

40. Jeffrey, *The Improvised State.*

41. Geremy Forman and Alexander (Sandy) Kedar, "From Arab Land to 'Israel Lands': The Legal Dispossession of the Palestinians Displaced by Israel in the Wake of 1948," *Environment and Planning D: Society and Space* 22, no. 6 (2004): 809–30.

42. Kozlovsky, "Temporal States of Architecture," 146.

43. The word *he'ahzut* is similar to *ma'ahaz,* meaning a civilian settler outpost camp created later in the West Bank.

44. David Ben-Gurion, *Recollections* (London: Macdonald, 1970), 103; Michael Feige, *Settling in the Hearts: Jewish Fundamentalism in the Occupied Territories* (Detroit: Wayne State University Press, 2009), 198; Gorenberg, *The Accidental Empire,* 67.

45. As Uri Davis reflects, many of the kibbutzim "created after 1948 were, in fact,

initially established as Nahal outposts." See Uri Davis, "Palestine into Israel," *Journal of Palestine Studies* 3, no. 1 (1973): 88–105, 91.

46. After the 1967 war such camps were also extensively created in the occupied territories (the Sinai Peninsula, the Golan Heights, the Gaza Strip, and the West Bank); see chapter 6.

47. Arieh Sharon, *Physical Planning in Israel* [in Hebrew and English] (Jerusalem: Government Press, 1952).

48. Sharon, *Physical Planning in Israel*, 4.

49. Sharon, *Physical Planning in Israel*, 4.

50. Sharon, *Physical Planning in Israel*, 4.

51. Eighteen New Towns were built between 1948 and 1951, and ten more by 1957. The British project consisted of "only" eleven New Towns between 1946 and 1955. Zvi Efrat, *The Israeli Project: Building and Architecture, 1948–1973* [in Hebrew] (Tel Aviv: Tel Aviv Museum of Art, 2004), 998–99.

52. Arieh Sharon, *Kibbutz + Bauhaus: An Architect's Way in a New Land* (Stuttgart: Karl Kramer Verlag; Givatayim: Massada, 1976), 79.

53. Scott, *Seeing Like a State*, 256.

54. Sharon, *Physical Planning in Israel*, 3.

55. Efrat, *The Israeli Project*, 996.

56. Sharon, *Physical Planning in Israel*, 3.

57. Haim Darin-Drabkin, *Housing and Absorption in Israel* [in Hebrew] (Tel-Aviv: Gadish, 1955); Kozlovsky, "Temporal States of Architecture," 144.

58. Kozlovsky, "Temporal States of Architecture."

59. Susan G. Solomon, *Louis I. Kahn's Trenton Jewish Community Center* (Princeton: Princeton Architectural Press, 2000), 17.

60. Naomi Klein, *The Shock Doctrine: The Rise of Disaster Capitalism* (London: Allen Lane, 2007).

61. Eshkol, quoted in Segev, *1949*, 143.

62. Wendy Pullan, "Interventions in the Political Geographies of Walls," *Political Geography* 33 (2013): 55–58.

63. Yehouda Shenhav and Yael Berda, "The Colonial Foundations of the Racialized Theological Bureaucracy: Juxtaposing the Israeli Occupation of Palestinian Territories with Colonial History," in *The Power of Inclusive Exclusion: Anatomy of Israeli Rule in the Occupied Palestinian Territories*, ed. Adi Ophir, Michal Givoni, and Sārī Hanafī (New York: Zone Books, 2009), 337–74.

64. Yonathan Paz, "Ordered Disorder: African Asylum Seekers in Israel and Discursive Challenges to an Emerging Refugee Regime," *New Issues in Refugee Research*, Research Paper no. 205 (2011), UNHCR Policy Development and Evaluation Service, http://www.unhcr.org/4d7a26ba9.html.

65. Smadar Sharon, "Not Settlers but Settled: Immigration, Planning and Settlement Patterns in the Lakhish Region in the 1950s" [in Hebrew] (PhD diss., Tel-Aviv University, 2012), 50.

66. Efrat, *The Israeli Project*, 995.

67. Bauman, *Modernity and Ambivalence*, 7.

4. Forced Pioneering

1. Beginning in the summer of 1950, most newly arrived immigrants were sent straight from the ship to the ma'abara camps. This government practice, which enabled

the population-dispersal policy to be imposed on the newly arrived migrants, is discussed in chapter 3.

2. See Pnina Motzafi-Haller, *In the Cement Boxes: Mizrahi Women in the Israeli Periphery* [in Hebrew] (Jerusalem: Hebrew University, Magnes Press, 2012), 15.

3. These pioneers of the kibbutz and moshav collective settlements and their settler tent camps are discussed in chapter 2.

4. The Negev is located between Egypt (which, at that time, controlled Sinai and the Gaza Strip) and Jordan. The entire region was historically inhabited by Bedouin tribes, who used to pass freely between these areas and maintained active commercial connections before firm national borders were established between what became enemy states. After Israel was established, the movement of the Bedouin was perceived as a security threat. See further discussion in chapter 5.

5. Zair, a member of Gan Shmuel kibbutz, met Yoseftal coincidentally and asked him whether he could help with the absorption of immigrants. Yoseftal mentioned Tel-Yeruham as a potential project, and Zair volunteered to pursue it. See Amnon Zair, *Vienna-Gan Shmuel* [in Hebrew] (Jerusalem: Gan Shmuel, 1980), 113. Gan Shmuel kibbutz, a kibbutz founded as a tent camp of Zionist settlers, is also the kibbutz of Arieh Sharon, the architect of Israel's National Plan.

6. The criminalizing term "infiltrators" was used to refer to every Arab person who entered Israel without permission after November 1947. See Alina Korn, "Military Government, Political Control and Crime: The Case of Israeli Arabs," *Crime, Law and Social Change* 34 no. 2 (2000): 159–82.

7. The difference between the government's Planning Department and the Jewish Agency, which was not a governmental organization but external to state institutions, is discussed in chapter 3.

8. Sharon, "Not Settlers but Settled," 56–58.

9. Letter from Lieutenant Colonel Harsina, head of the IDF Operation Department Settlement Branch, to Lieutenant Colonel Yuval Ne'eman, head of the IDF Planning Department, quoted in Sharon, "Not Settlers but Settled," 35.

10. Osnat Shiran, *Points of Force: The Policy of Settlements in Relation to Political and Security Destinations before the State and in Its First Years* [in Hebrew] (Tel Aviv: Ministry of Defense Press, 1992), 97.

11. See Il Seo and Y. Alex, "From Disorderly Dispersion to Orderly Concentration: Frontier Villages at the Korean Border, 1951–1973," *Scroope* 27 (2018): 43–58, 49.

12. John P. Augelli, "Nationalization of Dominican Borderlands," *Geographical Review* 70, no. 1 (1980): 19–35.

13. Hanina Porat, "The Plan for the Negev Settlement and Development, 1948–1951" [in Hebrew], *Cathedra* 78 (1995): 122–45.

14. Ben-Gurion at a Mapai center meeting, 8 January 1948, quoted in Porat, "The Plan for the Negev Settlement and Development," 129. Agricultural settlements like those that had been used by Zionist settlers in the prestate period to occupy the frontier were seriously considered. Establishing agricultural settlements in the Negev was feasible owing to 190 kilometers of water pipes, bought after World War II from London's fire brigade, which had used them during the blitz. It was only later that the government realized that agriculture in the area could not be considered because of the soil salinity. See Mordechai Naor, *The Settlement of the Negev: 1900–1960* [in Hebrew] (Jerusalem: Yad Yitzhak Ben-Zvi, 1985).

15. Ben-Gurion in a government meeting, 3 May 1949, quoted in Hebrew in Smadar

310   Notes to Chapter 4

Sharon, "The Planners, the State, and the Planning of the National Space in the Beginning of the '50s" [in Hebrew], *Theory and Criticism* 29 (2006): 31–57, 49.

16. Porat, "The Plan for the Negev Settlement and Development," 143.

17. Zair, *Vienna-Gan Shmuel*, 113. *Bir* is Arabic for "water well."

18. Chezy Laufban, *A Man Goes unto His Brethren: The Story of Immigrant Absorption in Israel* [in Hebrew] (Tel Aviv: Am Oved, 1967), 229.

19. "The Ma'abara in the Arava" [in Hebrew], written 10 January 1951 (author unknown), published in *Davar Hashavua*, 20 February 1951. It is important to note that *Davar* was a left-wing newspaper for the general public, showing the wide consensus under which such frontier settlements were constructed at the time. The wall and tower settlements, created as fortified camps during the years of the Arab Revolt (1936–39) during the British Mandate period, are discussed in chapter 2.

20. S. L., interviewed by the author, Ashdod, Israel, 16 August 2012. All interviews in this book were conducted in Hebrew and translated into English by the author.

21. Unknown author, *Ma'ariv* [in Hebrew], 18 January 1951, Yeruham Archive.

22. Zair, *Vienna-Gan Shmuel*, 114, 115.

23. See Kozlovsky, "Temporal States of Architecture," 151.

24. Yoseftal, quoted in Hacohen, *Immigrants in Turmoil*, 218.

25. Letter to the J. A. from Regional Doctor Y. Perl, Tveria, 29 May 1953, file 149/20, 57.0/2–651, 18/6/68, Israeli State Archives.

26. Committee for the Coordination of Social Services in the Ma'abarot, Ministry of Labor, July 1954, quoted in Kozlovsky, "Temporal States of Architecture," 151.

27. S. L., interview, Ashdod, 16 August 2012.

28. Darin-Drabkin, *Housing and Absorption in Israel*, 36.

29. Michael Biton, Yeruham's mayor, interview, 11 April 2013.

30. A. B., interview, Yeruham, 7 April 2013.

31. The possibility that Tel-Yeruham's wooden huts might be relocated in the future was indeed raised by the Jewish Agency. See Jewish Agency meeting protocol, 25 February 1953, Yeruham Archive.

32. Ronit Matalon, *The Sound of Our Steps* (New York: Metropolitan Books), 34.

33. Scott, *Seeing Like a State*, 127.

34. Darin-Drabkin, *Housing and Absorption in Israel*, 36.

35. S. L., Yeruham's head of planning, interview, Yeruham, 10 August 2012. S. L. came to Yeruham's second ma'abara with his family in the early 1960s.

36. Agamben, *Homo Sacer*, 188.

37. Dov Rozen, *Ma'abarot and Immigrant Settlements from the Ministry of Interior Point of View* [in Hebrew] (Jerusalem: Ministry of Interior, 1985), 217.

38. See Ofer Aderet, "Petition Demands Release of Classified Israeli Documents on 1950s Immigrant Transit Camps," *Ha'aretz*, 1 January 2019, https://www.haaretz.com/israel-news/.premium-civil-rights-group-petitions-israel-high-court-shin-bet-must-reveal-documents-1.6804312.

39. Zair, *Vienna-Gan Shmuel*, 115–17.

40. See Esther Shelly-Newman, "The Night Journey: Meetings between New Immigrants to Their New Place" [in Hebrew], in *Between Immigrants and Veterans: Israel during Mass Immigration 1948–1953*, ed. Dalia Ofer (Jerusalem: Yad Yitzhak Ben-Zvi, 1996), 285–98. Arieh (Loba) Eliav, one of Eshkol's assistants, remembers that immigrants who were brought to remote settlements often refused to get off the trucks, and in order to force them off, the truck's platform would be tilted so they slid off against their will. See Loba Eliav, "Redeemed or Deceived: Israel's Mizrahi Jews" [video in Ger-

man; Hebrew subtitles], interview, YouTube video, https://www.youtube.com/watch?v =iemUWpXtqOs.

41. A. B., interview, Yeruham, 22 August 2012.

42. Laufban, *A Man Goes unto His Brethren*, 97–98.

43. Hacohen, *Immigrants in Turmoil*, 194.

44. Daniel Plezenshtine and Ariyeh Shahar, "The Geography of the Ma'abarot," in Naor, *Olim and Ma'abarot*, 94.

45. Committee for the Coordination of Social Services in the Ma'abarot, July 1954, in Kozlovsky, "Temporal States of Architecture," 153.

46. Deborah Bernstein, "Immigrant Transit Camps: The Formation of Dependent Relations in Israeli Society," *Ethnic and Racial Studies* 4, no. 1 (1981): 26–43; Katchensky, "The Ma'abarot," 82–83.

47. Bernstein, "Immigrant Transit Camps," 33.

48. Unknown author, *Davar*, 18 January 1951, Yeruham Archive. However, this initial planning was interrupted by the mine companies themselves, which created their own labor camps adjacent to the mines, severely reducing this source of employment. See a letter on the subject of Tel-Yeruham by Tamir (a Labor Office representative) and Zigel (a JA Absorption Department representative) to Labor Minister Golda Myerson (Meir), 2 March 1953, file 6171/16 C, Israeli State Archives.

49. Giora Yoseftal, *Giora Yoseftal—His Life and Works* [in Hebrew] (Tel Aviv: Mapai, 1963), 92, quoted in translation in Deborah Bernstein and Shlomo Swirski, "The Rapid Economic Development of Israel and the Emergence of the Ethnic Division of Labour," *British Journal of Sociology* 33 (1982): 64–85, 82.

50. Darin-Drabkin, *Housing and Absorption in Israel*, 78, quoted in translation in Kozlovsky, "Temporal States of Architecture," 153.

51. Herzl, *The Jewish State*, 19.

52. Victor Na'im, interviewed by Lea Shakdiel, 2 November 1988, Yad Ben Zvi, Yeruham Archive.

53. These low-wage workers created great value for others. For example, the draining of Lake Hula by low-paid ma'abara dwellers created forty thousand dunams of agriculture land, which was mostly handed to kibbutzim. See Bernstein, "Immigrant Transit Camps," 32–34.

54. Yiftachel, *Ethnocracy*, 109–110.

55. During the Yishuv period, public organizations like the Histadrut (the organization of Jewish trade unions in Eretz Yisrael) were managed by their own high officials outside the organization's own formal regulations, leaving principal decision-making outside formal democratic frameworks, without the members' participation and with no public supervision.

56. See Bernstein, "Immigrant Transit Camps," 35–38. In addition, over the years after Yeruham became a town it suffered from long periods of contested leadership and was controlled by leaders appointed from outside by the state.

57. Bernstein, "Immigrant Transit Camps," 29.

58. Jewish Agency Absorption Department, 11 January 1953, in Segev, *1949*, 171; Yehuda Berginsky, at a meeting between the Jewish Agency and the government, 10 December 1956, quoted in Shalom Shitrit, *The Mizrahi Struggle in Israel, 1948–2003* [in Hebrew] (Tel Aviv: Am Oved, 2004), 73–74.

59. Guy Ben-Porat, "The Ingathering: Reasons of State, Logic of Capital and the Assimilation of Immigrants in Israel, 1948–60," *Immigrants and Minorities* 22, no. 1 (2003): 63–85. In the prestate period, approximately 90 percent of immigrants came from Europe

and 10 percent from Asia and Africa. J. D. Matras, "Some Data on Intergenerational Occupational Mobility in Israel," in *Integration and Development in Israel*, ed. S. N. Eisenstadt, R. Bar Yosef, and H. Adler (New York: Praeger).

60. See Louis Althusser, "Ideology and Ideological State Apparatuses (Notes towards an Investigation)," in *The Anthropology of the State: A Reader*, ed. Aradhana Sharma and Akhil Gupta (Oxford: Blackwell, 2006 [1970]), 86–88.

61. Bernstein and Swirski, "The Rapid Economic Development of Israel," 68.

62. Ben-Gurion, quoted in Bernstein and Swirski, "The Rapid Economic Development of Israel," 81–82.

63. Arie Gelblum, *Ha'aretz*, 22 April 1949, quoted in Ben-Porat, "The Ingathering," 70.

64. Zair, *Vienna-Gan Shmuel*, 115–17.

65. Quoted in translation in Bernstein, "Immigrant Transit Camps," 38.

66. Henriette Dahan Kalev, "You're So Pretty—You Don't Look Moroccan," *Israel Studies* 6, no. 1 (2001): 1–14, 1.

67. Shay Hazkani, *Dear Palestine: A Social History of the 1948 War)* (Stanford: Stanford University Press, 2021), 134–35, 194.

68. Government report recommending the removal of young people from the ma'abara, away from the influence of their parents. Report in the Central Zionist Archives, quoted in Ben-Porat, "The Ingathering," 72–73.

69. Ben-Gurion, quoted in Sammy Smooha, *Israel: Pluralism and Conflict* (London: Routledge and Kegan Paul, 1978), 88. In *The Arab Jews*, Yehuda Shenhav questions the dichotomy between Arabs and Jews promoted in Zionist discourse. See Shenhav, *The Arab Jews: A Postcolonial Reading of Nationalism, Religion and Ethnicity* (Stanford: Stanford University Press, 2006).

70. Sharon, "Not Settlers but Settled," 39–40.

71. Samuel Z. Klausner, "Immigrant Absorption and Social Tension in Israel: A Case Study of Iraqi Jewish Immigrants," *Middle East Journal* 9, no. 3 (1955): 281–94, 294.

72. S. L., Yeruham's head of planning, interview, Yeruham, 10 August 2012.

73. D. V., interview, Yeruham, 9 January 2013. D. V. came to Yeruham with his parents in 1962 at the age of twenty from Casablanca. A *mellah*—from the Arabic and Hebrew word for salt—was a Jewish quarter in a Moroccan city, not as isolated as a European ghetto. From the fifteenth century the Jewish population lived in fortified *mellahs*, which for their protection were originally located next to the royal palace or the ruler's residence. They were seen as privileged places but later deteriorated, becoming crowded and poor. The Jews used the whole Islamic city while living mostly in the *mellah*, which was used by Muslims for economic and cultural purposes. See E. Gottreich, "Rethinking the 'Islamic City' from the Perspective of Jewish Space," *Jewish Social Studies*, 11, no. 1: 118–46.

74. Shimon Balas, *HaMa'abara* [in Hebrew] (Tel Aviv: Am Oved, 1964), 51. See also Kozlovsky, "Temporal States of Architecture."

75. Balas, *HaMa'abara*, 146.

76. Shay Fogelman, "Exposed: In Emek Hefer Ma'abara, in 1952, the First Mizrahi Rebellion in Israel Erupted, Which Was Buried in the Pages of History" [in Hebrew], *Ha'aretz*, 22 January 2010, http://www.haaretz.co.il/misc/1.1185791.

77. Laufban, *A Man Goes unto His Brethren*, 259.

78. Immigrants had to linger in ma'abarot because only around 30,000 immigrants a year received permanent housing, and immigrants were still arriving in the country.

At the end of 1963, 15,300 immigrants still lived in ma'abarot, more than ten years after they were erected. See Hacohen, *Immigrants in Turmoil*, 301.

79. Hacohen, *Immigrants in Turmoil*, 210, 216.

80. Senior Jewish Agency worker, quoted in Plezenshtine and Shahar, "The Geography of the Ma'abarot," 93.

81. Letter from Arieh Sharon, head of the Planning Department in the prime minister's office (Tel Aviv) to the Local Authorities Department, Home Office (Jerusalem), 8 May 1951, quoted in Rozen, *Ma'abarot and Immigrant Settlements from the Ministry of Interior Point of View*, 209. On Sharon, head of the Planning Department during these years, see chapter 3.

82. Schmitt, *The Nomos of the Earth*, 33.

83. Zair, quoted in Altschuler, Berster, and Enav, "Fifty Years of Periphery," a seminar work for the Academic College Tel Aviv-Yafo, 1998, 21, Yeruham Archive.

84. Letter from Michael Aberman, Yeruham, to the Ministry of Labor, 18 May 1952 (Israeli State Archive, file 242/18595); emphasis in the original.

85. Shlomo Tamir, *Mission Chapters* [in Hebrew] (Tel Aviv: Culture and Education Projects Publishing House, 1967), 142.

86. Letter from Shlomo Tamir, manager of Tel-Yeruham on behalf of the Jewish Agency, to Prime Minister David Ben-Gurion, 2 October 1952, Yeruham Archive.

87. Letter from Ben-Gurion to Shlomo Tamir, 29 October 1952, quoted in Tamir, *Mission Chapters*, 138.

88. Letter from Giora Yoseftal of the Jewish Agency to Mr. Eilam at the Ministry of Labor, 27 November 1952, file 2421/52797, Israeli State Archive.

89. Letter from Shlomo Tamir to Ben-Zion Dinur, minister of Culture and Education, 17 January 1953, file 2077/3-1222, Israeli State Archive.

90. Protocol from a meeting held at the Jewish Agency regarding Tel-Yeruham ma'abara camp, 25 February 1953, Yeruham Archive.

91. Letter from Eshkol to Minister of Labor Golda Myerson (later Meir), 30 August 1953, file 2421-348, Israeli State Archive.

92. See, for example, a letter from David Tene to the minister of labor stating that "the Prime Minister has decided to start construction works in Yeruham-Village" (21 September 1953, file 2421-36387, Israeli State Archive); and a letter from Levi Eshkol to Golda Myerson in which he wonders "who will solve the mystery of the existence and essence of the place" (15 October 1953, Yeruham Archive).

93. Letter from Ben-Gurion to Dov Yosef, minister of industry and commerce, 17 July 1953, quoted in Tamir, *Mission Chapters*, 140.

94. Eliezer Brutzkus, "The Planning of the Negev and the Establishment of the Development Towns" [in Hebrew], in Naor, *The Settlement of the Negev*, 159. Other planned urban centers in the Negev that started as ma'abara camps were Faluga (Kiryat-Gat), Kurnub (Dimona), Mitzpe-Ramon, Imara (Ofakim), and Muhraka (Netivot). Like Yeruham, S'derot development town was also not included in the National Plan and was created on the site of the Gevim-Dorot ma'abara as a result of pressure from residents and the Jewish Agency. By contrast, towns such as Besor and Tzihor were planned but never built.

95. Brutzkus, "The Planning of the Negev," 164.

96. As Brutzkus stated, other camps as well as Yeruham were developed into permanent settlements outside the National Plan, such as Shlomi in the north. As a result of

their long years of continuous temporary status, these towns suffered greatly from weak material and human foundations. See Plezenshtine and Shahar, "The Geography of the Ma'abarot", 96.

97. Bitan, quoted in Motzafi-Haller, *In the Cement Boxes*, 17.

98. Rachel Kallus and Hubert Law-Yone, "National Home / Personal Home: Public Housing and the Shaping of National Space in Israel," *European Planning Studies* 10, no. 6 (2002): 765–79.

99. Alona Nitzan-Shiftan, "Contested Zionism: Alternative Modernism; Erich Mendelson and the Tel-Aviv Chug in Mandate Palestine," *Architectural History* 39 (1996): 147–80.

100. Sharon, *Physical Planning in Israel*, xxviii, xxiv.

101. Scott, *Seeing Like a State*, 346.

102. Efrat, *The Israeli Project*, 172.

103. Kallus and Law-Yone, "National Home / Personal Home," 774; emphasis added.

104. David Kishik, "Paragraphs on Modern Cities," in *Giorgio Agamben: Legal, Political and Philosophical Perspectives*, ed. Tom Frost (Abingdon: Routledge, 2013), 162–73, 163.

105. Haim Alalluf, interview, Yeruham, 10 April 2013.

106. Various interviews with Yeruham's residents conducted in 2013.

107. Saadia Mandel, Yeruham's town architect between 1976 and 1982, interview, Hertzelia, 25 December 2013.

108. Homi K. Bhabha, "Culture's In-Between," in *Questions of Cultural Identity*, ed. Stuart Hall and Paul Du Gay (Newcastle: Sage, 1996), 58.

109. Zair, *Vienna-Gan Shmuel*, 123.

110. Giora Yoseftal, conference for ma'abara managers, August 1954, Petah Tikva, file 2347/15-C, Israeli State Archives.

111. Scott, *Seeing Like a State*, 4–5.

112. Quoted in translation in Bernstein, "Immigrant Transit Camps," 39–40.

113. Aziza Khazzoom, "Did the Israeli State Engineer Segregation? On the Placement of Jewish Immigrants in Development Towns in the 1950s," *Social Forces* 84, no. 1 (2005): 115–34. Also see Yiftachel, *Ethnocracy*.

114. Motzafi-Haller, *In the Cement Boxes*, 2.

115. Sami Shalom Chetrit, "Mizrahi Politics in Israel: Between Integration and Alternative," *Journal of Palestine Studies* 29, no. 4 (2000): 51–65.

116. Dalia Gavrieli-Nuri has argued that the ma'abara camps for Mizrahi Jews were written "out of Israeli history." Gavrieli-Nuri, "Why Have Transit Camps for Mizrahi Jews Been Written Out of Israeli History?," *Ha'aretz*, April 18 2015, http://www.haaretz.com/news/features/.premium-1.652197. Nevertheless, it is important to note that there is an increased interest in the ma'abarot in recent years, reflected in two recent Israeli TV series and a planned national museum on the subject.

117. Also known as Camp Ariel Sharon, this large military training facility, built to house over ten thousand soldiers, was opened in 2015 in order to relocate IDF training facilities from former British military camps in the coastal area in order to "release" land for civic use. While the intention was also to boost the Negev's (Jewish) "development" by strengthening weaker settlements such as Yeruham, it appears that the IDF's contribution to civic growth in the area is limited. On the research of Meirav Aharon-Gutman of the subject, see Eric Mirovsky, "The Training-Base City Did Not Become a Growth Engine to the Negev Settlements" [in Hebrew], *The Marker*, May 23, 2017, https://www.themarker.com/realestate/1.4110060.

5. Unrecognized Order

1. Also known and Rachme and Rahme. Only lately, a label with the name of the settlement has been added to Google Earth.

2. See Ghazi Falah, "Planned Bedouin Settlement in Israel: The Reply," *Geoforum* 16, no. 4 (1985): 440–51.

3. See Mansour Nasasra, "The Ongoing Judaisation of the Naqab and the Struggle for Recognising the Indigenous Rights of the Arab Bedouin People," *Settler Colonial Studies* 2, no. 1 (2012): 81–107, 91; and Korn, "Military Government, Political Control and Crime," 162.

4. Ismael Abu-Saad and Cosette Creamer, "Socio-Political Upheaval and Current Conditions of the Naqab Bedouin Arabs," in *Indigenous (In)Justice: Human Rights, Law and Bedouin Arabs in the Naqab/Negev*, ed. Ahmad Amara, Ismael Abu-Saad, and Oren Yiftachel (Cambridge, Mass.: Harvard University Press, 2012), 19–67, 27. On the subject, see also Avinoam Meir, *As Nomadism Ends: The Israeli Bedouin of the Negev* (Boulder, Colo.: Westview Press, 1997); and Yiftachel, *Ethnocracy*, among others.

5. See Ronen Shamir, "Suspended in Space: Bedouins under the Law of Israel," *Law and Society Review* 3, no. 2 (1996): 231–57.

6. The two other zones are the northern military government zone in the Galilee, which included forty-five closed areas, and the military zone in the central region, which included around thirty Arab towns and villages.

7. See Mansour Nasasra, "Two Decades of Bedouin Resistance and Survival under Israeli Military Rule, 1948–1967," *Middle Eastern Studies* 56, no. 1 (2020): 64–83; and Nasasra, "The Ongoing Judaisation of the Naqab," 99–100.

8. Nasasra, "Two Decades of Bedouin Resistance," 70–71.

9. Ghazi Falah, "The Development of the Planned Bedouin Settlement," *Geoforum* 14, no. 3 (1983): 311–23. In a 2003 study by the Israeli Central Bureau of Statistics, the seven planned townships were at the bottom of the list of the poorest settlements in Israel.

10. See, for example, Mansour Nasasra, Sophie Richter-Devroe, Sarab Abu-Rabia-Queder, and Richard Ratcliffe, eds., *The Naqab Bedouin and Colonialism: New Perspectives* (London: Routledge, 2014). The use of indigeneity to describe the Bedouin has been adopted by scholars who oppose treating the Bedouin as an ethnic group that differs from the rest of the Palestinians in Israel, arguing that this serves the vision and policies of the state in colonizing the Negev and co-opting the Bedouin. See Nasasra, "The Ongoing Judaisation of the Naqab," 88. The concept of "indigenous people" is adopted as a form of Bedouin community's resistance and identity, while rejecting the exotic nature of the scholarly discourse around the Bedouin that reinforces the Palestinian society's ethnic fragmentation (Muslim, Christian, Bedouin, and Druze). However, some Bedouin leaders have expressed unease with the indigeneity approach, and others who stressed the Arab–Palestinian national identity have voiced reservations about the term "indigenous" and are reluctant to identify with it, pointing to the characteristics of primitiveness and vulnerability associated with the term. See Nasasra, "The Ongoing Judaisation of the Naqab"; and Amara, Abu-Saad, and Yiftachel, *Indigenous (In)Justice*, 325. In this book, I see the Bedouin as part of the Palestinian society in Israel, including the practices and policies of campization and abandonment directed by Israel to Palestinian IDPs in other areas.

11. See Hillel Cohen, "The Internal Refugees in the State of Israel: Israeli Citizens,

Palestinian Refugees," *Israel–Palestine Journal* 9, no. 2 (2002): 43. These encampments were often erected on the outskirts of existing Palestinian villages or adjacent to the confiscated villages; for example, Ein Hawd, established by Palestinians who were displaced from their original village, which became the Jewish artists' settlement Ein Hod, while the Palestinian IDPs' village was fully recognized only in 1992.

12. Bert de Muynck and Malkit Shoshan, *One Land Two Systems* 1, nos. 4–8 (2005), Foundation for Achieving Seamless Territory (FAST), https://issuu.com/seamlessterritory/docs/onelandtwosystems.

13. See James Tully, "The Struggles of Indigenous Peoples for and of Freedom," in *Political Theory and the Rights of Indigenous Peoples*, ed. Duncan Ivison, Paul Patton, and Will Sanders (Cambridge: Cambridge University Press, 2000), 36–60.

14. See Michal Rotem, "Stop Calling the Bedouin Settlements in the Negev 'P'zura'" [in Hebrew], *Siha Mekonit*, 30 October 2014, https://www.mekomit.co.il/.

15. Shamir, "Suspended in Space," 236.

16. Ismael Abu-Saad, "Towards an Understanding of Minority Education in Israel: The Case of the Bedouin Arabs of the Negev," *Comparative Education* 27, no. 2 (1991): 235–42.

17. Ghazi Falah, "Israeli State Policy toward Bedouin Sedentarization in the Negev," *Journal of Palestine Studies* 18, no. 2 (1989): 71–91, 72.

18. Meir, *As Nomadism Ends*; and Aref Al-Aref, *The Bedouin Tribes in Be'er-Sheva District* [in Hebrew] (Tel Aviv: Bustenai, 1937).

19. Gideon M. Kressel, Joseph Ben-David, and Khalil Abu-Rabia, "Changes in the Land Usage by the Negev Bedouin since the Mid-19th Century," *Nomadic Peoples* 28 (1991): 28–55.

20. Meir, *As Nomadism Ends*, 84, states that the Bedouin were cultivating five hundred thousand dunams by the end of the British Mandate.

21. Kressel, Ben-David, and Abu-Rabia, "Changes in the Land Usage by the Negev Bedouin," 86.

22. Rodolfo Stavenhagen and Ahmad Amara, "International Law of Indigenous Peoples and the Naqab Bedouin Arabs," in Amara, Abu-Saad, and Yiftachel, *Indigenous (In)Justice*, 158–93.

23. Yiftachel, *Ethnocracy*, 12.

24. Wolfe, "Settler Colonialism and the Elimination of the Native," 387–88. See also Caroline Elkins and Susan Pedersen, *Settler Colonialism in the Twentieth Century: Projects, Practices* (New York: Routledge, 2005).

25. Gordon and Ram, "Ethnic Cleansing."

26. Harney and Moten, *The Undercommons*, 18.

27. Moshe Dayan, interview in *Ha'aretz*, 31 July 1963, quoted in Shamir, "Suspended in Space," 231.

28. See Morgensen, "The Biopolitics of Settler Colonialism"; Atkinson, "Encountering Bare Life in Italian Libya and Colonial Amnesia in Agamben"; and Mbembe, "Necropolitics."

29. Henry Reynolds and Richard Nile, eds., *Indigenous Rights in the Pacific and North America: Race and Nation in the Late Twentieth Century* (London: Sir Robert Menzies Centre for Australian Studies, 1992). See also Yiftachel, *Ethnocracy*, 27.

30. Alexandre Kedar, Ahmad Amara, and Oren Yiftachel, *Emptied Lands: A Legal Geography of Bedouin Rights in the Negev* (Stanford: Stanford University Press, 2018).

31. Kimmerling, *Zionism and Territory,* 7. The meaning of "frontier" here, according to Kimmerling, is "free land."

32. Kimmerling, *Zionism and Territory,* 146.

33. On changes in control over the land, see also chapter 3. See also Yiftachel, *Ethnocracy,* 136–43. Yiftachel presents seven major steps through which the character of the Israeli land system was shaped. These practices of land Judaization included demolition of over four hundred Palestinian villages, denying Palestinians (including Bedouin) refugees the right of return, extensive expropriation of Arab land by the state, and a complicated legal apparatus that allowed land to be transferred to Jewish rather than Israeli (and therefore also Arab) hands.

34. Cole Harris, "How Did Colonialism Dispossess?," *Annals of the Association of American Geographers* 94, no. 1 (2004): 165–82, 177; Wolfe, "Settler Colonialism and the Elimination of the Native," 396.

35. Stavenhagen and Amara, "International Law of Indigenous Peoples," 165–66.

36. Wolfe, "Settler Colonialism and the Elimination of the Native," 396.

37. See Clinton Bailey, *Bedouin Law from Sinai and the Negev: Justice without Government* (New Haven: Yale University Press, 2009).

38. Ismail Abu-Saad, "The Bedouins' Complaint: 'How Can We Be Called Intruders If We and Our Ancestors Have Been Living in the Naqab for Thousands of Years?'" [in Hebrew], *Land (Karka)* 57 (2003): 31–34; quoted in translation in Thabet Abu Ras, "Land Disputes in Israel: The Case of the Bedouin of the Naqab," *Adalah's Newsletter* 24 (April 2006): 2, https://www.adalah.org/uploads/oldfiles/newsletter/eng/apr06/ar2.pdf.

39. These state practices used to permanently uproot Bedouin will be discussed later in the chapter.

40. Shamir, "Suspended in Space," 236, 240.

41. This data is taken from two sources: one governmental and one nongovernmental: Authority for the Regularization of Bedouin Settlement in the Negev (ARBSN), *A Social Survey of the Bedouin Dispersion [P'zura] around Yeruham (Rakhma)* [in Hebrew] (Be'er Sheva: ARBSN, 2011); and a report by Bimkom (a central Israeli planning-rights NGO), "Rakhma—Guiding Principles for the Planning and the Development of the Settlement" (2010), http://bimkom.org/wp-content/uploads/Rachme_final_screen.pdf.

42. The IDF has frequently engaged in the transfer and relocation of Arab communities, mainly Bedouin, since Israel's early years, ostensibly for security, military, or settlement needs, as part of the state's efforts to gain control over its frontier territories. However, while today this practice is criticized in the media and in court, in the past such events were almost unmonitored and received little attention. See Amira Hass, "From Yamit to the Jordan Valley, the IDF Continues to Force Arabs from Their Homes," *Ha'aretz,* 16 April 2012, http://www.haaretz.com/news/features/from-yamit-to-the-jordan-valley-the-idf-continues-to-force-arabs-from-their-homes-1.424503; and Anshel Pfeffer, "Sharon Ordered Expulsion of 3,000 Bedouin, New Biography Reveals," *Ha'aretz,* 12 February 2014, http://www.haaretz.com/news/diplomacy-defense/.premium-1.573778.

43. Shlomo Swirski and Yael Hasson, *Transparent Citizens: Government Policy toward the Bedouin in the Negev* [in Hebrew] (Tel Aviv: ADVA Center, 2005), 13.

44. The military governor's authority was established under the Mandatory government's Emergency Defense Regulations, which included Article 109 (forbidding certain people to be present in specific areas), Article 111 (enforcing administrative detention), Article 124 (imposing a curfew to control disturbances), and Article 125 (closing certain

areas while restricting movement in or to these areas); Article 125 was the one most frequently used. The Bedouin were also prohibited from entering Jewish settlements in the area, enforcing their separation from the Jewish population. See Nasasra, "Two Decades of Bedouin Resistance," 66. The IDF archive, for example, contains a 1963 document that specifies "a list of [Jewish] settlements which minorities are forbidden to enter"; the list includes Yeruham. File 21-564/1965, IDF Archive.

45. See Nasasra, "The Ongoing Judaisation of the Naqab," 99–100.

46. Yiftachel, *Ethnocracy*, 197.

47. Harney and Moten, *The Undercommons*, 80.

48. For example, see the IDF's file on the Abu-Karinat tribe, file 60-677/1959, IDF Archive.

49. The Israeli authorities officially recognized nineteen sheikhs as leaders of the remnant Bedouin tribes, some of whom had not been sheikhs before but had been chosen for their history of cooperation with the authorities and kibbutz leaders and their willingness to publicly swear allegiance to Israel, forcing Bedouin tribal leaders to become agents of the Israeli government based on their loyalty to the state. See Nasasra, "Two Decades of Bedouin Resistance"; and Swirski and Hasson, *Transparent Citizens*, 14.

50. Haia Noah, *The Existent and the Non-Existent Villages: The Unrecognized Bedouin Villages in the Negev* [in Hebrew] (Haifa: Pardes, 2009), 37.

51. Besides geopolitical reasons, concentrating the Bedouin was also justified by planners' concern about the cost of servicing and planning for dispersed populations. See Yiftachel, *Ethnocracy*, 201. This consideration, however, did not stop the state promoting land-control settlement strategies that included small-scale Jewish settlements, such as "single farms" *(havot bodedim)* in the Negev.

52. Oren Yiftachel, "Critical Theory and 'Gray Space': Mobilization of the Colonized," *City* 13, nos. 2–3 (2009): 246–63.

53. Among the reasons the Bedouin lacked landownership documents are the recognition of Ottoman and British Mandate rule in internal Bedouin landownership agreements, and the fact that there was only a two-month period during the British Mandate in which Bedouin were allowed to register their land. Mansour Nasasra shows the hypocrisy of Israeli policies dealing with Bedouin landownership. Among other examples, he quotes Lord Oxford, assistant district commissioner of Be'er-Sheva in 1943 during the British Mandate, as saying, "We did not oppose Bedouin land ownership, nor did we force them to register their land." Nasasra, "The Ongoing Judaisation of the Naqab," 95–97. Also see Yuval Karplus, "The Dynamics of Bedouin Space Construction in the Negev" [in Hebrew] (PhD diss., Ben Gurion University, 2009), 92; and Swirski and Hasson, *Transparent Citizens*, 9.

54. The transfer was accomplished by relying on the fact that according to the 1858 Ottoman Land Code, there were no permanent settlements in the area. Plia Albek, who chaired the committee that made the recommendation, served in the same capacity in the 1980s, when she approved the erection of over a hundred Israeli settlements in the Palestinian occupied territories, claiming that they were being constructed on state land (see discussion in chapter 6).

55. The ILA united the three major bodies in charge of land issues in Israel: the JNF, the Development Authority, and the State of Israel. The ILA moved between different government offices, including the Agriculture Office, the Housing and Construction Office, and the National Infrastructure Office. Most of these moves were made by Ariel

Sharon, who took the ILA with him to any government department where he served. Swirski and Hasson, *Transparent Citizens*, 15.

56. Salem Ubu Mariam, quoted in Swirski and Hasson, *Transparent Citizens*, 15.

57. In 2013, only three Bedouin, out of a total of seventy-five workers, were working in the Bedouin Authority. See Yanir Yagne, "In the Authority for Bedouin Settlement in the Negev Work Only 3 Bedouin" [in Hebrew], *Ha'aretz*, 20 March 2013, http://www .haaretz.co.il/news/education/1.1970867.

58. Interview with with S., working with the ARBSN, 18 August 2014.

59. Fanon, *The Wretched*, 40; Shenhav and Berda, "The Colonial Foundations of the Racialized Theological Bureaucracy," 346.

60. Swirski and Hasson, *Transparent Citizens*, 17; Michal Tabibian-Mizrahi, *A Background Document on the Subject of Invasion to Lands and Structures* [in Hebrew] (Jerusalem: Knesset Research and Information Centre, 2004), 5.

61. When I interviewed O. N., the temporary head of the Green Patrol, he showed me the various certificates in his wallet. O. N., interview, 5 August 2014.

62. Swirski and Hasson, *Transparent Citizens*, 17; Bimkom, "Rakhma—Guiding Principles," 16; and interviews.

63. See Adalah, "Report to the UN Special Rapporteur on the Right to Adequate Housing: NGO Report; Re: Spatial Segregation in Israel," 3 June 2021, 22, https://www .ohchr.org/Documents/Issues/Housing/SubmissionsCFIhousingdiscrimin/Adalah.docx.

64. ARBSN, *A Social Survey of the Bedouin Dispersion*; Bimkom, "Rakhma—Guiding Principles," 5. Also see Bimkom—Regional Council for Unrecognized Bedouin Villages (RCUV), *Master-Plan for the Recognition of the Un-Recognised Villages in the Negev* [in Hebrew] (Be'er Sheva: Bimkom-RCUV, 2012), 66, http://bimkom.org/wp-content/uploads /bedouins_Mars2012_final_screen.pdf.

65. Interview with S., Rakhma, 10 April 2013.

66. Israel's categorization of the state's Arab citizens is well expressed in their different relationships to the Israeli army: compulsory service for Druze and voluntary service for Bedouin, many of whom serve as trackers, while Palestinian Muslims are excluded from serving.

67. This conclusion is based on my interviews and on ARBSN, *A Social Survey of the Bedouin Dispersion*, 13–15.

68. Amiram Oren, "The Infrastructure and Alignment of the IDF in the Negev: Environmental Influences" [in Hebrew], *Ecology and Environment* 1 (2012): 54–61.

69. M. Z., interview, Rakhma, 5 April 2013.

70. S. Z., interview, Rakhma, 10 April 2013.

71. ARBSN, *A Social Survey of the Bedouin Dispersion*, 6.

72. S. Z., interview, Rakhma, 10 April 2013.

73. Yiftachel, *Ethnocracy*, 206–7.

74. Eliezer Goldberg, *Commission to Propose a Policy for Arranging Bedouin Settlement in the Negev* [in Hebrew] (Jerusalem: Ministry of Construction and Housing, 2008), 27, 34.

75. Goldberg, *Commission to Propose a Policy for Arranging Bedouin Settlement*, 33

76. Goldberg, *Commission to Propose a Policy for Arranging Bedouin Settlement*, 5.

77. "Cabinet Approves Plan to Provide for the Status of Communities in, and the Economic Development of, the Bedouin Sector in the Negev," Prime Minister's Office,

Jerusalem, 11 September 2011, press release, https://www.gov.il/en/departments/news/spokenegev110911.

78. Thabet Abu Ras, "The Arab Bedouin in the Unrecognized Villages in the Naqab (Negev): Between the Hammer of Prawer and the Anvil of Goldberg," *Adalah's Newsletter* 81 (April 2011), https://www.adalah.org/uploads/oldfiles/upfiles/2011/Thabet_English_2.pdf.

79. Dana Weiler-Polak, "UN Panel Urges Israel to Shelve 'Racist' Bedouin Relocation Plan," *Ha'aretz*, 26 March 2012, http://www.haaretz.com/news/national/un-panel-urges-israel-to-shelve-racist-bedouin-relocation-plan-1.420692; Ofer Aderet and Jonathan Lis, "Israeli Government Halts Controversial Plan to Resettle 30,000 Bedouin," *Ha'aretz*, 12 December 2013, http://www.haaretz.com/news/national/1.563200.

80. Plans 652-0767921 and 624-0765792. See Adalah, "The Illegality of Israel's Plan to Transfer Palestinian Bedouin Citizens of the State into 'Refugee Displacement Camps' in the Naqab (Negev)," *Adalah*, 10 December 2019, https://www.adalah.org/en/content/view/9888. See also "Israel to Build Camps as Preparation for Displacing Arab citizens," *MEMO: Middle East Monitor*, 8 October 2019, https://www.middleeastmonitor.com/20191008-israel-to-build-camps-as-preparation-for-displacing-arab-citizens/.

81. Southern District Planning and Building Committee, Plan 652–0767921, "Temporary Residential and Public Building Solutions for the Bedouin Population in the Negev" [in Hebrew] (Be'er Sheva, 2019), 11, https://mavat.iplan.gov.il/SV4/1/6001025561.

82. Yaacov Havakook, *From Goat Hair to Stone: Transition in Bedouin Dwellings* [in Hebrew] (Tel Aviv: Ministry of Security Publishing House, 1986), 77–79. See also Yossef Ben-David, *The Bedouins in Israel: Land Conflicts and Social Issues* [in Hebrew] (Jerusalem: Institute for Israel Studies, 2004), 192; and Karplus, "The Dynamics of Bedouin Space Construction," 140, which identifies the same pattern in other Bedouin settlements.

83. During my visits to the tribe's family clusters, I was first accompanied to the shig, where the first interviews were usually held. Residents sometimes invited me to the internal space of the cluster, often mentioning that this was only because I am a female researcher. For male researchers, they said, this space would probably remain off-limits.

84. S. Z., interview, Rakhma, 10 April 2013.

85. During my first visits I was always accompanied by a tribe member, whose presence signaled that I was an invited guest. When I became lost on village roads on the way to a family cluster to which I had been invited, someone always came out of one of the clusters to find out the reason for my presence.

86. N. H., interview, Rakhma, 9 April 2013.

87. J. A., interview, Rakhma, 6 April 2013.

88. Yaara Manor-Rosner, Yodan Rofe, and Sarab Abu-Rabia-Queder, "The Unrecognized Bedouin Villages: Internal Spatial Order as the Basis for Development," in *Vernacular Heritage and Earthen Architecture*, ed. Mariana Correia, Gilberto Carlos, and Sandra Rocha (London: CRC Press; Taylor and Francis, 2014), 531–36, 532. See also Ben-David, *The Bedouins in Israel*, 192; and Karplus, "The Dynamics of Bedouin Space Construction," 140.

89. Nikolaas John Habraken, *The Structure of the Ordinary: Form and Control in the Built Environment* (Cambridge: MIT Press, 1998), 226, 227.

90. Jean-François Lyotard, *The Differend: Phrases in Dispute* (Minneapolis: University of Minnesota Press, 1988).

91. Bauman, *Modernity and Ambivalence*, 7–8; Bergson, quoted in Robert Venturi, Denise Scott Brown, and Steven Izenour, *Learning from Las Vegas*. (Cambridge: MIT Press, 1977), 52.

92. Yossef Ben-David, *Settling the Negev Bedouin: Policy and Reality, 1967–1992* [in Hebrew] (Jerusalem: Institute for Israel Studies, 1993), 69.

93. S., authority for the regularization of Bedouin settlement in the Negev, interview, 18 August 2014.

94. Yiftachel, *Ethnocracy*, 205, 195; Abu-Saad and Creamer, "Socio-Political Upheaval," 27.

95. Bimkom, "Rakhma—Guiding Principles," 4.

96. Karplus, "The Dynamics of Bedouin Space Construction," 141.

97. J. A., interview, Rakhma, 6 April 2013.

98. S. Z., interview, Rakhma, 10 April 2013.

99. A., RCUV, interview, Be'er-Sheva, 18 August 2014.

100. A Bedouin Authority building inspector describes a "cats-and-dogs" game, in which Bedouin try to bypass the current building freeze by quickly erecting new houses and disguising them with old tin sheets and mud. Y. S., interview, Be'er-Sheva, 5 April 2013.

101. M. Z., interview, Rakhma, 5 April 2013.

102. N. H., interview, Rakhma, 9 April 2013.

103. S. Z., interview, Rakhma, 10 April 2013.

104. S. Z., interview, Rakhma, 10 April 2013.

105. Ramadan, "Spatialising the Refugee Camp"; Sanyal, "Urbanising Refuge"; Sigona, "Campzenship."

106. Bruno Latour, "From Realpolitik to Dingpolitik," in *Making Things Public: Atmospheres of Democracy*, ed. Peter Weibel and Bruno Latour (Cambridge: MIT Press, 2005), 16.

107. Jacques Rancière, *Dissensus: On Politics and Aesthetics* (London: Continuum, 2010), 37.

108. The authorities' alternative proposal was for children aged three to six to attend the kindergarten in another village, thirty kilometers away—an unsatisfactory solution given the young age of the children and the unsafe journey on dirt roads. See petition no. 241/09 to Be'er-Sheva Regional Court, 5 March 2009, https://law.acri.org.il/pdf/petitions/hit241.pdf. Mirkam Ezori is a Yeruham residents' NGO, working to help Rakhma achieve government recognition and meanwhile improve its living conditions. Most members of this voluntary group were not brought to Yeruham by the state but are religious residents of Ashkenazi origin who settle in Yeruham as a form of ideological Zionist social and national activism. While this group is very active in relation to the Bedouin and Yeruham itself, and many of its members have lived in the city for about two decades, they form a specific population group in Yeruham.

109. Association for Civil Rights in Israel (ACRI), "The Court: There Is a Need to Open a Kindergarten at Rakhma by the Beginning of the Next School Year" [in Hebrew], *ACRI*, 20 May 2010, https://law.acri.org.il/he/2488.

110. Interviews with Rakhma's residents and their representatives.

111. See Oren Ziv, "This Is How the Residents of Yeruham Recruited Themselves for the Establishment of a School in the Unrecognized Village" [in Hebrew], *Siha Mekonit*, 30 June 2019, https://www.mekomit.co.il.

322 Notes to Chapter 5

112. Stavenhagen and Amara, "International Law of Indigenous Peoples," 174.

113. See Harris, "How Did Colonialism Dispossess?," 165–82; Yiftachel, *Ethnocracy*; Tzfadia and Yacobi, *Rethinking Israeli Space*.

6. Camping, Decamping, Encamping

1. Gorenberg, *The Accidental Empire*, 40.

2. See chapter 5 on the post-1948 war zones managed under military rule until 1966.

3. Eshkol played a central role in the creation of Israeli settlements as part of his role in the Jewish Agency and later in government. See chapters 3 and 4.

4. Most Israelis, writes Tom Segev, were unaware of and stunned by the miserable conditions in the camps. Some saw the camps in the late 1950s during the occupation of the Gaza Strip in the Sinai campaign, yet this was not publicly discussed. See Segev, *1967: Israel, the War, and the Year That Transformed the Middle East* (New York: Metropolitan Books, 2007), 526.

5. Amos Eilon, *Ha'aretz*, 18 June 1967, 2, quoted in Segev, *1967*, 525. See similar comments in *Ma'ariv*, 15 September 1967, 13; *Ma'ariv*, 17 September 1967, 9; *Yediot Ahronot*, 16 July 1967, 8.

6. Segev, *1967*, 525.

7. Ben-Gurion and Eshkol cited in Segev, *1967*, 525.

8. Frank Giles, "Golda Meir: 'Who can Blame Israel?,'" *Sunday Times*, 15 June 1969, 12.

9. The refugee camps in the West Bank and the Gaza Strip were targets for Israeli cross-border attacks during the 1950s and 1960s, years before their occupation. They came to be deemed places of terror with the emergence of the Palestinian resistance movement and consequently were targets for armed incursions, aerial bombardments, sieges, and massacres. See Jean-Pierre Filiu, *Gaza: A History* (Oxford: Oxford University Press, 2014).

10. On the importance of the material elements of these camps, see Katz, "Mobile Colonial Architecture."

11. Rather than receiving aid from the humanitarian agencies, the refugees were hoping to receive assistance from the Arab cities and settlements they reached. Their attempts to cross the armistice border and seek care elsewhere, however, were blocked by the Arab armies, which forced them to remain contained in camps. See Fatina Abreek-Zubiedat, "The Palestinian Refugee Camps: The Promise of 'Ruin' and 'Loss,'" *Rethinking History* 19, no. 1 (2015): 72–94, 75. The crisis of the Nakba was also accompanied by widespread hunger, which overrode the ethics and practices of mutual care in the competition over basic resources; the local Palestinians of Gaza found it difficult to share with the refugees what they did not have.

12. Aid organizations working in Palestine during the war included the International Committee of the Red Cross (ICRC) and the Quaker organization American Friends Service Committee (AFSC).

13. Julie Peteet, *Landscape of Hope and Despair: Palestinian Refugee Camps* (Philadelphia: University of Pennsylvania Press, 2005), 48.

14. UNRWA was responsible for twenty-five camps under Jordanian control (twenty-one of them in the West Bank), eight in the Gaza Strip, eleven in Syria, and fifteen in Lebanon.

15. Peteet, *Landscape of Hope and Despair,* 208. Nabatiyyeh camp in Lebanon, for example, was preplanned, and Nahr al-Bared was an "accidental" camp formed by refugees who were not able to cross from Lebanon to Syria.

16. On the British Military camp as Jewish immigrant camps, see chapter 3. Nuseirat camp in the Gaza Strip, for example, was established in a British military facility. Peteet, *Landscape of Hope and Despair,* 59. UNRWA's director's report of 1951 described the various types of habitation of the refugees in the Gaza Strip: out of nearly two hundred thousand persons, around 44 percent lived in tents, 8 percent in barracks, and 48 percent in towns and villages. See Norma Nicola Hazboun, "The Resettlement of the Palestinian Refugees of the Gaza Strip" (PhD diss., University of Leeds, Department of Politics, 1994), 36.

17. See chapter 1 on the camp as a space of ambiguous sovereignty. On the Palestinian camps, see Ramadan and Fregonese, "Hybrid Sovereignty and the State of Exception"; and Oesch, "The Refugee Camp."

18. See Kjersti Gravelsater Berg, "From Chaos to Order and Back: The Construction of UNRWA Shelters and Camps, 1950–70," in *UNRWA and Palestinian Refugees: From Relief and Works to Human Development,* ed. Sari Hanafi, Leila Hilal, and Lex Takkenberg (Abingdon: Routledge, 2014).

19. Peteet, *Landscape of Hope and Despair,* 110–11. Another form of unauthorized movement was created between the closed camps and the outside world. As the refugee agency provided only minimal employment with modest payments for the refugees, many found informal employment around the camps. They also tried to cross the cease-fire lines and sell food to the internally displaced Palestinians within Israel or to bring back crops and olives from their abandoned homes. These "infiltrations," which continued until the mid-1950s, troubled the Israeli army and politicians, who tried to fight them. They were also another form of resistance, not only to the conditions of encampment but also to the international agreements that restricted movement to significant material and human resources and connections that were still within reach. On the Bedouin as infiltrators, see chapter 4; also see Abreek-Zubiedat, "The Palestinian Refugee Camps," 79–80.

20. Because people from the same towns and villages were often displaced at the same time or found one another later in the scattered spaces of displacement, many families originating from the same village remained together in one site, and neighboring villages in Palestine also occasionally became neighbors in exile. Consequently, spaces in the camps were organized by defining areas according to groups of refugees coming from the same village or those related by families or of similar descent, and these areas were also named after the refugees' original villages. These patterns of spatial and social organization were also understood by relief agencies that communicated directly with the *mokhtars,* the heads of the Arab villages in Palestine. Yet the villages were not fully recreated in the camps, and the relations between them significantly changed: while parts of villages were scattered in different camps, others, with more significant demographic presence, imposed their new weight and power on smaller ones. See Peteet, *Landscape of Hope and Despair,* 112–13; and Abreek-Zubiedat, "The Palestinian Refugee Camps," 78.

21. Peteet, *Landscape of Hope and Despair,* 103, 109. Public spaces in the camps were created only a few years after their establishment. Between 1954 and 1956 UNRWA began providing tents for public facilities such as schools and health-care clinics and later on a water infrastructure was added.

324 Notes to Chapter 6

22. The cost of two tents was equal to the cost of a nine-square-meter concrete structure. As a result of the storms in the winter of 1951–52, during which 5,120 tents were destroyed and around 10,000 were badly damaged, fifty-six thousand refugees were left with no shelter. See Allweil, *Homeland*, 196; and Hazboun, "The Resettlement of the Palestinian Refugees," 36. Although in the Gaza Strip tents were replaced with shelters by 1953, in camps elsewhere, more permanent shelters were built from the end of 1956 to the beginning of the 1960s.

23. Emanuel Marx, "Palestinian Refugee Camps in the West Bank and the Gaza Strip," *Middle Eastern Studies* 28, no. 2 (1992): 281–94, 283.

24. See Gravelsater Berg, "From Chaos to Order and Back," 113.

25. UNRWA and the host governments had to agree to these spatial changes, which were necessary in order to accommodate the growing families in the camp, yet they almost abdicated responsibility for construction activities, no longer carrying out maintenance work on refugee dwellings. See Marx, "Palestinian Refugee Camps," 287; and Peteet, *Landscape of Hope and Despair*, 94–95, 101. UNRWA and the host countries eventually allowed the refugees to expand their homes, but refugees also did so without approval.

26. Eyal Weizman, *Hollow Land: Israel's Architecture of Occupation* (London: Verso, 2007), 228.

27. Abourahme, "Assembling and Spilling-Over." In Dheisheh camp, 80 percent of the houses have two floors or more, and cement-based concrete makes up the vast majority of the material used for the construction of houses in the camp.

28. Abourahme, "Assembling and Spilling-Over," 212.

29. Abourahme, "Assembling and Spilling-Over," 202.

30. Agamben, *Homo Sacer*, 188. See previous discussion on the subject in chapter 4.

31. See Hagar Kotef, "Ba'it (Home/Household)," *Mafte'akh: Lexical Review of Political Thought* 1 (2010): 1–22. This is also based on the Aristotelian strict division between the *polis* (urban center and political community) and the *oikos* (household).

32. Minca, "Geographies of the Camp," 78.

33. In a conversation with Zygmunt Bauman on the function of camps as laboratories of power, Agamben suggested seeing the Palestinian camps as "counter-laboratories." The fact of "the people living there . . . wanting to remain there in order to maintain the idea of a possible return," he reflected, means that a possible consequence of these actions is the idea of destroying the power of those who encamp, re-creating the camps as spaces of resistance against the powers that displaced them and prevent their return. See Zygmunt Bauman and Giorgio Agamben, "Archipelago of Exception: Sovereignties of Extraterritoriality," Centre de Cultura Contemporània de Barcelona, 10 November 2005, http://www.cccb.org/en/multimedia/videos/archipelago-of-exception/225684.

34. Weizman, *Hollow Land*, 229.

35. Peteet, *Landscape of Hope and Despair*, 134, 162, 94.

36. See Weizman, *Hollow Land*, chap. 7.

37. See Katz Feigis, "Spaces Stretch Inward."

38. Jennifer Hyndman, *Managing Displacement: Refugees and the Politics of Humanitarianism* (Minneapolis: University of Minnesota Press, 2000), xxv.

39. Gilles Deleuze and Félix Guattari, *A Thousand Plateaus: Capitalism and Schizophrenia* (Minneapolis: University of Minnesota Press, 2002 [1987]), 291; and Deleuze and Guattari, *Kafka*.

40. Harney and Moten, *The Undercommons*, 39, 74–75.

41. See also Niki Kubaczek and Sheri Avraham, "Urban Undercommons: Solidarities before and beyond the National Imaginary," in *Capitalism and the Commons: Just Commons in the Era of Multiple Crises*, ed. Andreas Exner, Sarah Kumnig, and Stephan Hochleithner (Oxon: Routledge, 2020), 103–16.

42. Pasquetti, "Negotiating Control," 709.

43. Edward W. Said, *After the Last Sky: Palestinian Lives* (New York: Columbia University Press, 1999), 38.

44. Ronit Lentin, *Thinking Palestine* (London: Zed Books, 2008).

45. Filiu, *Gaza*, 71.

46. Filiu, *Gaza*, 95–100, 127.

47. Segev, *1967*, 523–42; Filiu, *Gaza*, 134. The population of Gaza dropped from 385,000 in June 1967 to 340,500 in 1969. The suggestion that the Gaza Strip be annexed was made by Eshkol, Allon, Meir, Galili, Dayan, and others. Hazboun, "The Resettlement of the Palestinian Refugees," 122; and Filiu, *Gaza*, 134–35. Dayan's "open bridges" policy, which secured the free flow of Palestinians between the Gaza Strip, the West Bank, and Jordan, also incited departures to Jordan and special coaches were set up to implement those journeys, yet those who traveled were seldom informed that their journey was irreversible. Between twelve thousand and thirty thousand Palestinians left Gaza between 1967 and 1969.

48. Dayan, quoted in Filiu, *Gaza*, 92.

49. Sartre, quoted in Filiu, *Gaza*, 120.

50. The agitation was partly sparked by the 1968 battle of Karameh, in Jordan, between Palestine Liberation Front (PLF) and Fatah fighters and the Israeli army in the Jordan Valley; by the 1970 Black September (violent clashes between the Jordanian army and the PLO); and by the death of Abdelkader Abu al-Fahm from Jabalia (in the Gaza Strip), who died following a hunger strike in an Israeli prison.

51. Weizman, *Hollow Land*, 68, 69.

52. Jabalia was nicknamed "Vietnam Camp" for its enduring resistance. Filiu, *Gaza*, 138.

53. Many refugees were relocated to encampments in Sinai, to camps described as more like detention camps than places for refugees. During this violent restructuring of the Gaza Strip and its camps, the eyes of the world were fixed on the PLO's attempts to establish a Palestinian "state within a state" in Jordan until Black September in 1970 and its retreat to Lebanon.

54. Weizman, *Hollow Land*, 70; Filiu, *Gaza*, 140.

55. See Nasser Abourahme and Sandi Hilal, "The Production of Space, Political Subjectivication and the Folding of Polarity: The Case of Deheishe Camp, Palestine" (presented at Peripheries: Decentering Urban Theory, University of California, Berkeley, February 2009), 5–7, http://www.campusincamps.ps/wp-content/uploads/2012/12/Nasser-Abourahme-and-Sandi-Hilal_Deheishe-Paper.pdf. Also see Alessandro Petti, Sandi Hilal, and Eyal Weizman, *Architecture after Revolution* (Berlin: Sternberg Press, 2010), 46.

56. Hazboun, "The Resettlement of the Palestinian Refugees," 121–22.

57. Sharon even planned to establish a compensation fund to bring the issue to closure. Filiu, *Gaza*, 143. Sharon's plan would divide the Gaza Strip into four controllable sections with five Israeli "settlement fingers," with the southern finger built in the Rafah Salient. As part of this plan, in January 1972 Sharon uprooted from five thousand to twenty thousand Bedouin from an area of at least eighteen square miles, bulldozing

their orchards, tin shacks, and concrete housing and blocking their water wells. See Weizman, *Hollow Land*, 97–98.

58. Hazboun, "The Resettlement of the Palestinian Refugees," 121–22.

59. Quoted in Hazboun, "The Resettlement of the Palestinian Refugees," 116.

60. Filiu, *Gaza*, 199. For this Palestinian organized resistance Israel created a special prison camp, named Antzar 3, in the Negev desert, where thousands of Palestinian civilians were detained during the second intifada.

61. Stephen Graham, "Bulldozers and Bombs: The Latest Palestinian–Israeli Conflict as Asymmetric Urbicide," *Antipode* 34, no. 4 (2002): 642–49.

62. Tsadok Yeheskeli, "I Made Them a Stadium in the Middle of the Camp," *Yediot Aharonot*, May 31, 2002; translated by Gush Shalom, http://zope.gush-shalom.org/home /en/channels/archive/archives_kurdi_eng.

63. Graham, "Bulldozers and bombs," 642.

64. Nurhan Abuji, *Urbicide in Palestine: Spaces of Oppression and Resilience* (London: Routledge, 2019), 199.

65. Fatina Abreek-Zubiedat, "In the Name of Belonging: Developing Sheikh Radwan for the Refugees in Gaza City, 1967–1982," in *Making Home(s) in Displacement: Critical Reflections on a Spatial Practice*, ed. Luce Beeckmans, Alessandra Gola, Ashika Singh, and Hilde Heynen (Leuven: Leuven University Press, 2022). See also Fatina Abreek-Zubiedat and Alona Nitzan-Shiftan, "'De-Camping' through Development: The Palestinian Refugee Camps in the Gaza Strip under the Israeli Occupation," in Katz, Martin, and Minca, *Camps Revisited*.

66. Hazboun, "The Resettlement of the Palestinian Refugees," 131.

67. Filiu, *Gaza*, 152. See also Abreek-Zubiedat and Nitzan-Shiftan, "'De-Camping' through Development," 143.

68. Abreek-Zubiedat and Nitzan-Shiftan, "'De-Camping' through Development," 144.

69. Hazboun, "The Resettlement of the Palestinian Refugees," 113.

70. Abreek-Zubiedat and Nitzan-Shiftan, "'De-Camping' through Development," 148, 151.

71. Eisenberg, quoted in Abreek-Zubiedat and Nitzan-Shiftan, "'De-Camping' through Development," 151.

72. Dayan, quoted in Hazboun, "The Resettlement of the Palestinian Refugees," 242.

73. See Philipp Misselwitz and Sari Hanafi, "Testing a New Paradigm: UNRWA's Camp Improvement Programme," *Refugee Survey Quarterly* 28, nos. 2–3 (2009): 360–88, 362. See also Dorota Woroniecka-Krzyzanowska, "The Right to the Camp: Spatial Politics of Protracted Encampment in the West Bank," *Political Geography* 61 (2017): 160–69.

74. See UNRWA, "Infrastructure and Camp Improvement Implementation Plan, 2010–2011," November 2009, https://www.unrwa.org/userfiles/file/AdCom_en/2009 /ICID_HIP_2010_11.pdf; Linda Tabar, "The 'Urban Redesign' of Jenin Refugee Camp: Humanitarian Intervention and Rational Violence," *Journal of Palestine Studies* 41, no. 2 (2012): 44–61.

75. Zygmunt Bauman, "In the Lowly Nowherevilles of Liquid Modernity," *Ethnography* 3, no. 3 (2002): 343–49, 345. Quoted in Abourahme and Hilal, "The Production of Space," 15.

76. Abourahme and Hilal, "The Production of Space," 15.

77. Ahmad H. Sa'di and Lila Abu-Lughod, *Nakba: Palestine, 1948, and the Claims of*

Memory (New York: Columbia University Press, 2007), 128–29. A similar approach of rebuilding the camp according to its predestruction layout was also adopted by the residents of the destroyed Nahr al-Bared camp in Lebanon.

78. See, for example, Gideon Levy, "Jenin Camp Rebuilt to Accommodate Tanks," *Ha'aretz*, 10 June 2004.

79. Tabar, "The 'Urban Redesign' of Jenin Refugee Camp," 56. Tabar analyzes the urban planning process and its actual outcomes, which include houses that are more conveniently accessed not only by the residents but also by Israeli jeeps.

80. Tabar, "The 'Urban Redesign' of Jenin Refugee Camp," 58.

81. In Dheisheh, for example, a pedestrian bridge was built to connect the new refugee city of Doha and the "old" camp, connecting the camp and its spillover while destabilizing UNRWA's secluding camp borders and working against Israel's rules forbidding bridges over Area C roads. It also rearticulated the pathological conceptualization of the "helpless refugee" through an everyday yet subversive spatial action. See Abourahme and Hilal, "The Production of Space," 1–3.

82. See Henri Lefebvre, *Writings on Cities* (Oxford: Blackwell Publishers, 1996); and Woroniecka-Krzyzanowska, "The Right to the Camp," 167. Similarly, Peter Grbac has defined "the right to the camp" as the right of refugees to appropriate the camp's space and participate in its creation. See Grbac, "*Civitas, Polis,* and *Urbs*: Reimagining the Refugee Camp as a City," RSC working paper series 96 (2013).

83. See Alessandro Petti, "The Concrete Tent," Campus in Camps—Dheisheh refugee camp, 26 June 2015, http://www.campusincamps.ps/projects/the-concrete-tent/.

84. Segev, *1967*, 574.

85. Eshkol, quoted in Segev, *1967*, 574.

86. See Yigal Kipnis, *The Golan Heights, Political History, Settlement and Geography since 1949* (London: Routledge, 2013); and Segev, *1967*, 575–76. As Gordon and Ram show, only 7 villages remained of the 139 Arab agricultural villages and 61 individual farms registered prior to the war. Gordon and Ram, "Ethnic Cleansing", 21.

87. Yehuda Harel, a leader of the settlers on the Golan Heights, interview in the *New York Times*, 31 August 1975. See Ann Mosely Lesch, "Israeli Settlements in the Occupied Territories, 1967–1977," *Journal of Palestine Studies* 7, no. 1 (1977): 26–47, 26.

88. See Theodor Meron, "A Memo on Settlement in the Administered Territories" [in Hebrew], Foreign Ministry, 18 September 1967, document classified as "top secret," https://www.thelawfilm.com/inside/wp-content/uploads/2013/02/meron-memo.pdf. Meron became a leading international legal figure and was later the president of the UN's International Residual Mechanism for Criminal Tribunals. See also Gorenberg, *The Accidental Empire*, 99; and Segev, *1967*, 576.

89. Meron, "A Memo on Settlement in the Administered Territories," 2; emphasis added.

90. Allon, quoted in Gorenberg, *The Accidental Empire*, 121.

91. Weizman, *Hollow Land*, 58.

92. The core members of Elon Moreh made eight consecutive attempts in three years to create a settlement in the West Bank's mountain region near the Palestinian village of Sebastia without government permission. In 1974, Shimon Peres, serving as minister of defense in Yitzhak Rabin's Labor government, allowed the settlers to remain in a section of the military base of Qadum, near Nablus. See Weizman, *Hollow Land*, 88–89; and Katz, "Mobile Colonial Architecture."

93. Weizman, *Hollow Land*, 103.

94. Lesch, "Israeli Settlements in the Occupied Territories," 26.

95. Lesch, "Israeli Settlements in the Occupied Territories," 26–28.

96. See chapter 5, note 57; and Weizman, *Hollow Land*, 118.

97. See B'Tselem, "Fake Justice: The Responsibility Israel's High Court Justices Bear for the Demolition of Palestinian Homes and the Dispossession of Palestinians" [in Hebrew], February 2019, https://www.btselem.org/hebrew/publications/summaries/201902_fake_justice.

98. See Katz, "Mobile Colonial Architecture."

99. Sharon, quoted in Weizman, *Hollow Land*, 133.

100. See Ariel Handel, "Gated/Gating Community: The Settlement Complex in the West Bank," *Transactions of the Institute of British Geographers* 39, no. 4 (2014): 504–17.

101. See Ilan Pappe, *The Biggest Prison on Earth: A History of the Occupied Territories* (London: Oneworld, 2017).

102. Reviel Netz, *Barbed Wire: An Ecology of Modernity* (Middletown, Conn.: Wesleyan University Press, 2004), 130.

103. Netz, *Barbed Wire*, 62–69.

104. Jeff Halper, "Dismantling the Matrix of Control," *Middle East Report Online*, 11 September 2009, https://merip.org/2009/09/dismantling-the-matrix-of-control/.

105. Gush Emunim master plan for settlement in Judea and Samaria 1980, 15, quoted in Sivan Hirsch-Hoefler and Cas Mudde, *The Israeli Settler Movement: Assessing and Explaining Social Movement Success* (Cambridge: Cambridge University Press, 2021), 100.

106. Weizman, *Hollow Land*, 80–81

107. See Yotam Berger, "Revealed: Israeli Taxpayers Helped Bankroll Illegal West Bank Outposts for Decades," *Ha'aretz*, 25 October 2018, https://www.haaretz.com/amp/israel-news/.premium-revealed-israeli-taxpayers-helped-bankroll-illegal-west-bank-outposts-for-decades-1.6581982.

108. Former settler now working for Peace Now (an organization promoting a two-state solution), interview, West Bank, 14 April 2019. Interestingly, Bedouin and Palestinians building without permits in Israel and the West Bank are using a similar method of constructing permanent structures within tents to camouflage the process until it is finished, as legally, it is much easier for the Israeli authorities to demolish a structure during the construction process, when they can demolish it immediately, than after the construction is finished, when they need a legal document to do it. See chapter 5; and Wafa Butmeh, "Static Displacement, Adaptive Domesticity: The Three Temporary Geographies of Firing Zone 918, Palestine," in Beeckmans, Gola, Singh, and Heynen, *Making Home(s)*.

109. Robert Young, *Postcolonialism: An Historical Introduction* (Oxford: Blackwell, 2011).

110. Harris, "How Did Colonialism Dispossess?"

111. See Gabriel Schwake, "The Community Settlement: a Neo-rural Territorial Tool," *Planning Perspectives* 36, no. 2 (2021): 237–57, https://doi.org/10.1080/02665433.2020.1728569.

112. According to the 2021 Peace Now statistics: Peace Now, "Population," https://peacenow.org.il/en/settlements-watch/settlements-data/population.

113. Taamallah, quoted in Zena Tahhan, "What an Israeli Army Closure on Ramallah Looks Like," *+972 Magazine*, 15 December 2018, https://972mag.com/israeli-army-closure-ramallah/139220/.

114. As the enduring temporariness of the occupation continues, territorial encamp-

ment is still part of the apparatus that consolidates Israeli control while spatially and legally segregating the Palestinians into different groups and spaces in what rights groups define as a nondemocratic apartheid regime. While the population of Jewish Israelis (around 6.8 million in 2021), including those living in the occupied territories, are managed under one legal system of the Israeli law, the Palestinian population (of around the same size) is divided into four groups: Palestinian citizens of Israel, East Jerusalem residents, West Bank ID holders, and Gaza ID holders (not including those scattered as refugees beyond the territory, who are not allowed to return). On the Israeli apartheid regime, see the 2020 and 2021 reports of human rights organizations such as Yesh Din, B'Tselem, and Human Rights Watch, and the 2022 report by Amnesty International. And see, for example, Oliver Holmes, "Israel Is Committing the Crimes of Apartheid, Rights Groups Says," *The Guardian*, 27 April 2021, https://www.theguardian.com/world/2021/apr/27/israel-committing-crime-apartheid-human-rights-watch.

115. See Michael Crowley and David M. Halbfinger, "Trump Releases Mideast Peace Plan That Strongly Favors Israel," *New York Times*, 28 January 2020, https://www.nytimes.com/2020/01/28/world/middleeast/peace-plan.html.

116. Ophir, "A Time of Occupation," 61.

117. Raja Shehadeh, "The Countersettlement," *Latitude* (blog), *New York Times*, 17 January 2013, https://latitude.blogs.nytimes.com/2013/01/17/palestinians-fight-israels-settlement-policy-with-settlements-of-their-own/.

118. See Gorgio Agamben, *Means without End: Notes on Politics* (Minneapolis: University of Minnesota Press, 2000), 58–59.

119. Former UK prime minister David Cameron called it a "prison camp." See Nicholas Watt and Harriet Sherwood, "David Cameron: Israeli Blockade Has Turned Gaza Strip into a 'Prison Camp,'" *The Guardian*, 27 July 2010, https://www.theguardian.com/politics/2010/jul/27/david-cameron-gaza-prison-camp.

120. See Nicolas Pelham, "Gaza's Tunnel Phenomenon: The Unintended Dynamics of Israel's Siege," *Journal of Palestine Studies* 41, no. 4 (2012): 6–31, 7.

121. Diggers and smugglers were taxed through the Interior Ministry's Tunnel Affairs Commission. With an investment of millions of dollars, what began as only a few dozen tunnels in mid-2005, with trade revenue averaging $30 million per year, had grown by the end of 2008 to at least five hundred tunnels and trade revenue of $36 million per month. Pelham, "Gaza's Tunnel Phenomenon, 7.

122. James Hider, "Gaza Mud Houses Are Answer to a Prayer for the Homeless," *The Times*, 19 June 2009, https://www.thetimes.co.uk/article/gaza-mud-houses-are-answer-to-a-prayer-for-the-homeless-chm2kxxf7f9.

123. Ben Piven, "Gaza's Underground: A Vast Tunnel Network That Empowers Hamas," *Al Jazeera America*, 23 July, 2014, http://america.aljazeera.com/articles/2014/7/23/gaza-undergroundhamastunnels.html.

124. S'derot is an Israeli town established as a ma'abara camp on the lands of the Palestinian village Najd, whose residents lived as refugees in the Strip after 1948.

125. The number of Gazans killed is according to the UNHRC; numbers vary according to different reports.

126. See United Nations Office for the Coordination of Humanitarian Affairs, "Humanitarian Snapshot: Casualties in the Context of Demonstrations and Hostilities in Gaza," *OCHA*, 12 July 2018, https://www.ochaopt.org/content/humanitarian-snapshot-casualties-context-demonstrations-and-hostilities-gaza-30-march-12-0.

127. See the beginning of this chapter. Also see Seraj Assi, "Gaza's Refugees Have

330   Notes to Chapter 6

Always Haunted Israel. Now They're on the March," *Ha'artez,* 29 March, 2018, https://www.haaretz.com/israel-news/gaza-s-refugees-have-always-haunted-israel-now-they-re-on-the-march-1.5958265.

128. See Melanie Lidman, "Ten Years of Limbo: Gush Katif Evacuees Still in Trailers," *Times of Israel,* 28 July 2015, https://www.timesofisrael.com/ten-years-of-limbo-gush-katif-evacuees-still-in-trailers/.

7. In the Desert Penal Colony

1. See images and description in Yoav Zeitun, "A First Glimpse of the Infiltrators' Facility: A Tree, a Court, and a Fence" [in Hebrew], *ynet,* 7 March 2012, https://www.ynet.co.il/articles/0,7340,L-4199518,00.html.

2. See Paz, "Ordered Disorder"; and Barak Kalir, "The Jewish State of Anxiety: Between Moral Obligation and Fearism in the Treatment of African Asylum Seekers in Israel," *Journal of Ethnic and Migration Studies* 41 no. 4 (2015): 580–98.

3. Zeitun, "First Glimpse of the Infiltrators' Facility."

4. Goffman, *On the Characteristics of Total Institutions;* and on total institutions, see chapter 1.

5. See Paz, "Ordered Disorder"; and Renana Ne'eman, "Settling the Unsettled: Holot Facility in the Mytho-History of the Negev Desert," in Scott-Smith and Breeze, *Structures of Protection?,* 97–108.

6. Matthew J. Gibney, *The Ethics and Politics of Asylum: Liberal Democracy and the Response to Refugees* (Cambridge: Cambridge University Press, 2004), 4.

7. The fence was built at a cost of ILS 1.6 billion. See Gad Lior, "Cost of Border Fences, Underground Barrier, Reaches NIS 6bn," *ynet,* 30 January 2018, https://www.ynetnews.com/articles/0,7340,L-5078348,00.html.

8. See HCJ verdict 8665/14 [in Hebrew], Desta et al. vs. The Knesset et al., verdict dated 3 February 2015, 46, https://www.refworld.org/cgi-bin/texis/vtx/rwmain/opendocpdf.pdf?reldoc=y&docid=56af90844. Also see Ne'eman, "Settling the Unsettled," 105.

9. See "'I Was Left with Nothing': 'Voluntary' Departures of Asylum Seekers from Israel to Rwanda and Uganda," International Refugee Rights Initiative, September 2015, 6, https://reliefweb.int/sites/reliefweb.int/files/resources/IWasLeftWithNothing.pdf.

10. "Israel's Anti-Infiltration Law Is a Disgrace," editorial, *Ha'aretz,* 11 January 2012, https://www.haaretz.com/1.5163102.

11. See Lucy Mayblin, *Asylum after Empire: Colonial Legacies in the Politics of Asylum Seeking* (London: Rowman and Littlefield, 2017); and Thom Davies and Arshad Isakjee, "Ruins of Empire: Refugees, Race and the Postcolonial Geographies of European Migrant Camps," *Geoforum* 102 (2019): 214–17.

12. Mbembe, "Necropolitics," 21.

13. Haim Yacobi, "'Let Me Go to the City': African Asylum Seekers, Racialization and the Politics of Space in Israel," *Journal of Refugee Studies* 24, no. 1 (2010): 47–68, 52.

14. Yacobi, "'Let Me Go to the City,'" 48–49; Paz, "Ordered Disorder," 5.

15. Eli Shani, Shira Ayal, Yonatan Berman, and Sigal Rozen, "No Safe Haven: Israeli Asylum Policy as Applied to Eritrean and Sudanese Citizens," Hotline for Refugees and Migrants, December 2014, https://hotline.org.il/wp-content/uploads/No-Safe-Haven.pdf.

16. See, respectively, Karin Fathimath Afeef, "A Promised Land for Refugees? Asy-

lum and Migration in Israel," New Issues in Refugee Research working paper no. 183 (Geneva: UNHCR, 2009), 11; Sarah S. Willen, "Lightning Rods in the Local Moral Economy: Debating Unauthorized Migrants' Deservingness in Israel," *International Migration* 53, no. 3 (2015): 70–86, 79; Yacobi, "'Let Me Go to the City,'" 57; Paz, "Ordered Disorder," 5.

17. This reverses the movement of the early 1950s, when Jewish immigrants who arrived in Israel's coastal cities were taken by night buses to the Negev. See chapter 4.

18. Yacobi, "'Let Me Go to the City,'" 57.

19. Sharon Rotbard, *White City, Black City: Architecture and War in Tel Aviv and Jaffa* (London: Pluto Press, 2015).

20. Loïc Wacquant, *Urban Outcasts: A Comparative Sociology of Advanced Marginality* (Cambridge: Polity Press, 2008); Rotbard, *White City, Black City*.

21. Rony Lifshitz, "Operation Order: Expel 300 Infiltrators Each Day" [in Hebrew], *ynet*, 2 March 2008, https://www.ynet.co.il/articles/0,7340,L-3515502,00.html.

22. See Dan Izenberg, "State Defends 'Hadera-Gedera' Asylum-Seekers Policy," *Jerusalem Post*, 29 July 2009, https://www.jpost.com/breaking-news/state-defends-hadera-gedera-asylum-seekers-policy.

23. Jonathan Darling, "Forced Migration and the City: Irregularity, Informality, and the Politics of Presence," *Progress in Human Geography* 41, no. 2 (2017): 178–98.

24. Yishai quoted in Dana Weiler-Polak, "Eli Yishai: Infiltrators Pose Existential Threat to Israel," *Ha'aretz*, 22 November 2010, https://www.haaretz.com/1.5142930; see also Harriet Sherwood, "Israelis Attack African Migrants during Protest against Refugees," *The Guardian*, 24 May 2012, https://www.theguardian.com/world/2012/may/24/israelis-attack-african-migrants-protest.

25. Thomas Leitersdorf (Holot's project architect), interview, Tel Aviv, 27 August 2018.

26. See Leitersdorf Ben-Dayan Architects, "Ktzi'ot—Detention Facility" [in Hebrew], 1 May 2019, http://www.lb-arch.co.il/en/פרויקטים/ktsiot/.

27. Thomas Leitersdorf, interview, Tel Aviv, 27 August 2018.

28. Leitersdorf Ben-Dayan Architects, PowerPoint presentation showing the facility and its design, undated, shared with the author in August 2018. It includes documents presented at planning meetings dated January 2011, as well as photos from the completed center.

29. Weizman, *Hollow Land*, 111–16.

30. See Leitersdorf Ben-Dayan Architects, "Ktzi'ot."

31. Simon Turner, "Suspended Spaces: Contesting Sovereignties in a Refugee Camp," in Hansen and Stepputat, *Sovereign Bodies*, 322.

32. See Foucault, *Discipline and Punish*.

33. See, for example, Sarah Gibson, "The Hotel Business Is about Strangers: Border Politics and Hospitable Spaces in Stephen Frears's *Dirty Pretty Things*," *Third Text* 20, no. 6 (2006): 693–701.

34. Orvar Löfgren, *On Holiday* (Berkeley: University of California Press, 2003), 256.

35. See also Ne'eman, "Settling the Unsettled." For a thorough discussion of the Negev desert in Zionism, see Yael Zerubavel, *Desert in the Promised Land* (Stanford: Stanford University Press, 2018).

36. Adi Drori-Avraham, Sigal Rozen, and Nimrod Avigal, "Where There Is No Free Will: Israel's 'Voluntary Return' Procedure for Asylum Seekers," Hotline for Refugees

332 Notes to Chapter 7

and Immigrants and ASSAF (Aid Organization for Refugees and Asylum Seekers in Israel), April 2015, http://assaf.org.il/en/content/report-where-there-no-free-will-israels -voluntary-return-procedure-asylum-seekers.

37. Yishai, quoted in Omri Efraim, "Yishai: Next Phase—Arresting Eritrean, Sudanese Migrants," *ynet*, 16 August 2012, https://www.ynetnews.com/articles/0,7340,L -4269540,00.html.

38. HCJ 7385/13 Gabrisilasi et al. vs. The Knesset et al., verdict dated 22 September 2014, 4, https://hotline.org.il/wp-content/uploads/2018/10/Gabrislasi-Verdict-092214 -abrogation-of-the-fourth-amendment-to-the-Anti-Infiltration-Law-Eng.pdf.

39. Allison Kaplan Sommer, "'Remember You Were Strangers': Ultra-Orthodox Jews Step in to Help Asylum Seekers in Israel," *Ha'aretz*, 16 April 2018, https://www.haaretz .com/israel-news/.premium-ultra-orthodox-jews-step-in-to-help-asylum-seekers-in -israel-1.6008184.

40. All names of asylum seekers included in this chapter are pseudonyms, as they appear in related publications. Ahmed, "Photo Diary: Inside 'Holot' Detention Center for Asylum Seekers," Activestills and *+972 Magazine*, 4 February 2014, https://www.972mag .com/photo-diary-inside-israels-holot-detention-center-for-asylum-seekers/.

41. Jacobsen, Karlsen, and Khoravi, *Waiting and the Temporalities of Irregular Migration.*

42. Yosi Mizrahi, "Love and Violence between the Fences: A Glimpse into Life in Holot Facility" [in Hebrew], *Mako*, 31 May 2014, https://www.mako.co.il/news-israel /education/Article-4a2f75928335641004.htm. See also Rotter, "Waiting in the Asylum Determination Process."

43. Hilo Glazer, "The Singing of the Sands: Near the Open Detention Facility Grew an Area That Tries to Bring Back Taste to Life" [in Hebrew], *Ha'aretz*, 17 December 2015, https://www.haaretz.co.il/.premium-1.2800294.

44. Brun, "Active Waiting and Changing Hopes," 24. See also Arendt, *The Human Condition*; Deleuze and Guattari, *A Thousand Plateaus* and *Kafka*; and Moten and Harney, *The Undercommons.*

45. Na'ama Angel Mishali, "'Holot' Facility in the Negev: Tens of Makeshift Structures Built by the Detainees Were Demolished" [in Hebrew], *Makor Rishon*, 8 January 2016, https://www.makorrishon.co.il/nrg/online/1/ART2/747/325.html.

46. HCJ verdict 8665/14, 40. See also Ne'eman, "Settling the Unsettled," 105.

47. HCJ verdict 8665/14, 110; emphasis in the original.

48. Lefebvre, *Writings on Cities*. The idea of the "right to the city," also discussed in chapter 6, calls for the reclamation of urban inhabitants' ability to change themselves by reshaping the city while exercising their collective power to alter urbanization processes, rather than leaving them only to strong, and often capitalist, forces. See also David Harvey, "The Right to the City," *New Left Review* 53 (September/October 2008), https://newleftreview.org/issues/ii53/articles/david-harvey-the-right-to-the-city.

49. HCJ verdict 8665/14, 110.

50. Tewalda, quoted in Yana Pevzner, "Forgotten in the Desert" [in Hebrew], *Mako*, 10 November 2016, https://www.mako.co.il/weekend-articles/Article-f63d71f9e4d4851004 .htm. The beginning of this quotation is the epigraph of the chapter.

51. Quoted in Pevzner, "Forgotten in the Desert."

52. Quoted in Pevzner, "Forgotten in the Desert."

53. Gidi Weitz and Hilo Glazer, "How Israel Tried to Dump African Refugees in Blood-Drenched Dictatorships," *Ha'aretz*, 25 December 2020, https://www.haaretz.com /israel-news/.premium.MAGAZINE-how-israel-tried-to-dump-african-refugees-in-blood -drenched-dictatorships-1.9398948.

54. A., who spent eighteen months in Holot before returning to Tel Aviv, interview, Neve Sha'anan Street, Tel Aviv, 20 August 2018.

55. D., who spent two years in Holot, interview, Neve Sha'anan Street, Tel Aviv, 20 August 2018.

56. Interestingly, the function currently under consideration for Holot, rather than its previously proposed military use, is to be a cultural and business center for hosting festivals in the Negev, a touristic use that formed part of its architectural design. See Josh Breiner, "Holot Facility, Used for the Detention of Asylum Seekers, Is Expected to Turn into a Business and Cultural Center" [in Hebrew], *Ha'aretz*, 5 October 2021, https://www.haaretz.co.il/news/education/.premium-1.10265462.

57. Michel Agier, *Managing the Undesirables* (Cambridge: Polity Press, 2011).

58. Foucault, *Discipline and Punish*.

59. See Saskia Sassen, *The Global City: New York, London, Tokyo* (Princeton: Princeton University Press, 2001); and Irit Katz, "The Global Infrastructure of Camps," *Insecurities*, Museum of Modern Art (MoMA), 10 January 2017, https://medium.com/insecurities/the-global-infrastructure-of-camps-8153fb61ea30.

60. Harsha Walia, *Undoing Border Imperialism* (Oakland, CA: AK Press / Institute for Anarchist Studies, 2013).

61. Didier Bigo, "Detention of Foreigners, States of Exception, and the Social Practices of Control of the Banopticon," in *Borderscapes: Hidden Geographies and Politics at Territory's Edge*, ed. Carl Grundy-Warr and Prem Kumar Rajaram (Minneapolis: University of Minnesota Press, 2007), 3–33, 9.

62. Ayelet Shachar, *The Shifting Border: Legal Cartographies of Migration and Mobility* (Manchester: Manchester University Press, 2020).

63. Nandita Sharma, *Home Rule: National Sovereignty and the Separation of Natives and Migrants* (Durham: Duke University Press, 2020), 3.

64. See Brown, *Walled States*, 36; also see Hagar Kotef, *Movement and the Ordering of Freedom: On Liberal Governances of Mobility* (Durham, N.C.: Duke University Press, 2015).

65. Enforced mobility is often an active practice to manage inmates in this "camp infrastructure"; many countries—the United States, Australia, the United Kingdom, Italy, and others—frequently move irregular migrants within the system, transferring them between camps as part of the detention routine. See Alison Mountz, Kate Coddington, Tina Catania, and Jenna M. Loyd, "Conceptualizing Detention Mobility, Containment, Bordering, and Exclusion," *Progress in Human Geography* 37, no. 4 (2013): 522–41.

66. Irit Katz, "Between Bare Life and Everyday Life: Spatialising Europe's Migrant Camps," *AMPS: Architecture, Media, Politics, Society* 12, no. 2 (2017): 1–21.

67. See Sam Okoth Opondo and Lorenzo Rinelli, "Between Camps / Between Cities: Movement, Capture and Insurrectional Migrant Lives," *Globalizations* 12, no. 6 (2015): 928–42.

68. Nicholas De Genova, "Spectacles of Migrant 'Illegality': The Scene of Exclusion, the Obscene of Inclusion," *Ethnic and Racial Studies* 36, no. 7 (2013): 1180–98.

Conclusion

1. See Meiches, "A Political Ecology of the Camp"; Katz, "Mobile Colonial Architecture"; and the reflections on the camp's materiality in chapter 1 and in the discussions of camps that appear throughout this book.

2. See discussion in chapter 1 and throughout the book.

3. Carl H. Nightingale, *Segregation: A Global History of Divided Cities* (Chicago: University of Chicago Press, 2012).

4. Forth, *Barbed-Wire Imperialism*, 2–3. See also chapter 1 in this book.

5. Arendt, *The Origins of Totalitarianism*, 128.

6. Netz, *Barbed Wire*, 130.

7. Foucault, *Society Must Be Defended*, 241; and see chapter 1.

8. Hansen and Stepputat, *Sovereign Bodies*, 24. This permanent state of exception endures as long as the colonial state continues. On the colonial state of exception see, for example, Hansen and Stepputat, *Sovereign Bodies*; Derek Gregory, *The Colonial Present: Afghanistan, Palestine, Iraq* (Malden, Mass.: Blackwell, 2004); and John Pincince, "Decentering Carl Schmitt: Colonial State of Exception and the Criminalization of the Political in British India, 1905–1920," *Política Común* 5 (2014), http://dx.doi.org/10.3998/pc.12322227.0005.006.

9. These camp types could be linked to the ghetto, the enclave, and the citadel analyzed by Peter Marcuse as the different forms of ethnically and class-defined spatial concentrations of population in the post-Fordist U.S. city. The ghetto, like the camps that contain and expropriate, is the result of the involuntary spatial segregation of a racialized subaltern group. By contrast, the enclave and the citadel, like the camps that protect specific populations during colonial expansion, are developed to enhance the position of more privileged groups. Yet unlike the urban forms Marcuse identified, the camps described in this book have roles primarily linked to territorial control and national struggles, a geopolitical and spatial genealogy in which relationships to race and ethnicity are also central. See Peter Marcuse, "The Enclave, the Citadel, and the Ghetto: What Has Changed in the Post-Fordist US City," *Urban Affairs Review* 33, no. 2 (1997): 228–64.

10. Irit Katz, "A Network of Camps on the Way to Europe," *Forced Migration Review* 51 (2016): 17–19.

11. Bauman, *Modernity and Ambivalence*, 7.

12. Wallace Stevens, *The Collected Poems of Wallace Stevens* (London: Faber and Faber, 1955), 215.

13. Agier, "Between War and City," 336. Liisa Malkki argues that the heterogeneity Agier describes in the camp is relatively unusual and that it is not helpful to discuss the camp as not-yet-city while conceiving the city as a "stage" that the camp cannot reach. See Liisa Malkki, "News from Nowhere," *Ethnography* 3, no. 3 (2002): 351–60, 355.

14. Peter Grbac, *"Civitas, Polis, and Urbs,"* working papers series 96, Refugee Studies Centre, Oxford Department of International Development, University of Oxford, 2013; Pasquetti, "Negotiating Control," 711.

15. Sanyal, "Urbanizing Refuge," 558; Diana Martin, "From Spaces of Exception to 'Campscapes': Palestinian Refugee Camps and Informal Settlements in Beirut," *Political Geography* 44 (2015): 9–18; Lucas Oesch, "An Improvised Dispositif: Invisible Urban Planning in the Refugee Camp," *International Journal of Urban and Regional Research* 44, no. 2 (2020): 349–65. For further reflection on the camp and the city, see Diana Martin, Claudio Minca, and Irit Katz, "Rethinking the Camp: On Spatial Technologies of Power and Resistance," *Progress in Human Geography* 44, no. 4 (2020): 743–68.

16. See Malkki, "News from Nowhere"; and Alsayyad and Roy, "Medieval Modernity."

17. See Minca, "Geographies of the Camp."

18. Abourahme, "Assembling and Spilling-Over," 200; see also Katz Feigis, "Spaces Stretch Inward."

Notes to Conclusion   **335**

19. Other protest camps, not discussed in this book, were erected in Israeli cities as acts against social upheavals; the 2011 camps of the social protest in Tel Aviv and elsewhere are examples.

20. Arendt, *The Human Condition*, 177. See also Irit Katz, "From Spaces of Thanatopolitics to Spaces of Natality," *Political Geography* 49 (2015): 84–86.

21. Deleuze and Guattari, *A Thousand Plateaus*, 291; Harney and Moten, *The Undercommons*; see discussion in chapter 6.

22. Shehadeh, "The Countersettlement."

23. On other forms of resistance in the camp see, for example, Owens, "Reclaiming 'Bare Life'?"; and Agier, *On the Margins of the World.*

24. Zygmunt Bauman, *Modernity and the Holocaust* (Cambridge: Polity Press, 1989), 39.

25. Shamir suggests this in relation to the Bedouin, but it could also be the case with other displaced Palestinians; see Shamir, "Suspended in Space," 254.

26. Hannah Arendt, *The Promise of Politics* (New York: Schocken Books, 2005), 108, 129.

INDEX

Page numbers in italics refer to figures and maps.

abandonment, 2, 31, 33, 40, 46, 129, 130, 135–40, 164, 165, 174, 175, 178, 266, 282, 283, 315n10
Abercrombie, Patrick, 109
Abourahme, Nasser, 54, 207, 216
Abreek-Zubiedat, Fatina, 218, 219
Abu-Saad, Ismail, 159, 172
Abuji, Nurhan, 218
actor-network theory (ANT), 52–53
Adalah, 176, 180
Aden, 20, *97, 101. See also* Geula transit camp; Hashed camp
Agamben, Giorgio, 19, 29, 38, 40, 44, 52, 140, 209, 217, 237, 284, 292n22, 294n5, 298n83; biopolitics and, 26; camps and, 5–6, 39, 41, 47, 134; colonialism, 298n78; modern state and, 30; theory of, 6, 17, 48
agency, 6, 42, 122, 208; political, 7, 275; spaces of, 41
Agier, Michel, 41, 268, 284, 334n13
agriculture, 69, 166, 167, 173, 174, 176, 177, 178, 309n14, 311n53, 318n55, 327n86; developing, 125; restrictions on, 164
Aida camp, *203, 205, 207*
Al-Aref, Aref, 166
al-Arish, 215
Albek, Plia, 230, 318n54
al-Bureij, 242

al-Fahm, Abdelkader Abu, 325n50
Aliyah, 93, 107, 293n31, 304n45
Allenby, Edmund, 59, 301n5
alleyway, *205*, 206
Allon, Yigal, 226, 325n47
Allon Plan, 226
al-Shawa, Rashad, 218
Am'ari, 223
American Friends Service Committee (AFSC), 322n12
Anderson, Benedict, 37
anti-Semitic, 13, 69, 287
Antzar 3, 326n60
Arab–Israeli war (1948), 9, 11, 14, 17, 83, 120, 124, 197
Arab Jews, The (Shenhav), 312n69
Arab Legion, 196
Arab Revolt (1936–39), 310n19
Arabs: Palestinian Arab citizens, 171, 303n40, 305n59; Palestinian Arabs, 196, 319n66
Arab uprising (1936), 61, 72, 74, 78, 84
architecture, 16–22, 45, 49, 87; ad hoc, 64–67; adrenaline, 252–55; Bauhaus-style, 251; emergency, 25; modern, 2, 150, 153
Arendt, Hannah, 19, 25, 26, 39, 280, 289; on camps, 5, 6; natality and, 262, 285; nation-state and, 38; political time and, 51; "We Refugees," 5
Ashkenazim, 14, 100, 114, 140, 141, 142
Asi River, 72, *73*
assimilation, 48, 70, 108, 141

Association for Civil Rights in Israel (ACRI), 190
asylum policies, 250, 258, 260
asylum seekers, 269; African, 15, 17, 21, 48, 118, 245, 247, 248, 250–51, 252, *261*, *262*, 263, *263*, 264–65, 267, 276, 278; arrests of, 259; camps and, 265, 267; deportation and, 22, 258, 265, 266; detention of, 22, 247–48, 265, 266; as infiltrators, 247, 252, 254; marginalization of, 251–52; politics and, 249
Atlit Detention Camp, 80, *80, 81,* 82, 83, 84
Auschwitz death camp, 298n81
authoritarian regimes, 2–3, 28
Avidar, Yosef, 77
Azazma-Sawachana Bedouins, 166, 172–73
Azoulay, Ariella Aïsha, 19, 195

Bab al-Shams, 236, *238*
badawi, term, 166
Balas, Shimon, 144
Balfour Declaration (1917), 59
banishment, 258–60, 262–63; space of, 21, 269
Baqa'a refugee camp, *204*
Barbed Wire: An Ecology of Modernity (Netz), 231, 271
Barbed-Wire Imperialism (Forth), 57
bare life, 5–6, 39–42, 47, 209, 285
Basic Law: Israel as the Nation-State and Jewish People (2018), 193
Basis for Planning: Land, People, Time, 110
Bauhaus, 51, 150
Bauman, Zygmunt, 23, 24, 91, 92, 118, 183, 287, 324n33; "Century of Camps" and, 2; modernity and, 8, 20, 283
Beach camp, *206*
Beauvoir, Simone de, 215
Bedouin, 11, 17, 159, 163, *167*, 176, 179, 184, 185, 193, 208, 228, 258, 263, 283; British Mandate and, 156, 318n53; concentration of, 175, 318n51; land-ownership and, 166, 168, 171, 172, 174, 175, 318n53; martial law and, 173, 174, 175; Palestinians and, 161–62, 164,

288; prestate territorial divisions of, *162*; spatial order of, 180–83; transfer of, 174, 180, 317n42; urbanization and, 170, 173, 175
Bedouin Authority, 175, 176–77, 184, 191, 319n57, 321n100
Bedouin encampment, *168,* 172
"Bedouins' Complaint, The" (Abu-Saad), 159
Bedouin settlements, 21, 48, 72, 157, 159–60, 166, 173, 179, 182, 193; unrecognized, 174, 175, 190
Bedouin villages, 164, 180; environment of, 188–89; map of, *165*; unrecognized, 183
Be'er-Sheva, 121, 128, 136, 137, 138, 255
Be'er-Sheva police station, 130
Beit-Alfa kibbutz, 73
Beit Hanoun, *241*
Beit Hashita kibbutz, 70
Beit Jala, 65
Beit Lid immigrant camp, *98, 100*
Beit Yosef wall and tower camp, *76*
Bellamy, Edward, 91
Ben-Gurion, David, 93–94, 99, 107, 109, 124, 141, 143, 148, 197, 258, 309n14, 309n15; on immigration, 98; Tel-Yeruham and, 147
Benjamin, Walter, 3, 5, 26, 30, 83
Bentham, Jeremy, 257
Ben-Zvi, Yitzhak, 147, *148*
Berda, Yael, 115, 176
Bergson, Henri, 51, 183, 300n130
Bhabba, Homi, 154
Bigo, Didier, 268
Bil'in village, 236, 237
Bimkom, 184
biological existence (*zoë*), 39
biopolitics, 5, 26, 34, 52, 119, 140, 275, 278, 279, 284, 285, 288; camps and, 35–42, 92; modern, 272; racism and, 36; of settler societies, 168–70
Bir Rakhma, 124
black bodies, racialized, 143, 249
"black city," 251, 258
Black September (1970), 325n50, 325n53
blocks, *113*; cement, 128, 202; huts and, 151–54; military/colonial, 62–64

Bodin, Jean, 27–28
Boers, 24, 296n43; Boer War, 231, 281, 296n40; camps, 32–33, 298n84
Bourdieu, Pierre, 105
Brecht, Bertolt, 87
Brenner, Neil, 45
British Empire, 11, 19, 57, 65, 301n4
British Mandate, 13, 61, 82, 84, 90, 94, 125, 160, 161, 172, 247, 278; Bedouins and, 166, 318n53; camps of, 17; end of, 85; militarization during, 67; regulations by, 30
Brown, Wendy, 268
Brun, Catherine, 50
Brutzkus, Eliezer, 109, 148, 313n96
Budeiri, Muna, 223
building materials, 64–65, *74*
Butler, Judith, 38, 39

Camp Ariel Sharon, 314n117
Camp d'Arenas ("Jewish Camp"), 102, *102*
Camp David Accords (1978), 228
campness, 172, 174, 179, 183, 193, 208, 224, 283; Bedouin, 164, 184, 278
camps: alignment of, 17, 267–68, 274; characteristics of, 7–8, 110, 126, 272; country of, 93–103, 105–10; creation of, 2, 11, 17–18, 20, 40, 54, 64, 72, 74, 76, *89*, 92, 133, 277, 278, 288; eliminating, 215–18; framework of, 225–28, 230; governance, and, 31–32, 273; hybridizing, 149–51; investigation of, 6, 7, 16, 52; Israeli–Palestine, 2, 4, 5, 7, *10*, 11, 12, 15, 17, 18, 22, 33, 41–42, 48, 55, 286, 288; laboratory of, 2, 11, 288; makeshift, 14–15, 16, 33, 239; political implications of, 9, 17, 273; right to, 221–24, 327n82; role of, 19–20, 22, 115; social meanings of, 17, 41, 288; as spatial entities, 1, 2, 3–4, 6, 7, 9, 17, 22, 25, 26, 40–41, 45–46, 50, 57, 84, 128, 210, 274, 281–84, 286, 288, 289; temporary, 49, 112, 146, 149, 157, 259; territorial/spatial/material instrument of, 42–55, 279–81; types of, 16, 17, 19, 59, 92, 118, 274, 275, 279, 280, 281, 288
camps de regroupement, 33
camp spaces, 4, 6, 8, 9, 16, 30, 40, 42, 48,

164, 177, 188, 269, 272, 274, 282; complexities of, 41; ethnicized, 144
camps-villes, 284
campus, 3
Campus in Camps, 223
caravillas (caravans), 227, *242*
cement, 64, 128, 151, 208, 239; urbanization and, 207
central place theory, 109
"Century of Camps," 2
chaos, 25, 282; order and, 92
Christaller, Walter, 109
Christian Church, Jews and, 287
Christians, population of, 60
citizenship, 171, 215, 224, 268, 272, 284; institution of, 38; nation-state and, 37; rights, 179
city-camps, 284
Civil Administration, 230
civilization, 46–47, 255; barbarism and, 3; sacred trust of, 60; state of exception and, 47
colonial camps, 24, 33, 39
colonialism, 8, 12–13, 16, 22, 25, 32, 53, 79, 90, 171, 233, 249, 273; camps and, 20; forms of, 33–34
colonial settler societies, 19, 34. *See also* settler colonialism
colonial wars, 32, 39–40, 53, 54
Colonist, The, 68
colonization, 25, 42, 77, 90, 92, 107, 149, 193, 272, 281; dispossession and, 171–72; double, 83; economic, 293n29; ethnic-survival form of, 293n29; internal, 110, 146, 274; international, 141
community, 25, 37, 222–23, 258, 268; political, 37, 51–52
concentration camps, 7, 14, 40, 53, 151, 231, 281; colonial, 6, 32–33, 295n38; German, 291n8; Italian, 33; Japanese American, 33, 279; makeshift, 33; Nazi, 18, 24, 29, 32, 100–110, 179; techniques at, 5
"Connoisseur of Chaos" (Stevens), 283
Connor, Walker, 36
construction, 48, 73, 76, 137–38, 150, 160, 204; plans, 193n33; process, 66, 328n108

Construction and Housing Office, 176
containment, 15, 270; instruments of, 85; space of, 21; technologies of, 31
countersettlement camps, 286
Covenant of the League of Nations, 60
culture, 141, 144, 285; Bedouin, 161, 163, 166, 167–68, 170, 171, 173, 177, 178, 186; cultural hegemony, 5, 45; cultural life *(bios)*, 39; cultural rules, 182, 282; dominant, 49; functional, 154; Israeli, 145, 234; material, 22, 52; Mizrahim, 143; spatial, 22
Culture and Imperialism (Said), 23
Cyprus, 80, 84, 101, 305n65; camps in, 82–83

Davar Hashavua, 310n19
Dayan, Moshe, 170, 215, 220, 325n47
death, 6, 40, 224; ritualizations of, 27, 35
death camps, 14, 136; Nazi, 18, 30, 39, 41, 197
decampment, 214–15, 218–21, 224
Declaration of Independence, Israeli, 30, 93, 94
Declaration of the Rights of Man and of the Citizen, sovereignty and, 37
dehumanization, 6, 39, 41, 90, 118, 134, 143, 144, 145, 262, 273, 275, 285, 289
Deir Jarir, 233, 235
Deleuze, Gilles, 53, 210, 262; camp spaces and, 8; political emergence and, 286
Demilitarized Zone, frontier villages in, 123
demographic changes, 15, 84, 250, 274, 276, 287, 289
de Muynck, Bert, 165
Department of Public Works, 220
Department of Refugee Affairs (PLO), 222
deportation, 248, 265, 266
detention, 1, 259, 260, 265, 269
detention camps, 1, 2, 6, 7, 11, 15, 17, 20, 21, 30, 47, 61, 84, 96, 254, 255, 256, 267, 269, 279, 281; British, 58, 80–83; creation of, 59; desert, 246; offshore, 44; site plans for, 80–81, *80*
development, 76, 122, 124, 214–15
Development Authority, 318n55
development towns, 88, 149, 154

Dheisheh, 223, 327n81
diamond industry, camps for, 296n41
Dimona, 49, 313n94
discrimination, 19, 88, 142, 156, 193; development of, 140; ethnoracial, 156
displaced persons, 23, 82, 305n64
displacement, 1, 11, 214, 268, 274; homemaking in, 209; spaces of, 255, 323n20; time-space rupture of, 300n130
dispossession, 38; colonization and, 171–72
Dominican Republic, agricultural colonies in, 124
Druze, 60, 319n66

East Jerusalem, 195, 224, 237, 329n114; settlements in, 230
economic dependence, 137, 139
education, 37, 121, 129, 143, 190, 201, 223, 279
Efrat, Zvi, 150
Eilat, 149, 251, 265
Eilon, Amos, 197
Ein Gev camp, 77
Ein Harod kibbutz, 69, *70, 71*
Ein Hawd, 316n11
Ein Hod, 316n11
Eisenberg, Dov, 220
Elden, Stuart, 43, 44, 45
electricity, 128, 160, 187; connection to, *129*
Eliav, Arieh (Loba), 310n40
Elon Moreh, 228, *229,* 327n92
Emek Heffer ma'abara, 145
emergency regulations, 30, 123, 171, 172, 317n44
encampment, 23, 166–73, 211, 227, 243, 255, 274; encamping, 230–36; global reality of, 22; infrastructure of, 268; makeshift, 239; resisting, 236–37
environment, 132, 133, 134–35, 151, 182, 204, 222; camp, 208, 211, 223; material, 208; ordered/disordered, 283; shifting, 201–3, 209; urban, 144, 275
E1 zone, 236, *238*
Eretz Yisrael (Land of Israel), 12, 13, 68, 69, 83, 93, 94, 197, 226, 293n31

Eritrea, 245, 259, 265, 267

Esh Kodesh, *234*

Eshkol, Levi, 98, 103, 115, 147, 196, 197, 224, 225, 240, 310n40, 313n92, 322n3, 325n47

Ethiopian Jews, 15, 118, 278

ethnic cleansing, 34, 225

ethnic minorities, 12, 16, 34, 40, 141, 271

ethnoracial regimes, 168, 279

Etzion, Kfar, 196

Exception and the Rule, The (Brecht), 87

exclusion, 4, 20, 92, 173–75, 189, 193, 211, 288; camps and, 45–46, 274; resisting, 178–80

Exodus (ship), 305n64

expansion, 23, 25, 164, 230, 249, 274, 279, 281, 282; nation-state and, 280; territorial, 196, 280; urban, 108; Zionist, 13

expropriation, 16, 20, 163, 164, 165, 173–75, 249, 274, 280, 288; resisting, 178–80

expulsion, 16, 20, 163, 164, 173–75, 274, 281, 282, 288; camps of, 280; darkness of, 175

extermination camps, 24, 54

Ezori, Mirkam, 321n108

Faluga, 313n94

family clusters, 180, 181, *185, 186, 188,* 320n83

famine camps, 5, 32

Fanon, Frantz, 18, 46, 176

Fatah, 214, 325n50

fedayeen, 197, 215

fire zones, 177, 178, 245

Flavius Josephus, 5

For Space (Massey), 44

Forth, Aidan, 13, 57

Foucault, Michel, 5, 19, 26, 30, 35, 39, 45, 257, 268; biopolitics and, 297n57; on biopower, 35, 36; on freedom/ governmentality, 31; on genealogy, 9; on territory, 44

Fourth Geneva Convention, 225

freedom, 28, 35, 289; governmentality and, 31

freedom fighters, 197

frena, 151, 152, *152,* 153, *153,* 154, 283

French Revolution, 28

frontier, 121, 142, 171, 192–93; opening/ closing, 47; Zionist discourse and, 48

frontier camps, 47–48, 67, 79, 86, 128, 130, 136, 137, 143, 151; immigrants to, 135; paramilitary agricultural, 196

Galilee, 105, 165, 315n6

Galili, Israel, 79, 325n47

Gan Shmuel kibbutz, 309n5

Garden Cities of To-morrow (Howard), 91

Garden City, 109

Gavrieli-Nuri, Dalia, 314n116

Gaza City, *206,* 218, 220, 239

Gaza Strip, 21, 59, 66, 122, 166, 195, 200, 204, *216,* 218, 219, 221, 225, 226, 228, 241, 246; blockade of, 15, 238, 239; camps of, 11, 196, 197–98, 214–15, 217, 218, 219, 220, 239, 322n9, 325n53; disengagement from, 242; evacuation of, 11; occupation of, 231; Palestinians and, 219, 325n50; plan for, 217; population of, 325n47; settlement in, 216, 230; tunnels in, 238–40, 242–43

Gaza–Tel Aviv railway, 215

genealogy, 8, 9, 17, 22, 41, 273, 277, 279, 286

genocide, 18, 32, 33, 54

geopolitics, 2, 7, 12, 16, 17, 43, 55, 57, 88, 118, 268, 289

German Southwest Africa, camps in, 33

Geula transit camp, 101, *101. See also* Aden; Hashed camp

Gevim-Dorot ma'abara, 313n94

Gibney, Matthew, 247

Gilroy, Paul, 5, 38, 79

Ginosar kibbutz, 72

Goffman, Erving, 32

Golan Heights, 15, 21, 195, 224, 225, *227;* camps in, 196; settlement in, 226, 230

Goldberg, Eliezer, 179

Goldberg Committee, 179

Gordon, Neve, 327n86

governance, 17, 20, 29, 54, 118, 120, 155, 278; camps and, 31–32, 273; centralized, 139–40; colonial laboratory of, 32–33; hybrid modes of, 201; military, 174; modern, 32–33; modes of, 30–31,

164, 275; state, 30–31, 272; strategies for, 173–75
Governmental Planning Department, National Plan and, 108
Graham, Stephen, 48, 217, 218
Grbac, Peter, 327n82
Greater London Plan, 109
Great March of Return, 240, 241
Green Patrol, 177, 319n61; Supervision Unit in Open Areas, 176
grid, deterritorializing, 203–4, 207–8
Grosz, Elizabeth, 51
Guantánamo Bay, camps at, 299n95
Guattari, Félix, 210, 262; *agencement* and, 53; camp spaces and, 8; political emergence and, 286
Gur, Shlomo, 73, 79, 304n45
Gush Emunim, 226, 227–28, 229, 232
Gut hut (Gut Gourevitz, Engineers), 65, 66
Gvati, Haim, 224

Ha'apala, 305n58
Habraken, John, 182
Ha'dera, 252, 303–4n44
Ha'gana, 73, 76, 79
HaHityashvut HaOvedet, 70
Haifa, 61, 95, 108, 109, 135, 136, 142, 197, 220; riots in, 156
Haifa Technion, 303n43
Halper, Jeff, 232
halutzim, 13, 69
Hamadia camp, 77
Hamas, 239, 329n125
hamula clusters, 180, 181, 182
Handel, Ariel, 231
hangars, 69
Hansen, Thomas Blom, 32
Harel, Yehuda, 225, 327n37
Harney, Stefano, 79, 262; on governance, 174; on settlers, 170; undercommons and, 211, 286
Harris, Cole, 234
Hashed camp, 101, 101. *See also* Aden; Geula transit camp
Hazboun, Norma Nicola, 216, 325n47
HCJ. *See* High Court of Justice
he'ahzut, 107, 307n43

health care, 37, 121, 129, 201, 323n21
Health Ministry, 307n23
Herero, camps for, 33
Herut movement, 105
Herzl, Theodor, 91, 92
High Court of Justice (HCJ), 227–28, 248, 259, 263
Higher Arab Committee, 303n40
Hilal, Sandi, 216
Histadrut, 311n53
Hitler, 80, 136
Hobbes, Thomas, 27–28
Hobsbawm, Eric, 37, 38
holiday camps, 6, 256
Holocaust, 18, 36, 100, 140, 145, 298n81; surviving, 14, 305n64
Holot camp (Holot Residence Center), 17, 21, 48, 115, 248, 248, 250, 251, 257, 257, 258, 261, 261, 262, 267, 268, 269, 278, 284; asylum seekers and, 260, 265–66; design of, 247, 252–53, 254–55, 256, 263; entrance of, 249; human/physical context of, 270; incarceration in, 245, 246, 264–65; leisure area outside, 264; protest at, 26
homines sacri, 6, 41
homo sacer, 5, 39
Homo Sacer: Sovereign Power and Bare Life (Agamben), 5
Hosen moshav, 105; tents in, 106
Hotel Panopticon, 255–58
hotels, 246, 253, 255, 256, 258
housing, 144, 150, 153, 156, 159, 163, 220, 221; Bedouin, 169, 186, 187–88; building, 94, 324n27; demolition of, 187; immigrant, 103, 149; permanent, 128, 146, 210; public, 151; refugee, 208, 209; stone, 106, 208
Housing and Construction Office, 318n55
Housing Ministry, 137–38
Howard, Ebenezer, 91, 109
Human Condition, The (Arendt), 35, 51
humanitarian disasters, 5, 105
humanitarianism, 197, 200, 210, 211
human rights, 28, 38, 235, 247
Hussein–McMahon Correspondence, 59
huts, 62–64, 81, 133, 184, 302n16; blocks and, 151–54; canvas, 100, 140; flooring

for, 128; kitchen, *127*; ma'abara, 150; military, *67*; ready-made kit, 126; Swedish, 131; timber, 71, 84, 126, 128, 140; wooden, 310n31. *See also* Nissen huts; Quonset huts

hygiene, 5, 256, 297n60, 307n23

Hyndman, Jennifer, 210

identity, 3, 142, 149, 153, 278, 287; collapse of, 143–45; cultural, 141, 210; Jewish, 90, 141; national, 37, 43, 252, 271, 315n10; political, 204, 289; social, 204, 210

ideology, 38, 141, 170; cultural, 168; Marxist, 209; modern, 14, 108, 155; nationalist, 38, 143; Zionist, 90, 118, 143, 293n31

IDF. *See* Israeli Defense Force

IDP camps. *See* internally displaced persons camps

ILA. *See* Israel Land Authority

immigrant camps, 2, 15, 34, *68*, 83, 87, *95, 96, 98, 100,* 103, 105–6, 114, 125, 142, 281; closing, 20, 137; Israeli, 14, 302n27; Jewish, 274; plan and, 94–99; second-generation, 115, 118; state of emergency and, 94–99

immigrants, 34, 84, *95, 96, 97, 98,* 102, 103, 111, 118, 121, 126, 135; absorbing/settling, 143, 155; dispersing, 106–7; influx of, 139; managing, 122; mass appropriation of, 119; as pawns, 20; transferring, 136; well-being of, 113–14. *See also* Jewish immigrants; Moroccan immigrants; Polish immigrants; Romanian immigrants

immigration, 7, 23, 25, 82, 98, 135, 143, 168, 259; controlling, 24, 102–3; illegal, 34, 269, 305n64. *See also* Jewish immigration; mass immigration

indigenous populations, 48, 171, 192, 193; destruction of, 34; expelling/enclosing/separating, 169–70; settlers and, 168–70

industrialization, 24, 83, 84, 94, 131

infiltrators, 126, 171, 247, 252, 254, 309n6, 323n19

Infrastructure and Camp Improvement Programme (ICIP), 222

infrastructures, 15, 22, 36, 51, 53, 54, 64, 65, 66, 76–77, 163, 173, 174, 186, 196, 207, 231, 233–34, 273, 274, 277; camp, 267–70; civilian, 61, 67; global, 269, 270; modern, 160; open, *206*; road, 78–79, 234; transportation, 125

"Ingathering of Exiles," 93, 114

instruments: of abandonment, 135–40; camp, 35, 54; of containment, 85; political, 57; settlement, 226; spatial, 276; spatiopolitical, 4–9, 17, 23, 24, 25, 52, 54–55, 285; tactical, 83–86

internally displaced persons (IDP) camps, 2, 11, 163, 165, 173, 276, 281, 306n2, 306n3

International Committee of the Red Cross (ICRC), 260, 322n12

international law, 36, 46, 60, 225, 232

internment camps, 5, 80, 85; British, 101, 296n40

In the Penal Colony (Kafka), 245

intifada, 11, 15 153, 222, 231, 239, 326n60

IPS. *See* Israeli Prison Service

Iraq, 60, 214

Iraqi Jews, 101

Iraq Petroleum Company, 125

Israel Housing Survey Committee, 114

Israeli army. *See* Israeli Defense Force

Israeli Black Panthers, 156

Israeli Central Bureau of Statistics, 315n9

Israeli Defense Force (IDF), 83, 107, 123, 125, 142, 160, 173, 174, 215, 223, 226, 233, 236, 252, 255, 256, 319n66, 325n50; Arab communities and, 317n42; camps used by, 11, 14–15; Palestinian camps and, 210; standards for, 254; training for, 314n117

Israeli Prison Service (IPS), 246, 252, 253, 259

Israeli Supreme Court, 179, 254

Israel Land Authority (ILA), 175, 176, 318–19n55

Israel Nature and Parks Authority, 177

Jabalia, 215, 315n50, 325n52

Jaffa, 59, 61, 197, 220, 304n44

Jaffa riots (1921), 61

Jamal, Amal, 51

Jayyusi, Lena, 195
JDC. *See* Joint Distribution Committee
Jeffrey, Alex, 31, 105
Jelazone camp, *202*
Jenin refugee camp, 222; ground zero of, 217–18, *217*
Jerusalem, 59, 108, 197, 226, 236, 251; bombing in, 305n65
Jewish Agency, 66, 73, 78, 96, 98, 101, 103, 118, 124, 128, 137, 139, 145, 147–48, 149, 172, 193, 225, 274; Absorption Department, 123, 136, 140, 311n48; camps of, 14, 142; Settlement Department, 146, 147, 224; Technical Department, 131
Jewish Colonial Trust (JCT), 68
Jewish Colonization Association (JCA/ICA), 68
Jewish Diaspora, 92, 93, 120, 137, 150, 152, 293n31
Jewish immigrants, 13, *63*, 66, *81*, *82*, 83, 94, 109, 121, 122, 142, 197, 201; absorbing, 20, 60, 93, 108; arrival of, 140, 331n17; camps for, 34; distancing of, 141; flow of, 115; illegal, 11, 59, 61, 80, 81–82, 83, 85, 305n58, 305n59; population of, 88, 122; quota of, 80; Zionist limitations on, 303n30
Jewish immigration, 11, 13, 84, 93, 94; absorbing, 86
Jewish National Fund (JNF), 19, 72, 73, 105, 172, 225
Jewish population, 16, 18, 60, 93, 122, 230; dispersing, 86, 278; geopolitical changes for, 88; growth of, 234, 303n40; prestate, 100; racial division of, 14; size of, 14
Jewish question, 60
Jewish settlements, 76, 121, 165, 174, 198, 230–31; agricultural, 59; expansion of, 157
Jewish state, 91, 138
Jewish State, The (Herzl), 91
Jews: European, 14, 18, 100, 142; North African, 102; reunification of, 67–68; wandering, 69, 287
Jezreel Valley, 70, *71*
JNF. *See* Jewish National Fund

Joint Distribution Committee (JDC/Joint), 14, 101
Jordan, 122, 171, 195, 200, 204, 214, 221
Jordan Valley, 200, 224, 226, 230, 236, 325n50
Judaization, 157, 179, 196, 258, 317n33

Kafka, Franz, 245
Kafr Malik, 233
Kahn, Louis, 114; site plans by, *116–17*
Kalev, Henriette Dahan, 142
Kallus, Rachel: public housing and, 151
kaolin mines, 125, 137
Karameh, 325n50
khaima, 291n5
Khoury, Elias, 65, 236
kibbutz, 69, 72, 73, 107, 108, 124, 145, 163, 225, 226, 284; movement, 70; settlers in, 14, 70, 76
Kibbutz + Bauhaus: An Architect's Way in a New Land (Sharon), 110, 112
Kibbutz Ein Gev, 74, 75
kibbutzim, 71, 72, 139, 167, 311n53
Kibbutz Tel Amal, 72, 303n44
Kida, *234*
Kimmerling, Baruch, 34
kindergarten, 190–91, *192*, 193, 266, 285, 321n108; tent, *191*
King David Hotel, bombing of, 305n65
Kiryat-Gat, 313n94
kites, 238–40
Klausner, Samuel Z., 143
Klein, Naomi, 115
Knesset, 98, 179, 227
Kokhav Ha'Shahar, *233*
Ktzi'ot, 251, 253

labor, 34, 112; conquest of, 69, 138; organized, 137–39
Labor Battalion, 69, 301n1
labor camps, 226, 296n41, 311n48
Labor Settlement movement, 70
Lamar, Howard, 47
Land and Desire in Early Zionism (Neumann), 70
Land Day, protests on, 240
Land of Israel Pavilion, 78
landscapes, 50, 64, 85, 110, 120, 134, 144,

159, 176, 189, 224, 232, 269, 283; contested, 157; desert, 131, 132, 167; institutional, 221–22; morphology of, 182; physical, 88; spatial, 42; Zionist, 151

Lanzmann, Claude, 215

Large Crater, 137, 178

Latour, Bruno, 53, 189

Law-Yone, Hubert, 151

Lebanon, 200, 221; class A mandate for, 60

Lefebvre, Henri, 43, 45, 223

Lefort, Claude, 28

leisure area, makeshift, *264*

Leitersdorf, Thomas: Holot and, 252–53, 254, 256, 257, 258

"Letters from the Palestinian Ghetto" (Jayyusi), 195

Leviathan (Hobbes), 27

Lewinsky Park, 251

Libya, 214; Jews from, 102

life that resists, 39–42

Likud Party, 156, 230

Liquid Modernity (Bauman), 23

Lod, 61, 67, 197

Löfgren, Orvar, 256

logistics, 7, 24, 53, 54, 55, 64, 84, 131, 256, 273, 274, 277

Looking Backward: 2001–1887 (Bellamy), 91

Lyotard, Jean-François, 182

Ma'abara, The (Balas), 144

ma'abara camps, 20, 34, 87, 88, 90, 103, *104*, 105–6, *105*, 107, 110, 113, 114, 121, 122, 125, *127*, 128, 128, 128–29, 131, *133*, *134*, 140–44, 142, *152*, 154–55, 156–57, 164, 174, 184, 197, 214, 218, 277, 279, 281, 282, 283, 284, 287; alignment of, 139; black, 145; building, 132, 149, 278; dwellers at, 135, 137; environment of, 132, 134–35; frontier, 136, 143, 146, 274; liquidation of, 183; manual labor in, 139; population management and, 149; privacy and, 133; public housing and, 151; temporariness of, 130, 145–46, 151, 142

Ma'ale Adumim, 236, 253, 254

mahane, 3

Mahane Yisrael, *67,* 96

mahanot olim, 87

malja, 202–3

Malkki, Liisa, 3

Mandatory Palestine, 48, 60, 72, 83, 94, 102; Jewish migration to, 274, 305n58; map of, *58*

Mandel, Saadia, 153

Manning Portable Colonial Cottage for Emigrants, 64, 302n20

Mapai, 140, 309n14

Marcuse, Peter, 334n9

Mariam, Salem Ubu, 176

martial law, 161, 171, 173, 174, 175, 196

Massey, Doreen, 44, 271

mass immigration, 14, 15, 17, 19, 20, 87, 113–14, 118, 122, 141; absorbing, 93–103, 105–10, 128; emergency of, 146; shelter during, 155

Matalon, Ronit, 132

materiality, 7, 26, 53, 54, 84, 131, 189, 190–91, 208, 237, 272; Bedouin, 188; building, 64–65, *74*; external/internal, 184; mobile, 201; modern, 22, 52, 277; provisional, 51; shifting, 275; temporary, 183, 186, 262

Mau, 24, 33

mawat, 171, 175

Mbembe, Achille, 18, 19, 39, 40, 47, 249, 285

mechanisms, 16, 45, 277; biopolitical, 34, 35, 94, 279; camp, 275, 277–79; educational, 137; spatial, 4–9, 12, 42, 279, 286, 288

Meiches, Benjamin, 53

Meir, Avonoam, 47–48, 293n29, 325n47

Meir (Myerson), Golda, 147, 197, 311n48, 313n92

mellahs, described, 312n73

Merom Golan kibbutz, 225

Meron, Theodor, 225, 226

Mesopotamia, Jews from, 144

military camps, 11, *134,* 226, *228;* appropriation of, 85–86; British, 14, 19, *58,* 60–67, *62, 63,* 83, 84, 93, 95, *95,* 201; building, 59, 62–64; Jordanian, 77; Roman, 5

military zones, 161, 180, 315n6

mining camps, 6, 32
Ministry of Defense, 177, 219, 252
Ministry of Education, 190
Ministry of Foreign Affairs, 218
Ministry of Interior, 184, 329n121
Ministry of Labor, 129, 147
Ministry of Tourism, 255
minoritarian becoming, 211, 262, 286
Minority Treaties, 38
Mirkam Ezori, 190
Mitzpe-Ramon, 313n94
Mizrahim, 14, 40, 100, 114, 122, 135, 140, 141, 142, 144, 151, 153, 155, 156, 193, 258, 278; immigration of, 143; marginalization of, 251
mobile homes, *119, 234*
mobility, 26, 54, 193, 273, 279, 289; enforced, 333n65; political, 189; spatial, 71; technologies of, 25; transnational, 280
modernism, 20, 52, 108, 119, 150; primitivism versus, 141–43
modernity, 2, 8, 34, 52, 54, 113, 283; attributes of, 23, 24, 60; camps and, 90–93, 273; changes of, 28, 91; material ontologies of, 53; politics of, 23
Modernity and Ambivalence (Bauman), 91
Modernity and the Holocaust (Bauman), 287
modernization, 28, 141, 142, 149, 183
"Monster's Tail, The" (Ophir and Azoulay), 195
Moroccan immigrants, 101, 144, *152*, 153, *154*
Moses, 98
Mossad, 99, 305n64
Moten, Fred, 79, 262; on governance, 174; on settlers, 170; undercommons and, 211, 286
mukhayyam, 3
Muslims, population of, 60

Nabatiyyeh camp, 323n15
Nablus, 229, 234, 327n92
Nahal camps, 15, 107, 177, 226, 227, 280
Nahal Dekalim outpost camp, *228*
Nahal El Al outpost, *227*
Nahal Oz kibbutz, 215

Nahr al-Bared camp, 323n15, 327n77
Nakba, 18, 88, 165, 197, 239, 278, 294n38, 322n11; camps created during, *89*; mural in, *212*
Nakba Day, protests in, 240
Nama, 24, 33
Namibia, 33, 296n45
Naqab, 160, 172
Nasasra, Mansour, 159, 178, 318n53
Nasser, Gamal Abdel, 214
nation, 37; as civic religion, 38; race and, 38
National Infrastructure Office, 318n55
nationalism, 12, 37, 38, 219
National Plan, 107, 108–10, 115, 118, 119, 120, 128, 146, 150, 157; changing, 147–49; contents of, 110, 112–14, 259; mass immigration and, 110
nation-building, 2, 87–88, 141, 149, 249, 271
nation-state, 23, 34, 36–38, 44, 47, 109, 119, 268, 271, 273, 288; camps and, 6, 7, 40; establishment of, 43, 168; European, 38, 39; expansionism and, 280; modern, 32, 278; Zionism and, 37
nation-state-territory triad, 43, 44, 273, 278. *See also* state-people-territory triad
Native Americans, 172, 295n38
natives, 40, 79, 126; settlers and, 168–73
Natural Reserve Authority, 178
Nazi Germany, 33, 302n24, 303n40
necropolitics, 177–78, 275, 278, 288; camps and, 35–42; natality/political emergence and, 285–86
Negev desert, 21, 95, 121, 122, 123, 126, 147, 148, 149, 160, 161, 169, 171–75, 177, 182, 183, 186, 189, 193, 230, 270; agriculture in, 166; Bedouins in, 124, 164, 166–68; camps in, 15, 20, 48, 78, 179, 245; farms in, 318n51; map of, *162, 165*; marginalization of, 258; militarization of, 258; natural materials of, 124; urban centers in, 313n94
Netanyahu, Benjamin, 235, 252
Netz, Raviel, 271
Neumann, Boaz, 70
Neve Dekalim, 228
New Towns, 90, 109, *112*, 308n51

New York Times, 225
NGOs. *See* nongovernmental
 organizations
Nietzsche, Friedrich, 8–9
Nissen, Norman, 62
Nissen huts, 62–63, *63*, 65, 82, *82*, 84, 114
Nitzan Beit, 242, *242*
Noar Halutzi Lohem. See Nahal camps
nomadism, 167, 170–73, 184
nomos, 6, 46, 47, 170–73, 279
nongovernmental organizations (NGOs),
 176, 184, 220, 251
Nuseirat camp, 323n16

Ofakim, 313n94
oikos, 40, 134, 284, 324n31
Oil Road, 125
Old New Land (Herzl), 91
Olmert, Ehud, 252
One Million Plan, 93–94, 95–96, 100,
 119
open-gates policy, 103, 115, 118
Operation Kadesh, 214
Operation Magic Carpet, 101
Operation Protective Edge, 239
Ophir, Adi, 46, 50, 195, 236
ordered disorder, 90, 115, 118–20
Oren, Elhanan, 304n45
Organization of Military Rule in the
 Occupied Territories, 231
Origins of Totalitarianism, The (Arendt),
 32, 280
Oslo Accords, 15, 220, 221, 222, 232, 236,
 239
Ottoman Empire, 57, 60, 106, 161, 166,
 230, 318n53
Ottoman Land Code, 318n54
outpost camps, 12, 15, 72–73, 76, 78, 107,
 196, 226, *227*, *228*, 277–78; Israeli, 48,
 237, 243; Zionist, 125
Owens, Patricia, 41
Oxford, Lord, 318n53

Palestine: depicting, 12; as frontier territory, 84; partition plan for, 13; PLO
 and, 325n53
Palestine Jewish Colonization Association
 (PICA), 68

Palestine Royal Commission, 78
Palestinian Authority, 221–22
Palestinian camps, 34, 201, 208, 211, 214,
 218; nature of, 223; political/symbolic
 role for, 197; resistance and, 198; right
 to, 221–24; spaces of, 210
Palestinian Catastrophe, 18, 88. *See also*
 Nakba
Palestinian Liberation Front (PLF),
 325n50
Palestinian Liberation Organization
 (PLO), 209, 222, 325n50; Oslo
 Accords and, 221; Palestinian state
 and, 325n53
Palestinian refugees, 15, 21, 40, 48, 66,
 93, 118, 171, 195, 196, 197, 200, *202*,
 203, 204, *204*, 211, *221*, 224, 240, *241*,
 276; camp spaces of, 198, 306n2,
 306n3; population of, 88, 214; shelters
 for, 61, 86, 220; transferring and, 217,
 219
Palestinians, 11, 118, 193, 196, 263,
 305n59; Bedouins and, 164, 288;
 discrimination against, 193; exclusion
 of, 193; land of, 171; martial law and,
 171, 173; objectives of, 221; population
 of, 15, 21, 60, 164, 196, 227, 234, 286,
 329n114
Palestinian struggle, 11, 18, 88, 209, 211,
 217, 224; camps and, 198
Pappe, Ilan, 231
paramilitary camps, 226
Paris World Exposition (1937), 78
Partition Plan of Palestine, 107
Pasquetti, Silvia, 211
Paz, Yonathan, 115
Peace Law (1980), 175
Peace Now, 328n108
Peace of Westphalia (1648), 43
Peel Commission, report by, 78
penal colonies, 22, 248, 250, 257,
 258–60, 262–63, 265
Peres, Shimon, 218, 327n92
Peteet, Julie, 201, 210
Physical Planning in Israel, 108
plague camps, 5
planning, 45, 105, 132, 148; comprehen-
 sive, 149; government, 174; long-term,

29, 155; physical, 87, 150; Tayloristic, 256; urban/regional, 108, 284
Planning and Construction Law (1965), 175
Planning Department, 20, 118, 123, 146, 147–48, 309n7
PLO. *See* Palestinian Liberation Organization
pogroms, 197, 293n29
police force, 76, 176–77
polis, 40, 134, 284, 324n31
Polish immigrants, 140, 296n40
political action, 1, 35, 41, 285; in Rakhma, 188–93
political becoming, spaces of, 198, 200–204, 207–11
political formation, 22, 25, 34, 211, 272, 289
political objectives, 12, 49, 276
political thought, 6, 8, 27–28
politics, 5, 6, 18, 22, 25, 42, 46, 51–52, 86, 97, 98, 190, 208, 211, 223, 275, 276, 277, 287; asylum, 249; camps and, 23, 24, 26–34, 285; changing, 7; freedom and, 289; global, 269; modern, 1, 4, 8, 23, 24, 26–34, 39, 54, 272; national, 210; nonrepresentational, 285; Zionist, 151
Popular Committees, 222
Popular Front for the Liberation of Palestine (PFLP), 214
power, 2, 31, 246, 249, 273, 276; affective/generative, 53; camps and, 7, 48–52; colonial, 40, 272; domain of, 275; forms of, 8; hegemonic, 45; national, 40; political, 30, 42, 43, 275, 289; postcolonial, 272; sovereign, 5, 28, 29, 32, 40, 41; state, 263
Prawer Plan, European Parliament and, 179
prisoner of war (POW) camps, 32, 83
prisoners of war (POWs), 31, 83
Production of Space, The (Lefebvre), 44
propaganda, 14, 93, 99, 140, 197; Zionist, 14
property rights, 170, 171, 175
protest camps, 2, 6, 31, 52, *235, 237, 238*, 335n19; function of, 1; Palestinian, 15, 21, 48, 198, 236, 285

protesters, 24, *262*
protests, 11, 260, 266
Pullan, Wendy, 115
Pundak, Yitzhak, 219
p'zura, 166, 182

Qadum, 327n92
Qasmiyeh, Yousif, 50
Quonset huts, 63

Rabin, Yitzhak, 327n92
Rabin Square, *261*
racial formations, 34, 35–42
racism, 33, 36, 171
Rafah, *221*, 238, 239
Rafah Plain (Rafah Salient), 228, 325n57
Raffestin, Claude, 294n5
Rakhma, 17, 21, 159, 160, *161*, 164, 174, 180, 183, 184, *185, 186, 188, 189, 191, 192*, 283, 287; clan/social clusters of, 181; economy of, 178; environment of, 182; formation of, 172–73; image of, *160*; livelihood of, 177, 178; master plan and, 179; political action in, 188–93; residents of, 185; spatial actions in, 189; spatial distress of, 186–87; Yeruham and, 191
Ram, Moriel, 327n86
Ramallah, 65, 235
Ramla, 61, 197
Rancière, Jacques, 190
Ras el Ain RAF supply camp, 66, *68, 69*, 96
Ratner, Yohanan, 73, 303n43
Raustiala, Kal, 44
refuge, spaces of, 198, 200–204, 207–11
refugee camps, 1, 5, 6, 7, 11, 22, 29, 31, 47, 96, 195, 203, *204*, 214, *216*, 224, 239, 242–43, 252, 255, 256, 270, 279, 281; decamping, 219; existence of, 197; Israeli future and, 215; liquidation of, 216, 222; Palestinian, 9, 14, 17, 21, 48, 54, 88, *199*, 200, *200*, 201, 207, 209, 218, 240, 243, 274, 275, 278, 282, 283, 284, 285; reorganizing, 219; situation in, 196–97; as spaces of struggle, 197–98; techniques at, 5
Refugee Rehabilitation Unit, 219

refugees, 7, 23, 82, 84, 202, 203, 266, 269; controlling, 24; exposing, 223; influx of, 250; political issue of, 222; rights of, 218, 261, 327n82

Regev, Miri, 252

Regional Council for Unrecognized Bedouin Villages (RCUV), 178

resettlement, 90, 137, 174, 216, 218, 266

resilience, 21; cultural, 151–54; spaces of, 145–54

resistance, 21, 39–42, 189, 214, 286; anti-British Jewish, 65; Bedouin, 178–80; Palestinian, 14, 214, 215, 223, 238, 322n9; spaces of, 7, 53, 145–54, 198

right of return, 14, 197, 201, 210, 218, 222, 223, 317n33

right to decide, sovereignty and, 26–30

right to the city, 223, 264, 332n48

roads: construction of, *138*; paved, 94, 160

Rodinson, Maxine, 68

Roma, 24, 29, 33

Roman Empire, camps of, 79

Romanian immigrants, *127*

Rosh HaAyin, 66, *68, 69*, 96, *97, 99*

Rotbard, Sharon: on "black city," 251

Rousseau, Jean-Jacques, 28–29, 31

Royal Air Force (RAF), 61

Royal Engineers, 62

Russo-Turkish War (1877–78), 301n4

Rykwert, Joseph, 292n12

Saharonim, 253

Said, Edward, 23, 68, 211

San Remo Conference (1920), 60

Sarafand El-Amar, 61

Sartre, Jean-Paul, 215

Schmitt, Carl, 5, 26, 39; decisionism and, 28–29, 146; legal/moral/political values and, 47; on *nomos*, 46; on sovereignty, 29

Scott, James, 20, 109, 133, 150, 155

S'derot, 239, 313n94, 329n124; camp in, *119*

Sea of Galilee, 74, 75, 77

Sebastia, 228, 229, 327n92

security, 43, 81, 123, 126, 135, 160, 216, 228, 256, 268; Israeli, 232; national, 252; threat to, 171

Seeing Like a State (Scott), 155

Segev, Tom, 105, 322n3

segregation, 4, 134, 164, 265; camps and, 33; ethnoracial, 279; spatial, 20

separation, 19, 85, 130–35, 288; camps and, 274; modes of, 131, 134; social, 4; spatial, 4, 130

Sephardi, 142

settlements, 1, 2, 48, 64, 68, 72, 112, 168, 171, 225, 226, 230, 231, 233, 234, 243, 258; agricultural, 15, 70, 108, 124, 309n14; civil, 79, 123; factory, 112; illegal, *233*; military, 226; moshav, 14, 107, 108, 284, 309n3; neocolonial, 25, 274, 276; permanent, 76, 146, 242; plan, 108, 110; spontaneous, 173, 182; temporary, *10*, 126, 128–30, 243, 259; Zionist, 69, 70, 78, 171, 196, 280, 286. *See also* Bedouin settlements; Jewish settlements

settler camps, 2, 107, 224–28, 230–40, 277–78, 287; agricultural, 59; Australian, 79; fortifying, 72–74, 76–79; frontier, 279; Israeli, 21, 198; prestate, 13; Zionist, 13, 17, 48, *58*, 67–79, 86, 90, 114, 196, 242, 277–79

settler colonialism, 12, 79, 90, 91, 242, 271; camps and, 33–35; territoriality and, 169; white, 193; Zionism and, 68. *See also* colonial settler societies

settlers, indigenous populations and, 168–70

Settling Department, 98, 147

Sha'ar Aliya immigrant camp, 95, *95, 96*

Shacham Plan, 231

Shamir, Ronen, 172, 335n25

Sharett (Shertok), Moshe, 78

Sharma, Nandita, 268

Sharm el-Sheik, 226

Sharon, Arieh, 20, 110, 112, 150, 309n5; National Plan and, 108; on population, 108–9

Sharon, Ariel, 215, 216, 231, 325n57; on camp location, 146; Gaza Strip and, 215, 217, 218, 219; ILA and, 318–19n55

Sharon Plan, 108, 109

Shati camp, *206*, 218, 220

Shati Rafah, 215

Shehadeh, Raja, 237
Shejaiya quarter, *240*, 241
shelters, 61, 86, 137, 204, 208, 209, 220, 252; concrete block, *203*; emergency, 155, 256, 269; permanent, 202; prefabricated, *127*, 128; steel, *104*; temporary, 203, 269
Shenhav, Yehuda, 115, 176, 312n69
shig, 181, 185, *185*
Shin Bet, 135
Shock Doctrine, The (Klein), 115
Shoshan, Malkit, 165
Shweiger, M., 55, 301n1
Sinai Peninsula, 15, 21, 59, 171, 175, 195, 219, 225, 226, 228, 238, 239, 247, 266; campaign, 214; camps in, 196; settlements in, 230
site plans, *116–17*
Six-Day War (1967), 11, 18, 21, 195, 214, 224
siyag zone, 160, 161, 162, 170, 173, 196; concentration in, 174
social contract, 28–29
Social Contract, The (Rousseau), 28
social engineering, 87, 122, 155, 265, 288
social life, camp, 260
social meaning, 7, 152, 209
social order, 20, 46, 274
social relations, 49, 181, 182
social services, 36, 129, 155
sociopolitical attributes, 17, 26
solar panels, 185, *187*
sovereignty, 5, 13, 26–34, 37, 41, 43, 108, 176, 222, 264, 268, 283, 287
spaces, 6, 9, 24, 44, 45, 47, 48, 57, 123, 151, 269; Bedouin, 287; black, 145; development of, 52, 274; encamping, 224–28, 230–40; extraterritorial, 26, 139; humanitarian, 208, 286; in-between, 272, 287; ordered/chaotic, 9, 22, 286; Palestinian, 196, 224–28, 230–40; political, 7, 53, 285; private, 134, 204, 208–10; public, 134, 151, 204, 209, 323n21; temporary, 51, 183–88, 227. *See also* camp spaces
spatial actions, 41, 52, 152, 188, 189, 193, 196, 201, 204, 210, 214, 239, 255, 262, 263

spatial arrangement, 29, 49, 181
spatial formations, 11, 22, 48, 188, 210, 211, 272
spatiality, 54, 149, 155, 182, 256, 273, 274, 275, 281–84, 289; ordered/chaotic, 283; unarticulated, 130–35
spatial order, 46, 151, 180–83
spatiopolitics, 16, 17, 66, 135, 191, 273, 276, 281
state-building, 17, 21, 22, 103, 272, 288
statehood, 13, 43, 60, 95, 108, 171, 278
state of emergency, 15, 20, 29, 30, 31, 39, 50, 65, 87, 90, 92, 93, 114, 115, 118, 120, 139, 296n46; immigrant camps and, 94–99
state of exception, 29, 47, 115
State of Israel, 180, 235; Bedouins and, 166; establishment of, 83, 85, 108
state of nature, 27, 29
state-people-territory triad, 54. *See also* nation-state-territory triad
State Prosecutor's Office, 230
Stepputat, Finn, 32
Stevens, Wallace, 283
Stoler, Ann, 33, 46
structures: camp, 84, 85; governmental, 24, 120; makeshift, *153*, 154, *154*, 174, *183*, 184, 185; political, 23, 24; portable, *237*; prefabricated, 62–64, *227*, *248*; social, 149
subjectivities, 6, 285, 289; political, 4, 188, 273; refugee, 208
Sudan, 245, 259
Sudanese protests, 250
Suhmata, 105, *106*
sukkah, building, 233
sumud, 175, 186, 189
surveillance, 160, 174, 187, 246
suspension, 16, 164, 270; architecture of, 124–26, 128–35; resisting, 178–80
Sykes–Picot Agreement (1916), 69
Syria, 60, 200, 221, 322n14, 323n15

Tabar, Linda, 223, 327n79
Tamir, Shlomo, 147, 311n48
technology, 22, 24, 26, 28, 31, 35, 36, 37, 45, 53, 55, 64, 91, 94, 202, 272, 273, 282
Tegart forts, 305n69

Tel Amal, 73, 78; wall and tower camp, *73*
Tel Aviv, 61, 65, 108, 109, 111, 150, 153, 239, 253, 258, 260, 261, 262, 284; asylum seekers in, 251–52, 264, 265, 266; camps in, 335n19; protests in, 266–67
Tel Hai, 70
Tel Sheva, *136,* 175
Tel Yosef kibbutz, 72
Tel-Yeruham camp, 17, 124, *127,* 129, *129, 131, 132, 133,* 134, 135, 137, 138, 139, 142, 145, 147, *148,* 149, *152,* 154, 193; arrival at, 136; described, 125–26; establishment of, 121–22, 123, 147–48; settlements near, 146; temporariness of, 130, 131; wooden huts of, 310n31
temporality, 3, 48–52, 254, 300n130
temporariness, 18, 49, 50, 51, 52, 54, 85, 128, 130, 151, 164, 188, 204, 207–8, 254, 282; permanence and, 145–46; resisting, 147–49; spatial, 20, 22, 71, 157, 163, 184, 191, 278, 287, 288
"Temporary Residential and Public Building Solutions for the Bedouin Population of the Negev," 179–80
tenement blocks, 21; hybridizing, 149–51
tent camps, 61, 70, *71,* 135, 196, *229, 235, 238,* 239–40; composition of, 11, 201; Zionist, 19, 34, 84
tents, 3, 84, *99, 106, 127,* 181, 191, 208, *200, 203, 228, 241;* hybrid, *202;* makeshift, 239, *240;* transient, 202
terra nullius, 47, 170–73
territoriality, 186; ethnoracial, 191; settler colonialism and, 169; territory and, 42–44
territory, 20, 26, 85, 184; changes in, 11, 276, 289; development of, 274; space and, 44; territoriality and, 42–44; unincorporated, 46
thanatopolitics, 285
Thompson, Leonard, 47
Time Travels (Grosz), 51
tradition, state restriction and, 183–88
transformations, 25, 122, 204, 276; geopolitical, 57, 288; political, 30, 277; spatial, 211; territorial, 277
Trans-Israel Highway, 180
transit camps, 6, 11, 20, 34, *63,* 83, 87,

88, 100–103, *101, 104,* 105–6, 218, 284; immigrant, 17, 123, 279, 294n38; Jewish, 14; living in, 146
transportation, 53, 78–79, 90, 94, 125, 135, 147
Trump, Donald, 235
Trumpeldor, Yosef, 70, 301n1
Trust Fund for the Economic Development and Rehabilitation of Refugees, 218
Tunnel Affairs Commission, 329n121
tunnels, 238–40, 242–43
Tz'rifin, 61

undercommons, 4, 211, 262, 275, 286, 289
UNHCR. *See* United Nations Commissioner for Refugees
United Nations, 36, 260; indigenous populations and, 168; partition plan and, 13, 107, 123; Prawer Plan and, 179
United Nations Commissioner for Refugees (UNHCR), 267, 329n125
United Nations Declaration on the Rights of Indigenous Peoples, 192
United Nations General Assembly Resolution 194, 197
United Nations Relief and Works Agency for Palestine Refugees in the Near East (UNRWA), 14, 19, 88, 202–3, 204, 207, 209, 219, 220, 274, 283; community participation and, 222–23; relief and, 200–201
United Nations Relief for Palestine Refugees (UNRPR), 200
Unit for Strategic Planning of Settlements Department, 232
UNRWA. *See* United Nations Relief and Works Agency for Palestine Refugees in the Near East
urbanization, 221, 275, 332n48; Bedouins and, 170, 173, 175
utopia, 90, 91; utopian vision/ideology/idea/rational/self-image/order, 12, 87, 92, 93, 118, 122, 288

violence, 22, 40, 47, 96, 172, 173, 177, 221, 223, 247, 272, 279, 280; anti-Semitic,

287; camp, 26; force and, 44–45; Israeli, 224; random/unaccountable, 281; state, 36; symbolic, 135
Virilio, Paul, 85

Wadi Salib riots, 156
Walia, Harsha, 268
wall and tower camps, 13, 19–20, 72, *73*, 74, *76*, 103, 125, 310n19; building, 76, 78, 304n45; watchtower, 131
war on terror, 2, 299n95
water, 94, 124, 125, 128, 143, 144, 146, 160, 167, 176, 185, 201
Weber, Max, 25, 26
Weizman, Eyal, 215
West Bank, 15, 21, 195, 200, *203*, 204, 205, 214, 217, 221, 225, 226, 233, 235, 237, 240, 253; annexation of, 236; areas of, 231, 232; camps of, 11, 196, 197–98, 223, 322n9; controlling, 12; occupation of, 231; population of, 234; settlements in, 216, 230
white, 79, 141, 143, 172, 251; labor, 34; settlement, 171
"white city," 251, 258, 265
White Paper (1939), 78, 80, 302n24, 304n45
Wolfe, Patrick, 169, 172
work camps, 59, 61, 291n8
World War I, 38, 57, 59, 77
World War II, 59, 61, 64, 78, 84, 93, 94, 279
Woroniecka-Krzyzanowska, Dorota, 223

Yamit, 228
Yemen, 96; Jews from, 66–67, *97*, 101
Yemenite children affair, 307n23
Yeruham, 21, 121, 122, 133, *134*, 143, 144, 147, *150*, 152, 153, 155, *156*, *156*, 160,

164, 178, 190, 193, 283, 287, 313n92; baking in, 154; desert around, 159; establishment of, 20, 157; leadership of, 311n56; population of, 285; Rakhma and, 181, 191; settlement in, 149; spatial order in, 151
Yiftachel, Oren, 13, 47–48, 175, 293n29
Yigal Allon, 72
Yishai, Eli, 252, 258
Yishuv, 82, 139, 141, 143, 311n55; term, 68
Yokneam ma'abara, 110, 112, *112*; building blocks for, *113*
Yom Kippur War (1973), 226
Yoseftal, Giora, 121, 126, 128, 147, 155; Tel-Yeruham and, 122–23
Young, Robert, 233

Zair, Amnon, 123, 124, 126, 135–36, 142, 147
Zanun, Udah, 190
Zionism, 48, 70, 79, 107, 125, 142, 150, 160–61, 236, 286, 312n69; colonial/ ethnonational elements of, 12–13, 68; development of, 90, 100; ethnoracial and dehumanizing aspects of, 143, 145; as national ideology, 37; quasi-, 226; transformation of, 91
Zionist movement, 13, 15, 18, 48, 60, 124, 150, 166, 279
Zionist organizations, 84, 88, 90, 91, 101, 120, 167; Palestine Land Development Company, 70; World Zionist Organization, 232
Zionist project, 12, 74, 78, 88, 92–93, 94, 120, 278
Zionist settlers, 12, 19–20, 57, 59, 83, 85, 107, 122, 167, 171, 172, 280
Zionist strategies, 90, 125

Irit Katz is assistant professor in architecture and urban studies at the University of Cambridge and Bye-Fellow of Christ's College. She is coeditor of *Camps Revisited: Multifaceted Spatialities of a Modern Political Technology.*